A Force Such as the World Has Never Known

Has Never Known

Women Creating Change

A Force Such as the World Has Never Known

Women Creating Change

edited by

Sharon G. Mijares, Aliaa Rafea and Nahid Angha

INANNA Publications and Education Inc.
Toronto, Canada

Published in Canada by
Inanna Publications and Education Inc.
210 Founders College, York University
4700 Keele Street, Toronto, Ontario M3J 1P3
Telephone: (416) 736-5356 Fax (416) 736-5765
Email: inanna.publications@inanna.ca Website: www.inanna.ca

The publisher is also grateful for the kind support received from an Anonymous Fund at The Calgary Foundation.

Note from the publisher: Care has been taken to trace the ownership of copyright material used in this book. The author and the publisher welcome any information enabling them to rectify any references or credits in subsequent editions.

Front cover photograph: From left to right, Christine Oatis, Blanesta Ada, Angela Willis and Sharmin Ahmad. Photo: Gerardo Romero, UN University for Peace, Costa Rica.

Printed and Bound in Canada.

Library and Archives Canada Cataloguing in Publication

    A force such as the world has never known : women creating change / edited by Sharon G. Mijares, Aliaa Rafea and Nahid Angha.

Includes bibliographical references.
Issued in print and electronic formats.
ISBN 978-1-77133-056-5 (pbk.). — ISBN 978-1-77133-057-2 (pdf)

    1. Women—Social conditions—21st century. 2. Women social reformers. 3. Women's rights. 4. Social change. 5. Feminism. I. Angha, Nahid, editor of compilation II. Mijares, Sharon G. (Sharon Grace), 1942-, editor of compilation III. Rafea, Aliaa, editor of compilation

HQ1161.F67 2013   305.42   C2013-902597-9
                                                C2013-902598-7

MIX
Paper from
responsible sources
FSC® C004071

*This book is dedicated to Elinore Detiger-Huber,
who is truly an embodiment of the world mother,
tirelessly serving in so many ways.*

*It is also dedicated to all people, both male and female,
who are similarly striving to make our world
a healthier place for all life.*

Table of Contents

*If ever there comes a time when the women of the world
come together purely and simply for the benefit of [hu]mankind
It will be a force such as the world has never known!*

—attributed to British poet, Matthew Arnold (1822-1888)

Acknowledgements

We are grateful to all the contributors who have shared their caring and their stories in this book. The Table of Contents alone evidences the vast areas of concern that have been addressed throughout it.

This most inviting book cover was first inspired by Luciana Ricciutelli and then photographed by Gerardo Romero at the United Nations University for Peace in Costa Rica. We want to thank Gerardo along with the women in the image, namely, Christine Oatis, Blanesta Ada, Angela Willis and Sharmin Ahmad.

We would also like to thank all the many people who have inspired us, the editors, throughout our lives as each of these persons has made a contribution to who we are and what we inspire to be and do. Their teachings and presence are the background of this book.

Certainly, Inanna Publications is the right publisher for this book and we are more than pleased that Luciana Ricciutelli, Editor-in-Chief, and her team worked through the manifestation of this polished and completed volume you are holding in your hands. It has been a perfect blend of professionalism and personal care.

We have created this gift in the hope of inspiring many other women to come forward, bringing increasing feminine presence. Together, we can create a balanced world, one in which the presence of women, men children and all aspects of nature are respected and cherished—for this is a foundation for peace.

—Sharon Mijares, Aliaa Rafea and Nahid Angha
August 2013

Foreword

JEAN SHINODA BOLEN

THE TITLE OF THIS ANTHOLOGY—*A Force Such as the World Has Never Known*—came from a quote that is familiar to me. I had used it myself in *Urgent Message from Mother: Gather the Women, Save the World* and in my mind is linked with Victor Hugo's famous quote, "There is nothing as powerful as an idea whose time has come."

The editors, Sharon Mijares, Aliaa Rafea, and Nahid Angha bring together contributors to this anthology who are seasoned, fiercely compassionate activists who are making a difference. They are women who rescue, teach, and empower girls and women and are advocates for positive change in judicial and religious institutions. They tell us about the lack of equality and the results of this for women in Syria, Japan, Costa Rica, Brazil, Bangladesh, Tibet, India, China, Israel, Palestine, Egypt, Liberia, United Kingdom, Iran, Uganda, Venezuela, Sweden, Canada and the United States of America. We learn about the discrimination and abuse that inspired their activism, about what reality can mean for girls and women. They tell about what has worked: educating girls in circles, liberating a country, recognizing rural women leaders, seeking justice, doing conflict resolution, providing sanctuaries, and creating innovative solutions. In their activism on behalf of others, they are also personally growing in wisdom, faith and courage themselves. This is an anthology whose authors draw from differing and deep spiritual traditions.

For years now, I have been going to the United Nations when the Commission on the Status of Women meets and when non-governmental organizations (NGOs) present panels, speakers and workshops. Each year, I am inspired by the vision, effort, work, and accomplishments of these mostly "on the ground" non-profits, and their leadership. I also continue to be appalled and moved by what I learn. Reality can be terrible and should not be happening to anyone. There is genital mutilation of young girls done in the name of religion, the trafficking of women and girls into prostitution, depriving girls of food when there is scarcity, the notion in parts of the world that education is only for boys, there are the child brides and marital rape. It is a reality that when economic conditions worsen, that domestic violence increases. It is learning about the preventable deaths in childbirth, and how untreated fistulas from lack of obstetrical care doom a woman to physical misery. It is about how AIDS is brought home by husbands, and leaves children to raise themselves after the death of their mothers for lack of treatment. There is so much more—and it will continue until human rights mean equal rights for everyone and decisions that affect the family and the world are made by mothers *and* fathers.

I had mistakenly assumed when I first went to the United Nations in 2002, that there would be another women's conference in 2005. There had been four previous ones, the last in Beijing in 1995, and I expected the fifth one would happen in 2005. Not only was this not the case, but I learned that there would be no further women's conferences. My book, *The Millionth Circle: How to Change Ourselves and the World: The Essential Guide to Women's Circles* had been published in 1999. It turned out to be a seed packet, seeding circles with a sacred center, and leading several women who had attended the World Parliament of Religions in South Africa to discuss forming "a millionth circle initiative." I was contacted by Peggy Sebara who asked if they could use the name and if I could come to an organizing meeting. Avon Mattison from Pathways to Peace, Elly Pradervand from Women's World Summit Foundation (one of the authors in this anthology) and Ann Smith who was then with Global Education Associates were founders or executive directors of these UN-affiliated organizations, who with others added that one of the intentions would be to bring circles to the UN and to UN NGOs.

As a result of this, I came to the UN and there I became the initial grassroots activist for 5WCW (shorthand for 5th World Conference on Women). The "millionth circle" was a metaphoric number inspired by the story of the "Hundredth Monkey," which in turn had inspired the anti-nuclear proliferation activists to "keep on keeping on" when conventional wisdom said it was unrealistic to think that ordinary citizens could stop the nuclear arms race between the superpowers. The hundredth monkey was an allegory, based on the premise of theoretical biologist, Rupert Sheldrake's "morphic field theory," which postulates that the behaviour of an entire species changes when a critical number of individuals within the species adopts a new way of behaving.

The morphic field for humans is the same as the collective unconscious of Carl G. Jung, only its emphasis is more on the collective than the individual. It was an explanation that fit how women in consciousness-raising circles in the United States and elsewhere, who brought ideas such as stereotyping, sexism, feminism, patriarchy into the culture, could bring about a change in laws and attitudes in less than a decade.

Just as each of the contributors to this anthology took on doing something meaningful, once they were moved to do so—which I call taking on *an assignment*—so it is that my assignment was furthering 5WCW—not as an end in itself, but a big step on the way to reaching the "millionth circle." This is the critical one that tips the scales and ends patriarchy. Either through the morphic field or through geometric progression, which Malcolm Gladwell described in *The Tipping Point*: when a critical number of women or people change their perceptions, attitudes, and behaviour, patriarchy will end and culture evolve. Each circle supports each woman in it to believe in herself and live authentically, to be who she could be and to do what she is moved to do, with support from the circle and by energy from Spirit—by whatever name.

The proliferation of women's circles—which form easier and faster, the more there are—would result in a world fit for all children and therefore for all on the planet. When there are a critical number of empowered, aware women, then what can result is what every woman wants for her own children and what all children are entitled to have. This is mothers' agenda: clean air to breathe, safe water to drink, nourishing food, universal education and access to excellent health care, where all have opportunities to develop intellectually, emotionally, and spirituality, where there is compassion and justice, and *no one* lives in fear of abuse or violence. This is an *idea* whose time has come, this will depend upon women in circles reaching a tipping point, to become the *force* such as the world has never known.

REFERENCES

Bolen, Jean Shinoda. *The Millionth Circle: How to Change Ourselves and the World: The Essential Guide to Women's Circles*. Berkeley, CA: Conari Press, 1999. Print.

Bolen, Jean Shinoda. *Urgent Message from Mother: Gather the Women, Save the World*. Berkeley, CA: Conari Press, 2005. Print.

Gladwell, Malcolm. *The Tipping Point: How Little Things Can Make a*

Big Difference. Boston: Back Bay Books, 2002. Print.

Sheldrake, Rupert. *A New Science of Life: The Hypothesis of Formative Causation*. Los Angeles: J. P. Tarcher, 1981. Print.

Sheldrake, Rupert. *The Presence of the Past: Morphic Resonance and the Habits of Nature*. New York: Vintage Books, 1988

CONNECTING POINTS

As women connect around our circular earth, we are creating networks—circles within a larger circle—all part of this spiraling galaxy and an expanding field of creative form and force. We carry within us a spark of light initiated with the big bang—that same creative power that birthed the universe. It is time to manifest feminine potential and restore right balance and healing as obviously the force is with us.

—Sharon G. Mijares

I.
Women Gathering

An Introduction

SHARON G. MIJARES, USA/COSTA RICA

A SPIRITUAL LEADER FROM AFRICA is speaking at a conference in the USA. He notes "it is women's time." He comments on the importance of women in this era "as they will bring much needed changes to our world." He sits on a stage with three male disciples behind him, as he requests that the women from his group gather in front of the stage on the floor below. He introduces, thanks, and dismisses them, as he moves on to other content within his speech. He does not invite any of these women to join him on that stage. To do so, would recognize and make a great contribution to this most needed equality, and create equal opportunity amongst the members of the global family. Our male partners still dominate political, economic, religious and social arenas. While it is true that increasing numbers of men are recognizing the role of women in global transformation, few are willing to share the stage, or to step aside to allow gender equality.

Women need to recognize and value their potential for themselves. It is time for women to claim their equality as human beings and to take leadership along with men in order to promote a healthier humanity and environment. A 1999 research study by the World Bank investigating differences between men and women in relationship to governmental corruption supports this statement. After investigating a vast number of behavioural studies in this area it was disclosed that women were "more trust-worthy and public-spirited than men." The researchers found that the results indicated that women "should be particularly effective in promoting honest government. Consistent with this hypothesis, [they found] that the greater the number of women in parliament, the lower the level of corruption" (Dollar, Fisman and Gatti).

The feminist movements of the past, as well as modern women's rights movements, have created both change and division; generations have not always agreed nor supported one another. To be truly successful it

1

is time for the focus to be one of both women and men working side by side to create a better world—one that is focused on human rights and the caretaking of all life on this planet. But it is the authentic feminine nature that is to illuminate the way.

A Force Such as the World Has Never Known: Women Creating Change includes selected stories from women around the world, many of whom are already making a difference in varied ways as they strive to leave a better world for future generations and for the entire human family. In this spirit, each contributing author provides a unique perspective from her part of the world. All of these women are working toward a truly peaceful, egalitarian world, rather than one dominated by violence, aggression, and war.

Speaking at a United Nations gathering in 2000, then-Secretary General Kofi Annan recognized and affirmed the role of women in creating peace:

> [W]omen, who know the price of conflict so well, are also often better equipped than men to prevent or resolve it. For generations, women have served as peace educators, both in their families and in their societies. They have proved instrumental in building bridges rather than walls. They have been crucial in preserving social order when communities have collapsed.... We in the United Nations know, at first hand, the invaluable support women provide to our peacekeepers—by organizing committees, non-governmental organizations and church groups that help ease tensions, and by persuading their menfolk to accept peace.

But why wait for further wars and devastation to show what women are capable of? Human beings have the capacity to facilitate global change, one that can save us from war, economic and environmental devastation. The patriarchal paradigm, with its extreme emphasis on corporate power, greed and related wars, is moving all of organic life rapidly into extinction. It is time for all humanity to make choices and related actions that create peace, economic security and environmental care for all—rather than for a small segment of humanity, a specific race, religion or gender.

This needed change will not happen if women are excluded from playing their part. This is not only because women have been playing significant roles in community development, or because they care more for a peaceful social and natural environment, but also because excluding women from having opportunities in leadership is itself an unjust approach and a violation of human rights. The tendency to make women take subordinate positions regardless of their individual capabilities mars the principles of justice, freedom and equality.

It is time to appreciate and utilize the feminine perspective and for both men and women to promote gender-balanced leadership in order to spur these critically needed changes in all segments of life.

A TIME FOR CHANGE

We are living in a wonderful time when we consider how the world has become connected through the information technology revolution along with the ability to easily travel to other lands. Rather than using this advantage for the sake of working together to improve the quality of life of all people throughout the world, and to collaborate to save our environment and enrich one another from the beautiful variety of cultural heritage, numerous political leaders compete in attempts to control and dominate the world, along with its resources. This spirit of competition and exercise of power emerged as a result of patriarchal models of control, and omission of an egalitarian model of empowerment. It manifests in unlimited corporate power where the rich get richer while the ranks of the poor increase.

One of the devastating impacts of the patriarchal model has been its disconnection from the natural world. Patriarchy emphasizes hierarchy and domination based on power. Hierarchical structures in religion, political and economic ideals have brought us to the brink of destruction. Their style is what we called in *The Root of All Evil* a "feminine model," using the psychological background of Carl G. Jung, and other traditions that define the archetypal characteristics of feminine and masculine (Mijares, Rafea, Falik, and Schipper). The latest manifestation of corporate power is motivated by greed and encourages vast consumption, while it depletes natural resources on a monstrous scale—destroying life rather than cultivating it. The world is desperately in need of an egalitarian model where collaboration rather than domination prevails. This can only be achieved if feminine voices contribute.

IT'S NOT MALE VS. FEMALE

We often take the expression "feminine model" as a metaphor that emphasizes equity and integration, rather than power and domination.

This model is the opposite of the patriarchal model, rather than an opposition to actual masculinity, and it is important to acknowledge that many men also represent an egalitarian paradigm. Men like Gandhi and Martin Luther King were concerned with the well-being of the entire human family, and with the environment. These men evinced the maternal qualities found within parents who would rather nurture than dominate, plunder, and control. It is common to see many men who are not domineering, who relate in kind and sympathetic ways.

And women are not always kind. Both men and women have been conditioned by thousands of years of patriarchal ideologies and behaviours. Each gender needs to embody the authentic feminine in order to aid in the creation of a gender-balanced world.

WOMEN MUST HEAL THE BAD MOTHER—GOOD MOTHER SPLIT

Women need to heal their relationships with other women in order to clear out dominating and destructive behaviours. For some time this has been one of the major factors undermining decades of feminist work in the United States, as younger and older generations of feminists find themselves in conflict with each other. As Susan Faludi suggests, focus is lost, and instead of a "feminist movement" we have a proliferation of opposing agendas, contributing to more confusion defining feminine nature.

Many psychologists have written about an unconscious split found in people who are unable to maintain positive relationships and who, instead, always project an internal psychic split on others. The mother is the first primary relationship in the world. If the offspring is unable to hold the fact that the mother has different emotional and mental facets with related mood changes, the psyche fragments. The split is exacerbated if the mother does not provide the needed nurturing for healthy psychological development. This results in what is called a "good mother/bad mother split." When the internalized "good mother" is predominant, one projects idealism in relationships and excitement about life, but because there is no internal cohesiveness this can quickly change. When the internalized "bad mother" is predominant, the projection changes and other women are viewed in a negative way. They are no longer nurturing figures, but rather destructive ones.

One also sees this split encouraged in religious tales, such as the "virgin" rendition of the birth of Jesus and similar myths related to Guatama Buddha's birth, as well as those of other historical male figures. The "virgin," which actually means someone who is whole in herself, is distorted to represent a woman who is sexless, and whose only role is to be a "pure" vehicle to birth great men. Other women then end up holding the projected opposite—the whore, the bitch, or the demonic figure.

Many women hold this split within their own psyches, acting out these archetypal energies. For example, they are unable to get along with one another. They will diminish another woman's work, personhood, etc., in order to assert their own dominance and power, and also to gain positions of importance.

This psychic split is also a result of patriarchal influence, resulting in the inability to know one's own feminine value. Thus, when we are unable to recognize our own human value or believe in our ability to manifest our intentions in the world, the tendency is to turn against self and others.

Women—as mother figures—are supposed to have the capacity to nurture others. But a woman influenced by this internal feminine split might present herself as a mothering caretaker, while projecting her shadow side onto another woman. Her style could be to engulf and influence others in order to draw attention away from other women, with the goal of making herself more important than others. She has become prey to hierarchical influences inherent within patriarchal structures.

A mother might, consciously or unconsciously, feel her daughter to be a threat to her own status, or the daughter might vie to have more power and influence than the mother. Sisters are often envious, resulting in emotional and mental violence to one another. A female manager may take advantage of her role and be overbearing to other women (or men). Women often mistrust other women, and thereby enact behaviours that increase this mistrust. Thus, many women have embodied the same competitive behaviours that have defined their male counterparts. This has created many problems for the feminist image, and, therefore, its resolution is a crucial step in the work toward equality for all.

Fairy tales often depict destructive relationships between stepmothers (or some evil feminine witch, etc.) and daughters who are pure of heart. The late psychologist Rollo May (1909-1994) wrote about the lack of and need for positive myths—myths that encouraged healthier living and transformation. Refreshingly, in recent years new myths related to the transformation of the feminine are manifesting. For example, in Disney's version of *The Little Mermaid* (1989), based on the Hans

Christian Andersen original, the mermaid Ariel literally gives up her voice in order to become human and marry the prince. She had negotiated this agreement with Ursula, the sea witch. In a later version (2000), Ariel and Eric the prince have a daughter named Melody. This daughter fights Ursula's sister, Morgana without the help of a prince or a father. Drew Barrymore's portrayal of Cinderella in the 1998 post-feminist film, *Ever After,* is another example of an evolving myth in that Cinderella saves the prince and then has the wicked stepmother and her daughters sentenced to working in the palace laundry-room.

The eponymous *Mulan* (1998) saves her people by pretending to be male and going to war in her elderly father's place. *Whale Rider* (2002) portrays the tale of Paikea "Pai" Apirana, the only living grandchild of a Maori tribal chief. Pai achieves victory after victory amongst the young men of her tribe, but her grandfather refuses to acknowledge her until Pai rides a whale to lead a pod of beached whales back to the safety of the sea. In so doing, a girl embodies tribal legend, and is therefore given its leadership. The recent *Alice of Wonderland* directed by Tim Burton (2010) puts Alice in a more empowering role, and Pixar's *Brave* (2012) presents a princess, Merida, who is both courageous and caring. In this story, the mother and daughter heal their relationship and then work together to rescue all from destructive forces.

Snow White and the Huntsman (2012) touches on the core issue of an evil step-mother determined to destroy the pure and beautiful daughter. The wicked Queen must *breathe in* the youth from young women and destroy Snow White in order to be "fairest of them all." This fairy tale relates how women have only known power (and, in many cases, safety) through seductive beauty. If a woman is not the fairest, or if she is aging, other women can be seen as a threat. In this revisioning, Snow White learns to wield the sword, leading the well-intentioned males to free themselves from the evil control of the Queen.

Another good example of the emerging feminine is seen in Katniss Everdeen, the heroine of Suzanne Collins' young adult novel, *The Hunger Games.* Katniss is not a princess, but rather a sixteen-year old woman of the village who has the power to be present with her depressed mother, sacrifice for her younger sister, to work alongside men, and to save the community in which she lives. She is at home with nature and with her own beliefs, and is free from envy and destructiveness. Katniss is skilled with the bow and arrow (a trope she shares with *Brave's* Merida) and she has the maternal expression of caring for others. Such stories are indicators of a significant social reconstruction of the feminine as these conceptual images move from the archetypal into ordinary reality, creating healthier relationships and a sustainable world.

These are examples of transforming myths, liberating woman and freeing her from an evil feminine power. Princes, fathers and other male figures are not saviours; instead, she is the one who steps forward with pure and empowered motivation. Mythological stories reflect an impetus from the collective unconscious. They portray the coming of women into true beauty and power in order to restore life to right balance. But this is only the beginning as women still need to form positive and supportive relationships with the eternal feminine and with other women.

Where men have projected evil upon other ideologies, nations, religions and races, women have tended to project it on close others. For example, while men have developed and used physical and military strength in order to have power over others, women have enacted more subtle, often unconscious, negative behaviours on family members, social or workplace relationships. As Carl Jung, and also Sigmund Freud, so rightly point out, what remains in the unconscious acts out in hidden ways. Thousands of years of repression encourage anger, with the tendency to displace it on other women, sisters, friends, co-workers. Because women in general have been suppressed, many are eager to have the power to achieve more influence in the world. If they are insecure at some level, they will find a way to eliminate other women from their work, social and home environments as they project the "bad" mother/ woman archetype upon them.

In short, dominating and destructive behaviours are not simply a male prerogative, but rather are part of a social structure that has emphasized power over others and all of nature. Therefore, we need to be more receptive to inner and outer forms of guidance enabling us to embody a new understanding of the feminine and gender balance. If women and men have a healthier understanding and the opportunity to exercise their creative power in the world—they do not have to resort to violence and negative competition due to envy resulting from limited self-worth. Many of our destructive behaviours have been rooted in this irrational fear.

GOOD MOTHER—POWERFUL MOTHER

Many years ago I was taking a creative writing course. The students were given an assignment to write from the perspective of an object in nature. We could be a rock, a tree, a fallen branch, etc. I decided to write as though I were the earth herself. My plan was to go for my usual sunrise walk in a nearby redwood forest, and then come back and write. The words were written down automatically as they flowed into conscious attention:

> *You walk upon my paths, and acknowledge my beauty.*
> *But you do not know my power—*
> *the power to push forth mountain peaks and open valleys for*
> *oceans to fill.*

As I awaited the next words, an earthquake moved the ground beneath my feet. By astonishing synchronicity, the epicenter was in the location where I was writing.

While my ritual had been planned to create a space for creative writing, it turned out that something much larger was taking place. Think of this! The feminine (and nature) are often portrayed as beautiful (a term used for both women and nature), but "her" power is rarely acknowledged. The force within nature to move mountains, to shift continental plates as oceans fill the vast spaces between them, and to produce new life is immense! Does a woman truly recognize this force for transformation is within her? Do we even know how feminine power would differ from masculine power? The source of the earth's capacity to shift the ground beneath us comes from a deep inner core.

We have been filled with religious and cultural indoctrination telling us that to be feminine means that one must be receptive, loving, kindly, nurturing, submissive, obedient (especially the latter two), but never forceful. In fact, the image of feminists as "aggressive" in the 1970s was engineered in order to weaken their message and their struggle for equality. This strategy successfully prevented many women, not wanting to be perceived as aggressive, from joining in the movement.

The majority of women have no sense of feminine power as women's identity has been greatly influenced by men through male interpretation of religious texts. This influence has dominated throughout the world, and culturally, women have been deemed to be "second best." It is a fact that women have been victims of socially-approved male dominance, domestic control, and violence for much of recorded history. Overall, men have dominated every segment of social organization, dispensing their beliefs and practices in religion, health, economic, education, and political arenas.

Although it has been recognized by The World Bank that a gender balance, wherein traditional male and female characteristics have been balanced within the individual or the culture, results in a healthier society, for the most part it has not been realized in the world. Historical evidence confirms the degree to which women have been excluded from equal contribution to the advancement of our human civilization.

MODELS OF POWER

It is time for women to gather—to know, to speak and act with a compassionate and powerful balance that recognizes the value of all life. It is a necessary prerequisite for change.

One would hope that by increasing the numbers of women in leadership roles, we will establish a more gender-balanced world, and therefore create a more egalitarian and truly democratic world. In order for this to become a reality, women need to be watchful and assure that they do not simply recreate "more of the same" by emulating a patriarchal model. They must recognize the difference that occurs when embodying a feminine approach to life.

A women's way of using power differs from the patriarchal stance of "power over" others (Starhawk 9). *Power over*, or dominating rule, is supported by fear. Earlier feminists, such as psychoanalyst Alice Miller, explained that this "poisonous pedagogy" is based on "the overriding importance of our early conditioning to be obedient and dependent and to suppress our feelings" (19-20). Overall *fear* has been the overriding influence found in patriarchal dominance. It has led to ongoing and ever increasing wars. It keeps its citizens in subservient roles and projects threats upon *the other*.

Considering the many ways that adults have been trained to be good citizens, many rarely question the decision for war. They just go along with the status quo—especially if they believe there is something to fear. Then they particularly fail to observe, question and research what is taking place before them and within them. This was evidenced when the United States diverted its attention from pursuing Bin Laden and Al Qaeda in favour of controlling Iraq and its oil. Later when people learned that the war had been built on false information that Iraq had weapons of mass destruction, the U.S. citizens did not recoil in indignation and shame for what had been wrought on countless innocent inhabitants killed or maimed by war. Even though the news stories were abundant, the people of the United States did not question that it was wrong to destroy a country, and then send in big companies who would earn a lot of money to rebuild it.

Control of financial resources also plays a large part in patriarchal domination. This is evidenced in the immense power of the corporate models that care little for their impact on the average person (or the environment). The dollar is, typically, the bottom line.

More positive forms of power include the knowing of our inherent power as a human being. In the larger and deeper sense this *power-from-within* means that we are speaking from an authentic place with clarity (and typically with wisdom and compassion as these accompany "authenticity"). Educating women makes an important contribution to the development of this attribute, for it is true that "knowledge is power." When women cultivate their potential skills, widen their vision to the world, appreciate who they are, and get motivated to contribute change within their societies, they are likely to be at peace with themselves, and thus are acting on a powerful force from within. In short, education builds confidence and ability, while providing opportunities to learn about injustice and ways to heal it.

A third form is *power with*, and this has been a model encouraged by modern feminists. It means we share our knowledge and gifts with others, recognizing they likewise have something to share. It is based on mutual respect as opposed to a hierarchical model.

ANCIENT DEPICTIONS OF THE FEMININE: LISTENING TO THE ANCESTORS

Spirituality is part of human experience, but often religious dogma purveys a negative influence on gender. Few people are even aware that *the first written document* including a signed attribution was written by a woman named *Enheduanna*, living and writing approximately six-thousand years ago (Dalglish *Humming the Blues* 13). Her stories depict Sumerian goddesses illustrating the inherent spiritual and earthly power of the feminine, along with its wisdom.

Later, when the Greeks translated the *Book of Proverbs* from the Hebrew Bible, *Sophia* was the name they used for the manifestation of Holy Wisdom (in Hebrew, *Hochmah*). Neil Douglas-Klotz in *The Genesis Meditations* discusses how Hochmah is given a place of power and authority, and elsewhere considers how she holds a space for all the different voices within ourselves needing attention and integration (*Desert Wisdom* 145). The first chapter of the *Book of Proverbs* declares "Wisdom crieth without; she uttereth her voice in the streets.... I will pour out my spirit unto you, I will make known my words unto you" (1:21-23). Hochmah's gifts are noted throughout the canonical Proverbs, along with the impending perils upon ignoring her voice. But she is also seen as a gatherer who invites all to her table. "Wisdom

10

hath builded her house ... she has also furnished her table. She hath sent forth her maidens.... Come eat of my bread, and drink of the wine which I have mingled. Forsake the foolish and live: and go in the way of understanding" (9:1-5). For the most part, however, the Judeo-Christian paradigm has ignored the feminine voice and unifying presence of wisdom.

The *Haggadah,* a later Talmudic book, describes one version of the creation of the archetypal human being, Adam (historically, there are many differing origin stories). In this story, God is concerned about which entrance to use for placing the soul within Adam. If the soul were inserted through the mouth, he might "speak ill of his fellow men. In the eyes? With them he will wink lustily." So it was decided to breathe "her" into his nostrils "as they discern the unclean and reject it." The narrative explains that "the perfections of Adam's soul showed themselves as soon as he received *her* [emphasis original]" (28-29). But this was not the creation narrative chosen for placement in the Bible—instead, we have the story of Eve, who being created from a rib is obviously "second best," who is influenced by evil and thus condemns humankind.

Compassion and mercy closely denote the spirit of motherhood that embraces humankind with love. These divine qualities are also highlighted in Islam where every *Surah* (chapter) in the Qur'an begins with "the name of God the most compassionate and most merciful." In Arabic the two words that denote compassion and mercifulness are driven from the root *Ra Ha Ma,* the same root of *rahem,* meaning the "womb," and within that root is a verb which means "acts with mercy." But, just as in Judaism and Christianity, the feminine roots were ignored, and the actualized living woman was demonized by religious dogmas propagating inequities.

The recognition of the feminine as *wisdom* and *compassion* appears in the Far East, where one incarnation is known as *Quan Yin,* a Bodhisattva of Mercy and Compassion in the Buddhist tradition. Legends relate that as she was about to enter the heaven realms of Nirvana, Quan Yin heard the cries of people in the world. In her compassion, she opted not to enter into absolute peace, and, instead, vowed to remain with all life until everyone and everything entered into the great enlightenment. Never have we needed the wise and compassionate feminine more than we have in this era. If we continue to ignore the cries of people due to poverty initiated by greed and power, we are humanity without a soul.

Tara is a Tibetan deity honoured for her twenty-one divine attributes. She appears in many forms, such as White Tara, Red Tara, Green Tara and so forth. The feminine deity Green Tara is revered as a dispenser of wisdom, fearlessness, and compassion. The feminine holds many attributes that can seed a new future. In fact, the Dalai Lama has noted the global need for gender balance. He recognizes the need for right balance between feminine and masculine energies, and has publically proclaimed that the world will be saved by Western women (Chan) although, as this book reveals, women are waking up throughout the globe.

India has a rich mythology of feminine deities. Columns of temples and religious iconography are adorned with images of feminine sensuality. Everywhere there are temples dedicated to Kali Durga, representative of loving mother and powerful transformer. Yet, as a result of patriarchal dominance, the living woman has not received the same venerations as statutes and relics based on mythologies.

Overall, the Indigenous traditions of the world have maintained an understanding that gender balance is a requirement of harmony between heaven and earth. Stories of *Ama-terasu Omikami*, the Shinto goddess, *Mama Quilla*, the moon goddess and *Pachamama*, the earth goddess of Peru, *Pele* of Hawaii, *Huitaca* of Chibcha, *Mbaba Mawana Waresa* of the Zulu people, the Hopi legends of *Spider Woman*, the *Maya* moon goddess, the Aztec mother of the gods, Cōhuātlīcue; and numerous other divine feminine depictions are abundant. Their influences are still felt and honoured, although even in many of these Indigenous cultures the living female has been abused through domestic violence and rape (Mijares et al. 228).

As we listen to the voices of our feminine ancestors we also begin to bring forth their inherent *wisdom, power,* and *beauty.* Our world is in desperate need of this feminine wisdom, along with her power to nurture and guide. Her energy holds the potential to heal the current threats to our planet and the many life forms upon it. It is egalitarian rather than hierarchical, conveying a caring awareness of past, present and future.

HONOURING OUR DIFFERENCES

There are many women who are already achieving small or larger miracles in creating needed change. Their stories are shared in this book. Our authors represent various cultures and life styles. Some are making small, but felt, influences in various groups. True change must come from within the individual community as each one differs in so many ways. We can make changes in ways that slowly spread. We can also create larger movements. The authors present a variety of cultures, as each one has its own unique needs and inherent gifts.

A GATHERING OF WOMEN

After several thousand years of indoctrination, the larger majority of women are freeing themselves and awakening to their inherent creative and relational power—a power that is beautiful in itself and truly ordained by God as all of creation is endowed with the power to become its full potential—from the seed to the tree, from the infant girl to the fully manifest woman. We need to be open to *new understandings of feminine power to guide us in wisdom and right change.*

Gender balance is the ultimate goal, but both women and men first need to compassionately recognize and heal the many obstacles within themselves in order to support the needed shift from the patriarchal paradigm, and its ally, the corporation, to an egalitarian paradigm that benefits all. Because women have not been given the chance to express their authenticity as compassionate, loving, intelligent, and equally powerful beings, they need to come together, support one another, and take off the veiling masculine traits that hide the beauty of the authentic feminine nature. Men also need to relinquish their dominant positions, and step aside to make room for their female counterparts and the receptive side of themselves.

It is not easy for women to move into their full potential as so many obstacles have been placed in their paths. Let us not forget that many other women may be so overburdened with poverty and the task of simply finding food and water for themselves and their children that they do not have the time or means to ponder these efforts and ideals. These women need to be supported by women outside of the system who can help them find inner and outer resources to free themselves from such overpowering forces. There are also women who live in war zones, where safety and life preservation of self and family dominate each day. *It is time to change this paradigm.*

Our authors discuss the many obstacles that they have personally experienced in their own cultures. Some authors present theories and visions, and show what they or other women are doing to create change. Others describe concrete instances of political oppression and violence against women, including the longtime and widespread use of rape in times of war. These women tell stories of rape, murder, forced sterilization, exile and other horrendous experiences that women have endured as a result of the masculine, military model.

Women are coming forward and supporting one another as they speak out against these offenses. They are no longer accepting that the burden of shame is their own. They may be threatened or even jailed, but they stand for human rights and nothing stops them. There are also women who live in more peaceful lands, but even in these nations, women are working for equality in parliament, in the justice systems and in their communities. They work to awaken women to their own feelings, their right to speak for and know what they believe, and, also, to take control of their own bodies, hearts and souls—to awaken from the *great lie* telling them they are unimportant and inferior in comparison to the male. Nutrition, environmental, birthing and health issues are also evolving as women work to create needed change. We can no longer sit by while the human race is poisoned by foods saturated with insecticides and injected with hormones for the sake of financial profit. There are creative and alternative ways to shift this paradigm.

Can women, as mothers, wives, grandmothers and friends, sit idly by as medical systems fail the basic human right for health care? Again, this is another example of greed where a few benefit while many others suffer—and in many cases needlessly die due to poor health care or the lack of it. This represents yet another failure in patriarchal systems. There was a time when women were the medicine healers. Is it any wonder that one of our chapters shows how *nurses* are working to change world health and to provide a more nurturing medical model encompassing care for all? Women were also the ones who assisted with birthing babies, as they still do in some parts of the world, where the western medical model has not dominated health care. Healthy models for birth promote healthy children, and therefore a better world.

The following chapters represent the visions, struggles, successes, and examples, of women making both small and large changes in the world. Each chapter is a unique fabric in the tapestry of this collection because each woman speaks from a very different historical and cultural perspective. We, the editors, are not concerned that our authors tell stories of oppression and violence enacted by another culture. We are more concerned that their stories be told. All religions and nations have enacted violence upon another group at one time or another, albeit some more and some less. Each author speaks for the benefit of the entire human family. We simply describe what needs to be changed. Each one speaks from the *womb of compassion, wisdom, and power*.

HEALING THE SPLIT

Comparative religions expert Geoffrey Parinder explains that in the transition to patriarchy there were mythologies that spoke of the split of father [spirit] and earth [form]. These myths reflected the onset of divisiveness taking place as males declared their dominance over females and nature, and patriarchy took root. Meanwhile, we find in the early Egyptian mythology and painting, the sky goddess *Nut*, representing the feminine power in the universe embracing the earth, *Gib*, the masculine element. Nut embraced, rather than dominated. Co-editor Aliaa explains that Egyptian mythologies focused on integration rather than separation. Ancient Egyptians did not have this idea of dichotomizing humans or the world to spirit and matter. The sky meets with earth on the horizon and completes it as one whole. This is the worldview uniting many Indigenous traditions, a belief that had been maintained despite the dominating influence of patriarchal ideology. It is time to heal this split and, together, create a healthy human family that lives in harmony with all of life.

As women join, influenced by this innate feminine wisdom, compassion and embodied power, we have the opportunity to create right balance in our world. We can co-lead and sponsor (embrace and embody) a new way of being. We will be able to manifest the words attributed to the British poet Matthew Arnold (1822-1888):

> *If ever the world sees a time when women shall come together purely and simply for the benefit of [Hu]mankind, it will be a force such as the world has never known.*

REFERENCES

Chan, Victor. "Western Women Can Come to the Rescue of the World." The Dalia Center for Peace and Education. January 25, 2010. Web.

Dalglish, Cass. *Humming the Blues*. Corvallis, Oregon: Calyx Books, 2008. Print.

Dalglish, Cass. "Poems by Enheduanna (c. 2350 BCE)." *Feminist Writings from Ancient Times to the Modern World: A Global Sourcebook and History. Part I: Feminist Writings, 2350 BCE – 1899, Vol. 1, No. 1.* Ed. Tiffany K. Wayne. Westport, CT: Greenwood, 2011. 1-4. Print.

Dollar, D., R. Fisman and R. Gatti. "Are Women Really the 'Fairer' Sex? Corruption and Women in Government." Abstract. Policy Research

Report on Gender and Development. Working Paper Series, No. 4. (October 1999). The World Bank. Web.

Douglas-Klotz, Neil. *The Genesis Meditations: A Shared Practice of Peace for Christians, Jews and Muslims*. Wheaton, IL: Quest Books, 2003. Print.

Douglas-Klotz, Neil. *Desert Wisdom: Sacred Middle Eastern Teachings from the Goddess through the Sufis*. San Francisco: Harper, 1995. Print.

Faludi, Susan. "American Electra: Feminism's Ritual Matricide." *Harper's* October 2010. Pp. 29-42. Print.

Freud, Sigmund. *Case Histories II* (PFL 9). London, UK: Penguin, 1988. Print.

Jung, Carl, P. Young-Eisendrath and T. Dawson. *The Cambridge Companion to Jung*. New York: Cambridge University Press, 1997. Print.

Haggadah. Book in The Other Bible. Edited with Introductions by Willis Barnstone. San Francisco: Harper, 1984. Print.

Karam, Azza, ed. *Women in Parliament: Beyond Numbers*. Stockholm, Sweden: Institute for Democracy and Electoral Assistance (IDEA), 1998. Print.

May, Rollo. *The Cry for Myth*. New York: W.W. Norton & Company, 1991. Print.

Mijares, Sharon G., Aliaa Rafea, Rachel Falik, and Jenny Eda Schipper. *The Root of All Evil: An Exposition of Prejudice, Fundamentalism and Gender Imbalance*. Exeter, UK: Imprint Academic, 2007. Print.

Miller, Alice. *For Your Own Good: Hidden Cruelty in Child-rearing and the Roots of Violence*. Trans. Hildegarde and Hunter Hannum. New York: Farrar, Straud & Giroux, 1983. Print.

Parrinder, Geoffrey. *World Religions: From Ancient History to the Present*. New York: Facts on File, 1983. Print.

Proverbs. *The Holy Bible. King James Version*. New York: University of Press, Cambridge. 1982. Print.

Starhawk. *Truth or Dare: Encounters with Power, Authority and Mystery*. New York: Harper Collins, 1990. Print.

World Bank. "Gender." Web.

2.
Rising Phoenix

Weaving Peace

SHARMIN AHMAD, BANGLADESH/USA

A S THE DAUGHTER OF TAJUDDIN AHMAD, the first prime minister of Bangladesh,[1] and my courageous and loving mother Syeda Zohra Tajuddin, I was raised with a deeply engrained sense of moral values, social responsibility and a love for the land in which I had been born—Bangladesh. My father and his family were on Pakistan military's death list as he organized and courageously led the war of liberation to victory. We witnessed the horrors of a genocide inflicted by the Pakistan military and the birth of a new nation in 1971. Although I eventually moved to my adopted home, the United States, Bangladesh continued to have a profound impact on my life. Living in the Washington, D.C. area, I easily and naturally gravitated into Human Rights endeavours. In particular, my work and support has been to advocate for women's rights.

Therefore, when my friend e-mailed me an announcement that Mukhtaran Mai—a woman from a remote village in Pakistan who was gang raped on the order of village tribal leaders in 2002, and has been since then a champion of human rights—was to be honoured publicly for "her courage to speak out against injustice," and that that event would be held in a mosque, I felt a silent revolution had taken place. The issue of rape, wife beating, and domestic violence are taboo issues and are seldom spoken of in mosque events. The majority of our community leaders are reluctant to address such issues of grave concern. So when I learned that a mosque as prominent as the All Dulles Area Muslim Society (ADAMS) would be hosting this event, in collaboration with KARAMAH: Muslim Women Lawyers for Human Rights and the Muslim Public Affairs Council, I was hopeful and determined to attend this unique event. I felt as if we were taking essential steps towards finally growing up.

The large social/prayer hall in which the event was hosted was fully packed with diverse groups of Muslims from various cultures and regions; I saw some western women in the women's section of the audience. Before Mai's presentation, a short documentary film was played in which the brutality inflicted on her was narrated—all because her then fifteen-year-old brother had been having a romantic relationship with a village girl. In the film, her brother told how he was gang raped and lost consciousness as he bled profusely. Mai, who was dragged into a room and gang raped, afterwards reappeared undaunted to press charge against the rapists and has been fighting her case in the nation's highest court since then. Her case is unique in a society where most rapes go unreported, rapists roam freely, and women's silence is deemed a high virtue. The film ended with a heavy silence. As Mai appeared in a tan-coloured traditional Pakistani suit, I approached her with tears in my eyes and congratulated her for her heroic courage to demand justice. Her hand felt soft as I shook it, and I shuddered at the thought of how her softness had been torn apart by a gang of beastly men. Mai spoke in Urdu, which was translated into English. Her speech was as soft as her appearance yet at the same time clear and bold.

Despite the fact that many atrocities against women in her culture are done falsely in the name of Islam, I found it amazing that she could maintain a grace of gratitude to Allah and was able to separate those abusive cultural practices from the religion. A teacher of the holy Qur'an, Mai, who does not know her exact age and guesses that she might be thirty-four, now runs full-time schools for both girls and boys in her village, a makeshift shelter for women, and a health clinic with the money she has received from the national and international communities. In 2005, she was named Woman of the Year by *Glamour Magazine*, and was introduced at the ceremony by actress Brooke Shields.

Mai, whose case has been pending nearly four years, said that she will never forgive the men who raped her until such time as the laws in Pakistan are changed to protect women. Mai, a woman from a poverty-stricken background with a limited amount of formal education, has proven to be rich and enlightened in heart. Among the students in her schools are children from her violators' families—a positive lesson of altruism, and a character trait that many people need to learn.

At the completion of Mai's presentation, women posed most of the questions. I happened to be the last questioner of the event, and as I held the microphone and shared my thoughts, I felt a deep sorrow and a searing pain running through my entire being. I was sharing the untold and forgotten stories of hundreds of thousands of women of Bangladesh, ranging from nine to ninety years, who were systematically raped by members of the Pakistani military during a genocide inflicted by the military government in 1971. I told Mai that as a woman I shared her pain and related to her as a member of the human race across the cultural barrier. I was not surprised, I added, that her case was still pending in Pakistan's court when the government of Pakistan has never confessed nor offered an apology to Bangladesh for its rape crimes against hundreds of thousands of its women.

I was interrupted by a sudden outburst of rage from the men's section of the audience. A man stood in the audience and while brandishing his fingers in the air flew into a fury. He yelled, "don't bring in the Pakistan government" and continued to yell until some men held him back attempting to calm him. A friend who was seated next to me held me tight, fearing the man might attack or throw something at me. The entire audience seemed to have fallen into a sudden state of shock. I was still holding the microphone while standing in a daze. Then I began where I left off. I repeated my last sentence at the point of interruption and concluded by urging women never to be afraid to tell the truth.

As I concluded, women burst into applause and congratulated me for being courageous enough to bring up this fact. A few men from Bangladesh applauded me for speaking up. Some women of Pakistani origin approached me and offered sincere apology for the crimes done by their government. I was also told that women's organizations in Pakistan demanded an apology to Bangladesh from their government, although the government of Pakistan did not pay heed to it. Most women, however, expressed their shock and surprise at learning for the first time what had happened to the women of Bangladesh at the hands of men who call themselves Muslims.

KARAMAH's founder, Dr. Azizah Al Hibri (who was among the participants in the panel discussion), was correct in her analysis when she said that we must fight injustice by cleaning our own houses first. I believe this act of cleaning and clearing must begin by shattering the shadows of our own silence.

This is how my journey of supporting rape victims and sharing their stories began. I wanted to learn more about the personal stories of women who dared to defy the cultural taboos, who tore the dark veils of tormenting silence. They made a difference by being themselves, and by being bold and creative. Thereby they made a difference in my own perspective. No longer would rape be someone else's problem: it was mine. The boldness of their message inspired me to look beyond, which is why each of these women represents my *Rising Phoenix*. In order to find and learn their stories I turned to the past and revisited a childhood/girlhood where the seed of my own story had been planted.

WEAVING PEACE

As city dwellers in Bangladesh, our yearly trip to our ancestral village home stirred tremendous excitement within our family. The village of Dardaria, which means "river entrance," stands on the banks of the Shitalakhma River, about 82 kilometers from Dhaka City in the Gazipur district. Green mango groves, tall palms, coconut trees, luscious banana orchards and the golden luster of rice fields laden with the perfume of an autumn breeze surround the area.

As a child, I was mystified by its natural beauty. Yet within this paradise, I was also intrigued by a group of women, composed of all ages, gathered to weave colourful threads together into an exotic handmade quilt. They were getting ready for the winter. In our predominantly Muslim neighbourhood, we had a number of Hindu neighbours. Some of them, who were also skilled in the art of quilt making, would often join the group. As these two groups of neighbours, both Hindu and Muslim, joined together, they became as one, with the singular mission of celebrating the joyful creation of a quilt. They would spread out the square or rectangular pieces of soft, old fabrics. They broke into small groups to work; yet remained "together." Sometimes they would speak in a whirl all at the same time; like the sudden fall of a monsoon rain, relieving their hearts after a day's work. Then just as suddenly, they would fall back into a deep, meditative silence, meanwhile continuing to guide the subtle course of each stitch into a unique design.

From the womb of this shared, yogic-like silence gradually emerged a magical world full of colourful stories embedded in the softness of a quilt. Apparent differences of faith, class, and outlook would collapse into this collective, creative adventure. Instead of individuals, the "Other" and "I" now merged into one—a grand dialogue between hearts, which allowed a blossoming that would be cherished forever. Observing this, at a nascent stage in my life, I embraced the idea of human relationships evolving through the connection of hearts: how we could transcend the superficial boundaries that hold us back from unfolding our human potential for a peaceful coexistence.

By relating my personal story, I would like to state that all grand accomplishments must begin at a personal level and must begin within our hearts. Unless we make an effort to have an honest dialogue with ourselves and to analyze our true selves, we cannot make peace with others, either within communities or in the world at large. A perfect example of one heart changing many is that famed American "golden girl" known as "Peace Pilgrim." Born Mildred Norman in 1908, her personal journey did not begin until she was in her mid-forties, yet she would eventually walk thousands of miles honouring peace initiatives. By the time of her death in 1981, she had covered far more than an astonishing 25,000 miles (she stopped counting in 1964) for the sole purpose of spreading peace. Peace Pilgrim taught that

> Ultimate peace begins within: when we find peace within there will be no more conflict, no more occasion for war. If this is the peace you see, purify your body by sensible living habits, purify your mind by expelling all negative thoughts, purify your motives by casting out any idea of greed ... and by seeking to serve your fellow human beings and by desiring to know and do God's will for you—inspiring others to do likewise.

However simple her words may seem to be, it's a struggle of a lifetime to purify our thoughts and actions. Destruction of others seems to have taken precedence over winning others over through our compassion and understanding.

In 1971, a violent incident occurred in Bangladesh which serves as testimony to what happens when a genuine dialogue between two different cultures and races fails to unfold. At that time we witnessed the deaths of millions of innocent Bengalis, a majority of whom were Muslims (although the victims included Hindus, Buddhists, and Christians), at the hands of the invading Pakistani army, who happened to be Muslims—all because of a shattered dialogue, a broken promise. Pakistan then had two "wings," separated by over one thousand miles, with India lying between; East was considered a colony to be exploited by West Pakistan. In Pakistan's *first ever* general election, the political party Awami League, representing the majority Bengalis who lived in East Pakistan, had won a landslide victory in favour of democracy, equality, social justice and fair distribution of resources. But the military rulers who lived in West Pakistan, and who were from a different ethnic background, declined to transfer power to the elected representatives. A sense of racial superiority within the

Pakistani military culture and a lust to retain power by any means, resulted in a genocide that killed millions of civilians within the span of only nine months.[2]

A new nation, Bangladesh, arose from the ashes consisting of millions of martyrs and the silent tears of thousands of raped women. The physical war had ended and a psychological war had begun. An estimated two hundred thousand girls and women were violated by Pakistan military and their accomplices.[3] Silence overshadowed their lives as though they never existed.

SHADOWS OF SILENCE

Bangladesh achieved its victory on December 16, 1971. Our all-girls' public school reopened in January 1972, but our reunion with schoolmates was mixed with both joy and sorrow. Almost everyone had a story to share—stories of houses burnt by the military, brothers joining the war of liberation, sisters organizing underground shelters, parents secretly listening to Swadhin Bangla Betar[4], etc. A few students, like myself, had taken shelter across the border in neighbouring India with their families in order to escape death. Ten million refugees had begun to return to their newly liberated home.

A few students remained silent. Their stories were too painful to share. Lira and Yen's parents had been shot to death in front of them. When the genocide began on March 25, 1971, they had escaped from the city and took shelter in the village. Soon, the military began to invade the villages, rounding up the villagers and killing them. Yen and Lira fell on the ground and miraculously survived. Their grandmother survived with nearly a dozen of bullets in her stomach and her aunt with three bullets on her back while she was carrying her two-year-old baby daughter. We heard such heart wrenching stories from neighbours, friends and relatives.

But we also learned about women called *Birangana*. In Bangla it literally means *heroine*. After 1971, the government of Bangladesh gave this honourary title to girls and women who had been violated by the Pakistan military and its supporters. The title, which was intended to restore their dignity, seemed instead to add a burden, given the stigma associated with rape. No woman came forward in public to identify herself as Birangana or a war heroine—not until many years later. She merely existed among the estimated two hundred thousand violated women whose stories were buried in silence. I, like most in my age group of that time, had not fathomed the extent of their sufferings nor had we understood exactly what had happened to them. Instead, we went about with our daily lives.

It was a balmy afternoon of spring in Bangladesh's capital city Dhaka. The tall trees and sprawling homes with spacious yards were the landscape of the city's suburbs in the early seventies. I was walking back home from school. My classmates and I were chirping about so many things. The country was liberated and we were back to school safe and unharmed. We were the lucky ones. We had been invited to the home of one of our classmates and had taken a different route than usual. As we approached a two-storied building with a balcony facing the street, a classmate whispered "look, look at the girl on the balcony—she is a *Birangana*." My eyes met the gaze of a slender young woman who quickly looked away and hurried inside. We met through our eyes for a few seconds—and then I walked on while capturing a memory of a lifetime.

"What had I seen in her eyes?" I often pondered. I saw the tormenting sadness wrapped in dark silence. I saw a wilted flower struggling to survive. I saw the surface of an ocean with all its secrets.

I passed by that street a few times afterward. Each time I looked at the two-storied house with the balcony draped in purple wisteria vines. My eyes searched for the slender young girl—the mystery woman—the *Birangana*. She was nowhere to be seen—ever. Like the untouchable caste in Indian society, she existed in limbo, never to be reached again. The sudden gush of spring breeze would blow away the purple petals strewn upon the path, like her untold stories, here and there.

The victims of rape in 1971 were silent for the longest time. Silence in many societies is regarded as part of womanhood; and bitterness and sorrow a part of wisdom and enlightenment. But silence is also a revolution in progress.

We hear of notable women throughout the world creating visible change, but this chapter acknowledges these silent women whose pain and bravery are also creating ripples of transformation in this world. The suffering is not only that of the many women who had been violated, but also of their babies, born of rape.

In the early nineties, I read the story of Ryan Badol Good in the leading national daily news in Bangladesh. The headline was "Badol is searching for his mother." Good, raised as a Canadian citizen, had returned to Bangladesh to find his mother, but after a long search left for Canada with a heavy heart: no one had come forward to claim him as her son. His narrative touched me a great deal. I clipped the story and filed it in my Bangladesh liberation collection. Ryan Badol

Good's story was featured among other victims of war in a Canadian documentary, Raymonde Provencher's award-winning *War Babies*, a decade later:

> My name is Ryan Badol. I have two mothers—one calls me Ryan, and the other calls me Badol. The one who calls me Ryan, I have known all my life. The one who calls me Badol, I have never met. I was born in Bangladesh to the Mother who calls me Badol. Three weeks later, I was born in Canada to the Mother who calls me Ryan. A Pakistani soldier raped the Mother who calls me Badol in 1971. I am a war baby.

As the documentary comments, "for as long as men have fought in wars, women have been part of the spoils of conquering armies."

Ferdousy Priyabhashini is one such booty of war, violated during an army invasion in 1971. She stayed silent for twenty-five years and then, like a volcano, erupted to defy and challenge cultural taboos. As a result, she recreated her destiny and thereby helped shaped others.

My first encounter with her was on April 17, 2008, in Dhaka, Bangladesh. April 17 is a significant date in the history of Bangladesh. On this same day in 1971, the First Cabinet of the Bangladesh Government had been sworn in officially as the Proclamation of Independence was read in the liberated area, in a mango grove, before a gathering of hundreds of foreign and local journalists. Thirty-seven years later, my mother, sister and I went to a meeting that had been organized to commemorate that event. Ferdousy was in the audience. She immediately caught my attention as she took her place near where I was seated. She wore an ordinary cotton sari, bangles, necklace made from bamboo or clay and a *tip* (a coloured dot on the forehead worn in south Asia for religious or fashion purpose), which I assumed was hand-decorated and matched her dress and jewelry. There seemed to be something special about her. Was it her artistic style? Her composed persona? I could not tell. Having immigrated to the USA over 25 years before, I did not know many locals so I asked my sister Rimi if she knew her. She whispered to me her name and added, "She is a fabulous artist. She makes sculptures out of ordinary stuff, like the rind of a tree and its branches and twigs. She was tortured by the Pakistan military." Though we had not been introduced at that time, I felt that I had found something important. I had found Ferdousy, who was able to create the extraordinary out of the ordinary and in so doing transform suffering into art. I had found a *Birangana*—an exceptional woman.

Six months after my return to the USA, I received a package from Bangladesh, containing a book, a collection of interviews with women professionals and activists on various socio-economic issues related to women. I had been interviewed for a chapter on violence against women and how to prevent it. As I leafed through its pages I came across Ferdousy's interview in which she spoke about the socio-economic emancipation of women. She introduced herself as a *Birangana*, and a brief background of her suffering in the hands of Pakistan military followed, although the subject of her interview was not related to the events of 1971. To the best of my knowledge she is the only one who has used the *Birangana* title in public and helped to raise awareness of the 1971 rape victims in a manner no one had dared before. I was intrigued and decided to interview her.

In order to appreciate the difference she has made by recreating her destiny, it is important first to understand her sufferings. Before she could make a difference, she had to go through a process. She went through stages of outer and inner turmoil before reaching the glorious height of a fearless equilibrium. By learning to overcome fear she achieved liberation. She encountered her destiny and molded it into art.

Born February 19, 1947, in Bangladesh, her maternal grandfather, Abdul Hakim (who held an important position in the government), had named her Ferdousy Priyabhashini. The name *Ferdousy* could be associated with one of the seventh heavens, which is named Ferdous in Islamic tradition, and also the medieval Persian poet Ferdowsi, who is widely known for his masterpiece and national epic, *Shahnameh*. *Priyabhashini*, a Bangla name which is uncommon for a girl in Bangladesh, means "pleasant tongue." At a fairly young age, Ferdousy married a man of her choice. She thought marriage would grant her the freedom she longed for. On the seventh day of her marriage she was forced by her husband to wear the burqa (an outer covering which conceals a woman's body and face). By age twenty she had become the mother of three boys and sole bread earner of her family. Her husband did not work and resorted to physical and verbal abuse against her. At age twenty-four she divorced her husband. In retaliation he kidnapped the children and moved to a different city. She was not allowed to see her children for many months.

Meanwhile the Pakistan military cracked down on the Bengali population on March 25, 1971. Prominent professors were killed in their university quarters; students, vendors, rickshaw pullers, and countless numbers of innocent men, women and children were killed indiscriminately the first night of the attack. The genocide continued. The Platinum Jute Mill in the Khulna district, where Ferdousy worked as a telephone operator and secretary, was closed temporarily due to the violence. Her mother and six younger siblings provided her moral support by staying with her during the turmoil, but they had to evacuate their home when one hundred twenty military trucks entered their town on March 27,1971. They took shelter along with other evacuees of the town in many different places. One night they hid inside a cow barn when a bombshell fell on a house nearby. Between March 28 and April 7, no one had been able to take a shower and they barely had enough food to eat. Everyone was running away from the military. Eventually, her mother proclaimed, "It's better to die at home than elsewhere," and Ferdousy and her family returned home. At this point they were so exhausted that they no longer feared death, until the day they witnessed the murder of fourteen members of a family who lived across the street. The neighbours were ordered to stand in a line in front of their house as the military opened fired on them. The mass murder of innocent people had taken place only two hundred yards from Ferdousy's home, so they fled again. This time they realized the danger of traveling in a big group. Her two brothers were also missing. Although they had heard from others that they had joined the resistance group, her mother went back to her home in Jessore district hoping to find the brothers. Ferdousy joined other families and kept running. Eventually she was captured by a non-Bengali. This was a segment of the non-Bengali and Urdu-speaking population who lived in what was then a part of East Pakistan. The majority of them supported the Pakistan military. The collaborator happened to be her colleague at the jute mill where she worked. He offered her safety, but instead locked her up in an elegant home in the heart of Khalishpur industrial town (a few miles from Khulna town) known as Muscut House and ordered her to be ready to "receive the military." She escaped with the aide of a sympathetic non-Bengali youth who informed her that every night soldiers occupied the house and raped the captured victims. Some girls who resisted were killed. Ferdousy did not waste a second. She ran away as discreetly as possible. She caught a rickshaw on the way and went straight to Crescent Jute Mill, which had recently reopened. She was a former employee of the mill and knew the managing director, Mr. Fidai, well.

Though a non-Bengali, Mr. Fidai had been a good boss, and treated her as his sister. Ferdousy trusted him. Mr. Fidai greeted her cordially and upon hearing her ordeal he gave her a telephone operator's job on the spot. Ferdousy thought that she would be safe under the protection of a non-Bengali boss. Little did she know that she had entered the hyena's den. For the next eight months she would live an unforgettable nightmare. She would become the booty—the spoils of war. First, her employer betrayed her, revealing her presence to a Navy commander Gulzarin, known to be a ruthless killer. After raping her, Gulzarin ordered the half-unconscious Ferdousy to eat dinner. In Ferdousy's words, "I couldn't look at myself. I felt paralyzed. I felt senseless and without any balance. The dinner in front of me was soaked by my unstoppable tears."

Her nightmare continued. Fidai had sent his wife and children to Pakistan. He used his two-storied home in Khalishpur town for nefarious activities. She was kept as a prisoner, and he raped her in his vacant home. Later she was taken to a different home, near the Khulna Rail Station. She was then gang raped by Fidai, Warsi (the prior editor of *Pakistan Observer*), and two military officers, captain Ishtiaq and major Gani. On an average two men would rape her daily. She was under close watch and her few attempts to escape were foiled. She had the courage to survive and live for the sake of her children and loved ones.

On October 28 she was sent to Jessore Cantonment (a neighbouring district) and was then gang raped by the military. There was a barrack for the soldiers, where village girls were regularly tortured and raped. One man, major Altaf Karim of 125 Brigade, was the exception. He did not participate in the rapes and expressed sympathy toward Ferdousy. Consequently he helped in her release from the military cantonment.

He was a single man and proposed to marry her. He even offered to take care of her children. He said that it would be difficult for Ferdousy to live in Bangladesh after what she had gone through. Given the conservative characteristics of South Asian society, she would be misunderstood and shunned. Ferdousy thanked him for his kindness, but respectfully rejected his proposal. She told him that it would be a betrayal to her country to marry someone whose own kind had destroyed her country and committed inhumane crimes. She would prefer humiliation and undergo starvation, rather than leave her country to settle in Pakistan.

Ferdousy's statement was put to the test. Her subsequent marriage to freedom fighter Ahsanullah Ahmed, in liberated Bangladesh, was fraught with many challenges. Her husband knew about her violation at the hands of Pakistan military, but loved her for who she was.

She spoke about her rapes to no one except her husband. However, people speculated all sorts of things. Unlike her husband, her in-laws put her through ignoble tortures and hurled attacks at her character. Her husband left his family behind, and walked away with her. His wealthy family, as a consequence, deprived him of a large sum of family assets. Everywhere she went she was shunned, and badly treated until she and her husband moved to a new part of Bangladesh.

RISING ABOVE GRIEF

Ferdousy buried her tormenting past in silence, and attempted a fresh start. She became her own counselor. When memories of genocide and torture became unbearable, she would meditate and surrender to God. She would seek inspiration from the songs of beloved Bengali poet and Nobel Laureate, Rabindranath Tagore.[5] As new buds slowly emerge from the volcanic ashes, she emerged as a human rights activist and powerful sculptor who created an unusual form of art. The natural world provided her with means to speak—to say things her lips could not repeat. Nature spoke to her and she spoke through nature. She saw differing forms and shapes in tree trunk, branches, twigs and rind. She would mold the differing parts of a tree into a story. The visitors in her sculpture art exhibitions saw expressions of the "genocide," "refugee camp" along with the "journey to victory," and the expressions of the poet Tagore, Mother Theresa, Abraham Lincoln etc.—all through the lens of nature. In Ferdousy's words, "beauty and new ideas are born out of suffering."

In 1996, Dr. Hamida Hossain, a well respected human rights activist in Bangladesh and founding member of 'Ain O Shalish Kendra, a human rights organization specifically focused on violence against women, asked Ferdousy to provide an oral history of the rape victims of 1971 from her area in Khalishpur-Khulna. She knew of her concern for human rights, and wanted her to get the testimony of a rape victim.

Ferdousy returned home deep in contemplation. She thought about the implications for her sons and daughters (she had three daughters with her second husband), their spouses and in-laws if her story became public. She feared the potential rejection of her friends and community. Then like the rising dawn, everything became clear to her. She explained to her husband, expressing her commitment and her willingness to lose family, friends and relationships with neighbours in the struggle for freedom and people's sacrifices for liberation. If all of her friends rejected her because of her history of rape, then let it be. She explained, "My life is mine alone. It doesn't matter what title I am given. I know who I am."

Ferdousy went to Hamida Hossain and told her her story. In a few years her story became public knowledge. Soon, it became national news.

Her children, their spouses and in-laws accepted her with pride. Her friends stood by her. Shahriar Kabir, renowned journalist and filmmaker on human rights, organized a huge reception in 1999, to honour her as a *Birangana* and wrote an extensive article about her experience in his book, which included testimonies of other rape victims. In 2000, at Hamida Hossain's initiative, she gave testimony as an eyewitness at a seminar on war crimes and violence against women in Japan. The younger generation was stunned by her story. Many youth came to her for courage and inspiration. In the street she would be spotted by many and greeted with respect. In 2004, she received a "Hero of the Month" award by *Reader's Digest* (Singapore Edition) for her courage and sacrifice.

At that point in time, people had nearly forgotten about the rape victims of 1971. Ferdousy's story was a turning point in raising consciousness about the issue and inspiring many other women to come forward and document their sufferings at the hands of Pakistan military and their collaborators. Young journalists began collecting stories from other women—stories that tore at the nation's heart. Stories that also spoke of the valor and strength of the soul. [6] Ferdousy's story emboldened the demand for the trials of those accused of war crimes committed in the Bangladesh liberation war.[7]

The biggest loss of a nation however is when it forgets its past and flinches from honouring a woman's sacrifice. This is why Ferdousy and stories of women like her are important in order to revive a nation from its collective amnesia. Their stories are the seeds of empowerment and transformation for women around the world.

The stories of women, which I have read and collected over the years, affirm my conviction that in order to transform all forms of injustice and violence we first need to examine ourselves on an individual level and change any internal beliefs that foster these manifestations. We need to work collectively against ignorance. Ignorance creates false notions of self-importance, and typically leads to the negation of others resulting in acts of greed, injustice and violence. In contrast, knowledge, infused with divine love, illuminates this unconscious darkness and increases light in our bodies, behaviours and hearts. This is the only way that we will be guided to sustainable peace, prosperity and development.

Many Muslim nations have forgotten the examples set forth by the Prophet Muhammad (peace upon him) in his kindly and egalitarian treatment of women. The then ignorant and barbaric Arab society (majority of Muslims are not Arabs and not all Arabs are Muslims), where it had been the custom among some tribes to bury female children alive, was transformed by the message of the Holy Qur'an, whose very first revealed word was *Iqra*, or "read." Unfortunately in recent years, we have witnessed the rise of extremism in many Muslim and non-Muslim societies. In Muslim societies, extremism has created obstacles, particularly against female education and her free movement. So long as this situation prevails, compounded by poverty and violence, society will not achieve peace.

In 2003, I published my first book, *The Rainbow in a Heart*,[8] to convey the importance of a woman's powerful role in shaping a non-violent society through knowledge and love. In this fictional story, the child searches for her perfect mother, who will be her teacher and guide her to embrace all that is beautiful, before she is even born. This story has been used in various schools and institutions in both the USA and Bangladesh. Currently, a peace education curriculum and teacher's guide are being developed by a team of teachers, researchers and myself, with the aim of using them in the grass roots in Bangladesh and other nations.

Only an awakened people can see the light and be the love and light.

[1]As the first Prime Minister of Bangladesh, he led people of Bangladesh to victory during the Bangladesh Liberation War in 1971. He initiated and organized the first independent government of Bangladesh with the vision and courage to resist foreign aggression and occupation. He was a gifted organizer and administrator, characteristics that were surpassed only by his integrity, love for humanity, deep-seated patriotism, and unflinching stand for fairness and justice. A seeker of truth, he rose with purpose and commitment to the rank of statesman (see www.tajuddinahmad.com).

[2]For further information on this, see Sheikh (24.)

During this time, many people of conscience stood by the suffering people of Bangladesh. World-renowned celebrities like musician Ravi Shankar and rock star George Harrison organized The Bangladesh Concert in 1971, and artists such as the singer Joan Baez also expressed solidarity with the people of Bangladesh. The U.S.Consul General Archer Blood's name is immortalized in the hearts of all truth-seeking people. He risked his career and spoke truth to power. He sent a cable, signed by twenty diplomats from the U.S consulate in Dhaka,

Bangladesh, on April 6, 1971. The cable, also known as "The Blood Telegram," strongly protested and denounced the U.S government's role in the genocide of the innocent people of Bangladesh. The Blood Telegram and the Bangladesh genocide are discussed at length in Hitchens (44-55). The genocide is also addressed in Anderson (255-314).

[3]Interviewee Ferdousy Priyabhashini mentioned Dr. Dufrey Davis, who worked with The Red Cross and came to Bangladesh, soon after the liberation, to provide medical support to the rape victims. He was quoted as saying that rape victims in reality exceeded 400,000 victims.

[4]Free Bangla Radio Centre founded by radio artist and broadcaster Belal Mohammad and later organized by the People's Republic of Bangladesh Government, from their place in exile.

[5]Rabindranath Tagore (1861-1941), the Bengali poet, is the only poet and songwriter whose two songs are the national anthems of two nations, i.e., India and Bangladesh.

[6]For stories of women in the Bangladesh liberation war see Amin, Ahmed and Ahsan.

[7]The movement to bring the war criminals to trial was first initiated and led by another courageous woman, writer and political activist, the late Jahanara Imam (http://en.wikipedia.org/wiki/Jahanara_Imam#War_of_Liberation).

[8]The Media Specialist for Montgomery County Public Schools (MCPS) of Maryland, ranked among USA's top public schools, has approved this bilingual (Bangla and English) book for their schools' English Language Arts curriculum.

REFERENCES

Ahmad, Sharmin. *The Rainbow in a Heart*. Dhaka: Pratibhas, 2003.

Anderson, Jack, with George Clifford. *The Anderson Papers*. New York: The Ballantine Books, 1974.

Amin, Aasha Mehreen, Lavina Ambreen Ahmed and Shamim Ahsan. "The Women in Our Liberation War: Tales of Endurance and Courage." Freethinker: Mukto-Mona. 16 December 2006. Web.

Hitchens Christopher. *The Trial of Henry Kissinger*. New York: Verso, 2001.

Kabir, Shahriar. "Ekatturer Dushshaho Smriti." Dhaka: Ghatok Dalal Nirmul Committee, 1999.

Norman, Mildred. "Chapter 8: The Way of Peace." *Peace Pilgrim: Her Life and Work in Her Own Words*. Peacepilgrim.com. Web.

Provencher, Raymonde, Prod. Dir. *War Babies*. Macumba International, 2003. Web.

Sheikh, Naveed S. *Body Count: A Quantitative Review of Political Violence Across World Civilizations*. Jordan: The Royal Aal Al-Bayt Institute for Islamic Thought, 2009.

3.

Women Building Peace Against All Odds

LEYMAH GBOWEE, GHANA/LIBERIA

THIS CHAPTER SHARES what it was like to live as women in Liberia's wars, while watching an entire community's ongoing suffering as an extremely patriarchal government went from bad to worse with the election of the warlord Charles Taylor in 1997. It also describes women's love and tireless efforts to create positive changes, demonstrating what is possible when women rise up and take a stand against violence and injustice. This is the story of how we, the women of Liberia, stopped a war, created the *Women in Peacebuilding Network* (WIPNET), and initiated the *Liberian Mass Action for Peace*. It is a story of women working to change a nation.

POLITICAL HISTORY

Imagine a country where mothers watch as their young daughters are kidnapped and raped, as their sons are drugged and trained to be boy soldiers. This was Liberia from December 24, 1989 to August 2003. As readers will see, the people of Liberia (as well as the whole of Africa) have struggled for peace and freedom for many years.

Nineteenth-century Africa was besieged by invading countries, imposing their rule in order to take advantage of its rich resources. European and American political and economic interests and practices had a major influence in the continent. It also supplied an answer for what the United States might do with its large African-American population, once slavery had been abolished.

Early in the 1800s, the United States conceived the idea of creating a colony in Africa, eventually named Liberia, for the purpose of housing former African-American slaves. Many of these African-Americans returned with differing political ideologies from Indigenous Africans, which has led to ongoing conflict. For example, in 1841, J. J. Roberts

33

became the first black Governor of the *Commonwealth of Liberia*. Roberts renamed it as the "Free Republic of Liberia," modeling its constitution after that of the U.S., while denying native Africans the right to vote. Indigenous Africans continued to fight against these impositions until around 1980 when Samuel Kanyon Doe, an ethnic Krahn, led a bloody *coup d'etat* against William Richard Tolbert and his primarily Americo-Liberian (i.e., of African-American descent) cabinet. This class distinction created ongoing strife and there was much discord between these groups. These tensions, combined with human greed for money and power (exemplified by the exploitation of rubber, diamonds, and other resources), have long controlled our country. With such influences, Liberia had become a dangerous combination of political and exploitative forces that set the stage for the warlord Charles Taylor to take rule.

CHARLES TAYLOR

Taylor was the son of Americo-Liberians, descendants of former American slaves, and was educated in the United States. He returned to Liberia immediately after Doe's assassination of Tolbert and the overthrow of the dominating influence of the African-Americans. Taylor won Doe's admiration when he walked in one morning and announced that he was now the head of Liberia's Government Agency Service, and, therefore, controlling its budget. This admiration soon disappeared when Taylor embezzled a large sum of money, and left for the United States. He was imprisoned in the U.S. under extradition rules, but soon reappeared in Liberia joining in efforts to overcome Doe's corrupt and violent regime. Eventually Taylor and his group of rebels formed the National Patriotic Front of Liberia. Doe was executed in 1990 in the midst of chaos, a political climate that Taylor both fostered and used leading to his becoming president of Liberia (Lovgren).

In 1996, Charles Taylor initiated his campaign for presidency of Liberia. His allies and supporters used the slogan "*he killed my ma, he killed my pa, but I will vote for him*" and, tragically, people voted this warlord into further power. At that time Ellen Johnson Sirleaf was running for office, but only won 10% of the votes: our people were afraid that we would revert to warring if Taylor were not in charge. Nothing got better. There were numerous executions and human rights violations.

During his presidency, it is alleged that Taylor smuggled arms and worked to support Sierra Leone's Revolutionary United Front (RUF) in kidnapping and recruiting boy soldiers, receiving blood diamonds in exchange for smuggled weapons. This is the leadership that would allegedly support vast murders of innocent people in Sierra Leone, along with the forced recruitment of boy soldiers and the rape of girls—all for blood diamonds. Also, in that Liberia was rich in timber, Taylor began to exchange timber for weapons.[1]

This man who would eventually be tried for war crimes for untold victims of murder, rape, kidnapping of children, for example, forcing drugs upon young boys as young as nine years old while training them to be vicious killers, was the man I faced in 2003.

A STORY OF FEMININE COURAGE, CARING AND UNITY

I grew up in Liberia, in a family of five girls. While my father spoiled us all, my mother was the disciplinarian; she had been strictly disciplined in her own upbringing and followed suit with her daughters. The girls learned to fight as well as boys. This fostered a deeply engrained foundation of discipline and determination. At the same time, as Christians we lived in a community where everyone was welcome in each and every home. We lived Jesus's advice to love our neighbours as ourselves. Children would be fed in any home they happened to be in. I also served as an altar girl in a Lutheran church, learning about Jesus Christ, the "Prince of Peace." This influence would later lead me to be stand up for peace in my own land.

Most people cannot imagine the horrible consequences of a bloody civil war and I hope that they never have to experience this. Some of these things include the rape of women, seeing boys as young as nine kidnapped from their villages, drugged, and made to commit horrible acts of inhumanity to their family and community members, seeing your neighbours' arms or legs being severed while others lay dying from being shot—numerous atrocities that no one should ever see, let alone experience. My depression was deep. How could I even focus or care about any of life's normal expectations, such as education or fulfilling any dreams?

There were so many tragic stories of suffering and loss. Although I was only in my twenties, I began to assist other women from the war-torn countries of Liberia and its neighbour Sierra Leone. These women in turn were helping me, because I could see that they had hopes and still carried dreams for the future. This was hard for me to understand as they had all suffered so much, but the women shared their belief that because they were *mothers* they had the power to change. Then I had a powerful dream telling me to gather Liberia's women so we could join in prayers for peace. I found myself in a leadership position, with these women looking up to me for guidance. This soon led to the formation of the Christians Women's Peace Initiative. The group included both Christian and Muslim women, joined together in our prayers for peace and healing. We decided that our official dress or uniform would be white t-shirts and scarves, without jewelry or makeup. Like Esther in the Bible, we were clothed in sack cloth and ashes as we petitioned God for peace.

Despite desire and work for peace, people were still dying and war raged on. In fact, over 200,000 people had been killed by 2002 and one in three persons had been displaced. Something different had to be done. We gathered and decided to use one of the oldest female tactics possible—if men chose to go to war, their wives would withhold sex[2]. The numbers of women increased as women developed more confidence and found strength in numbers and our shared unity of intention.

Finally, after weeks of seeking an audience with President Taylor, he agreed to meet with us, because our presence had created an impact. He responded to the pressure and began to conduct peace talks—but without bringing peace. The talks dragged on from weeks to months; after almost three months, amid a worsening humanitarian and security situation, we decided to block the entrance of the peace hall, preventing any of the Liberian delegates from leaving until some agreement for peace had been put in place. We had the men locked in. I had told the women to sit at the door, locking arms so no one could get out and the men would be forced into peace talks. Suddenly, on the overhead speaker we heard, "*Oh, my god. Distinguished ladies and gentlemen, the peace hall has been seized by General Leymah and her troops.*" We had no intention of moving until a peace agreement had been signed.

The idea was to keep the men without food and water so they experience what the people of Liberia were experiencing. One of the delegates decided to push the women out of his way forcefully. The chief mediator cautioned him against it. Upon threats from security men that they would arrest me for obstructing justice, I began to strip naked in front of them. This was the strongest act of indignation I could demonstrate. Even though many of these men had most likely raped other women, combining violence with sex, they were immensely shamed at my demonstration. Somehow my nakedness, along with the nakedness of my soul, brought them to disgrace.

After months of negotiations, we had a written peace agreement. We needed to simplify the wording so the average Liberian woman would be able to understand it, and, therefore, feel a greater sense of participation in the process. We held meetings and set benchmarks—making sure we were involved in all stages of the process—including the voting process.

The United Nations had been sent to Liberia to restore order and assure safety, but had been unsuccessful in impacting the men, but, we, the women of Liberia, were able to bring our nation into order. We watched as Charles Taylor was banished—eventually to be turned over to the United Nations and sent to the Penitentiary Institution, Haaglanden to undergo trials at the Hague for his numerous war crimes and crimes against humanity. We now took on the task of electing the first woman president in Africa.

Ellen Johnson Sirleaf was inaugurated in January 2006. We were all empowered as women who cared about our children, one another, and our nation. And the changes in our country reflect the worthiness of all we have endured and struggled to obtain. We also recognized the value of having a female president. In the later film depicting our story, *Pray the Devil Back to Hell*, I remarked that "our peace work was the cake; the female president was the icing."

ELLEN JOHNSON SIRLEAF

Sirleaf had a longtime political history in Liberia. She had served as assistant minister of finance in Tolbert's administration, and was lucky to escape death in 1980 when Tolbert was assassinated and twelve Liberian cabinet members executed as Doe came into power. Returning from exile in Kenya in 1985 she ran for Senate, and was briefly imprisoned for criticizing the Doe government. Because of this history she initially supported Taylor's regime, but ran against him in 1997. After Taylor was exiled, Sirleaf led anti-corruption reform efforts, and was the person chosen to be Chairperson of the Governance Reform Commission upon the formation of the National Transitional Government of Liberia (NTGL). After successfully transforming the reporting mechanism of the General Auditing Commission from the Executive to the Legislature, she was elected President of Liberia on January 16, 2006.

In her inaugural speech, she especially noted the importance of women and what we had achieved.

> *Until a few decades ago, Liberian women endured the injustice of being treated as second-class citizens. During the years of our civil war, they bore the brunt of inhumanity and terror. They were conscripted into war, gang raped at will, forced*

into domestic slavery. Yet, it is the women, notably those who established themselves as the Mano River Women Network for Peace who laboured and advocated for peace throughout our region. It is therefore not surprising that during the period of our elections, Liberian women were galvanized and demonstrated unmatched passion, enthusiasm, and support for my candidacy. They stood with me; they defended me; they prayed for me. The same can be said for the women throughout Africa. I want to here and now, gratefully acknowledge the powerful voice of women of all walks of life whose votes significantly contributed to my victory. My Administration shall thus endeavour to give Liberian women prominence in all affairs of our country. My Administration shall empower Liberian women in all areas of our national life. We will support and increase the writ of laws that restore their dignities and deal drastically with crimes that dehumanize them. We will enforce without fear or favour the law against rape recently passed by the National Transitional Legislature. We shall encourage families to educate all children, particularly the girl child. We shall also try to provide economic programs that enable Liberian women to assume their proper place in our economic revitalization process.[3]

Since she began her own term she has made elementary school education available at no cost. Her leadership has been peaceful, and she has engaged in progressive relationships with the Republic of Côte d'Ivoire, China, Germany, the United States, and has established a Truth and Réconciliation Commission to deal with the long years of war and their consequences. She is also a member of the Council of Women World Leaders. She is continually working to assure a healthy government—no easy task given Liberian history.

WOMEN AND THE FUTURE OF LIBERIA

Obviously, we women have been doing our part to improve the security and future of Liberia for all. Our story has been documented in the before-mentioned film *Pray the Devil Back to Hell*. It has been shown in the U.S. on PBS , and various places throughout the world, winning several awards including top honours at the Tribeca Film Festival. While we celebrate these awards and the global recognition there is still a lot more to be done in a nation that went through a period of such intense violence. However, our stepping out in to the "peace space" has afforded Liberian women (lettered and unlettered) the opportunities to shape and change their community and the nation. Currently women are involved from at every level from village to national in campaigns to stop violence against women. Women are stepping out and increasing their economic power by engaging in communal farming and small and medium scale businesses. Girls' leadership and empowerment has come to be my newest passion—we must prepare the next generation of women's leaders to continue the work that we and our mothers before us have started. Politically, Liberian women are no longer saying it is "the men thing." Instead, they are involved in political parties and are often seen lobbying in parliament for the passage of bills that will enhance the status of women.

[1] Although the United Nations imposed an embargo, Taylor was able to avoid it by using the Ivory Coast for smuggling purposes.

[2] This tactic was first recorded in ancient Greece when the eponymous Lysistrata, in the play by Aristophanes, led the women to refuse sex to their husbands if they chose to war. This ploy has reappeared in various forms in the last few decades.

[3] The entire inaugural address can be read on the Liberian Literacy Foundation website.

REFERENCES

Lovgren, Stefan. "Liberia President Taylor's Life of Crime." *National Geographic News* July 25, 2003. Web.

Pray the Devil Back to Hell. DVD. Gini Reticker, Dir. Abigail E. Disney, Prod. Kirsten Johnson, Dir. of Photography. Web.

4.

Empowering Women and Girls—
Empowering Nurses

Discovering Florence Nightingale's Legacy
of Global Citizenship

DEVA-MARIE BECK, CANADA

I REMEMBER THE DAY this story began, now more than twenty years ago in 1991. I was driving home into the mountains after my nursing shift at a hospital near Palm Springs. The road led steeply upwards, seemingly into the sky, winding back and forth with many switchbacks to reach the full 5,000-foot elevation from sea level. Back and forth I climbed, with my little car in first and second gear, the mountain peaks coming closer as I gained in altitude. This was my normal routine, for I had done this commute from a hospital in the desert to my home in the mountains once a week for more than a year, but, the drama of this journey was always present for me. This was especially true on that day, as it was summer and the daylight lasted longer, slowly turning to twilight as I drove.

Suddenly a switchback turned me to drive directly toward a mountain peak, just as the golden-pink sunlight shone upon its surface, creating the famous "aspenglow" effect of coral colour across the mountain's rock face. The clouds just near the peak also turned several shades of pink and lavender to create a spectacular sunset scene. I pulled over onto the widened side of the road, just to watch the sun's light creating beauty for a while, as I took several deep breaths, in and out, to capture the beauty into the "camera" of my memory.

It was then—in my own moment in time—that a new idea filled my mind and heart, surprising me with its global scale and yet with its individual simplicity: "Look to create a 'world well-being network' of like-minded friends wherever you can find them. This will be the way of the next century—people connecting with people, friends across the earth, to empower each other and to strengthen our collective ability to bring ideals into a global reality, where we each live, in our own neighbourhoods."

I wondered how this vision could possibly manifest? Already I sensed its immensity of scale. A global network would mean connecting thousands, maybe even millions of people on many continents. The network would have to consist of people who spoke different languages, coming from many cultures and religious perspectives. How could the connection happen? And, if we connected, what would we have in common? How would we stay in touch? What would we share with each other?

NOTING LIMITATIONS, ASKING MORE QUESTIONS

Questions and doubts already flooded my mind. I was familiar with fax machines. Faxes were indeed in common use then, displacing the need to send letters by post, allowing us to instantaneously send ideas to the other side of the world. A friend in Australia was busy using these to connect with me and other friends far away. I had heard of e-mail and the connecting of computers to create what was starting to be called the "Internet," but I had not seen evidence of this on a computer screen and had not yet tried to use e-mail myself. The nascent "world wide web" was in its very early stages of development even as I was wondering about the "how" for this vision, but I did not know about this. I had no real technical or travel experience to see how any of this could possibly become a reality. Yet this vision, my own moment in time—of perfect beauty and clarity—affected me so profoundly that I would come to trust this insight—this profound sense of inner guidance for my own future—against what seemed to me to be some pretty big odds.

I was well aware of my limits to realize this vision. I was a single, recently-separated woman, already in my early forties. I had been married for twenty years and had spent much of my energy on maintaining the relationship. We had not had children, so I was "free" of that responsibility. But, in general, it was a little disconcerting, being on my own, thinking of accomplishing something so big. I knew of people who might be able to help me to think about this vision. But none were my close friends or relatives. In fact, most of the people I knew would probably have laughed or even scoffed at such a dream. I had no savings and was working as a nurse just to pay my bills and to live in a modest apartment in the mountain village that I had loved since a girl. My car was the old stick-shift kind with high-mileage readings on my odometer. It would need major work soon. I had traveled a bit, once to Europe and three times to Australia and New Zealand, mostly to hike and experience the outdoors. I was just one nurse, making a living with what I knew, enjoying nature in my off-time. Free in many ways to do what I liked. But what? And how? How could I possibly create a global network of people I did not know, across continents and cultures, languages and limits to understanding? With no funding or technical resources? And, for what purpose?

WATCHING THE EFFORTS AND FAILURES OF OTHERS

With all these doubts and limitations, I did have a hint of the answer to that last question. For what purpose? Indeed! I was watching a phenomenon unfold around me at the global level. The United Nations Earth Summit, scheduled to be convened in Rio de Janeiro in the next summer of 1992, was on the planning horizon. In fact, it seemed that all around me, the people I met were talking about it. This Earth Summit was to take place in Brazil, specifically because of the vast tracks of tree-cover being clear-cut near and around Brazil's great Amazon River. Environmental concerns were more evident in places where nature was at risk. I lived in one of those places. It was well-known and discussed in my village, for instance, that deforestation, the clear-cutting of trees, does more than destroy the forest. The ecosystem depending on the forest is also at risk—from the smallest creatures and plants living in the forest, to the surrounding weather patterns and even the air we breathe.

A culture of understanding about these basic life principles—impacting all of us on a global scale—was emerging and gaining the support of concerned peopled across the world. Because of the approach of the Rio Summit, many around me were talking about these and related issues, such as toxic fuels and spills and non-recyclable wastes, man-made production of things to be used once and thrown-away to pile into landfills and dumped to pollute oceans. The culture of environmental activism was growing and I found, in this culture, a new home of shared concern with others I was meeting, including strangers who became friends.

Also discussed was the concern that many government leaders were not that keen to care about these issues. It was widely agreed that politicians counted on being elected by spending large donations from people and corporations who wanted to keep making short-term profits from unsustainable environmental practices. As well, government bureaucrats—the people who administer and implement laws once in place—are often appointed to jobs by these very politicians and not elected at all. These two groups were the same people who were allowing and even encouraging unsustainable environmental practices. This dynamic—of short-term profit, short term gain, short-term power and job security—was a great cause for concern among those who were actively participating in worldwide preparations for the Rio Summit. Already many were asking a key question: What if all of this energy, effort, time—to meet at a global conference and to discuss substantive concerns about the environment—would be wasted because the people actually attending the Summit were government politicians and bureaucrats who were only making a show of being there and not really concerned at all?

WATCHING NEW GLOBAL CULTURES EVOLVE

As I watched these concerns grow all around my awareness, I noticed something else that seemed to me to be more powerful still. Awareness about these issues was increasing at an awesome rate as the dates for the Rio Summit came closer. Newspaper articles and television shows were springing up, based on interviews with environmental activists. Beyond my village, many other villages and towns were mobilizing. Beyond the life-science experts who knew the most about these issues, people from all walks of life were also talking intelligently about their concerns. Teachers, lawyers, accountants, engineers, artists, musicians and entertainers were some of the people I was meeting. As well, young people and children were excited to be involved. Rock bands were writing related lyrics for popular songs. Schools were already developing special classes to learn more about the environment and even to plant trees in previously lifeless neighbourhood parking lots.

A culture of informed concern and relevant action was forming worldwide. A sense of collective awareness about shared global issues was creating "global citizenship"—a term I thought about myself, many months before I heard it used, more widely, by others who must have also coined the phrase. To me, this phenomenon seemed to be potentially even more powerful than the government "leaders" and bureaucrats who ultimately did go to Rio and seemed, even there, to ignore the Summit's mandate.

Perhaps I noticed this because I had been primed—by my earlier remarkable vision during that mountain sunset—to already be considering how people create networks with each other to support a common cause. Even after the Rio Summit convened—and experts reported that, in reality, no laws changed and very little government action occurred—it seemed to me that the real news was the more-sustained empowerment of an increasing number of people, worldwide, who would remain informed and concerned enough to continue their relevant activism. Global Citizenship! A new culture of active concern for global issues was being created, developing before my eyes!

THE COURAGE TO BECOME SOMETHING NEW—
LEAVING THE FAMILIAR BEHIND

I wanted to learn more and be actively involved myself. I had attended many local meetings, listening to the stories of others who planned to go to Rio and reading as much as I could. But, I did not yet have the strength of conviction or courage to fly to Rio myself—to join the activists who themselves had met there, demonstrating to make these issues more widely known. Now, I knew this courage would be my own next step—to begin to travel to places where this culture of activism for global concerns was practiced every day—to learn from doing the work beside those who were living this kind of life.

I also reviewed at my own career-path. I had become a nurse specialized in critical-care, and had worked in many related settings: emergency, cardiac, neurology, surgical recovery, endoscopy, telemetry. I had studied the holistic approach to nursing—where physical needs are considered beside equally-vital emotional, mental and spiritual needs. And, I had learned enough to write about this, publish a book and teach classes and workshops to nurses and to think about how to make hospitals more holistic in the delivery of healthcare. I had already exceeded goals I had earlier set for myself. But now, I also measured this "success" against my new vision and all that I was learning about global activism.

For the first time, I realized that the culture of nurses and doctors and hospitals could become as perfect as anyone could make them and that, even then, global factors—like poverty, toxic environments, disregard for human rights and wars over religious and cultural disagreements—would continue to keep people stressed, diseased, sick, wounded and dying. These inherent—also holistic—causes of suffering were global in scale, also needing to be addressed at global levels, by a culture of people—"global citizens"—who knew how to do so.

At first, I discussed these ideas with my nursing colleagues at work. Right away, I noticed that they kindly listened to me. But, they also wondered how I could even consider such issues. Nursing's culture was a far-different world. Nurses were not prepared to consider how people became sick, only to take the best possible care of them when they were ill. The causes were someone else's responsibility. This was especially true in the sub-culture of critical-care nursing. What was important, there, was to be able to care for patients while also watching monitors and machines for warning changes in the status of people who might otherwise die or suffer needlessly—if doctors and nurses did not intervene with sophisticated techniques and medicines. The underlying social and environmental causes of heart disease or brain injury or gastric bleeding or renal failure were not our problem. Treating the heart and the brain and the digestive tract and the kidney! That was enough to do! Some public health nurses—whom I did not know or work with—did look at community causes of sickness, as this was also in their scope of practice. But, for the most part, my nursing culture was a very narrow worldview of responding to these specialized needs of individuals and, sometimes, their families.

But, the wider worldview of global citizen activism was "calling"me and I responded, finally, with the courage to leave my familiar California world behind—to move away from my friends and family, to establish an entirely new life, first in Washington, DC, and then, in Ottawa, Canada. In both national capitals, where many global activists lived and worked, new networks of strangers became my friends. Eventually, some of these new friends even came to be like "family" to me, and, likewise, I would find a new home in Canada. During this time, I continued to work nursing shifts for many more years, but now, nursing seemed merely a means to an end, no longer a career in itself. I believed I was walking away from the limiting culture of nursing and learning to become a pro-active member of the wider global citizens' culture, eventually to establish this career, instead.

THE EMERGING CULTURE OF WOMEN IN THE GLOBAL ARENA

During my own initial steps, I also learned more about the worldwide needs of women and about the growing empowerment of women to address these needs. In 1995, the United Nations Women's Summit was convened in Beijing, China, with opportunities and challenges similar to the 1992 Rio Earth Summit. Here, women's issues—for examples: lack of rights to determine even when to have sex or bear children; forced work to do heavy menial tasks like carrying wood long distances for cooking fires; disregard for the education and value of girls, even the killing of infant girls, where boys were the ones preferred to eat scarce food—were some of the concerns of this global meeting. The barriers to these issues were much the same. Some key governmental leaders and bureaucrats were still "paid" to seek and stay in power—secured by those who would wish that these conditions stay the same. Here too, ancient cultures were often a key factor. If a lack of human rights was a woman's plight in some places, so be it. This was the way it had always been done—a patriarchal "tradition" never to be changed.

Yet, the same emerging culture of opportunity was also there, in fuller force even than in Rio. Non-governmental organizations (NGOs) of women working on these issues, from all over the world, flocked to be involved in the Beijing Summit. So much so that the predictable outcomes of the governmental meetings were actually eclipsed, in worldwide press coverage, by the empowering activities, concerns and solutions put forward by people working on women's rights from the world over. In fact, 25,000 citizen activists were granted visas to attend this Summit and convene related meetings. 25,000 more—who were denied visas because the Chinese government set this limit on attendance—still convened meetings of their own at the same time, in their own locales. There, they also networked with each other and the press, to keep these issues clear, across the global arena, in the minds of as many people as possible during this Summit and thereafter.

A SURPRISING RELEVANT ENCOUNTER WITH FLORENCE NIGHTINGALE

It was just then, in early 1996, that I discovered my own further clarity of direction in a surprising way. By then, I had established—with several of my new friends from many disciplines—a pilot program called "Wellness Dynamics" to discuss the global "holistic" connections between health and related issues of economics, environment, education, society and culture. We had been encouraged to present this program at the United Nations in New York City, in preparation for the United Nations Human Settlements Habitat Summit to be convened in Istanbul that summer. Our program looked at these health connections in the context of the places where people lived—the theme of this Summit, hence, we were invited to share our presentations at a number of the International NGO meetings to be convened there.

In the midst of the early planning I was asked if I knew that Florence Nightingale had begun her famous nursing work in Istanbul. "She did?" I asked, much surprised. At that time, all I knew of Nightingale was that she had somehow founded nursing education. I did not know how. The host of the Istanbul planning group, however, knew all about her and that Nightingale had indeed begun her famous nursing work—at a barracks hospital, still standing on the Asian side of Constantinople, now Istanbul, during the Crimean War (1854-56). It was agreed that it

46

would be a significant opportunity to honour Nightingale at this very site with a special United Nations tribute to her during this upcoming Summit. Two weeks later, this plan was confirmed. I was to collaborate with nursing educators in Istanbul to develop this event.

This encounter sent me to look, for the first time, at the significance of Nightingale's life, from the perspective of a nurse and a nursing educator. But, I wondered—beyond nursing wounded soldiers and contributing to nursing education—did Nightingale's life have any relevance to what we were exploring at a UN Summit focused on the quality of life in human habitats? Or to our "global citizen" efforts to make a difference, now in the coming twenty-first century? What I found was truly amazing! I discovered that after her initial famous nursing work in Turkey, Nightingale continued for nearly four decades to focus on the critical global health issues of her time. She accomplished this in many ways: changing political will by interacting with government leaders across the British Empire and elsewhere; improving the environment of both rural and urban peoples to sustain health; advocating for better conditions for women and children and for the poor, actively collaborating with the media of her time, while also to networking in correspondence with her friends and colleagues. Today, more than 14,000 of her letters exist in collections around the world. And, she called all of this "health nursing," noting that "health was not only to be well, but to use well every power we have" (qtd. in Dossey, Selanders, Beck and Attewell 288-297).

Florence Nightingale was the very model I was looking for! She was, indeed, a "global citizen nurse" who had worked, not only at the bedside and in nursing education, but also on the same broader issues I had come to understand and work upon myself! At the UN Nightingale Tribute, convened several months later in Istanbul, I spoke to the audience about my own renewed conviction, and clarified my focus for the years to come: "Florence Nightingale saw nineteenth century problems and created twentieth century solutions. We see twentieth century problems and we can create twenty-first century solutions. That's why we are here today" (Beck).

EVOLVING MY VISION, SHAPING A NEW CULTURE: WHAT WOULD NIGHTINGALE DO TODAY?

Florence Nightingale's legacy could well inspire the nurses of a new century to become, themselves, global citizens collaborating together to address global issues related to health, beyond the limits of their hospital culture. I would invest several more years of time and energy to develop this idea further. Much of this time would be in collaboration with new friends and colleagues, including several Nightingale scholars, who would also come to share this vision with me. In time, I became a Nightingale scholar myself. Focusing on the work Nightingale achieved near the end of her life, I wrote a doctoral dissertation to establish a stronger academic connection between the practice of nursing and Nightingale's global work. Based on this, I collaborated on a nursing textbook that has become a new model for studying Nightingale's life and its relevance to today's nurses (Dossey, Selanders, Beck and Attewell).

But, something was still missing and my co-authors and I knew it! It was all very well—and even important—to study a historical Nightingale and to establish in-depth academic relevance of her work to today's challenges. Yet, research and textbooks cannot, in and of themselves, achieve change. Ideas developed in books must be further developed by people working "on the ground" to establish sustainable improvements based on ideas. What next? We knew that even beyond the United States, Canada and Britain, in modern China, India and Japan, in Africa and the Arab world, in Turkey and the Caribbean, the South Pacific and all the Americas, Florence Nightingale had become widely known as an inspiring, heroic figure. We knew that this had occurred much because of her own extensive correspondence and through her own networking that had spread her ideas, out into the wider world. So, we asked ourselves, "what would Nightingale have done with fax machines, e-mail and the Internet? What kind of network can we build now?"

Like me, she had also had a vision—a "calling" to use her life to serve the suffering as a nurse. So clear was her sense of feminine intuition and connectedness, that, throughout her life, Nightingale took her own stand to courageously advocate—from a worldview of caring—for and about the needs of others. As a woman living in a world dominated by a patriarchal society, she gained a new ground of concern for the sick and impoverished people of the world. As well, she sought to remedy the causes of this suffering. Although she faced many cultural barriers stemming from a patriarchal worldview, she stood within her own conviction for changes that were necessary. In doing so, she became a catalyst for an emerging worldview that created nursing as we know it today. As a woman, she was an agent of change who set a culture of caring in motion—still continuing, even now, into the wider possibilities of the twenty-first century.

As a nurse, Nightingale challenged other nurses and leaders on every continent to raise their standards of practical concern for humanity. For Nightingale, nursing was a personal and worldwide service of caring and communicating her knowledge, skill and commitment. If today's nurses could become empowered and sustained in innovative ways, they too might become like Nightingale—effective agents of change and active global citizens. By bringing Nightingale's worldview to the global community of today, human health could become valued enough to create consensus and collaboration toward achieving a healthy world.

From these Nightingale insights, my original vision—to somehow create a "world well-being network"—became embedded in a compelling new idea that also incorporated the visions of my new colleagues and friends: the Nightingale Initiative for Global Health (NIGH). In 2004, NIGH was established—in Nightingale's name—to become a catalytic nurse-inspired grassroots movement to increase public awareness about the priority of health, in all of its facets. Further, NIGH has focused on using the continually-emerging tools now available on the World Wide Web to empower nurses, and as many concerned citizens as possible, with a voice to advocate effectively for the changes that are needed for such a priority to occur. Since its founding, NIGH has evolved, as of early 2010, to include more than 23,000 nurses and concerned citizens from 110 nations—many who are leaders representing millions of people around the world. NIGH is developing a new culture, a network of people using innovative approaches to caring for and about global health needs (NIGH).

EVOLVING CULTURES BY MATCHING COMMITMENTS
WITH GLOBAL NEEDS

The estimated 16 million nurses actively practicing around the world (ICN) are a specific niche of the overall 3.43 billion women alive today (Worldstat). Nurses are universal caregivers, revered and respected the world over. They are the end-deliverers of healthcare in every nation and the grassroots catalysts of health development. They are the arms and legs of health care and the body and soul of health care implementation, advancing the health of all humanity.

Most nurses, however, are women practicing a culture of caring for people in a worldview dominated by men—doctors whose worldview is based on medicine and the treatment of disease. As a result, many women feel disempowered by subservience to a masculine culture that is not truly their own. This is one of the key factors in the increasingly-severe global nursing shortage that is placing pressure on nurses everywhere and putting the sustainable health of everyone on the planet at risk.

But, what if a newly-connected caring culture of nurses, practicing around the world, could become empowered to evolve their more-limited, subservient culture, bringing nurses' commitments to publicly and pro-actively address the needs of the world? We asked ourselves, couldn't this evolution—in the way nurses see themselves, as well as the way the world sees nurses—actually address the global nursing shortage with positive, innovative, newly-empowering solutions, at the same time, pro-actively addressing the wider global need?

Meanwhile, in 2000, the United Nations established eight Millennium Development Goals (MDGs) that must be achieved for the twenty-first century to progress toward a sustainable quality of life for all of humanity. Of these eight, three—addressing child health, maternal health and disease—are directly related to health. The other five—addressing poverty and hunger, education and literacy, women's empowerment, environmental sustainability and creating global partnerships—are factors that determine the health, or lack of health, of people. We know that the three health-related MDGs will never be accomplished without involving the nurses who work hard to achieve these goals every day worldwide (UNDP).

Keeping the UN MDGs and related challenges and issues in mind, a global team of people, facilitated by NIGH, established 2010—the centenary of Florence Nightingale's death—as the International Year of the Nurse, to empower nurses to make major efforts at all levels and to create a nursing culture of global citizenship advocacy to achieve these Goals (STTI).

LESSONS I OFFER TO YOU

From all these experiences since my vision, now more than twenty years ago, I have learned these lessons. Seek quiet opportunities, as often as possible, to foster intuitions and guidance for living the life you would like to live—particularly for discovering how you can make your own difference in your time, with your talents and wisdom. Trust your intuitive guidance—write it down and use this reflective practice to establish further ideas, as often as you can, as you go along. Do not worry about how your vision will be established. Instead, focus on the "why." Stay committed to the reasons for your vision and the emerging "how" will be shown to you, over time.

As you continue, seek friends and collaborators who encourage your vision and have a similar vision themselves. Forget trying to convince those who would scoff at your vision. This is a waste of your valuable time and energy. Remember that ideas must also have legs, arms and hands. Develop empowering ways for others to share your vision and apply yourself to achieving something or things that demonstrate your vision so that, together, you can see tangible results—further perpetuating the empowerment you seek.

When you encounter barriers, do not assume they are insurmountable. There will be other ways around these barriers: look for them. Acknowledge your limits and, at the same time, see life as an opportunity to expand your limitations. Allow yourself new experiences to broaden your own horizons. Keep an open mind and heart. Allow yourself—and your vision—to be updated and upgraded, over time.

Globalization and related technological advances are providing all of us with unprecedented opportunities to network with others of like-mind and heart to strengthen and improve the quality of life in our global village. Most of today's youth have never known a world without the Internet. Unlike previous generations, they easily assume a sense of the global perspective as their birthright. Many are seeking global relevance in their priorities and activities, in their future plans, in the careers they choose and in their role models.

Keeping all of these above, in mind, remember that—with half of the world's population as women and girls, now some 3.43 billion females alive today—there is an unprecedented opportunity and potential to empower these people to become strong "global citizen" activists in our time. Even if we can develop approaches to empower the one billion of these who are currently less than twenty years old, the twenty-first century will look like no other in human history. These girls will be the grandmothers and great-grandmothers of the twenty-second century, and will play a significant role in the quality of life on earth—for decades and centuries to come.

REFERENCES

Beck, Deva-Marie. Private Notes, 1996.

Dossey, Barbara, Louise Selanders, Deva-Marie Beck and Alex Attewell. *Florence Nightingale Today: Healing, Leadership, Global Action.* Silver Spring, MD: American Nurses Association NursesBooks.org. 2005. Print.

International Council of Nurses (ICN). Web. Accessed: September 10, 2013.

Nightingale Initiative for Global Health (NIGH). Nightingaledeclaration. net. Web. Accessed: March 3, 2010.

Sigma Theta Tau International (STTI). Nursing Society.org. Web. Accessed: March 3, 2010.

United Nations Development Programme (UNDP). Millennium Development Goals. Web. Accessed: March 3, 2010.

WorldStat.info. 2011. Web. Accessed: September 10, 2013.

5.
Protecting Mother Earth

The African Women's Sanctuary — Stories of Support, Struggle and Success

DESPINA NAMWEMBE, UGANDA

CCESS TO AND CONTROL OF RESOURCES such as land continues to challenge women in Africa. Cultural and traditional stereotypes continue to dominate property decisions across levels, from the family and community to the national. Policy makers and implementers tend to think alike when confronted with issues of female property ownership. In these scenarios therefore, planning and protecting these resources becomes difficult because the owners, *the men,* are nurtured in communities that condone male supremacy and domination. The simple act of planting a tree has to have the consent of the head of the household: a man. If he is dead, then his son or brother succeeds him and becomes the one in charge of everything. Even if consent is given for a woman to plant a tree, or farm on a particular piece of land, if the man who owns that land feels like cutting the tree down or using that particular land for other things, the woman has no guaranteed protections. It is assumed that planning and developmental ideas are initiated and enforced by men. As the owner, the man can do whatever he pleases with the land and its natural vegetation. This culturally stereotyped thinking in favour of men's decisions has greatly damaged the environment in Africa. Although some men have contributed to environmental protection, the majority have instead contributed immensely to its destruction. Greed, selfishness, economic competition and the quest for easy success are some of the driving forces behind men's tendency toward environmental degradation in many parts of Africa.

Statistics indicate that 80 percent of Uganda's population is rural-based; almost all use biomass such as firewood for cooking food. According to the World Health Organization, smoke from burning biomass is the fourth leading cause of death and disease in the world's poorest countries. Indoor air pollution due to the use of firewood in traditional stoves while preparing family meals constitutes a serious health hazard to women, whose immune systems are already often compromised by poverty, gaps in contraceptive use, and a high fertility rate (in Uganda that stands at 6.7). These indices are even higher in rural areas because of the many factors that promote a huge family base. As the population continues to grow at this rate, much additional pressure is put on natural resources, so that competition for these limited resources leads to conflict either in the short or long run.

Many bills have been passed in recent years by the Ugandan Parliament but one, the Domestic Relations Bill (later renamed the Marriage and Divorce Bill) has been stagnant for years; it was first tabled in 1964. Different women's groups continue to exert pressure on Parliament to pass this bill, with positive indications of it being passed in the 8th Parliament, but it continues to meet heavy resistance on different fronts with the current one rejected after conducting community consultations. The resistance to passing this bill comes, for the most part, from the male members of Parliament who are in the majority of seats. Some of the articles of this bill allow for women to acquire and own property, including land. With a Parliament dominated by male seats, it becomes hard for women to pass legislation in their favour. Most men, whether learned or illiterate, still have reservations about women owning property. Estate plans are made in the names of male heirs, despite the fact that women are often more articulate and developed as compared to the men. In some tribes in Uganda, when a man dies, the women are asked to sit down and decide who the heir should be. They are asked to choose from their male siblings; if they have none then they must choose from their male cousins—never themselves. Once the male heir is selected, all powers to own property including the father's house, land, and related assets are turned over to him. The women can only farm on the land if the heir allows, but they do not participate in initiating any major developments. Owning land and protecting it is still a challenge for most women.

Legislation in Africa is also male dominated; to some extent this impedes the passage of policies that favour women in environmental protection processes and other related developmental sectors. The Ugandan government can be commended for its affirmative action in ensuring that at least one third of the representatives in Parliament and the local leadership councils are women. The onus, however, is again on the women themselves to make sure that those who are sent to these legislative levels are not merely window-dressing or "for show" to display gender equality in the legislative framework, but rather active participants ready to enforce laws that favour their fellow women. When the Honorable Beatrice Anywar, one of the most vocal of women Parliamentarians on the issues of the environment, led a demonstration against the give-away of one of the most resource-rich forest reserves to a sugar corporation, some men were not amused. They called her an "iron lady" who would not be "marriage material" because of her assertiveness. Most women, including myself, participated together with various civil society organizations to stop the give-away of this forest reserve by government. We participated in actions such as sending text messages, distributing brochures and holding sensitization meetings with key people in the policy-making arena. Some women are never politicians (including myself) but there are issues that require one to stand up and be part of the back-up team supporting a positive agenda that may well affect the future of our children.

One woman, Hilda, grew up in eastern Uganda knowing that water was free to all, but that getting it was a woman's job. But today the only borehole in her village that used to serve over 2,000 people has dried up. "It costs to access water in this village," she says. "The scarcity of water has crippled this village because it is now harder to survive without money." Nankuyo, who lives in the nearby village, no longer has enough time for cultivation because she and her children must spend hours looking for water. Shallow water wells and bore holes installed years back are no longer helpful, and people have to walk more than three miles to get water. "People had to dig deep holes in the dry river bed and then clean water would slowly appear and accumulate over time," says Nankuyo. "We would then use a smaller container to scoop it out and fill the bigger jerry cans (plastic containers used for fetching water). We have no option but to share the water sources with animals like cattle." Nankuyo continues: "The environment has been battered. People have been cutting down trees relentlessly, but now they are waking up to a crisis on their hands."

Traditionally in Africa, the young women and their daughters are in charge of making sure that there is food prepared for all family members. This can be both a risky and tedious process, even from the initial stages such as gathering fuel or collecting water. Young girls are put at risk of bodily harm such as rape because they are forced to venture far from the safety of their homes to fulfill their domestic roles. Because of environmental degradation, most streams close to human habitations have dried up. The tree branches that used to fall off the old trees naturally have been cut down. The vegetation traditionally used for medicinal purposes is long gone.

RECLAIMING WOMEN'S ENVIRONMENTAL PASSION

Most women have to walk long distances to gather traditional herbal medicine, which is mostly available in rural areas. Hospital medicine is not within their reach due to its high cost; mothers are not income-earners with their own money, but rather are seen only as "home organizers." Yet it seems that the women are the real owners of the home because of their role caring for and supporting the home. Their feminine nature, and sense of humanity, shows in their tenderness towards mother earth, which is also the *source* of survival of all humankind. A mother shares a strong bond with her children. She knows that their survival is dependent upon the productivity of mother earth, thus this bond between them is a strong and enduring connection. As the mother and child gently work together cultivating and experiencing their relationship with nature, their tender *nurturing* care supports a sustainable environment.

There has been a growing trend of women stepping up to reclaim the fight for the environment in a more *assertive* way. After decades of watching men selfishly and greedily destroy the environment, women in Africa are saying "no." They have been inspired by leaders like Wangari Mathai,[1] who not only did profound groundwork but also reached out to the policy makers for potential change at meetings such as the African Water Congress in Kampala (March 2010). Much environmental damage stems from ignorance; exploitation of the environment by men is simply "the way things are done" and is taken for granted. Having a deeper understanding of the environment by the women and how it can be sustainably used is an urgent necessity. Mothers tend to have a strongly holistic connection to the earth because family survival so greatly depends on them and on the well-being of the land.

The work I currently do with the United Religions Initiative (URI) is rooted in working with grassroots religious communities and groups of people of faith known as Cooperation Circles. As one of URI'S principles states, "We act from sound ecological practices to protect and preserve the Earth for both present and future generations." Another central principle encourages equal participation by both genders: "We practice equitable participation of women and men in all aspects of the URI." These have become some of the guiding principles for full women's participation in protecting the environment. Human beings are intimately connected to our surroundings and unless these surroundings are cared for, we as people of faith cannot leave meaningful lives.[2]

As an institution, we make periodical awareness programs to communities and in schools encouraging the youth, women leaders and community leaders in the villages to educate the local populations about environmental protection. We work against traditional cultural gender stereotypes by emphasizing the presence of women both young and old; otherwise the meetings become male-dominated. In one awareness campaign, some women told me that it was not even worth them taking a stand for the environment because they have no control over its use. One woman noted, "Our work is to help the men at home and in the fields to farm, harvest and give them the crops to sell." Another woman, Juliet, lamented, "We don't even ask what the sold harvest was worth, when the husband comes back.... If he treats you well, he can buy some meat for the family but in most cases he takes his gains to other women or even marries *more* women."

Juliet is one of many young girls who are married even before the age of fourteen by their guardians in order to supplement the family income. Early marriages, early pregnancies, and high illiteracy levels condemn most young girls to live dominated by inferiority complexes, helplessness, and naivety in their homes.

In situations like these, male involvement and emphasis on women's participation was found to be paramount. Gender issues and roles are discussed in these gatherings and to some men, it appeared to be the first time they had heard about this concept. One man, Mpaata in Namago village, lamented, "There is no way I can discuss with my wife anything about owning or planning for land. Of what value is she when it comes to taking care of the land? She can leave me and go to another man and disrupt my plans." But another man, Wakasa, had an altogether different opinion: "I am a teacher and I have little time for home and land issues. As long as my wife doesn't sell off my land then I have no issues with whatever she plants or cuts down—after all she is the mother of our children." That was hopeful indeed!

Campaigns for educating young girls have been intensifying from the family level to community leadership. Education is key to a confident, articulate and critical thinking person in society. Uneducated women in most cases fear the unknown and are less assertive. Educating the girl child leads to an open-minded and rational person who can look beyond what usually meets the eye. It leads to job creation and the potential for subsequent income generation. Although the proceeds of these earnings are currently debatable, there is an inner feeling of personal satisfaction and fulfillment within a woman. Early training in life skills helps young people to grow up with increased self-confidence, with skills of knowing and living with oneself and others, and with decision-making skills. The training of women as environmentalists is another important area that has been encouraged. Once women learn the importance of preserving the ecosystem, they can easily champion ecological campaigns. There is a difference between *knowing* and *understanding* the consequences of a poorly-protected environment. To most people *intellectual* knowing is loosely acted upon, while *understanding* comes with deeper reflection and commitment. Women who have been equipped with the necessary information foster recognizable changes in the perception, attitude and practical behaviour towards the environment within their communities.

INTER-RELIGIOUS INVOLVEMENT

The involvement of different religious leaders as key actors in our environmental campaigns has improved our advocacy strategy. For example, URI as an inclusive interfaith organization brings together people of faith from various communities. Mobilization of these communities is facilitated by the strategic use of leaders from different religious groups, which have developed communication channels for sharing information and getting key women leaders to further mobilize their fellow women. Sustaining these programs is made possible as they become more and more institutionalized. "If we use our faith as the doctrines tell us without selfish motives to address world environmental troubles, then this world can be a better place" said one religious leader. The lay perception of most religious leaders is of credibility and integrity, and they are held in high esteem. With the commitment of the religious leaders comes the support of a significant proportion of the community. Therefore, in some areas where we sometimes experience challenges in reaching out to women to partner in environmental awareness campaigns, we consult the families in the presence of their religious leaders. On the other hand, it should be noted that some religions and religious doctrines have contributed to the subordination of women. Therefore involving religious leaders in bringing women to the front during advocacy campaigns helps dispel some of these myths.

OTHER ENVIRONMENTAL APPROACHES

The climate-change induced water crisis hampers growth, increases the cost of operating power plants, and leads to load-shedding. The need to explore other sources of renewable energy, like solar and energy saving stoves, is an urgent part of advocating for change. Offering solutions to community energy problems is an area that needs to be critically assessed before advocating for environmental protection activities.

Although the issues put forth may be appealing, if the population has no fuel alternatives in order to prepare their meals or earn an income, then all of these efforts may be fruitless. Finding alternative sources of cooking energy, for example, is fundamental as it is the most common reason for destroying the environment.

Skills-training programs for the community in the use of solar cookers and the making of briquettes have been very useful. Providing finished products without giving skills is a temporary solution only; sustainable programs must equip communities with specific skills that can see them manage energy issues at that level for the long term. The making of biomass briquettes for use in cooking is an excellent example of a strategy that addresses a number of problems. The raw materials for making briquettes are agricultural waste; this reduces garbage problems, by re-using and recycling waste biomass into energy efficient fuel. The manufactures of briquettes also not only creates income for women, but reduces out-door air pollution, and protects the health of women by reducing smoke from cooking. Solar cookers, which use the sun as an energy source, are similarly useful because a woman can put food outside and carry on with her other chores—or even rest for a time under a tree. These are low-cost alternatives that appeal to rural-based people, and many communities are increasingly interested in being part of this program.

CONCLUSION

Campaigning and raising awareness without advocating for policy change is not enough. It is of great importance for women to take up leadership positions from the grassroots to national levels. Gender sensitive policies can only be influenced if women take the mantle of decision making in key positions at all levels. Non-activist women should support those women who choose to stand up and challenge the patriarchal perceptions that are so common in African societies.

It is also important to note that environmental intervention campaigns should be of a multi-sectored approach when addressing communities. For example, environmental awareness campaigns need to talk about the hazards of high population growth and its effects on the environment. Advocating for family planning and other reproductive health issues, and the need to encourage parents to educate the girls in our communities so that they stay longer in school in order to reduce population pressures is important. Providing alternative modes of income for the communities is another key strategy. People are more likely to continue destroying the forests and grasslands if they feel it is a matter of economic survival. Educating more girls and boys as environmentalists, and educating parents to groom their children into environmentally ethical persons, can also go a long way in creating a future generation that cares for the environment. Religious leaders, cultural leaders and lay leaders are encouraged to take the lead, to use the respect in which they are held in their communities as a force for change. Integrating environmental concerns into issues of peace too is very important: as humans, we cannot experience full peace without being at peace with the environment in which we live.

On an international level, environmental concerns should be paramount for everyone on the planet. These problems are global in effect, not isolated, and will eventually have an impact on all. The effects of greenhouse gases, cutting down trees, encroaching on the wet lands, unethical use of water, along with the general destruction of the ecosystem by inhabitants of this planet will not impact individual communities but also cause devastation for the entire spectrum of people from all geographic zones on earth.

Neither gender is the expert in environmental protection—rather a collective effort of all who live on mother earth is needed. Stereotyped actions cannot staunch the bleeding of our environment. Many people used to refer to Africa as a "land of plenty" when referring to its natural endowments—these natural features are quickly turning to artificial environments. Yet, Africa is still facing challenges in trying to catch up with the rest of the world in terms of technological advancement. Mechanical failure is rampant with no easy alternatives available. These deficits cannot favour deviation from the natural ecological set up as is the case, perhaps, in some other parts of the world. It is imperative to consider even beneficial technological change in the wider context of Africa's available resources.

African traditions and spiritual expressions have a very strong connection to mother earth and the environment. We feel that it is crucial, for the people to be healthy, that our food and medicines must be natural—we must be sustained by the land. This knowledge was known and shared by our great ancestors who had much respect for the land because of what it offers us, and its life- and health-giving qualities. Our African ancestors knew how to cultivate food and work with mother earth. Their actions both complimented and preserved nature. If the current generation wants a sustainable future for their great-grandchildren, commitment to the environment has to start now. Land ownership, involvement and participation of both genders from the small household and community interventions to the national and international arenas are required.

[1] Professor Wangari Mathai (1940-2011) was an international environmentalist and political activist, and the first African woman to win the Nobel Peace Prize (2004). She founded the Green Belt Movement International, which fosters good governance and cultures of peace by advocating for and empowering communities worldwide to protect the environment. She received many honours for her work.

[2] URI continues to recognize the continued support and good will from the religious leaders, and the importance of women and young people in promoting change. It is, therefore, the commitment of URI Great Lakes Region to work with women and young people, especially targeting girls as principal participants together with people of faith; further, URI encourages boys and men to commit more to peace and the environment.

REFERENCES

Mathai, Wangari. Greenbelmovement.org. Web.
United Religions Initiative (URI). Web.
World Health Organization. "Uganda: Country Cooperation Strategy." Brief, 2009. Web.

6.

Women's Movements
and the Democratic Transition Process[1]

The Effectiveness of Rights and Judicial Politics in Brazil

ROSANE M. REIS LAVIGNE, BRAZIL

I N THE POLITICAL DEMOCRATIZATION PROCESS in Brazil, women's movements are well known as having been strong and effective in the resistance[2] to the military dictatorship,[3] and in the construction, implementation, and enforcement of rights established in new paradigms that guaranteed structural change in social relations. They are present in laying the foundations of gender equality in all aspects and dimensions of life in society. This process, established in a formal plan, has provided a stable platform for developments in all areas of Brazil.

According to Guillermo O'Donnell and Philippe Schmitter's reasoning, the democratization process implies two transitions (27). The first is the transition of a government regime that gradually leaves authoritarianism to rule via democracy. This period of regime shift, away from an authoritarian standard to a democratic one, is the first stage of the process. The second stage starts with the strengthening of the democratic regime, that is, with the actual enforcement of democracy in society.

THE FIRST TRANSITION

The first transition period, which started with the restoration of democracy,[4] took place simultaneously with the appearance of a new feminist movement in Brazil. This movement challenged frames of mind and social reactions to the prevalent political oppression. It stirred thoughts and critical reflection related to women's issues and position in society, both in the public and private spheres, triggering a debate on measures to subvert the perceived "natural order of things" (Bordieu 15). In questioning this order, the feminist movement pointed to the social construction of the gender. Debates on the historical and social determinants of women's issues and the position of women in society started taking place. An institutional space was created in order to take action and give visibility to socially-constructed difference, leading to the rejection of inequality. Debate could only be valid or useful with the inclusion of women's voices: an unusual factor, since women had never been main participants in the public sphere, nor were they heard by the subjects of the discourse that ruled over life in Brazilian society.

Social reaction needed to be fine-tuned to the enforced political and institutional order, adding specific gender-sensitive items related to the liberating agenda in the making. It was understood that this inclusion would be articulated with different stakeholders in the consensus in favour of democracy. There was a clear, qualified reaction from women which was strongly articulated in the struggle over the constitutionalization process of rights, as another formal affirmation of much needed structural change.

At that historical moment, the internal pressure for institutional change arose with great intensity from a variety of civil society groups— an unprecedented phenomenon in Brazilian history. The explosion in demands that resulted provided a focal point around which these groups could organize, cutting across social categories, demanding the recognition of new political subjects, and the answers to specific issues. This active demonstration, made up of diverse identities, had an impact on the constitutional process that took place from 1987 to 1988, helping to incorporate into the embryonic constitution text enshrining the human rights platform supported by those groups.

The women's movement underwent many changes over time. The mobilization of Brazilian women in the struggle for democracy, especially in the 1980s, acquired distinct characteristics. There were women's groups who occupied certain thematic political institutions, one of the most important being the Centre for Brazilian Women (*Centro da Mulher Brasileira*). These groups formed part of the start of the second wave of feminism in 1975, which also included other groups which were concerned with reflecting on the female condition, with an emphasis on sexuality, for example the CERES group. Women also created autonomous spaces and organized the Feminist Forum and SOS-Women (SOS-*Mulher*), a group that provided direct assistance to the female victims of domestic violence, and non-governmental organizations which acted on the gender equality issue and public policy. Today's women's movement is the result of the expressions of many of these groups and other interested political parties.

The contribution of women's movements, such as the "Lipstick Lobby" (*Lobby do Batom*)[5] to the drafting of the 1988 Federal

Constitution is mentioned in many papers and is officially documented in the National Brazilian Report—a report on women's issues between 1985 and 2002,[6] prepared for the Convention on the Elimination of Discrimination against Women (CEDAW). The feminist movement grew as a political force in the national sphere due largely to the capacity of women across the country to organize, mobilize, and articulate through a supra-partisan alliance. The participation of women in the development of the first stage of the democratization process in Brazil is undeniable.

THE SECOND TRANSITION

The democratization of Brazil was not the consequence of a rupture in the established order, but rather a comprehensive, progressive and exhaustive bargaining process between the established political forces and civil society. Women's movements had already contributed significantly to the bargaining process with strategies and goals. They had to be tested by a broad spectrum of members of the democratic coalition since many resisted proposals for structural change aimed at ending gender asymmetry in Brazilian society.

The women's moviments developed numerous strategies to urge the State to implement social policies in line with new demands made by collective groups about specificities hitherto ignored by the government spheres. Contributions to other social mass movements were organized by area of interest: the need for daycare centers, land and agricultural land tenure regularization; political party agendas (especially the Workers Party [Partido dos Trabalhadores] and the Brazilian Democratic Movement Party [Partido do Movimento Democrático Brasileiro]); academia; fostering the creation of Women's Studies Centers (Núcleos de Estudos Interdisciplinares sobre a Mulher). Women's movements stand out[7] in this demand for equality, constantly re-affirming women's needs and differences.

New approaches to the study of gender are being developed; Nancy Fraser's ideas are striking, as she proposes a new social organization considering redistributive[8] politics and a politics of recognition that perceives the social status of each one of us, and takes into account the level of each individual, to overcome subordination and recognize the subaltern subject as a full member of society, capable of interacting with the other members as an equal. It deals with *recognition* demands as if they were *justice* demands within a broadened notion of justice.

The consolidation of rights, a characteristic of the second transition in the democratization process as suggested by O'Donnell and Schmitter, calls for a permanent re-assessment of action tactics and strategies. Hard-won constitutional rights and formal rules inaugurate a new scenario of mobilization and political activity for women, and guide action programs focused on implementing and interpreting the law, making the ways in which we think and exert power more sophisticated, encompassing a vision of equality not restricted by formal equality.

As a result, the Brazilian legal framework is gradually changing to a new constitutional order more in line with international human rights treaties. Leila de Andrade Linhares Barsted, for example, emphasizes the achievement of several state-related rights and obligations such as the recognition of equality between men and women in general, repudiation of domestic violence, equality of offspring, recognition of reproductive rights, etc. Nevertheless, change is slow, consequently radical action is still needed to offset historical inequities, inherited from substantive rights deficits that persist today.[9] Therefore, it is necessary to apply the entrenchment clause contained in section I, Article 5 of the Constitution: men and women have equal rights and obligations under this Constitution, thereby ensuring that formal equality becomes concrete practice.

The Constitutional Legislature in Brazil included affirmative action points for women with the aim of speeding up action[10] since it was aware of possible barriers to full implementation of the equality principle in social relations. Even though such a strategy makes the Brazilian Constitution stand out as one of the most progressive in the world, the principle of equality between men and women, the cornerstone of the legal framework, is not tangible in reality, according to recent surveys like the 2008/2009 National Household Sample Survey. As a recent study by Maria Celina D'Áraújo attests, women are far removed from decision-making positions. Democratic insufficiency is fed by never-changing inequalities. This divide takes gigantic dimensions if race is considered in addition to gender, as studies carried out by the Economic, Historic, Social and Statistical Racial Relations Studies Labouratory (*Labouratório de Análises Econômicas, Históricas, Sociais e Estatísticas das Relações Raciais da Universidade Federal do Rio de Janeiro*) show.

Nevertheless, in the last twenty years both the Executive and Legislative Powers have heard the claims made by women's movements and have thus become involved with issues related to the feminist agenda and to the position women have in power relations. It is the beginning of the shifting of feminist agenda claims set forth in documents like Feminist

Alerts (*Alertas Feministas*) published in election years[11] about public policy.

THE EXECUTIVE AND LEGISLATIVE POWERS

Both the Executive and the Legislative Powers have been more responsive to the broad claims of women's movements. In 1982, the political nature of Brazilian States was reformulated by direct elections of the head of the Executive Power. States assumed different democratic nuances, expressing the distinctive political contexts of the federation. Women's movements obtained governmental positions, filling all possible gaps, with the creation of a *locus* of their own: the Women's Rights Councils (*Conselhos dos Direitos da Mulher)*[12] at national, state and municipal level, set up by democratic criteria of popular participation.[13] More recently, the Special Secretary of Policies for Women (*Secretaria Especial de Políticas para as Mulheres*)[14] was created under the Presidency of the Republic and the National Council of Women's Rights (*Conselho Nacional dos Direitos da Mulher*) is part of its structure.

This pioneering experience opens a new social control modality in public administration: on the one hand, by directly influencing state decision-making and implementing innovative public policy, and on the other hand by pinpointing existing vacuums in planning and enforcement of those policies, generally through budgetary constraints. For that reason, women focused on gender-oriented[15] participatory budgetary activities.

New power spaces, especially Women's Rights Councils set up during the state restructuring phase, were gender-equality sensitive policy-making incubators, cutting across government areas with ideas, bringing government closer with proposals to reduce existing asymmetries in favour of women's advancement. Women took advantage of these spaces to articulate needed policies—many implemented to date—with greater efficiency. Coordination centers and commissions were set up, multiplying structures and presence, disseminating ideas and proposals in different ministries, secretaries and state entities. Action programs at the Executive level set out short, medium and long term targets to advance gender equality, bringing light to priority areas in the women's agenda: education and culture, health and reproductive rights, work, violence and justice, legislation, environment and communication.

The National Brazilian Report for the Committee on the Elimination of Discrimination Against Women (CEDAW), 1985-2002, provides a summary that portrays progress made by global policies that fostered long lasting measures to address specific needs of the female part of humanity.

As far as Women's Rights Councils are concerned, the VI Brazilian Official Report, 2001-2005, addresses important activities carried out specifically by the National Council of Women's Rights (CNDM).[16] These agencies within the executive were successful in their undertaking. According to the above mentioned official report:

> Apart from specific action as the National Council for Women's Rights, the Council also focused on advancing women's rights councils in Brazilian states and municipalities. In order to do so, it partnered with existing councils, reported on the council's activities, answered requests and drafted registries with data collected. In 2003, there were 90 Municipal Councils and 20 State Councils. The Council's Secretary registered 204 Councils: 24 State Councils (including the brand new Amazonas State Council of Women's Rights) Pernambuco, Rondônia and Sergipe State Councils under way; and 180 Municipal Councils. (Please note that this figure refers to identified and contacted municipal councils.) [*translation mine*]

This report, presented at the CEDAW[17] Committee on July 25th, 2007, details recent steps in the implementation of the Convention in Brazil. It reflects efforts made in Brazilian universal policies for the advancement of women at the Executive and Legislative levels. It also comments on initiatives to make the Judiciary enforce women's international human rights instruments and contribute to the advancement of the principle of equality, with the goal of a subsequent transformation in Brazilian culture, achieving gender symmetry in power relations.

Drafting unofficial reports is an international practice. *Shadow Reports* prepared by women's organizations follow the same process as official reports, and are also submitted to CEDAW Committee at the same time with the purpose of providing information and input for comparison of versions submitted by States Parties. Counter reports (see Agende) submitted by Brazilian women acknowledge significant progress in advancing women's rights in the country, but it is clear that some state policies are more successful and long lasting, like pioneer services introduced for women in Public Safety with Police Stations for Women (*Delegacia Especializada de Atendimento à Mulher*, or DEAMs). Apart from gender-sensitive human-resource training, these facilities provide greater visibility and efficiency in situations of gender-based violence against women.

Several publications on the task carried out by DEAMs are a proof of the worthy contribution these innovative stations make to unmask violence in a narrow or strict sense that afflicts women. These specialized police stations collect hitherto unknown data, thus creating a new statistical registry that shows that public policies in this area are yet to be implemented.

Guita Grin Debert goes on to describe these specialized police stations as follows:

> DEAMs are, certainly, one of the more visible faces of the politicization of justice to guarantee women's rights. It is a way to press the Judiciary about the criminalization of acts considered private issues. Their replication in the past twenty years—and the interest they provoke in power positions within the system of justice and in other institutions even when they do not share a feminist agenda—shows they are deeply rooted in our country. [translation mine]

Policies to advance gender equality in Brazil are present in The Plurianual Plan 2004/2007 that introduces in Annex I, Act n° 11.318, 2006, the Strategic Government Guideline, whereby:

> •Advancing gender equality, and focus on appreciation of different identities.
> •Cross-cutting gender, racial, ethnic, generational approach considering people with special needs and sexual orientation in public policy formulation and implementation.
> •Promotion of affirmative action policies, focusing on socially vulnerable groups' needs; broadening access to justice;
> •Eradication of domestic violence; eradication of violence against vulnerable social segments. Appreciate identities and preserve integrity and national sovereignty. [translation mine]

The representation of women's movements at the state level is achieved by the Women's Rights Councils—with a specific public agenda—and represents pioneering government action along the path of affirmative and exclusive action targeted for women. Through this approach, a gender perspective was included in the development of universal policies in different areas. These are landmark actions in the evolution of the feminist fight: the greatest achievement since the suffragette victory in 1934.

Government in Brazil is increasingly concerned with women's issues. At every level there is political commitment as evidenced by the broad support state governments and local representatives gave to the National Pact to Eradicate Violence against Women. This important initiative by the Special Secretary of Policies for Women, sets out a group of actions (supported by budget allocations) to prevent and eradicate all forms of violence against women, and especially violence against rural, black, or Indigenous women due to their greater social vulnerability.

As these initiatives took place within the Executive in the last two decades, the Legislature, with similar enthusiasm, created the Feminine Caucus in the National Congress, as well as creating alliances at different legislative levels in the country. This parliamentarian organization of women is still in force today. The caucus focuses on subjects related to women's issues and on democratic practices such as holding public hearings to encourage dialogue with civil society leaders. The Feminine Caucus in National Congress summarizes political representations for the advancement of women through the promotion of necessary articulations to create and improve institutional mechanisms to achieve gender equality and shape, step-by-step, an egalitarian power division between men and women, on the basis of the democratic rule of law, fairness, and solidarity: the foundations of the Brazilian republic.[18]

The purpose of presenting these issues is to trace a narrative of arguments and introduce information to elaborate and compare, in a summarized manner, how the Executive, Legislative and Judicial Powers are reacting to the struggle and mobilization of women's organizations in Brazil to speed up and broaden the effectiveness of women's rights.

THE JUDICIARY

If the Executive and the Legislative Powers are engaged with the advancement of women's rights,[19] how, assuming it is following a responsive and democratic approach, is the Judiciary performing in this area? The answer, alas, is "not well." In the last two decades, the Judiciary has been late, slow, and reluctant in its response to the urgent and unpostponable women's agenda. This position is confirmed by different official reports by the Brazilian government and in counter-reports and studies made by women's organizations and related stakeholders in documents for the implementation of CEDAW and the

Convention of Belém in Pará, Brazil, Plurianual Plans, Strategic Plans, and others.

For a long time the Judiciary abided by discriminatory archetypes reproduced in jurisdictional structures that made gender inequality prevail in social segments. It remained alien to the New Constitution until the *Maria da Penha Act*[20] – Prevent Domestic and Family Violence Against Women was passed in August, 2006. Only then did the Judiciary begin a slow and gradual process to align itself towards a new paradigm.

Examination of the past two decades of the justice system demonstrates that the criminal branch of the Judiciary shows the cruelest face of inequality between men and women, stained by violence that cuts across the boundaries of morals to step on criminal grounds. This area also shows the state's behaviour in these cases.

The first obvious example is that of "legitimate defense." This thesis was frequently used for many years to acquit men detained for murder of their current or former spouses, cohabitants and girlfriends. In such cases, legal decisions were based on arguments that showed that the male aggressor was trying to defend his "marital honour" through his behaviour, or the honour of his injured machismo, "stained" by the woman due to adultery or simply because she expressed the desire to end the relationship. In response to constant so-called crimes of passion that took place during the 1980s, women's movements coined the motto "Love does not kill." Debates, demonstrations, seminars, and publications flourished at the time to provide evidence for the absurdity of the possibility of being acquitted on the grounds of legitimate defense.

In 1991, a groundbreaking Superior Court of Justice case rejected the thesis of legitimate defense of honour, by a vote casted by Judge José Cândido de Carvalho Filho, in Special Appeal 1517. In spite of this, Case Law decisions still make reference to such a thesis.[21]

During those years significant papers were written on court decisions involving female victims, such as the Human Rights Watch report "Criminal Injustice: Violence Against Women in Brazil" and Danielle Ardaillon and Guita Grin Debert's "When the Victim Is a Woman." Both studies are based upon the same premise: the letter of the law *versus* the strength of cultural standards. Is the logic of criminal cases the same for men and women? For Ardaillon and Debert,

> ...it is worth noting that, in the legal discourse, victim and defendant are transformed into play characters and oddly enough, the main character in not the crime itself but the

sexual, professional and social characteristics and descriptions
of the characters. (5) [*translation mine*]

These first reports on the Brazilian state administration of the legal
system, produced by players involved in domestic violence episodes,
from the perspective of their relationship with the legal structure and
political actors, as well as by Case Law summaries in the country, show
the shallow perception the Judiciary has of the nature and magnitude
of gender-based violence. This stubborn deficiency makes the Judiciary
unable to provide the protection of rights women expect and deserve.

All the documents collected by the women's movement that describe
their helpless situation within the legal system supported action taken
to make the necessary changes in the system, especially in the Judiciary.
Action taken focuses on the Judiciary and strategies are set forth to
break the prevailing justice model that accepts the historical set of
conditions that perpetuate and make chronic the reproduction of the
serious social phenomenon of violence against women, as Suely Souza
de Almeida points out.

The barriers to change are slowly being dismantled, thanks to
actions promoted by women's governmental and non-governmental
organizations throughout the years to introduce a gender sensitive
perspective in the Judiciary and change the paradigm of legal decisions.
Before the *Maria da Penha Act* was passed, a dichotomy existed between
the international body of law that defended women's human rights and
the domestic legal framework that granted no special treatment to the
issue. For more than a decade, domestic violence cases were heard as
minor crimes according to Act 9.099, passed in September 26, 1995.
Together with appealing and challenging discriminatory discourses
that contaminated legal cases when the victim was a woman, a second
form of disregard of domestic violence by the Judiciary was created by
this Act: the distribution of food boxes to charitable institutions as an
alternative to criminal prosecution. A two-fold situation is created: the
violation of women's human rights versus a minor crime. How can a
crime that violates the human rights of a woman be considered a minor
crime?

Based upon empirical studies, countless academic papers as well as
reports published by organized feminist groups from different areas
such as women's health, unions, and members of the judicial system,
a common conclusion was reached: enforcement of Act 9.099/1995
in domestic violence cases perpetuates the trivialization of these cases,
increasing cases of violence against women. This situation conflicted

with the direction of international studies backed by the Brazilian State that set forth that violence against women constitutes a violation of human rights and undermines development.

Wide feminist articulation had for some years been working on the debate to implement strategies to change the existing frame of mind in the judicial system and change the Brazilian legal framework in human rights violation cases especially when related to domestic violence. For this purpose a working group was set up to take concrete action to address the discouraging situation as proposed in CEPIA's (*Cidadania, Estudo, Pesquisa, Informação e Ação)* (or, Citizenship, Study, Research, Information and Action) open letter (see Barsted and Reis Lavigne 2002).

The proposal to draft a Bill was the response to the domestic disagreement with international women's human rights legislation and the New Constitution. The Bill granted the Law Enforcement and Judiciary Systems the necessary instruments to advance gender-specific measures and respond to women's specific needs. The state had to respond with qualitative measures that in the face of concrete cases would advance the human rights paradigm and impact society deterring the infringement of these rights.

Thus, on August 7, 2006, Act 11.340—the *Maria da Penha Act*—was passed to prevent and eradicate domestic and family violence against women. Adjudication Centers, gender-sensitive legal policy hubs, were set up within the legal system. The Public Attorney's Office, the Public Defense and support services would also work along with jurisdictional structures with specific responsibilities, powers, and objectives to deal with issues related to domestic and family violence against women.

Nevertheless, initiatives taken so far fall short of expectations to trigger the longed for change in the legal framework. Barriers within the Judiciary prevail: a lack of understanding of gender issues and a low budget allocated to ongoing human resource training of magistrates, judiciary officials and support personnel; low enforcement of international instruments in favour of women's human rights in legal decisions; barriers to networking, especially in women-oriented multidisciplinary services in the Executive Power; disorderly response to specific women's care; lack of communication structures for ongoing dialogue with women's movements as well as for planning, monitoring, controlling and budgeting women sensitive action programs.

This is a brief summary of the many shortcomings the Judiciary has in the face of historic demands of Brazilian women's movements. Nevertheless, the fact that the Judiciary Reform by Constitutional

Amendment N° 45, was passed in December 2004 and Act 11.340—the *Maria da Penha Act*—passed in August 2006, renewed women's movements' momentum and hope for the implementation of a gender-sensitive law enforcement and judicial system in the country, one that would promote the exchange of ideas and actions to advance equality in the Powers of the Republic, and raise the bar of effectiveness of this constitutional mandate.

FINAL CONSIDERATIONS

The new 1988 Constitution has come of age. More than twenty years have gone by since women organized at the time of National Constitutional Assembly for the purpose of achieving gender equality and advancing the rights that would grant women in Brazil full enjoyment of citizenship on equal basis with men. The *Maria da Penha Act* was, indeed, a turning point in affirmative politics of women's movements in their quest to achieve in practice constitutional equality in Brazilian society.

The relationship that women's movements have with the Powers of a refounded Brazil, particularly with the Executive and the Legislative Powers, has triggered major shifts in the course of public politics and in the legal status of women. Agreement with our 1988 Federal Constitution, and with women's international human rights instruments of all subordinated legal instances, as well as ongoing systematic production of gender-sensitive public policies, has set change in motion at administrative levels and at state organizational structures, reducing the risk of continuity due to simple government rotation.

In order to transform women's demands into public policy platforms during post-constitutional processes, recently improved democratic practices such as public hearings at the state and municipal levels in women's conferences have taken place. These political interventions have resulted in the National Women's Policy Plans in place during the last eight years.

Within the Judiciary, the necessary transition to change in line with democratic harmony among the Powers of the Republic, a demand of the consolidating Rule of Law, is slow and more cumbersome due to inherent characteristics of the Judiciary, only changed by Constitutional Amendment N° 45, passed on December, 30, 2004.

The creation of the National Justice Council (*Conselho Nacional de Justiça,* CNJ)—the new mechanism introduced by the above-mentioned reforms—to interface between the Judiciary and civil society, has strengthened the relationship between the Judiciary and women's movements. While this policy is currently part of the justice system, it does not yet respond appropriately to women's needs. It is essential to continue to advance access to justice, still scarce for women, and to establish concrete actions and institutional mechanisms to create and modify government structures that will effectively raise the standard of gender-sensitive policies. There is an expectation regarding the role of the CNJ in constructing a common basis for the Judiciary with a balanced gender perspective. In this way, the different levels of Judiciary Power Administration would implement the actions designed by the CNJ with the tools to leverage policies that will equalize this Power with the other two: Executive and Legislative. These polices should have a specific focus on increasing programs and activities to advance gender equality.

Great progress has been made in Brazil to advance women's human rights, in all of its dimensions. Nevertheless, gender equality has not yet been fulfilled. It is in progress.

[1] This article presents some ideas that were developed during my Judiciary Masters Degree Program and research at FGV Direito, Rio de Janiero, Brazil. Research was conducted to determine whether women's rights were received by the National Council of Justice, the body responsible for new institutional design of the judiciary in Brazil. To this end, I examined the administrative acts of the CNJ, since its establishment in 2005. The research determined that a balanced gender perspective had not yet been fully implemented in judicial policies established by national judicial spheres of the administration.

[2] Some expressions of women's movements like the Women's Movement for Amnesty and Democratic Freedom, were essential players in the fight to end the military regime that ruled the country since the *coup d'état* on March 31, 1966.

[3] The military dictatorship lasted more than twenty years in Brazil (1964-1985) and imposed deprivation of political and constitutional rights, dissolved political parties, imposed censorship, repression of those against the regime and issued institutional acts or decrees. *Institutional Act n.º5*, AI-5, issued on December 13, 1968, during General Arthur da Costa e Silva's dictatorship, was the worst of all and the hardest blow of the military regime. This decree authorized the President of the Republic, without any judicial interference, to adjourn National Congress sessions; intervene states and municipalities; disfranchise parliamentarian mandates; impose a ten-year suspension of political

rights of all citizens; seize all goods considered illegal; and suspend habeas-corpus guarantees (available at <http://www.cpdoc.fgv.br/nav_fatos_imagens/htm/fatos/AI5.htm>).

[4]Act 6683 (*Amnesty Act*) passed by National Congress in August 28, 1979, is a landmark in this period.

[5]*The Lipstick Lobby* is the name given to a group of women that closely followed the constitutional process, raising awareness among house representatives and senators to consider the demands included in the "Letter from Brazilian Women to Representatives." This historic document advocated for legal framework that translated gender equality and reaffirmed the role of the State in advancing that legal framework (Pitanguy).

[6]In agreement with article 18, CEDAW, ratified by the National Congress in 1984, States Parties undertake to submit for consideration by the Committee a report on the legislative, judicial, administrative or other measures which they have adopted to give effect to the provisions of the present Convention. This official report is the first one and includes five reports in one. It includes information that should have been considered in 1985, 1989, 1993, 1997 and 2001 (see Brazil's Participation).

[7]Women's movements undergo fluctuations throughout time. From the moment Brazilian women organized themselves to advance democracy, in the '80s; the movement developed itself into different ones. Women's movements like the Center of Brazilian Women represent the beginning of the second feminist wave in 1975. Feminine reflection movements focused on sexuality, like CERES, autonomous women Feminist Forum, like SOS-Women, provided care for women victims of domestic violence until the moment non-governmental organizations appeared to include gender and public policy on the state agenda. At the present moment, the movement is the result of the expressions of many groups and political parties.

[8]Income concentration is very unbalanced in Brazil. Nevertheless there is a transformation under way due to income programs and better education, as shown by a drop in the GINI coefficient between 2001 and 2007 (see IPC-IG).

[9]The Gender Equality Observatory for Latin America and the Caribbean (*Observatorio de Igualdad de Género de América Latina y el Caribe*) presents disturbing indicators on women's situation in Brazil as, for instance, in decision-making.

[10]The VI Brazilian National Report to CEDAW contains information on the situation of women in the country from 1985 to 2002, and includes

affirmative action strategies for women, pinpointing legal innovations on the matter.

[11]Feminist Alerts are information publications published by feminist groups from various backgrounds during elections periods with claims for the advancement of women and with the goal of informing political candidates of women's interests.

[12]Councils of Women's Rights, as they were also called, are similar in nature, function, and structure in states and municipalities. They are collegiate bodies associated directly or indirectly to the head of the Executive Power, and have the main task of formulating and implementing gender-sensitive public policies. They are also enforcement-oriented. Most Council's basic structure include a deliberative body, subject-specific technical committees, and an administrative team.

[13]Membership to State Councils of Women's Rights, between 1988 and 2002, was recommended by several segments of women's movements through a triple list presented to State Governments with proportional representation of progressive political parties, unions, and women's independent groups.

[14]The mission of this agency was to "develop joint initiates with all Ministries and Special Secretaries with the challenge to advance women's agendas in public policies and empower women for full citizenship."

[15]The United Nations Development Fund for Women (UNIFEM) promotes studies and research on gender participatory budgets. Also related is the document "Women and Participatory Budgets: Women's Demands and Conquests Study, 2005 and 2006. Recife, Pernambuco State," by SOS Corpo, Feminist Institute for Democracy.

[16]The Council was created in 1985, under the Justice Ministry, to promote gender sensitive policies and achieve women's political, economic and cultural participation. The Council's functions and responsibilities have changed greatly with time. Under the current administration it serves under the Special Secretary of Policies for Women. The Council is made up by civil society and government representatives that take part in the social oversight of gender sensitive public policies and is chaired by the Madam Minister of the Special Secretary of Policies for Women.

[17]CEDAW consists of 23 experts, of "high moral standing and competence" in the field covered by the Convention (Article 17, 1), gives effect to the provisions, by States Parties, of the present convention CEDAW, and considers reports submitted by them (Article 18 Convention); makes suggestions and general recommendations (Article 21, 1 Convention); and considers communications from individuals or a group of individuals who claim to be victims of violations of the rights protected

by the convention. With the entry into force of the Optional Protocol to the Convention on 22 December 2000, the committee is entitled to two important additional functions: to receive and consider petitions from or on behalf of individuals or a group of individuals who claim to be victims of violations of the rights protected by the convention.

[18]In accordance with Part I, Article 3 of the Federal Constitution of 1988, a fundamental objective of the Federal Republic of Brazilia is to build a society free, fair and in solidarity with all its citizens.

[19]More recently, the Brazil Observatory for Gender Equality, under the coordination of the Special Secretary of Policies for Women, was set up to give visibility to, and strengthen, Brazilian State efforts in the advancement of gender equality and the protection of women's rights.

[20]Act 11.340, the *Maria da Penha Act*, was passed in August 7, 2006. The Act, a result of joint action by civil society and the State, provides mechanisms to prevent domestic and family violence against women, in accordance with Sec.8, Article 226 of the Federal Constitution, and with CEDAW and the Convention on the Prevention, Punishment and Eradication of Violence against Women. This Act also provides for the creation of Special Courts for Domestic and Family Violence against Women; and the amendment the Code of Criminal Procedure, the Penal Code and the Penal Execution Law, and other measures. The Act is named after biochemical pharmacist Maria da Penha, who was the subject of a domestic violence case in 1983, which reached the headlines after being subject to examination by the Inter American Commission of Human Rights. As a consequence of the unacceptable delay of the Judiciary, especially the Ceará State Court of Justice, and although the crime incurred represented a violation of human rights, almost 20 years went by without passing final sentence against the man who had twice tried to kill Maria da Penha and had left her paraplegic. Since no final sentence was passed and the aggressor was free, while his victim had no freedom to come and go as she pleased since she was bound to a wheel chair, in 1998, Maria da Penha, together with the Center for Justice and International Law and the Latin American and Caribbean Committee for the Defense of Woman's Rights, filed her case at the Inter-American Commission of Human Rights at the Organization of American States.

[21]Recent Rio de Janeiro State Court of Justice Decision, in an Appeal for Reversal of the Decision, not accepted by majority, on February 16, 2006. Majority vote does not accept the legitimate defense of honour thesis since "tradition does not authorize murder or verbal offense against honour." Nevertheless, it is worth mentioning the arguments made in the above-mentioned trial in favour of accepting the legitimate

defense of honour thesis: "...in effect, as appropriately mentioned in adverse opinion, the judges' decision is backed by oral proof in the records. In self-defense, the defendant claims he was humiliated by the victim, saying the defendant was a 'cuckold, a horned man, a fag and that if he felt sorry for her, he could be her lover's woman' [sic]" (fls. 94). The victim goes on to describe that she met her lover and that treason took place in the couple's home. Thus, legitimate defense of honour is typified and confirmed by the Court Decision Council of São Sebastião do Alto Judicial District, especially since it is a small town where everyone knows one another. These are the reasons why an appeal was granted, in the terms of adverse opinion, with dismissal for legitimate defense of honour.

REFERENCES

Ações em Gênero Cidadania e Desenvolvimento (AGENDE). Brazil and Compliance with CEDAW. Shadow Report of Civil Society to the VI National Brazilian Report to the Convention on the Elimination of Discrimination against Women, 2001–2005. June 2007. Web. Accessed: March 5, 2009.

Act 9.099, September 26, 1995. On Civil and Criminal Courts and other issues. Web. 24 Mar. 2009.

Act 10.933, August 11, 2004, on the Plurianual Plan for 2004/2007. Annex I as provided by Act 11.318, 2006. Web. 6 March 2009.

Ardaillon, Danielle and Guita Grin Debert. *When the Victim Is a Woman*. Brasília: CEDAC, 1987. Print.

Barsted, Leila Linhares and Rosane M. Reis Lavigne. "Domestic Violence Against Women Act Proposal. *CEPIA's Letter* 8.10 (Dec. 2002). Web. 22 Mar. 2009.

Bordieu, Pierre. *Male Domination*. 4th edition. Trans. Maria Helena Kuhner. Rio de Janeiro: Bertrand Brazil, 2005.

Brazil's Participation on the 29th Session of the Convention on the Elimination of Discrimination against Women (CEDAW). Brasília, 2004. Web. April 12, 2010.

Convention on the Elimination of Discrimination Against Women (CEDAW). Web. 9 March 2009.

D'Áraújo, Maria Celina. "Os ministros da Nova República; notas para entender a democratização do Poder Executivo." CPDOC/FGV, 2009. Web. Accessed: April, 2010.

de Almeida, Suely Souza. "Risking One's Life and Impunity: Indicators for Domestic Violence Judicialization Policy." *Domestic Violence:*

Foundations for Public Policy Making. Ed. Barbara Musumeci Soares, Marisa Gaspary, and Suely Souza de Almeida. Rio de Janeiro: Revinter, 2003. Print.

Debert G. G., Maria Filomena Gregori, Adriana Gracia Piscitelli. "Gênero e Distribuição da Justiça: as delegacias de defesa da mulher e a construção das diferenças." Campinas: PAGU/Núcleo de Estudos de Gênero da UNICAMP, 2006. Print.

Economic, Historic, Social and Statistical Racial Relations Studies Labouratory (*Labouratório de Análises Econômicas, Históricas, Sociais e Estatísticas das Relações Raciais da Universidade Federal do Rio de Janeiro*). Web Accessed: April 14, 2010.

Fraser, Nancy. "Recognition Without Ethics?" *Theory, Culture and Society* 18 (2,3) (2001): 21-42. Web. 3 Mar. 2009.

National Household Sample Survey, 2008/2009,. Web. Accessed: April 15, 2010.

Human Rights Watch. "Criminal Injustice: Violence Against Women in Brazil." An Americas Watch Report. New York, 1991. Web. Accessed: March 23, 2009.

International Policy Centre for Inclusive Growth (IPC-IG). "What Explains the Decline in Brazil's Inequality." Web. Accessed: June 19, 2010.

National Brazilian Report for the Committee on the Elimination of Discrimination Against Women (CEDAW), 1985-2002. Coordinated by Flavia Piovesan and Silvia Pimentel. Brazilian Foreign Affairs Ministry, Justice Ministry, and Women's Rights State Secretary, 2002. Print.

O'Donnell, Guillermo and Philippe Schmitter. *Transiciones desde un gobierno autoritario.* Buenos Aires: Prometeo Libros, 2010. Print.

Pitanguy, Jacqueline. *As Mulheres e a Constituição de 1988.* Web. Accessed: April 5, 2010.

"Sixth National Report of Brazil on the Convention on the Elimination of Discrimination against Women (CEDAW)." Brasília, 2008. Web. March 2, 2009. Print.

Special Appeal 1517 – 6th Chamber Judge José Cândido de Carvalho Filho 11.03.1991. Published in 04.15.1991. Web. Accessed: March 9, 2009.

Special Secretary of Policies for Women. "Facing Violence Against Women: Action Balance 2006-2007." Web. Accessed: 21 Mar. 2009.

7.
This Precious Human Life

How to Turn an Ordinary Life into an Extraordinary Adventure

ANAHATA IRADAH, USA/INDIA/NEPAL/BRAZIL

ONE OF THE REVELATIONS of Shakyamuni Buddha, twenty-five hundred years ago, was that nobility of the human heart is earned through practice and diligence, and not necessarily something acquired through birth. This is one of the teachings that makes Buddhism so extraordinary: that any human being may achieve an enlightened mind, independent of circumstances. This teaching is especially empowering for women, because it means that when we do our spiritual work internally it has a direct effect on our outer lives. There is an interpenetration between the inner realms and outer reality. This premise has been the basis of all of my social-action work throughout the world, and is the foundation of my personal spiritual journey.

I would like to share a legend from the Tibetan Buddhist tradition. When the *bodhisattva,* or Great Goddess, Tara was about to reach enlightened mind, she was told by her teachers that she could take any form. It was recommended that she take the body of a man. She thought about this, then vowed at that moment to always take the form of woman because, she declared, there was no difference between the body of a man or a woman in its capability of manifesting enlightened mind. His Holiness the Dalai Lama says that Tara may well have been the first feminist! This story is incredibly encouraging for women. In essence it means that by applying the six perfections to our ordinary everyday awareness: 1) generosity, 2) ethics, 3) patience, 4) effort, 5) concentration, and 6) wisdom), we too can reach the state of Buddhahood, the highest accomplishment within Buddhism.

I have been a practicing Buddhist for most of my adult life, and one thing I have found is that the essence of the teachings is applicable for all people, in all circumstances, at all times. I have lived and worked in many countries, but my outreach in non-English speaking cultures has been focused in Brazil, India and Nepal. There I have cultivated and contributed to many cottage industries that have served to support schools, nunneries, monasteries, senior citizens and numerous other venues of social justice.

It has been an interesting journey, how my life has unfolded and how all the projects have come into manifestation. There have been two main strands. The inner strand, my foundation, is the strength and fortitude that I gained from my path as a meditator, which helped me to cultivate qualities of endurance, patience, equanimity, loving kindness and compassion. The outer strand, or I could say the structure built on that foundation, is one of the most beautiful forms I have ever encountered, the "Dances of Universal Peace." The Dances emerged from an esoteric school of Sufism called the Sufi Islamia International, whose founder was Murshid Samuel L. Lewis of San Francisco, California. He in turn was inspired by the highly esteemed Sufi master Pir O. Murshid Hazrat Inayat Khan who came to the USA from India in 1910. The Dances of Universal Peace are based in the embodiment of the Sufi ideals of Love, Harmony and Beauty. Murshid Samuel Lewis received the inspiration for the Dances in the late 1960s and early '70s. Sacred phrases from one or more of the earth's spiritual traditions are recited, sung or chanted to music appropriate to that tradition while, holding hands, usually in a circle. When I encountered the tradition in the mid-eighties I was particularly lucky! I immediately had two wonderful teachers, Murshida Tasnim Fernandez and Murshid Saadi Neil Douglas-Klotz. I had a strong musical background and could play many instruments. I was a composer, and easily picked up each dance, and was soon able to accompany them on guitar. I achieved some recognition as a teacher in the USA and started to receive invitations from many places in the world to teach and share. I cultivated my skills, building my repertoire of Dances and infused my teaching from within this school of Western Sufism with my understanding and realizations from the Buddhist tradition. My meditation practice supported my teaching of the Dances from the earth's spiritual traditions, and my appreciation of the wisdom traditions of the earth helped to deepen my Buddhist practice. It was for me an auspicious confluence of inspiration.

In 1997, I was working on a beautiful sacred dance project, manifesting a book of Buddhist dances based upon the Brahma Viharas, The Heavenly Abodes of Consciousness. At this time I started to work with Prema Dasara. She came to New Zealand at my invitation to teach the Mandala Dance of the Twenty One Praises of Tara. I had already played the music of the dance for her in Seattle and wanted to offer the experience of dancing the Mandala of Tara to the women of New Zealand. When Prema arrived, we realized that we had much in common in terms of our commitment to sacred dance, music, and the wish to empower women and give them the tools to transform consciousness. Our wish was to teach, from the wisdom traditions, how to transform pain and suffering into wisdom and compassion.

Prema had been invited by His Eminence Jamgon Kongtrul Rinpoche II to take the Mandala Dance of Tara to the Tibetans in diaspora specifically to empower Tibetan refugee women, nuns, and children in India and Nepal. Since I had had some success in co-ordinating peace missions to the Middle East at an earlier time, I offered Prema my experience. It became our mission to take our first delegation of women to India and Nepal to dance with and for the Tibetan people. It was an awesome task and responsibility. We took our first delegation of 50 dancers in 1998 to North India and Nepal, our second delegation of twenty people to South India early in 2001 and, later that same year, our third delegation of over 90 dancers from 25 countries of origin.

All human beings appreciate their spiritual traditions being understood and honoured. By combining respect for their spiritual tradition with an invitation to participate in the sacred dance, we found a way to empower women, and the requests and wishes of H. E. Jamgon Kongtrul Rinpoche II were fulfilled. Through the Mandala Dance of the Twenty One Praises of Tara, the Tibetan women could recognize within themselves Tara's attributes of wisdom, compassion and power. Not only the Tibetan women benefitted: all the pilgrims of many nations who participated in the delegations were empowered to go home to their countries and communities to share the wisdom of interconnectedness.

In the Tibetan language, the word for "woman" historically also meant "lower caste." This translation speaks for itself. Female Tibetan practitioners were rarely taught the higher teachings, and were mostly the servants of the male practitioners. They sat at the back of the teachings. They cooked and served the food. They had no access to important cultural practices, such as the Cham-Sacred Dance, the Creation of Sand Mandalas or the Dialectic School of Debate. The nunneries were usually impoverished and neglected. One day during an audience with H. H. Dalai Lama, a Western nun asked His Holiness to imagine reversing the roles, to imagine that the men were only allowed to eat after the women, that they had to sit at the back of the room, that they had no access to the higher teachings and that the monasteries had inadequate infrastructure and no support to receive teachings. At the end of her description His Holiness wept and acknowledged that things had to change. He abolished the use of "woman" to mean "lower caste" from the Tibetan language, and systematically set about empowering woman at every level of Tibetan society, including the formation of a secular government in exile where woman now play very important roles and have equal rights.

When the Tibetan nuns escaped Chinese-occupied Tibet, they were not only escaping from the Chinese but also from an in-built bias towards the empowerment of men in their society and the lack of opportunity for women. Since 1959 there have been many monasteries set up in exile to receive Tibetan boys who wished to become monks, but very few opportunities for girls to enter the novitiate. This is now changing, largely due to the pioneering efforts of western women like Karma Lekshe Tsomo, who fought diligently for the right of the nuns to receive full ordination when hitherto they could only take the vows of a novice. Change is happening within Tibetan society, partly through the powerful work of Mrs. Rinchen Khondro, who established the Dolma Ling nunnery in Dharamsala, officially inaugurated by His Holiness the Dalai Lama in 2005. Now several nunneries are flourishing due to awareness and support both from within the Tibetan world and the international community. Within the Tibetan lay community the Tibetan Women's Association provides strength, wisdom and solidarity for the secular community.

I mentioned earlier that there were three subjects that women traditionally were not allowed to engage in Cham-Sacred Dance, the creation of Sand Mandalas, and the Dialectic School of Debate. Much progress has been made in all three domains. All the nunneries are now fully participating in the sacred art of creating sand mandalas. They are also doing very well in their debating schools. Prema, many members of Tara Dhatu, and I are very proud to be addressing the subject of Cham, sacred dance for women. The Kopan Monastery first invited us to teach the nuns of Khachoe Ghakyil Ling Nunnery in Kathmandu, who studied with us to the point where they could present certain dances in their overseas tours of Germany, USA, and Australia. Their touring programs allowed the nuns to raise money to support their rapidly growing nunnery in Kathmandu. Thousands of Tibetans still escape from Chinese-occupied Tibet; these nunneries are an essential part of the infrastructure of keeping Tibetan culture alive in exile, and providing a home and education for girls who aspire to become nuns. A few years ago, we were invited by Thrangu Rinpoche to teach the nuns of Tara Abbey, also in Kathmandu. With the assistance of

Andrea Abinanti, a classical dance master in the Newari tradition of Nepal, some of the nuns of Tara Abbey studied the Mandala Dance of Tara as part of their core curriculum in the nunnery. Every monastery and nunnery recites the Twenty-one Praises of Tara every day, but the dance takes it to a new level of manifestation.

What has this done for the nuns? Just imagine the nuns escaping from their homeland, where their religion is being systematically torn apart by the occupying forces. Where, if they carry a picture of the Dalai Lama, they are thrown into prison for years and years. Where women are being forcibly sterilized and not allowed to have more than one child. Imagine this and then imagine coming to a place where they can pray in freedom, where they have enough to eat, where they can receive an education that is not propaganda-based and where, in addition to all of this, they are told they are Tara! The Mandala Dance of the Twenty One Praises of Tara has played a significant role in the empowerment of women. It is not only nuns in the Mandala that are affected, but the entire nunnery. On festival days the whole community comes out to receive the blessing of the dance. The audience applauds the efforts of the dancing nuns to manifest themselves in all their glory as Tara, the Mother of the Buddhas, in all her forms and with all her attributes. The dance models power not imposed from above, but power from within and shared equally with each other. Each nun takes her turn to be in the center of the Mandala. Tara's declaration, that there is no difference between the form of a man or a woman in its capability of manifesting enlightened mind, is ritually enacted and embodied, bearing witness to the community at large that the Great Mother is alive and well and that we must sing and dance her Praises. This surely helps to dissolve the stronghold of patriarchal systems!

We have danced for His Holiness the Dalai Lama, who has expressed his sincere appreciation for our work on behalf of Tibetan culture. Many of the high Lamas have become personally involved, champion our efforts, and make strong prayers for us to be able to continue our work. We are truly blessed to be able to merge spiritual endeavour with social action. The image of women working with women, whether nuns or lay practitioners, cultivating appreciation for each other instead of competitiveness, is another non-patriarchal form because it is not based upon power-over but empowering each other.

Our work has been successful on many levels, and one of those levels has been the birth of our humanitarian projects. In the USA, we have created a non-profit organization, Tara Dhatu, which enabled us to receive tax-deductible donations. It is both moving and empowering to see circumstances in India and Nepal where we know we can make a difference. In the Sufi tradition I was taught always to ask the question "Is this mine?" when I saw a circumstance that needed attention. So I would ask this question frequently; when the universe answered "yes," then Prema and I would move gently into the space of trying to bring benefit to people, places, projects, and circumstances. We never sought out opportunities. They simply unfolded before us in a very natural and organic way. This resulted, for example, in the setting up of sustainable cottage industries that support the education of girls who would otherwise receive no education. In a speech I made at the Atisha School in Nepal, I said "Tara Dhatu is about responding in an appropriate way. Sometimes we respond with the inspiration of offering sacred dance to uplift and inspire humanity. Sometimes we respond with kind words or a prayer and sometimes we respond by offering financial assistance in the form of creating sustainable and dignified ways for people to earn a livelihood."

Atisha School is the poorest of the Tibetan communities in the Kathmandu Valley. After the invasion of Tibet in 1959 the Tibetans escaped into exile and many formed a colony in Jawalakhel. In 1998 we pledged our support to this community and have found sponsors for most of the school children. The largest percentage of the sponsor's money goes towards the educational expenses of the child, but a small portion goes to the family to assist them with living expenses. In addition to this Tara Dhatu has raised the money for traditional cultural clothing dance costumes that allows the community to keep their folkloric dances and songs alive. Tara Dhatu has also contributed to the Tibetan Refugee Reception Center (TRRC), where Tibetans first go when they escape Chinese-occupied Tibet.

The project that is nearest to my heart at this moment is the opening of a shelter for at-risk children in Nepal. Due to the recent civil war and economic chaos, many Nepalese families cannot afford to feed their children, and abandon them in sacred places like the Boudenath Stupa (a very large outdoor shrine). Our Nepalese friend Pabitra Lama lives in front of the great Stupa; when she finds abandoned children she takes them into her home, contacts me and I find sponsors for them. Pabitra was raised in one of Nepalese villages several hours from Kathmandu. She is very well known to the villagers and when a girl's life is in danger (due to the loss of parents, dire economic circumstances, illness of family etc.) they contact Pabitra. She first verifies that there is no other way of solving the problem and then with the support of the tribal community she brings the child to Bouda. In

2012, we formed an NGO named Bright Nepal. Pabitra's home was full of children from all over Nepal and we needed to take the next step of opening a shelter to house girls at risk of being trafficked in the sex trade. Thus Bright Nepal was born. At this present, moment we have thirteen girls in residence, receiving education and full accommodation. They return home to their villages for festivals and many of the girls have the aspiration to help others in their villages when they are in a position to do so.

Bright Nepal is on a firm foundation, and we are currently working on a project to found a home for elderly women without families or anyone to take care of them. It will be a little further out of the city and in the countryside. In this facility we will have a small farm of goats and cows and we will grow produce to be self-sustaining. Each grandmother will be especially connected with one girl. The wisdom of the elders will be shared with the children, and the joy of the girls will lighten the hearts of the women.

The small humanitarian projects we began in 1998 are still going strong and are lovingly supported by friends around the world thanks to the ease of communication provided by the Internet. And this is the background that brought us to Brazil.

THE DANCES AND PEACE WORK IN BRAZIL

During this intensive time working on projects in Asia, we also had many invitations to teach in Brazil. The Dances of Universal Peace took Prema and me throughout much of this vast country. In order for us to understand Brazilians, we needed to embrace two of the major influences on their spiritual life: Native Brazilian tribal traditions and the African Orixás. In the state of Bahia we encountered an amazing international community called *Terra Mirim*, under the directorship of a Brazilian shaman named Alba Maria. In a poor rural area outside the city of Salvador, they opened a free school called the "Ecological School" and offered classes in African dance, Capoeira (a Brazilian martial art), and music. The community's caring for the people around them won their hearts and their trust. One of my students, Rhavina Schertenleib, introduced the Dances of Universal Peace to the teenagers. Five extraordinary young people stepped forward and requested to be trained as leaders. Rhavina asked if Prema and I would go to Terra Mirim to assist her in this mission, and an unforgettable journey began. Early in her training, eighteen-year old Eliandra Moreno dos Santos said "The Dances of Universal Peace help me and the world. Doing them here in my community is going to help us with the violence. I believe that these dances bring peace."

Since the beginning of this work, many years ago, we suspected that the Dances could be used as a tool for peace-making and reconciliation and to help break the cycles of violence and drug abuse. It has proven to be true. Of course, it could never be a result of the Dances in isolation. The Dances are a tool to be combined with other consistent methods of mind training and education. In a community like Terra Mirim, the Dances of Universal Peace find fertile ground. The proclivity is towards health, well-being, enlivenment, honesty, healing, and balance. In this environment the Dances are an inspired tool, because they bring to life the spiritual ideals of unity and peace.

When we started training the young people I could feel that we were planting a seed in their hearts. They were dancing for peace. They were dancing for equality. They were dancing to increase dignity and to dissolve despair. After the second of our annual seven-day training retreats, Camila Angela Santana dos Santos wrote a report about her experiences:

This is my true identification. On May 23, 2009, Saturday, I participated for the second time in a retreat of Dances of Universal Peace training in São Paulo. Circles that go through all the world traditions cultivating peace.

Different from the last training this one touched me a lot, it had a base about my life purposes and I was able to see them better, things clarified in my mind, answers to some questions came without effort, I felt relieved in my heart and a voice saying to be calm, to relax and valorize each moment I was living there.

It was peace I am sure, once more entering my heart, and I followed the voice and relaxed, enjoyed every moment, every opportunity, every speech, every movement. It was really an unforgettable gathering, different, transparent and friendly.

I was needing this meeting, to see new people, to meet myself and to remember that peace exist. We just need to cultivate it inside of us and this is the purpose of this retreat. It is also my intention as a young being, that has been growing, learning every day with life that many times seems to be lacking in gratitude. We know that sometimes we are part of this lack of gratitude. but many times we do not want to be open to understand this and to do something for a better life, to dance the rhythm that life plays, to see things as they can be and not just as they are.

With all this I feel awake to life, I live better with myself and I am able to make some people happy with my transformation. I realized that I can accommodate peace inside me without not being who I am. I realized that it is much better to walk in peace, to understand and be understood by the others and to have responsibility and intelligence than cultivate intrigue and harm in my heart, than to live alone and without knowing myself. This WAS me.

There is something that I can say for sure and with strength that is "to that world I do not return," I am sure of this affirmative after participating in the training, everything was so moving, so true that I still feel all that energy on my skin, in my eyes, in my speech, it was really a remarkable meeting. I remember the smiles, people gazes happy to see young people cultivating peace and spirituality without choosing or rejecting any tradition.

I am grateful every day for my awakening, I ask for transformation of other children and young people that are the future of our country, our world. I want to contribute to strengthen the peace movement and the awakening of the young people in my community, drink more and more of "this water" that does so good to me, the more I drink the more I want to.

These are the words of a young woman that thought about going through a path she thought was the right one, deluded by the wrong things of life, believing that she was always correct. This young woman also knew that she could do everything, but, in the middle of the way she found people that held her hand and invited her to walk together and in a moment like this you need to be fast and smart to decide if you want to go or not with this person. You have free will. I asked myself: why should I follow this person? And I ended up giving a chance to myself without knowing what could happen from that moment, I just got that opportunity that was presented to me and it was the best day of my life and I will never forget it.

Today, in a place called Terra Mirim Foundation, together with these people that offered me their hand, I live every day and I try to show to other young people that I meet that there are better paths to follow. I am grateful for the strength of all these people and finally I can say thank to myself for having chosen this path, to be able to say that I love myself, I love what I do and I love life.

I am deeply touched and inspired by Camila's beautiful testimony. After Camila wrote this, I returned to Terra Mirim, and some of the senior citizens attended because they wanted to meet and dance with the woman who was influencing their young folk! It was really joyful for me to see the impact of my work touching young and old alike. If real and lasting global change is to happen, it must come from the heart of the people. Change is not easy; it can only happen through consistent effort and a willingness to relinquish old habits. As Mahatma Gandhi said, "You must be the change you wish to see in the world." When we live from that place, we touch all things through our presence.

It is deeply satisfying to inspire other human beings. When the gifts I have been given help to fine-tune the soul of another then I am fulfilled. It is vital that we each find the spiritual nourishment and guidance that gives a deeper meaning to our lives. It helps to shape our life's purpose. To empower another human being is the greatest gift I can give them. When I am empowered by another human being it is the greatest gift they can give me. This is how it is, the passing of knowledge and wisdom from soul to soul, from heart to heart, from age to age.

Only through great compassion, courage and love can we significantly change anything. It begins inside, flows outward to touch everything and everyone. This human life is precious because we have the capability of attaining deep and lasting peace, and we are able to radiate our loving compassion into the world for the benefit of all beings everywhere without exception. This is the meaning of my life and this is the meaning of my work in the world, touching beings one heart at a time.

8.
Advocating Women's Rights in Palestine

HANA KIRREH, PALESTINE

T HE WHOLE WORLD, in general, and Palestinian society in specific, need to allow women to take a more equal role in society. If women are given equal opportunities as men then the whole world will have better generations and a better future as well. In this chapter I will focus on Palestinian women and the importance of their involvement in social, political and cultural activities.

MOVING BEYOND DISCRIMINATION

No one denies that men and women are equal in their capabilities in almost every respect, provided that women are given the same opportunities as men for training, employment, and promotion, yet discrimination against women is still present in today's social and political vision. In order to tackle this problem, attitudinal change by both men and women is needed. Some women are highly aware of their rights and abilities and are trying to fight for that change; for example a group of highly-motivated women of differing ages associated with the *Fateh* faction of the Palestinian Authority stated that they simply "don't have time to wait for a social revolution." For decades, Palestinian women have shared in the struggle for national liberation, and have put off the struggle for their rights as women—waiting until they have a state. They have decided of late that they need to work on both at the same time. It has been always proposed that women's issues will be discussed after liberation, but I would say that liberation and obtaining women's rights have to go together and on the same stance: remember the experience of the Algerian women who participated in the liberation process but who were denied their rights afterwards.[1]
To assure this does not happen again, women activists and men who are conscientious and respectful of gender must take the initiative

to train women in public speaking, confidence building, non-violent communication, techniques to overcome domination, conflict resolution and negotiation. Women must be encouraged to seek both primary and higher education. By doing so we create women who are ready to become leaders of the future, who will refuse the unbalanced distribution of domestic roles and the double full-time jobs those women are performing inside and outside the home. Quotas must be established that will give women more opportunities to be involved in the process of politics in all its aspects. Furthermore, the concentration and division of women in limited service-sector occupations, such as nursing, hotel and catering, teaching, banking, public administration, finance and insurance must be expanded to allow the talents of women to be available in other arenas.

Women should no longer be looked at as inferior to men. As Qasim Amin, the Egyptian lawyer and judge who is considered the "father of Arab feminism," wrote, "The evidence of history confirms and demonstrates that the status of women is inseparably tied to the status of a nation" (26). Palestinian women must do their best to increase their representation in decision-making bodies and changing or applying the nation's laws. Women are able to become a successful judges, ministers, presidents, drivers and so on.

Discrimination against women is not acceptable. Nabila Espanioly notes that it "is a big challenge for all women in the Palestinian community inside and outside Israel. As a Palestinian woman in Israel, citizen of Israel, I live in a state which defines itself as a Jewish state, but if we are speaking about all issues relating to women's issues, then Palestinian women inside Israel are triply discriminated against" ("Women in the Middle East" 35).

VIOLENCE IS NOT ACCEPTABLE

Women are recognizing that they do not have to accept violence as a way of life. There are many faces of violence practiced against women in the Palestinian society. These behaviours weaken women who are also responsible for the other half of the society, namely, the men. So if the base is weak and shaken, what do we expect to achieve in life?

Nawal El Saadawi has stated that "Violence against women is not separate from violence against the poor, is not separate from violence against the black people in Africa or in Europe or in the States. Violence can be done by the state itself. It can be official violence" ("Women in the Middle East"). Like El Saadawi, I believe that in order to empower women we must eliminate the many kinds of violence practiced against them. And by violence, I mean all kinds: international violence; state and national violence; domestic violence; sexual and economic violence. A woman who lives in poverty is a disabled woman, and this is also a form of violence. Palestinian women must learn from other women's experience throughout the world. We need to make it clear that when Israel imposes political policies on the Palestinian people, it is women and children who suffer the most. This was especially clear in the Israeli attack on Gaza Strip that took place during the winter of 2008–2009, when Israeli forces launched a military attack on Gaza resulting in death and despair for its women and children. Due to the illegal Israeli checkpoints and the apartheid wall, which women need to cross daily to reach their universities and schools, the number of women seeking higher education has been steadily dropping. Because of the harassment and intimidation by Israeli soldiers, families are worried and are asking their daughters to stay home and get married instead. Therefore, we must have a strong transnational power to make change possible.

THE ROLE OF MEDIA

We should never ever ignore the role of the media and press in stereotyping gender. Women are only expected to perform traditional roles. Many films and TV series portray women only as housewives who escape man's domination by cunning and evil deeds. A good woman who is respected by society is a woman who knows how to cook well and serve her husband, who obeys orders and never says "no." Arab film makers must change this image of women. If they portrayed a real woman, one who has the ability to change this world into a better one, they could impact our society for the better.

Of course there are many Palestinian women activists who portray the power of Palestinian women through their work, including writers and poets such as Sahar Khalifa, a Palestinian woman from Nabulus (Sabbagh 62-78). There are female journalists such as Shireen Abu Aqlah and Chevara Al-Budari from Jerusalem, although journalism was traditionally perceived as a masculine pursuit. Female journalists were rejected and discouraged from entering the profession. Women researchers are assessing policies that might affect women more than men. By doing this we can develop more successful and inclusive policies to defend and protect the rights of women. Female documentary-makers are foregrounding these issues: *Masarat*, for example, is a documentary created by Palestinian women focusing on the role of Palestinian women in society.

WOMEN AND THE LACK OF JUSTICE

The Palestinian social and legal structure has restricted the development and meaningful societal participation of Palestinian women in numerous ways. As a result women are prevented from acquiring social justice and equality.

There are too many incidents of brutal "honour killings" that have shaken the Palestinian community. These deaths have prompted demands for a change to laws inherited from the days of Jordanian rule that deemed all women be considered "minors," under the authority of male relatives, and that provide a maximum of six months in prison for killings in defense of "family honour." Article 340 of the Jordanian penal code, which is still in effect in the West Bank, gives advantage to male relatives. Males benefit by a lessened sentence if their crime was murdering a female relative. In this model, it is considered an honour for a man to kill a woman because she violated his honour. It is the male who controls the sexuality of the females in his household, otherwise he is dishonoured.

In a so-called honour killing incident in May 2011, the body of university student Aya Barde'a, age 21, was found in a well; she had been drowned by her uncle because a young man kept asking Aya's family to allow him to marry her. The young man's persistence led the uncle to believe that there was a sexual relationship, and for this reason the uncle killed his niece. After huge protests and anger in the Palestinian society by different movements and organizations, Palestinian National Authority President Mahmoud Abbas issued a Presidential decree to annul Article 340 of the Jordanian Penal Code in the West Bank. Nevertheless, we still do not see this amendment translated on the ground—more needs to be done.

There are no laws to support a woman who finds her husband in "an unlawful bed." The fact that the Palestinian people have been successively under Ottoman, British, Egyptian and Jordanian rule has added to the suppression of Palestinian women. During the last fifty years or more, Israeli military orders have created obstacles for women by likewise victimizing them. Adding to this, traditional patriarchal values underlie the handling of many legal cases. These are dealt with under tribal law by the Mukhtar (tribal elder) or amongst members of the extended family. This is done only to cover up the crime, conceal the scandal and forbid it from spreading. The woman's cause is undermined by traditional patriarchal values influencing how the Mukhtar (tribal elder) or members of the extended family view and handle her case.

A women's testimony in court is not considered, ultimately because a woman's testimony is less valued than a man's. From this we can see a clear discrimination of legislation in laws, such as the personal status law. For example if a woman who has been raped is willing to go to court, she cannot go by herself. She can only do this if she is accompanied by her father or her brother. Therefore we can see that the freedom and mobility of women have been guided and determined by religious and socio-cultural norms and discriminatory laws.

WOMEN WORKING FOR JUSTICE

There are many women activists and NGOs who work hard to protect and empower harassed and abused women. For example, the founding of women's shelters for those who have suffered from domestic violence has resulted from their untiring efforts. At the same time, the presence of these centers and the women who use them challenges the patriarchal structure, and, of course, women who seek help from women's movements, the police and NGOs are always looked at as trouble-makers by their families.

Working to change this paradigm, the Women's Center for Legal Aid and Counseling (WCLAC) is working alongside the Ministry of Women Affairs and legislators to pressure the government to implement necessary changes. For example, the first police family unit, catering specifically to domestic violence, has been established in Bethlehem. Advocating women's rights, especially issues dealing with discrimination related to citizenship rights and receiving passports, has resulted in Palestinian women being able to obtain their own passports. Raising the minimum age of marriage to eighteen years old is another change to prevent girls from being married at young ages. But this work has been changing according to political situations, getting better and then worse. At the same time that positive improvements are introduced, such work is always confronted by opponents accusing them of sabotaging culture and tradition. Women who work in such institutions are always subject to harassment by males.

WOMEN IN GAZA UNDER HAMAS

Nowadays with all the violence taking place in Hamas-controlled Gaza, secular women are concerned that Hamas will undermine the relative freedom they once enjoyed under the rule of Fatah. In fact you can notice a dwindling percentage of women willing to be unveiled in public in Gaza. We always hear Hamas spokesmen say that they will not harass anyone, and that they are not going to impose a certain dress, but many women think that this is not the case. There are female students who feel discriminated against because they are not wearing a veil. Women are caught in the crossfire between new and old values. Some women also believe that they have less opportunity to be promoted at work if they have a conservative boss. It is always observed that in the way Hamas presents its understanding of Islam, the liberties of a woman are always subject to the consent of a male relative. They do not consider women as equal to men. When they indoctrinate women they always say that she has to obey the male in the family and that when she gets married she is to "obey her husband." If a woman needs to work, she must have her husband's permission. Regardless of these influences, we still hear voices from Islamic women activists such as Jamila al Shanti, a Hamas activist who wants to revive Islamic thoughts and heritage: "People think that Islamic law is about being veiled, and closed and staying at home, but that's wrong. A woman can go out veiled and do all kind of work without any problem" (qtd. in Johnston).

THE IMPACT OF THE OCCUPATION ON PALESTINIAN WOMEN

Thousands of women have endured the loss of their husbands, sons, daughters, their homes and land due to the brutality of the occupation. We need to emphasize that women are not immune to the Israeli policy of imprisonment. There were approximately sixty-five women political prisoners in Israeli prisons as of June 2009 according to statistics taken at that time ("Palestinian Women Political Prisoners"). When women are imprisoned, they are subjected to different kinds of abuse, humiliating treatment, and torture (either verbal or physical), and prevented from contact with their families.

The apartheid wall affects women's life negatively. It is 645 km long, and cuts off many families from their relatives and other family members. According to the Israeli authorities, the wall is "a defensive measure designed to block the passage of terrorists, weapons and explosives into the state of Israel" (cited in Amnesty International). The fact is that this wall has not been built on the Green Line between Israel and the West Bank, and therefore cuts off villages, communities and families from each other. It separates farmers from their land, Palestinians from their work, educational institutions, health care facilities and other essential services.

The wall has the largest impact on Palestinian women. It deprives them of access to their land, and also to educational institutions. Many women are deprived in many villages of seeking higher education because of the fact that the wall has created too large of a distance for them to access schools, colleges and universities. This also provides an opportunity for men to further dominate females. The wall combined with patriarchal dogma prevents women from seeking education. The reasons the men give are that women might get exposed to danger while trying to reach schools or colleges. So, the alternative to education is getting these women married in order to provide safety for them. And since the male is supposed to be the traditional breadwinner, the need is for women to be home—performing traditional chores.

The apartheid wall also causes women to suffer from lack of medical care. In many Palestinian villages there are no nearby clinics or hospitals that women can access without passing a checkpoint or travelling a long distance. This of course, puts women's lives at risk. There are many cases in which women have given birth at checkpoints, waiting for the soldiers to give them permission to pass to reach a hospital or clinic. In many cases, women die at checkpoints or lose the baby (Musleh 59-74).

Women have also been affected by the demolition of houses, where they are the ones who suffer the greatest losses. These women find themselves without shelter, having to seek help from family members, relatives, and humanitarian organizations.

There are many women who have been involved in resistance against these continued abuses. These women have sacrificed much by speaking up and working to create change. Many of them are active in student's circles and unions such as medical, engineering, and teachers' unions.

GENDER EQUITY

The Palestinian Personal Status laws are based on religious laws inherited from Jordan and Egypt, and are discriminatory in areas such as marriage, divorce, child custody and inheritance. Women rarely have any choice regarding whom they marry as this decision is made by the family. The separation wall has also added to this dilemma in that women are limited to specific neighbourhoods, which limits marital choices.

Polygamy is accepted in Palestine in that 95 percent of the population is Muslim. According to Islamic law a Muslim man can marry up to four wives. Obviously, the Islamic Personal Laws usually discriminates against women. Men dominate! Another example of this is the fact that the father is considered to be the guardian of his children rather than the mother (Uhlman). In cases of divorce, the mother has the right to custody of sons until the age of ten and of daughters until the age of twelve. If a woman remarries, she loses the right of custody of her children. Women cannot confer citizenship to their children. In the case of inheritance, women can inherit from her father, mother, husband, children—but her share is usually smaller than what a male inherits, and in many cases women are forced to give up their inheritance to their brothers or any other male relative. In spite of all these facts, I must say that for each rule there is an exception and that there is a growing number of Palestinians who are against violence against women and who find honour killing to be unacceptable.

More women are seeking higher education and reaching higher positions, but we still need change to take place at the roots of the problem in order to bring about a needed dramatic shift and to formulate laws that are equal for men and women. We have to listen to women's voices—to their needs and demands—so they can light the way for change and liberation.

PALESTINIAN WOMEN:
CHALLENGING AND CHANGING PATRIARCHAL SOCIETY

Even though I have been describing dire conditions, changes have been taking place for women within Palestine itself. For example, in the past women were not able to study engineering, but at this time we see increasing numbers of female engineers, ministers, college deans, bank managers, journalists, mayors, ambassadors, hotel managers, and others. In the past it was never allowed nor was it acceptable for a woman to have a position as a bank manager, but nowadays it is natural to work with a woman in such a position. Once a woman is empowered she will not accept being treated as an unequal member of society because of unjust patriarchal laws, discriminatory laws and occupation that perpetuate patriarchy within the Palestinian society.

EMINENT PALESTINIAN WOMEN IN ACTION

There are many examples of women working to empower other women and enable them to discover new potential. For example, Dr. Hanan Ashrawi, a member of the Palestinian Legislative Council, received the

2003 Sydney Peace Prize. As official spokeswoman for the Palestinian delegation, Ashrawi works alongside the fourteen negotiators in what is essentially a man's world. She believes that she brings a different perspective to politics—what she describes as a woman's approach based on the issues unclouded by self-interest. In her view, this means that she can present the main issues in a clear, honest and even daring way that breaks through the barriers. She says that she has "learnt how not to be scared of a man's world," adding that "women should always build support systems and networks for other women, and they should not be an excuse to exclude other women from politics."

Women are active in various areas of Palestinian government. Zahira Kamal, who founded the first grassroots movement for Palestinian women, also played an important role in the creation of the first Palestinian Ministry for Women's Affairs. She penetrated what is deemed to be a man's world, accepting the challenge to be an active woman surrounded by men who tried to marginalize her role and achievements. Another woman, Leila Shahid, was chosen by Yasser Arafat as the first woman to represent the PLO in Europe. She occupied several key positions in European Capitals before she moved to Brussels in 2006 to become the General Delegate of Palestine to the EU, Belgium and Luxembourg. Janet Mikhail was elected as the first Palestinian woman Mayor, in Ramallah in 2005. Recently, two Palestinian women were appointed to the judiciary, one from Ramallah and the other from Hebron. Maybe this movement will encourage women to trust the judicial system because they will feel more comfortable to talk about their cases with a woman judge as opposed to a male judge.

Despite these political activists, women remain under-represented in party politics. Therefore women have been active in non-governmental organizations and in civil society, where they have established a network of services for women to provide support, regardless of continuing conflict, and to help play a larger role in building a Palestinian state. These services include micro-credit loans, health and counseling, protecting abused women by instituting women's shelters, childcare, job creation, raising awareness about human rights and women's human and legal rights, preparing women to participate in elections, etc.

NGOS EMPOWERING WOMEN

NGOs are doing much to empower and protect women. The Jerusalem Center for Women, for example, provides women in East Jerusalem with venues for training in democracy, human rights, advocacy and life skills to advance women's status and roles in the decision-making process. Additionally, Bethlehem's Wi'am Conflict Resolution Center has a women's program that offers women of Palestinian society a space where they can form support networks, develop their leadership and work-related skills, and therefore take a more active role in their community and in Palestinian society at large. Wi'am Women's Project promotes women's advancement with programs that focus on their health, education, employment and legal rights. Wi'am conducts workshops for women on issues such as the democratic process, civil society development, reproductive health, communication, gender equality, conflict mediation, human security, methods for non-violence and treatment of domestic violence. Wi'am also provides assistance for women through income generating activities and employment opportunities.

These types of support help to build a healthier culture, one that is gender-balanced. As a result of this and similar efforts, in recent years we have witnessed women running in presidential elections. As an example, Samiha Khalil (1923-1999) ran against Yasser Arafat in 1996, and attracted 11.5 percent of voters—a good percentage. If we rebel against meaningless traditions and gender discrimination, and if we bring up a new, educated generation that is aware of gender and human rights, then we can make the difference we are seeking. Nawal El Saadawi noted that it is necessary that "Women must have a firm personal choice, strong will and have a strong desire to reach a leading role in society and politics by freeing her from all types of violence." Women in Palestine have now reached and won many seats according to the quotas both in the municipal elections and in the parliamentary elections. Thirteen women—six of them from Hamas—were elected under the new quota system that was introduced in 2005 to ensure that women make up 20 percent of the PLC (Pierson 10).

Charitable societies, women's movements, and NGOs are all making a difference by involving Palestinian women in diaspora in the struggle and resistance of women in the occupied territories. The curriculum taught at schools has been amended to portray women as valuable persons equal to men, who can be productive and not restricted to a domestic role.

Women are also experiencing their power in other areas of life, For example, Suzanne Al-Houby is the first Palestinian woman to climb Mountain Elbrus, the highest point in Europe, and other mountains in Africa and France. Having experienced such success, she has gone on to develop a charity foundation in order to support and provide for

Palestinian children in the Occupied Territories. When women become physically active, they also begin to have a sense of embodied power. Along those lines, Palestinian women's soccer is a new sport in the West Bank. Recently Jibriel Rajoub, Head of the Palestine Sports Association and former National Security Advisor to Yasser Arafat, formed the League of Women's Soccer Teams. He found his ideas a hard sell: "Once I took office I knew I wanted to form a women's soccer club, but as traditional as Palestinian society is, many sheikhs and clerics were appalled by the notion.... The Palestinian society is still struggling with women's liberation, so for me, soccer is a challenge" Rajoub quotes Honey Thaljieh, Captain of the Palestinian National Women soccer Team, as saying that "This is totally new to our Palestinian culture and traditions, but these women are saying we are here and you must accept us as we are" (Shaked).

Women artists have also been given the stage to express their identity, struggle and fears. See, for example, the 2007 book, *Palestinian Women Artists: The Land = the Body = the Narrative*, which features 41 Palestinian women artists whose achievements have garnered them long-standing recognition (Fadda).

WOMEN AFFAIRS TECHNICAL COMMITTEE

The Women Affairs Technical Committee (WATC) is a coalition of individual activists and women's organizations. Established in 1992, the coalition members work together for the elimination of all forms of discrimination against women in the pursuit of a well established, civic, democratic society that respects human rights. WATC works to mainstream Palestinian women's issues within the process of constructing a democratic society free of all forms of discrimination; to effect gender sensitive policies and legislation in various spheres of life; to develop the assertiveness of women using the latest methodologies in adult education and training; to enhance the involvement of women in political life at all levels, especially the decision making level; to lobby decision makers in Palestinian society to promote equal rights for women; and to empower and support existing women's committees and groups on the operational and organizational level. WATC attains its objectives through networking, advocacy, campaigning, training, and a media program.

Gender-oriented conflict resolution
All future planning and policies for conflict and peace operation must

be "gender proofed," and also include the consideration of gender at all stages of decision-making, allocation and policy development. I would focus on some recommendations regarding women empowerment and the increase of women participation in a transitional period and in the future Palestinian state.

These are but small examples of larger changes taking place for and by Palestinian women.

• Formulate clear policies; prepare police departments to be able to handle complaints by women.

• Form ministries such as ministry of education, ministry of health, ministry of sport and youth and other official bodies to hold responsibilities in dealing with violence and discrimination against women.

• Encourage effective NGOs to continue their work, and offer them any possible support to reach all woman victims.

• Conduct awareness campaigns that can reach women living in suburbs and villages and teach them to be able to defend their rights and stand for themselves.

• Assure that the Palestinian authority accepts the demands of Palestinian Women activists and NGOs to increase the representation of women in the Palestinian legislative council and in all branches of government and to be able to reach higher positions in ministries and diplomatic missions.

• Increase budget allocations and services for women's health programs, especially for women in rural areas.

• Abide by all international laws and conventions such as UN Resolution 1325 and CEDAW.

• Movements and NGOs must work more closely with the Palestinian police to overcome obstacles and bring change, and to improve co-operation , understanding and co-ordination between formal and informal sectors. Women NGOs and activists should be included in peace submissions and post-conflict planning.

• A good number of women must be trained in negotiation, mediation and facilitation skills to be able to take leadership positions.

• Create a networking system with other women from different backgrounds and geographical locations to enable women to learn from different experience and build bridges between women all over the world.

CONCLUSION

As a Palestinian woman activist I have a vision that our Palestinian society will witness a remarkable change in the near future. I believe in women—this gives me the motivation to conduct workshops and trainings for women and youth to light a candle for them to see their way. Through my work I have been able to convince many women that they have both the right and the power to live as human beings and to take the initiative to change their lives by making their own decisions and acting on their own future plans. In spite of the light of change we are seeing in some parts of the occupied territories, we still need to raise more and more awareness in society as a whole where women's rights and liberation and the existence of the Palestinian state will go together. Thanks to all the Palestinian women who sacrificed—and who are still sacrificing—challenging those who want to keep them marginalized and invisible. These women represent the future!

[1]This conflict between Algeria and France took place in between 1954 through 1962. For more on this specific topic, see Lazreg.

REFERENCES

Amin, Qasim. *Emancipation of Women*. Cairo: Dar Al-Ma'aref, 1970. Print.
Amnesty International. "Israel and the Occupied Territories: The Place of the Fence/Wall in International Law." February 19, 2004. UNISPAL Document Collection. Web.
El Saadawi, Nawal. Web.
Fadda, Reem, ed. and curator. *Palestinian Women Artists: The Land = the Body = the Narrative*. Palestinian Art Court, Al Hoash, Jerusalem, September 2007. Print.
Johnston, Alan. "Women ponder future under Hamas." *BBC News* Gaza, 3 March 2006. Web.
Lazreg, Marnia. "Gender and Politics in Algeria: Unraveling the Religious Paradigm." *Signs* 15 (4) (Summer 1990): 755-780. Print.
"Masarat: A Journey Through Palestinian Women's Lives." Europe Aid Feature. Documentaries. 2011. Web.
Musleh, Rose Shomali. "People Behind Walls, Women Behind Walls: Reading Violence Against Women in Palestine." *Violence and Gender in the Globalized World: The Intimate and the Extimate*. Ed.

Sanja Bahun-Radunovic and V. G. Julie Rajan. Surrey, UK: Ashgate Publishing, 2008. Web.

"Palestinian Women Political Prisoners and Detainees in Israeli Jails." Miftah.org. October 25, 2001. Web.

Pierson, Claire. "Political Participation of Palestinian Women and the Furtherance of Women's Rights in Palestine." The Palestinian Human Rights Monitoring Group (PHRMG). Web.

Sabbagh, Suha. "Palestinian Women Writers and the Intifada." *Social Text* 22 (Spring 1989): 62-78. Print.

Shaked, Ronny. "National Palestinian Women's Soccer Team takes field." SHAYnetnews.com. October 29, 2009. Web.

Uhlman, Kristine. "Overview of Sharia and Prevalent Customs in Islamic Societies-Divorce and Child Custody." Expert Law. January 2004. Web.

"Women in the Middle East: Progress or Regress? Panel Discussion." *The Middle East Review of International Affairs (MERIA) Journal.* 10.2 (June 2006): Article 2.

Women's Affairs Technical Committee (WATC). "Women in Palestine." Watcpal.org. Web.

9.

A Serving Nation

Gathering People Who Serve
to Create a World that Works for All

ELLY PRADERVAND, SWITZERLAND

H UMAN HISTORY CAN BE VIEWED in many different ways. One is to see it as a slow march toward unity and the consciousness of the oneness of all forms of life. For generations an invisible nation of "world servers" has been forming all over the planet—an invisible web of individuals who share distinctive traits and attitudes, dominated by a sense of service toward their neighbours, community and the world at large. This self-constituting "Serving Nation," without any territory, is an expression of the progressive opening-up of humanity to a more holistic and unified view of reality.

One meets the "citizens" of the Serving Nation all over the planet. They have existed since time immemorial. Although they have never heard of it, they belong to it by their spirit of disinterested service and by their way of life. They have pledged themselves to a certain quality of being, living, and sharing. They have made a commitment to human dignity and human rights—not always verbally, but by the integrity of their thoughts, actions, and life styles. They strive to "walk their talk." It has been said that "where there is no vision, the people perish" (Proverbs 29:18): if humanity presently faces challenging situations, it is first and foremost because there is no common human, social and ethical vision, which would harness our immense technical, financial and scientific means towards a constructive common goal.

The vision governing the membership of A Serving Nation (ASN) is extremely simple: a world that works for all, nature included, and where basic human needs are met. For the world to work for all parties concerned, including its so-called weaker members, it is essential that humankind strive to generalize "win-win" mechanisms and relationships in every single area of life. A meaningful future is one built through the inspiration of a vision. It is not only the result of our action, but first and foremost a result of the power of our vision.

ASN does not exist as a body nor as a legal entity, but as a metaphor for a virtual nation of world servers. It is at the heart of the work of the Women's World Summit Foundation (WWSF), an international, non-profit, humanitarian NGO serving the implementation of women's and children's rights and the UN development agenda. One of the major programs of the organization is to acknowledge rural women who are making a difference in their communities, by offering a Prize for Women's Creativity in Rural Life worth $1,000 USD. Since 1994, the Prize has honoured women and women's groups around the world exhibiting exceptional creativity, courage and commitment for the improvement of the quality of life in rural communities. The Prize aims to draw international attention to its Laureates' contributions to sustainable development, household food security, and peace, thus generating recognition and support for their projects. While rural women are vital in providing examples of sound practice in their communities, they still do not have full access to tools needed for development, such as education, credit, land rights, and participation in decision making. By highlighting and rewarding creative development models, innovations, and experiences enhancing the quality of rural life, WWSF works to promote women's empowerment and mainstreaming, and to eradicate rural poverty.

In 2007, the International Day of Rural Women (15 October) was declared a UN Resolution Day that invites UN Member States to commemorate the Day and give due credit to rural women's contributions. The Day was originally launched in 1995 at the Beijing Women's Conference by several INGOs; WWSF took the lead in annually promoting the day around the world to give visibility to the work of rural women. It continues to reach out to its rural women's network with a message of empowerment in the form of an Open Letter to Rural Women of the World and to share the profiles of our Laureates.

In 2012, WWSF honoured ten Laureates with the Prize for Women's Creativity in Rural Life. bringing the total number of awards since its beginning in 1994 to 385. Truly, these women exemplify what is possible when a woman recognizes her own needs and those of the people around her. Here are their stories.[1]

Julitte Ketehoundje, Benin: An Innovative Approach to Microfinancing

Juliette Ketehoundje (age 37), from the village of Allohounkodota in the Zakpota district of Benin, did not let poverty and illiteracy prevent her from becoming an uncontested leader in her community.

Juliette is extremely dedicated, intelligent, serious and dynamic, with an exemplary commitment to the eradication of famine and poverty and the mobilization of women. Working directly with rural women, she is helping them change their lives through an innovative microfinancing system known as the "African Women Food Farmer Initiative" (AWFFI). Beginning with a group of 20 women, that number doubled after one year. Now Juliette is the president of a group called "Soudjagbè" with 3,000 members, comprised of about 150 women's groups with approximately 20 participants each. Each group has its own internal autonomy, and they meet regularly (twice a month) to network. These meetings are considered so important that members who come late or who quarrel are sanctioned. At each meeting, members of the group deposit 200 West African francs (CFA), or around $0.40 USD, in a kitty. Amazingly, the rate of reimbursement in this microcredit scheme reaches 100 per cent. Their own group savings enable the women to assure the complete reimbursement of the group loans borrowed from AWFFI. The success has been such that AWFFI is now aiming at implementing Juliette's strategy in other areas. Juliette now wishes to start a system of scholarships for the schooling of girls. She herself aims at learning how to read and write so that she can present herself at local elections at the request of her community, which recognizes her rare honesty and leadership qualities, and her incredibly hard work.

Anne Stella Fomumbod, Cameroon: A Unique Charter for Widows

The rural women of northwest Cameroon produce 60 percent of the region's agricultural output. However, their methods are primitive, and they hardly enjoy the fruits of their back-breaking labour. Anne Stella (age 47) has set up a series of innovative programs to help them. She has created a group entitled "Fund for the mobilisation of women" to enable them to have access to microcredit to acquire their own farm, land, and goods. Through her organization, InterFaith Vision Foundation Cameroon (IVF Cam), she has brought together fifty different widows' groups, enabling them to be recognized by bodies like UNDP and to have greater freedom in their activities, including access to markets. To lighten their manual labour, she provided tools and seeds, resulting in productivity skyrocketing from 30 to 120 kilograms per month.

She has also facilitated access to microcredit for 40 other women's communities in the region, including women victims of HIV/AIDS, and promoted HIV/AIDS sensitization programs which warn against the dangers inherent in remarriage and the responsibility of parents. Anne

Stella has launched literacy programs for the women of the region to enable them to acquire much needed skills, which in turn encourages change in their communities. She organized training sessions to guarantee property rights and access to land for women, and brought together the widows of 43 communities around the deplorable status of widows in their communities. In a concerted effort, they assembled traditional chieftains together to educate them concerning the huge gap between customs and women's rights in their area, and to encourage them to re-examine traditional practices. But her most outstanding contribution was the promulgation of the "Metta Charter on Widowhood," a first in the history of her country enabling major progress for widows.

Dorothy Awino, Kenya: Land Rights for Women—A Development "Must"

The question of women's access to property is a major issue in many communities. In Kenya, women furnish 80 per cent of agricultural labour and produce 60 per cent of agricultural income, while only 5 per cent of them own land. The common belief is that women are not trustworthy and hence do not deserve to inherit and dispose of property, which acts as a major obstacle to the rights of women and children and constitutes a major hindrance for development. In 1992, after having been deceived and disinherited, Dorothy Awino (now age 47) was forced to leave her home with her two-year-old son. In 2003, she joined other women who had been disinherited to found the "Road Marks International," a community organization in Nyanza Province, where the traditions of the Luo tribe lead to the disinheritance of orphans and vulnerable women. Her investment in the project led to major changes for the women and children of her community. Dorothy won the trust of the Caucus for Women's Leadership, an organization aiming at reinforcing the abilities of local leaders to denounce violations of women's and children's rights. Thanks to this organization, the Elders' Council of the Luo has committed itself to protecting the rights of women, even enabling some of them to reestablish themselves on their ancestral lands. It is Dorothy's commitment to her community, and her knowledge and understanding of Luo culture that has enabled her to win the support of the elders of her tribe. She herself has become a member of the Elders' Council, and even coordinates their programs, something exceptional in that culture. Dorothy believes that poverty and some traditional cultural practices represent major obstacles to the protection of the rights of women and children, and need to be overcome. Her project has initiated major changes, measured by the fact that violations of women and children's rights have significantly decreased.

Wendy Jasmine Pekeur, South Africa: A Trade Union for Those Who Feed the Nation

Wendy Jasmine Pekeur (age 31) is the General Secretary of *Sikhula Sonke*, a South African trade union which represents rural women farmers. Wendy's ambitions were conceived in her childhood, when she worked on her grandparents' farm in Western Cape Province. At the age of six, she witnessed violence in her home due to her father's use of alcohol and drugs. At eighteen, she took her first steps in an organization called "Woman and Violence," which was campaigning to bring to justice a man who had killed his wife. Wendy explains her motivation: "I chose the cause of farm workers, because I had worked as one on a fruit farm and knew their life. Women farmers earn the lowest wages in South Africa, and it is grimly ironic that what they produce feeds the nation and brings profits [while] they live in the direst poverty, often virtually starving." She opposes domestic violence and discrimination against women farm workers. After ending her studies, Wendy worked as a volunteer for the organization Women of Farm Projects (WFP). This organization enabled Wendy and other women to acquire the experience and maturity needed to launch the trade union *Sikhula Sonke* for women, run by women. They have launched a series of community projects, such as the protection of children, the organization of transport for people living on isolated farms, and the fight for a minimum wage and stable work for women agricultural workers. An additional concern is workplace safety: women farm labourers, unlike men, often do not have protective clothing against pesticides. A major victory is to have obtained greater security for divorced and single women. Wendy wishes that men would sign a declaration committing themselves to end violence against women and children. She refuses all compromise on issues of gender.

Anna Mercy, India: Turning a Village into an Aquarium!

Despite her teaching obligations at a university, Anna Mercy (age 56) found time to develop a highly original pioneering project to improve living conditions in the village of Kumbala in the State of Kerala. After studying the breeding of ornamental fish, for the first time ever in India she successfully developed a technology for raising fifteen different species in the Ghats region. Anna convinced the Department of Technology of her country to give her funds enabling her to offer a five-day training programme to twenty women, teaching them all the different aspects of this process, from the building of aquariums to the production of food for the fish. By 2009, 300 persons had been trained. Anna encourages participants to start breeding fish in their own ponds and on their own terraces. One fifth of those who are trained establish aquariums in their own homes. Others have started building moulded glass tanks. Most participants in this experiment now earn an income of 4,000-5,000 Rupees (approximately $100 USD) per month thanks to the sale of fish, aquariums, plants for aquariums or fish food. Shops have been opened to sell fish and accessories for aquariums, which increases local income. The project has not only had a significant financial impact, but has also had other positive side effects. For instance numerous women suffering from hypertension or asthma have acknowledged the positive effects of this activity on their health. There has also been a drastic decrease in domestic violence and—especially important—most families now send their girls to school. To insure the continued success of the project, participants receive regular follow-up visits. Worldwide, ornamental fish breeding is an industry worth hundreds of millions and possibly billions of US dollars; India could certainly turn this into a significant source of income both for individuals and the country.

Narmada Baldeva Gond, India: A Gandhian Adivasi Warrior Changes a Whole Region

"Between silence and violence there is non-violence." Narmada Baldeva Gond (age 60) is an outstanding rural tribal woman of the Adivasi community. The Adivasis (aboriginal inhabitants) are among the most despised and disadvantaged people of the subcontinent. From an illiterate labourer who was expelled from her forest with thousands of others, struggling to make a livelihood of 20-35 Rupees per day (55-90 US cents), she became the main organizer of a whole region and has given back pride to the downtrodden. Twenty years ago Narmada participated in a training program of *Ekta Parishad*, a Gandhian organization that advocates non-violence as a means for empowering the rural masses of India to use the democratic space. She discovered that poverty was destined by karma as society taught, but was due to various social and economic conditions that could be changed. A few years later she convinced 200 families living in absolute destitution to occupy unutilised land. Despite vigorous police opposition, the Adivasi held out non-violently and managed to overcome innumerable obstacles. This was the first time Narmada declared herself a community leader. Training herself ceaselessly, she introduced numerous reforms in the newly-created village of Chilghat, including organizing a panchayat (village council) to which she was elected. In 2007, Narmada was among the activists supporting the organization in setting up a peaceful 30-day march of 25,000 landless peasants to New Delhi to claim their right to land, water and forest. The march sparked the creation of a National Commission for Agrarian Reform and major changes in the forest laws to effectively protect the Indigenous population. In the village of Chilghat, nineteen families obtained property rights by requesting that the law, which makes them land owners after they till the soil for five years, be applied. Much too often, government laws are not implemented, which is the reason for a new mobilization in 2012 with local and national actions, covered by the world's media. Jan Satyagraha, or "the force of truth" is a non-violent march for justice. The march was planned to unite, in its last phase, 100,000 deprived people to give an ultimatum to the New Delhi government regarding the necessary implementation of their fundamental rights. In fact, after a delegation met successfully with the government and negotiated significant advances, the march was halted at Agra. Narmada is the living illustration of someone who refuses the limits imposed by culture, gender and birth and becomes self-empowered. In Narmada's own words: "With Ekta Parishad, we have discovered another world! We were so ignorant, but now our eyes are opened. From slaves condemned to live in the slums of Delhi or Bombay, we have become human beings proud to fight for our rights."

Pratibha Rajesh Bukkawar, India: Revolution in Daryapur

In a world where around one billion people survive precariously on approximately one dollar a day, food is the number one basic necessity for survival. Born in Daryapur near Amravati, Maharashtra State, Pratibha (age 39) grew up in poverty, so it was easy for her to grasp this fact. Having acquired skills in the field of food processing, in 2005 she decided to start a food-based cottage industry called *Trinetra Mahila Gruh Udyog* (Third Eye Women's Cottage Industry). Starting with five rural women preparing special food formulas reproducing the tastes of certain dishes consumed locally, the number of women employed rapidly grew to 750, all illiterate, living below the poverty line, and working out of their homes. Further democratizing the process, she shared her Research and Development efforts with these women, enabling them to become stakeholders in the ingenious food production system she had created and involving them in policy decisions. She then started training courses not only to improve their knowledge and hands-on skills in food processing, but to expand their economic opportunities by offering

110

them training in fields as varied as catering, garment manufacture, and the production of printing materials and kitchen cloths, to name but a few. After making the food production unit self-sustainable, she decided to produce certain new food products from locally-available natural resources like tamarind chocolates, ambadi jam and jellies, various spices, etc., enabling the producers to expand their outreach into the national market. With the overall development of these women workers in mind, she became Founder President of the Indian Women's Development Organization, in view of stimulating skills development and employment generation at the local level. Another innovation of Pratibha was in forming the Amravati District Self-Help Groups (SHG) Association, uniting 1000 SHGs from minorities living below the poverty line, enabling the members to overcome for the first time numerous social and cultural barriers to work outside the home. With each passing year, Pratibha's efforts on behalf of women grow. This brief report cannot do justice to her very broad efforts for the rehabilitation of poor rural women and the handicapped, and her exceptional social work to empower the most disadvantaged classes of her community.

Santosh Bai Sahariya, India: Fighting Harmful Traditional Practices

Santosh Bai Sahariya (age 30) is a member of one of the most vulnerable of tribal communities, the Saharoya, who depend for their survival on meager forest products. Married at 15, she gave birth to two children; soon after her husband died. She then committed herself to ending harmful myths and practices, poverty and discrimination against women. She protested vigorously against a tradition which forced women to walk barefoot, saying that as long as men were not subject to the same rule, she would refuse to pay the 50 rupee fine for wearing shoes. She managed, in this manner, to eliminate a tradition that did much harm to women, and encouraged others to follow suit. She also managed to introduce penalties on violence against women—the most widespread and under-reported crime on the planet—thereby gaining much recognition amongst women. Santosh joined the *Swachh Pariyojna* (a local village group organization), as a volunteer. This enabled her to encourage young girls and women in her community to adopt more hygienic practices and especially to get vaccinated against sexually transmitted diseases, a privilege which was solely reserved to men. Thanks to this, the number of infected women decreased considerably. Elected to the *Gram Panchayat* (village council), she had to wage war against corruption and the blackmail of other elected Council members, including attempts to corrupt her. In her new function, she has become

111

an advocate for the poor tribals, widows and women who are separated, the handicapped and lonely, and makes a special issue of encouraging families to send their daughters to school. With remarkable daring, Santosh successfully initiated the banishment of shops selling alcohol so as to end or at least decrease violence against women. Notably, she has also managed to integrate other women in the *Gram Panchayat*, while at the same time undertaking major efforts to end deforestation.

Nuansy Ratanasithy, Laos: From Dependency to a Partnership of Equals

The director of a cotton business known as "The Ngeum Cotton Group," Nuansy Ratanasithy (age 44) has radically changed the lives of the women of her village. Although encountering serious problems taking care of her small children when her husband had to leave her region to work, Nuansy decided she wanted to also do something for the women of her village. Despite the fact that her basic training was in the field of medicine, she had the courage to branch out into a field that was totally new to her: cotton cloth production. She discovered the existence of an important niche market for a special kind of Asian brown cotton, the sales of which would enable women to fight poverty. Summoning her creativity and her modest capital, she invested in the creation of a small cotton factory employing 50 women. Eleven young women undertook a special four month training in the capital, Vientiane, to learn the various weaving techniques and methods. Thanks to this training, the women concerned could produce high quality products using new designs. The opinions and decisions of these women then began to be taken into consideration. As a result of this new village industry, the economy of northern Laos has become a little less dependent on the more industrialized productions of Thailand, which represented a real danger for the culture and the identity of the Laos weavers. The sales of cotton products have restored the pride of the men and women of the village who now work as equal and independent partners with their Thai neighbours. Nuansy represents a model of creativity for the young people of her region and enjoys the highest reputation.

Nurcan Baysal, Turkey: Happiness is Part of Development

While working as a teaching assistant at one of her country's top universities, Nurcan Baysal (age 35) packed her bags to return to her hometown in Diyarbakir. Turning her back on a brilliant academic career, she decided to fight for the underprivileged of her region. Significantly, she persuaded the Ozyegin family, who are among Turkey's most prominent philanthropists, to partially fund a project which rapidly led to a country-wide integrated rural development program and one of the most ambitious efforts to tackle poverty and inequity in Turkey, the "Ozyegin Foundation Rural Livelihoods program." It has a unique philosophy linking the development of economic opportunities with tools for empowerment and social mobilization.

The vision of the program is a process geared to eliminating social disparities and ensuring a decent life for all, which includes happiness (something rarely if ever mentioned in development jargon!)—in Nurcan's words, "re-building lives and living spaces that were once shattered and taken away from people." For Nurcan, rural development is not only about income generation and infrastructure building, but about listening to people to comprehend what it is they actually need, desire and dream of—and then furnishing them the opportunities and tools to turn their visions into reality. Thus, painting workshops for children can be as important as animal husbandry! Rebuilding relations, women's empowerment, art, preserving positive values and customs are all part of the complete picture. In other words, the program has given qualitative measures an importance equal if not superior to quantitative output. After only one year in operation, there has been measurable progress. Among the main features of the program outlined by Nurcan, its integrated program design, emphasis on social capacity building and livelihoods, its framework of basic rights and services, including a human rights dimension at the core of the program, and an authentic participatory effort (often mentioned but rarely practiced in the field of development) all stand out.

Konomi Kikuchi, China and Chile: Walking, Walking ...To Protect the Environment

Since childhood, her love of exploring has led Konomi Kikuchi (age 44) to open the way for other women. Devastated by the suicide of her first husband, she decided to transform this tragedy in a manner that would be of service to all. During a long march of 1,000 kms undertaken with her second husband, Paul Coleman, she planted trees across China, Korea and Japan. During her march, she met thousands of people and shared powerful messages on the environment. Her march met with an extraordinary attention in China and her experience was broadly relayed through the media, encouraging other countries to welcome the march. At times, she slept outdoors in freezing temperatures, experiencing hunger for the first time, and facing constant physical pain. But she just marched on, courageously and with a smile, undaunted by these challenges. She started an online community "Marching across the planet, planting trees," which attracted thousands of on line members. Konomi walked another 3,300 kms for eleven months from Hong Kong to Taijin, China. Other persons from abroad (Great Britain, New Zealand, Japan, China) joined her in the walk. During this trip, she was especially disturbed by the effect on human health of the water pollution in the province of Shandong, where river water, in which women washed vegetables and children, was heavily polluted with chemical products poured directly from factories, as well as human feces. She organized protests to present documentaries on the environment in China and to propose sustainable solutions. She currently works in Chile with her husband in an isolated region of Patagonia, on a sustainable house-building project. In a country recently rocked by a devastating earthquake, they are demonstrating the benefits of sustainability and an alternative economy to the local villages.

FUTURE WORK

At present, we see the concept of A Serving Nation as a pedagogical tool to help develop the sense of oneness and increase the recognition of the work of these and other women's contributions, which are part of serving nations, adding to a steady and positive global transformation.

With time, and when right, ASN will take on a more structured form and for its members to develop the ability to significantly influence national and world decisions. It does not aim at being one more humanitarian organization. It simply aims at empowering citizens, you, me—to act where they are, but with a new consciousness and understanding that the solution of the world's great problems does not reside in cleverer technologies, better organization, greater freedoms of world markets, and other similar approaches, but in the worldwide dissemination of a spirit of disinterested world service, respect for human rights and responsibilities, and integrity in action. Without any attachment to a religious institution, in the long run, ASN could end up as a "community of consciousness"—a spiritual family.

[1]"Empowering Women and Children." WWSF *Global Newsletter* September 2010: 18A. Print.

10.
Tibetan Women

Devotedly Defiant

TENZIN DHARDON SHARLING, TIBET/INDIA

IN THE HISTORY OF HUMAN STRUGGLE, women have played a significant role. While the actions of a few extraordinary women may stand out, the efforts of ordinary women remain in the background. Early Tibetan history does not boast of heroines, and even in the early twentieth century, there was no tradition of women political leaders or government officials, and no vision that things would change with modern education. But when the fate of the nation and its people reached a critical juncture in 1959, Tibetan women united as one and conjoined the movement. Thus, for the first time in Tibetan history, women's voices became visibly pertinent.

On March 12, 1959, Lhasa, Tibet's capital and seat of His Holiness the Dalai Lama, was filled with the sounds of feet stamping the pavement and shouted pleas for freedom: with hands raised high in the air, Tibetan women stood united against the Chinese communist regime's unlawful occupation of their nation. An estimated 15,000 unarmed Tibetan women took to the streets of Lhasa to oppose the violent Chinese occupation of their country. As the defiant crowd grew in number, a few women spontaneously took charge. One of them was Ghurteng Kunsang who stepped forward and spoke out forcefully urging that "Tibet should fight back not with violence, but with peace and compassion in the effort to force the Chinese back to their own land" (cited in TWA "Breaking the Shackles" 8). This day marked the first active, women-led non-violent protest against the Chinese occupation and laid the foundation for peaceful resistance in Tibetan history.

Following the historic uprising, women took part in successive protests and resistance against the repressive Chinese regime. The Chinese military responded brutally, opening fire upon the crowds. Many of the women who stood up on that epic day sacrificed their lives in pursuit of freedom. Those that escaped with their lives found themselves imprisoned and subject to inhuman torture. The surviving, exiled elders are the last generation of women left to tell the story of the Women's Uprising, and to transmit their cultural legacy. More than half-century after Tibet's national uprisings, reality in Tibet remains smoke-screened by Chinese Government. News and knowledge make it through a veil of repression only through the efforts of courageous men and women who risk their lives to make their stories heard.

In the early decades of the last century, there was no tradition of Tibetan women standing shoulder-to-shoulder with men in public affairs. As the Tibetan adage of the time pronounced, "the mother is the precious jewel-at-home, the father the external fencing." In a period when women remained totally home-bound to care for the family, cocooned thus in a corner of the walls of time, the communist Chinese occupiers created havoc; women stood against this repressive regime and to this day have, with utmost resilience, courage, and dedication, driven the movement forward.

WOMEN INSIDE TIBET REMAIN DEFIANT

While Tibetan women continue to be the victims of the repressive policies of the Chinese government—systematic oppression, coercion, and sadistic state-sanctioned violence—the spirit of Tibetan Women refuses to rest. As the official website of the Office of Tibet, New York suggests, "the present Chinese policy, a combination of demographic and economic manipulation, and discrimination, aims to suppress the Tibetan issue by changing the very character and the identity of Tibet and its people."

For those remaining in occupied Tibet, the struggle continued, often with dire consequences. Women, in time of crisis, have stepped forward and assumed the mantle of political leadership. Nun Thinley Choedon from Nyemo region in Tibet emerged as a renowned guerrilla leader in the large-scale rebellion; she led a group of Tibetan freedom fighters in the 1960s and fought fierce battles with the Chinese. Her fame spread even in the prisons at the time where the inmate Douche Konchog Tenaha composed an unprecedented praise for her, saying; "you, Thinley Choedon, who risked her life to defend the faith are the supreme heroine in the defense of the faith. All Tibetans behold you as an example to be emulated. We shall remember you for ever." (cited in TWA "Breaking the Shackles" xiv).

Thinley Choedon was captured and executed by Chinese military forces on September 26, 1969. Thirty-four others were also executed that day (Goldstein, Ben, and Tanzen).

THE SPIRIT OF TIBETAN NUNS: THE DRAPCHI FOURTEEN

Tibetan nuns constitute an important subset of the Tibetan female population; they are considered to be of a higher class than ordinary Tibetan women as they belong to the sacred realm of Tibetan Buddhism. But, in particular, the Buddhist nuns are revered more for their defiance than their devotion. The stories of the Buddhist nuns and their endurance of endless sufferings under the repressive Chinese regime stand witness to the indomitable courage and strength embodied by these female members of the monastic community.

The case of the Drapchi Fourteen, a group of fourteen nuns imprisoned in Drapchi Prison after the 1987 and 1989 peaceful protests in Lhasa, Tibet, is exemplary of human courage. Even incarcerated, these patriots never gave in. In 1993, imprisoned nun Ngawang Sangdrol and thirteen other Tibetan nuns managed to smuggle out a secretly recorded cassette tape, filled with songs of freedom, resistance, and religious dedication. The recordings first reached Lhasa, and from there, the international community. The power of the music immediately served to galvanize support for the Tibetan cause. It revealed not only the harrowing conditions within Drapchi, but also the immense courage of the political prisoners confined behind the walls.

For this "rebellious" act of mutual consolation, the nuns received extended sentences, ranging from five to nine years. After eleven years of incarceration, Ngawang Sangdrol walked out of Drapchi prison and back into the free world. Though she was beaten, tortured, and systematically humiliated as the object of a campaign of terror that sought to break her physically, mentally, and spiritually, upon her release Ngawang Sangdrol spoke unflinchingly about love, compassion, and joy, even within this living nightmare. Instead of expressing anger or hatred for her oppressors, she regarded this cruelty as "an opportunity to develop compassion." Instead of the pit of despair it was meant to be, Drapchi prison "became [her] nunnery and the prison guards became [her] gurus" (TWA "Light in the Abyss" 51).

The Drapchi Fourteen illustrate an enduring expression of freedom in the face of tyranny, and the profound power of faith and compassion in resistance to authoritarian might. In dedication to Tenzin Gyatso, His Holiness Dalai Lama, and to all the sentient beings of the world, the nuns while imprisoned prayed:

May the suffering and hardship of us, poor prisoners,
Never be suffered by any sentient being.
In the heavenly realm of the land of snows
The source of limitless benefit and peace
May Avalokiteshvara Tenzin Gyatso
Reign supreme throughout all eternity.
("Songs from a Tibetan Prison" Song 12)

The nuns embody positivity and keeping alive hope in times of great turmoil, each song of the Draphci Fourteen fundamentally reveals the hope that carried them through the torture, deprivation, and degradation. "They never surrendered to despair and lived everyday with the faith of a better tomorrow.'" (TWA "Light in the Abyss" 38).

The white cloud from the east
Is not a patch that is fixed
The sun from behind the clouds
Will certainly appear one day.
We feel no sadness.
If you ask why,
Even if the day's sun sets,
There is the moon at night.
("Songs from a Tibetan Prison" Song 13)

PROTECTING WOMEN'S REPRODUCTIVE RIGHTS

As staunch Buddhists, Tibetan women consider motherhood to be sacred, and traditionally, Tibetan families idealized having as many children as possible. Tibet is a largely agricultural land, with most of the population either nomadic or farmers; increased numbers of children means more human resources and better prosperity for the family. The family planning policies initiated and implemented by the Chinese government began a tragic chapter in the lives of the Tibetan mothers, as they underwent abortion, sterilization, intimidation and coercion. "Birth control in Tibet was tightened, imposing on the Tibetans a punitive family planning program which included reports of abortions and sterilizations and even, allegedly, infanticide" (Craig 308).

The story of a woman recently interviewed by the Tibetan Women's Association and published in *Tears of Silence* (TWA 105) also shows the continued prevalence of sterilization of Tibetan women as a form of population control. The courage and growing strength of Tibetan women to fight against all odds is evident in the story of Chemi Lhamo (b. 1967) who dared to give birth to four children despite the stringent implementation of the two-child policy in her village, Runpatsa in Kham. After giving birth to her second child, she ran back and forth to Lhasa to hide her identity and gave birth to her third and fourth child at Lhasa. She was levied with heavy fines for failing to abide by the family planning law and going ahead in giving birth to her third and fourth child, and faced forced sterilization after giving birth to her fourth child. She was later imprisoned and tortured in prison for possessing a photo of His Holiness the Dalai Lama and for having in her possession the phone directory of the Tibetan Government in Exile. But despite all the hardships, she later managed to smuggle her four children to exile in India in pursuit of better education.

TIBETAN WOMEN'S ASSOCIATION

Following the 1959 invasion, many Tibetan women fled across the border, seeking asylum along with His Holiness the Dalai Lama. When these women reached Kalimpong, East India, they worked to establish an organization for women in exile. As the women in Tibet were struggling to find steady footing, the women in exile fought to help them from the free side of the border. Although in those days some ninety-nine percent of the members were illiterate, with selfless service and dedication, they demonstrated their capabilities and made sizeable achievements in politics, social welfare and other fields.

On September 10, 1984, under the advice and guidance of His Holiness the Dalai Lama, the Tibetan Women's Association (TWA) was reinstated in Dharamsala, India, the present seat of the Tibetan government in exile. The TWA took off at once as a bird does to the sky and quickly gained a reputation on the world stage, rubbing shoulders with women from progressive countries and discussing issues with them in roundtable forums as equals.

Since its initial inception in 1959 in Lhasa, Tibet, the Tibetan Women's Association has made unwavering efforts in mobilizing political participation, in the preservation and promotion of Tibetan religion and culture, in building the identity of Tibetan women and in empowering women on the educational and leadership fronts.

The TWA incorporates Buddhist nuns within the scope of its work to ensure that all sections of Tibetan women benefit equally. For this purpose, it set up the Tibetan Nuns Project that reaches out to Buddhist nunneries in other Himalayan regions as well as to nuns in other countries. The nuns themselves have worked very hard, have made great progress, and have achieved a great deal in the field of education, and continue to persevere further. This precious journey is not by a few nuns nor for a few nuns but for generations of Buddhist nuns to come. In the effort to become modern, they have not misplaced their souls.

His Holiness the Dalai Lama has over the years expressed His deep admiration and gratitude for His countrywomen in their fight for Tibet's freedom. During a special audience for the members of TWA in 1995, His Holiness said that, "Tibetan women hold a powerful significance in rebuilding their community and offering outstanding examples of spiritual and peaceful leadership to the world." TWA strives to justify the confidence he has placed in Tibetan women.

WOMEN'S STRUGGLE PERSISTS

More than 50 years later, Tibetan Women lead the revolution that is now two-fold: inside and outside of Tibet.

Women Inside Tibet

Despite suffering losses owing to the worsening political situation inside Tibet, women in Tibet have resisted Chinese repression and risen beyond the horizon. Their perseverance is palpable and laudable. Since 2009, more than a hundred Tibetans have resorted to self-immolations as a form of political protest and of them more than a dozen are women. They called for the "dignified return of His Holiness the Dalai Lama back to Tibet," and "freedom inside Tibet," even in their final acts of defiance.

Brave contemporary women writers in Tibet like Tsering Woeser continue to write and express despite threats of detention and torture. The gallant writings on her blog "Invisible Tibet" challenges the Chinese Government despite being under house-arrest. The series of international recognition conferred on to her speaks to the effect of the valiant and indomitable spirit of Tibetan women inside Tibet.

In Exile

From their principal refuge in Dharamsala to small settlements scattered across the globe, Tibetan women have become the architects and builders of the new Tibet in exile. In exile, woman like Jetsun Pema is revered as *Amala*, the Tibetan word for mother. Her tireless contribution to champion the cause of education and empowerment of Tibetan children in exile remain phenomenal. The University of San

Francisco president, Stephen A. Privett, while honoring Jetsun Pema with an honourary doctorate in December 2012 said, "she models the Jesuit ideal of being a woman for others" (USF).

Having faced imprisonment in Chinese prisons in Tibet for twenty-seven years, Ama Adhe, now 77, lives in exile and speaks to the world about how she endured endless torture but never lost courage; she stands as a living testament to a woman's strength and spirit in times of adversity. In her book, *A Voice that Remembers*, she writes, "I am free now. There are no guards outside my door. There is enough to eat. Yet an exile can never forget the severed roots of beginnings, the previous fragments of the past carried always within the heart. My greatest desire is to return to the land of my birth."

For women inside and outside Tibet, their goal is singular—to nurture the future generations and to inculcate in them the knowledge of their cultural heritage, spiritual wisdom and strength of character. Tibetan women continue to share the wisdom and fortitude that bridge their worlds, ancient and contemporary. Their stories are a celebration of the female spirit.

Tibetan women have received messages of encouragement from His Holiness the Dalai Lama, who stated:

> Today, when there is a new understanding among the women in the Tibetan community, and the assumption of new responsibility among them, leading to the gaining of a new experience, there is a new determination and fruitful results in endeavours undertaken in every aspect of public life. When, thus, the term "Tibetan women" becomes a recognized force on the world stage, I am gladdened by a new sense of happiness and pride; and I have a new sense of confidence. (cited in TWA "Tibetan Women's Association marks its 25th anniversary")

The spectacular story of Tibetan women warrant the confidence and conviction His Holiness placed in them.

The English poet Matthew Arnold (1822-1888) is said to have predicted that, "If ever the world sees a time when women shall come together purely and simply for the benefit of mankind, it would be a power such as the world has never known" ("Wise Words"). Undeterred and unyielding, Tibetan Women have seen light in the abyss, have become the beacon of hope, the bastion of optimism and the illuminating light for the emancipation of the oppressed. Tibetan women, who have lost everything, survived decades in prison, and braved a perilous escape

121

across the Himalayas have managed to transform the brutality of invasion into a community of compassion and courage, of devotion and defiance.

REFERENCES

Adhe, Ama (as told to Joy Blakeslee). *The Voice that Remembers: A Tibetan Woman's Inspiring Story of Survival.* Boston: Wisdom Publications, 1997. Print.

Craig, Mary. *Tears of Blood: A Cry for Tibet.* Washington: Counterpoint, 1992. Print.

Goldstein Melvyn C., Jiao Ben, Lhundrup Tanzen. "Chapter 6: The Capture of the Nun." *On the Cultural Revolution in Tibet: The Nyemo Incident of 1969.* Berkeley: University of California Press, 2009. 137-161. Print.

Office of Tibet, New York. Web.

"Songs from a Tibetan Prison: 14 Nuns Sing to the Outside World." *News from Tibet, October-March 1994.* TIN News Review, Tibet Information Network, London, 26 April 1994. 18-21.

Tibetan Women's Association (TWA). *Breaking the Shackles: 50 Years of Tibetan Women's Struggle.* Dharamsala: TWA Publications, 2009. Print.

Tibetan Women's Association (TWA). *Light in the Abyss.* Dharamsala: TWA Publications, 2009. Print.

Tibetan Women's Association (TWA). *Tears of Silence.* Dharamsala: TWA Publications, 2009. Print.

Tibetan Women's Association (TWA). "Tibetan Women's Association marks its 25th anniversary in Exile." Dharamsala, September 10, 2009. Web.

University of San Francisco (USF) Office of Communications. "University of San Francisco Honors 'Mother of Tibet, Jetsun Pema.'" December 13, 2012. Web.

"Wise Words for Human Rights Activists." Alliance for Human Rights in Santa Cruz County. Web.

11.
Women and Wisdom-Culture in India

RENUKA SINGH, INDIA

I N THE COMPLEX AND HIERARCHICAL social fabric of India, development concerns in general and women's empowerment in particular still remain on the agenda for twenty-first century intellectuals, activists, bureaucrats, and religious actors. Ever since U.N. designated 1975 as International Women's Year, with the objectives of promoting equality between men and women and encouraging women's participation in the process of development and maintenance of world peace, both governmental and non-governmental efforts have been made in India to assess women's needs and problems, and enhance their status. Many scholars have also described the imbalances created and resolved by the processes of development, urbanization, modernization, and globalization.

It is generally considered that the relative status of women in India has deteriorated in post-independence India. In spite of constitutional protection for women in India, the drop in their numbers (the sex ratio, or number of females per 1000 males, fell from 945 in 1951 to 914 in 2011), life-expectancy, literacy rate, and economic participation *vis-a-vis* men all denote a situation at odds with women's welfare (UNFPA). Amniocentesis or ultra-sound examinations leading to the selective abortion of female foetuses, female infanticide, widespread harassment of brides, rape, and other forms of increasing violence against women speak all too clearly of women's deprivation and discrimination.

When academicians and activists highlight the scarcity syndrome experienced by a majority of the ignored and marginalized rural women in India—their struggle to procure the most basic necessities of life such as food, fuel, and water, their minimal control over the conditions and the products of their labour, their passive role in the decision-making process within the family—one may then wonder about the spirit that keeps these women alive and ticking.

Needless to say, if women are to engage seriously in the task of self–development, they must first identify areas of conflict and interest. The Beijing World Conference on Women in 1995 identified twelve critical areas for women's development, elimination of poverty and armed conflict, education, health, access to political and economic rights, career advancement, and nurturing of the girl child. Ideological, religious and cultural differences have been acknowledged yet peace and progress for women remains a common aim. Empowerment of individual women has to go hand in hand with a wide range of opportunities for both men and women, and building a basis for action at the family and community level may be the key to social development in the future. However, in recent years new patterns have emerged in the ways in which urban women view and seek to empower themselves. Although many women have attempted to develop their lives by drawing power through external sources of financial support, polity and society, others have tried to sustain strength and confidence by seeking a path of spirituality or culture of wisdom expressed in terms of peaceful and non-violent ethos based on love, nurturance, receptivity and the experiential.

In India, women's involvement in public life began with Mahatama Gandhi's call to participate in the freedom struggle. Way back in 1937, it was the establishment of Congress Party that gave impetus to women's active role in the field of education, politics and society. In post-independence India, even though political freedom had been won there was no guarantee of economic independence for women. However, each political party had its own women's wing (all right and left wing parties) that worked towards the raising-up of women, but it is still a debatable issue whether or not they fulfill feminist objectives ("Towards Equality"). In our constitution and Law, women theoretically enjoy complete equality, whereas in reality even today many discrepancies remain along with weak enforcement of laws.

Rural India has been a stage for different struggles and movements waged by women. For instance, the Self Employed Women's Association (SEWA) was established in 1972 in Gujarat by Ela Bhatt, who also subscribed to the Gandhian values. Women in her organization work in different trades in the informal sector, especially as street vendors, but share common oppressive conditions with very poor remuneration. SEWA aimed and succeeded in improving the working conditions through training, technical aid and collective bargaining to create a culture of honesty, dignity and simplicity for these women. There are many similar sites of women's activism. The Shahada in Dhulia district of Maharshtra was a leftist movement related to anti-price rise agitation. The Bhil tribal landless labourers protested against the exploitative practices of non-tribal land-owners. This began as a folk protest, but eventually women became more active and resisted physical violence at the hands of their husbands associated with their alcoholism. Hence, women in groups stormed liquor shops and destroyed liquor pots.

In 1970s, sharecroppers' movement was renewed in Telengana, Andhra Pradesh, where women actively participated in the landless labourers' movement. Women mobilized themselves against wife-battering and landlord rape along with resistance against Dowry, especially in the countryside.

The burning of Roop Kanwar on the pyre of her husband in Rajasthan has informed the public of the sufferings and plight of women here, and prompted mobilization against Sati in the 1980s.

Ecological concerns have been expressed through Chipko movement, for example. This in an historical case of women's resistance in order to prevent denuding and destruction of forest by timber contractors.

Interestingly, participation in the women's movements has not only contributed to the development of gender studies in terms of theoretical and methodological debates in the field, it has forced us to reconsider the boundaries between the sacred and the secular.

In general, gender studies challenge the generation and distribution of knowledge. Shifting the focus from androcentricity to a frame of reference that validates women's different and differing ideas, experiences, needs, and interests forms the basis of epistemology and pedagogy. Power relations are clearly visible in current knowledge frameworks, practices and access. So, as in the West, in India too, the setting up and teaching of such courses is a political act; theoretical analysis is connected to social change, broadly defined as the recognition and analysis of women's oppression that requires elimination in patriarchal and capitalistic societies. Feminism and the women's movement can certainly be questioned in terms of structure, ideology and agenda, nonetheless different waves of feminism have insisted on the importance of sisterhood, the personal being political, the public and private spheres having a false boundary, and a recognition of the common element of women's oppression. Post-modern theorists however remind us of the difference and diversity in terms of race, ethnicity, sexuality, class, age and levels of disability challenging a totalizing philosophy of feminism. Post-modernism rejects epistemological assumptions, refutes methodological conventions, resists knowledge claims, and literally obscures all versions of truth.

Although postmodernism has been a preoccupation of academia for a while, it is difficult to generalize about the character of the postmodern condition. Nonetheless, there is found everywhere a commitment by society to heterogeneity, fragmentation and difference which has been applied to various conflicting socio-cultural projects. Instead of generating insights in terms of universals, postmodernists have been emphasizing difference in the understanding of gender issues—linguistic, cultural, socio-economic, political, social and psychological. Conventional schools of thought have assumed that women can be agents of change and transformation. However, many postmodernists, as Lois McNay suggests, through deconstruction of unified subjectivity into fragment subject positions, have questioned this assumption by suspending all forms of value judgement, such as truth, freedom, and rationality for all emancipatory movements (1).

The connection between the new spiritual concerns of postmodernism and its need for an ethical code, Edith Wyschogrod argues in *Saints and Postmodernism*, can serve as a new normative structure after the dismissal of Marxism. Thus, according to Geraldine Finn, experiences of excess, disjuncture, difference, chaos and chance are necessary and indispensable conditions of ecstasy, creatively, change and critique (205). This attitude towards religious beliefs, practices and organizations and the seemingly strange resurfacing of the spiritual imperative at the core of secular thought has become largely a global affair.

There is a breakdown of boundaries and power balance as globalization manifests in many forms all around us. Whether we deny postmodernity or try to update it, the idea of globalization carries serious implications for culture and identity. According to post-modernists, liberation and oppression are two sides of the coin in the process of globalization. People have a plurality of cultural choices and meanings that they can pick from and thus strengthen or modify their identity. This ever-changing and expanding world with its rapid exposure might lead to uncertainty, chaos, cultural disorder and confusion. Anthony Giddens ' urges us to be reflexive about our lives, our very sense of self. In the past, studies of religion have dealt with different ideologies, teachings, and prescriptions that determine to a great extent the identity, role and status of women. Neglected are the implications that religion has for self-perception and enlightenment. Even though religions are still a site of struggle for many women, for a majority of cultures around the world, religion thoroughly permeates and certainly affects the everyday business of survival and hope. The role played by women in India to remove the divide between secularity and spirituality and to synthesize the sacred and profane through their intuitive wisdom and culture of non-violence is commendable and inspirational, as I have shown in my 1997 study of urban Indian women's experiences of spirituality, *Women Reborn*.

MAJOR RELIGIONS IN INDIA

Four major, often called "great," religions originated in India: Hinduism, Jainism, Buddhism and Sikhism. Buddhism, however, spread to other Asian nations such as China, Japan, Korea, Vietnam, Cambodia, Thailand, and Sri Lanka. In recent years, some scholars have used the distinction between the "Great" and the "Little" traditions to distinguish between mainstream formal expression of a particular religion and its local variations and expressions, particularly at the village and folk level. Whether "Great" or "Little," religion has had an undeniable impact on societies in all continents. Be it cultural affairs or political development, religion has often been instrumental in legitimizing, suppressing or inspiring government, aesthetic experiences and movements, and different philosophies. In our present turbulent times, if religion has inspired individuals to live up to exalted personal standards, it unfortunately has played a provocative role in bringing out the baser nature of human beings as well.

Resistance to feminism in the world at large and to feminist analysis in the study of religion in our given patriarchal contexts is not difficult to understand. Adherents and practitioners have much at stake in terms of losing their worldview, position, and divine conception as mostly all religious positions and participants in religious activities have traditionally been men. Once women question masculine authority and hegemony in religious affairs, men can no longer retain their hitherto-held power in the sacred domain. As Darlene Juschka aptly suggests, "[g]ender ideology is used within societies so that activities, roles and social locations produced within the social domain are naturalized and made to appear as if they are not a product of social relations (relations defined hierarchically and oppressively) but found in "nature." Gender ideology is then internalized so that men and women believe that the differences mapped out within the social domain are in fact located in nature." Rituals, symbols, and mythology tend to lose their certainty and objectivity once feminist analysis enters into the picture. In fact, divine design gets questioned and goes topsy-turvy. Feminism points to the gender encoding of all knowledge, including the spiritual.

Religions that originated in India have posed paradoxical situations for women. In Hinduism, the unity of all created beings is juxtaposed with differences in status and the role of individuals. The hierarchical structure of Hindu society remains, even though the modern laws of India prohibit discrimination against people on the basis of caste. Dalit women—women from the lowest rung of Indian society, who do not belong to the honoured castes and strata—thus are doubly oppressed. More generally, if divinity and eternal peace are promised to one and all, then why have women been excluded from attaining Moksha (salvation) in a female body? Simply because women have bodily secretions that they cannot control, while men are considered to have the capacity to withhold their semen. Today's feminists have questioned the fundamental premise of various religious texts and reinterpreted and reinvented traditional religious texts and literature. The orthodox division of labour with little or no prospects of mobility has been addressed through modern forms of competition in education, employment and new class formations that provide relatively greater flexibility.

Motherhood still emerges as the highest ideal for Indian women, and women are thus very important for the continuation of society. Their chastity raises much concern in religious texts and epics; female sexuality is viewed as something that must be controlled. An ambivalent attitude towards women is still prevalent in Indian society. Ideally they are honoured and worshipped as goddesses, but in reality, they are dehumanized and seen as not to be trusted. The *Manusmriti* (an ancient text ascribed to the sage Manu) contains ample evidence of such contradictory sayings that impinge upon the nature of gender relations and authority patterns in highly-stratified Hindu society. Indian feminists, of course, have been very critical of these orthodox views and arrangements. Yet self- control is what emerges as a common theme in both traditional and modern contexts today.

Jainism in India has propounded and promoted the philosophy of *anekantavada*, a doctrine of manifold aspects, multiple viewpoints, and comprehension, making space for that which is not self but other. It is a form of tolerance (required acutely in our violent and conflict-ridden world) that gives latitude to people to blossom authentically.

This kind of bliss and freedom prevents violence from being inflicted upon others. Women are suitable vehicles to effect both subtle and radical change based on non-violence, and create a world order of ecology and compassion. The symbol of the dove hence has been linked with women representing peace, purity, patience, and simplicity. Clearly, women are seen to encourage a desire for transformation inherent in one's innermost being.

In Buddhism, initially women were not taken into the fold of Sangha but upon the insistence of Buddha's disciples and aunt, were inducted into it at a later stage. Patriarchal domination and preferences could not be wished away despite such a radical move. Although women were believed to have the same potential as men for enlightenment and Buddhahood, the position of the mother is again valourized. The ideal of "loving kindness" is seen as akin to the feelings and affection a mother has towards her only child, and particularly a son. Thus, being mother of Buddhas holds the mothers in high esteem and wisdom, and emptiness is the feminine principle operating here. Wisdom in this tradition is greater than acquiring possessions; and loving kindness more than hatred and aggression.

There is a particularly striking contrast between the representation of women as evil or wise. Rita Gross suggests that the body, sexuality, menstruation taboos, death, inauspiciousness, and witch-like behaviour are linked with the complex issue of evil, which is the antithesis of the spirit of Wisdom and compassion in the representation of the female Buddhisattva. In early Buddhism, let us not forget, the greatest possible female aspiration was to be reborn as a man for spiritual attainment. Today, much has changed and women now participate in the activities of the International Buddhist Women's Association. The *Sakyaditta* (named after the Buddha's daughter) conferences are organized by women regularly to take up issues and problems faced by nuns and lay women.

Sikhism, a modern religion considered by some scholars to be a reformist movement, claims to have revolutionized the status of women, giving credit to the male *Gurus* (teachers). Eleanor Nesbitt observes and confirms that previously women were considered ritually unclean as a result of menstruation and childbirth. Girls were viewed as a liability, since a hefty dowry had to be paid for their marriage. Widows were regarded as inauspicious and the bearers of misfortune. Results of these beliefs included female infanticide, a ban on widows' remarriage, and the practice of *Sati*, the self-immolation of widows on their husbands' funeral pyres. The Gurus have consistently condemned these customs but conventional reality has not usually matched their teachings. In Sikhism there have been ten historical Gurus, the first being Guru Nanak and the last one Guru Gobind Singh. Thereafter, the sacred text or holy book *Granth Sahib* was given the status of the future Guru or Ultimate teacher. Renunciation has not been applauded in Sikhism and salvation has to be achieved while performing your worldly household and family duties. Householdership is advocated as the natural way to one's salvation and women do not need to be reborn as men in order to attain Moksha. Divinity and family responsibility are closely linked, while celibacy is not the idealized state for men. Guru Nanak says:

> It is through woman, the despised one, that we are conceived and from her that we are born. It is to woman that we get engaged and then married. She is our lifelong friend and then survival of our race depends on her. On her death a man seeks another wife. Through women we establish our social ties. Why denounce her, the one from whom even kings are born? (*Adi Granth* 473)

Women, therefore, are not perceived as seductresses or temptresses, or as a threat.

Motherhood obviously is seen as a source of power and authority in Indian society. However, the conventional social roles of women as mothers, wives and daughters are also being expanded not only into modern professions but also into spiritual vocations, such as nuns, ascetics, mystics, and healers; women are emerging as alternative power centers. Sri Aurobindo affirms, the *Purusha* and *Prakriti*[1] symbolize the male and female divine principles in the Universe—the Stri or unborn Female Energy, is the executive divinity of the Universe, the womb, the mother, the bride, the mould and instrument of all joy and being (*On Women*).

In India today, further political empowerment of women is actively being sought even though a statute, the 73rd Amendment of Indian Constitution (1992), has brought about a 33 percent quota for women representatives to the Panchayati Raj local governments in rural areas. This has provided an opportunity for women to get a foothold in the arena of politics. At the national level, a fifty percent quota for women is becoming the current demand; this bill should see the light of day in the parliament. In the meanwhile, the United Nations Development Fund has sponsored the project "Enhancing the Role of Women in Strengthening Democracy," that aims to create a pool of one thousand women across the country and train them to be part of the expanding political landscape. Nonetheless, we have to be wary of the rise of religious fundamentalism and the virulent rhetoric used by some women as speakers and targets and ensure that they do not end up being the key players in such fundamentalist games. With the advent of globalization, pauperization and marginalization of women workers is taking place and undoubtedly the current patriarchal structures do pose greater difficulties for women.

Therefore, increased economic and political empowerment should have a salutary effect on violence against and abuse of women in India, with its resulting humiliation, betrayal and loss of self-worth. Women's religious upbringing can at times produce guilt and isolation to such an extent that they feel totally trapped as secular treatment options clash with their given value-systems. Synthesizing the secular with the sacred thus requires tremendous wisdom and courage.

In the Indian tradition, although aggression has been used as a means for conflict resolution, non-violence is the supreme weapon against any form of oppression and discrimination. Paradoxically, passivity, cooperation, tolerance and sacrifice become empowering virtues. Ultimately the purifying power of stillness equips women to face modern life, characterized by political and economic upheaval, insecurity, and fear. This seems to be the most effective way to bring about global transformation. Women do not advocate a separatist option which is exclusively meant for women or children alone in the patriarchal society as it would change very little. While they create their own autonomous world in their given cultural contexts, of course, they negotiate their daily existence not by destroying the system but by working within it, reforming, recasting, and reinventing. Thus, Panchayati Raj Institution has successfully tapped the power of women in the domain of rural politics. Other developments such as gender sensitization, the emergence of peace initiatives, women's studies centers in various Indian Universities and innumerable non-governmental organizations working in the area of health, education and employment are indeed changing the complexion of local and global feminisms. Their greatest and deepest impact lies in the discovery of a new sense of self and awareness of others in a new light that liberates and democratizes society. However, this does not preclude the rising violence against women and the paradoxes of Indian society in terms of the ever-expanding infrastructure meant for promoting educational, economic and technological growth and communication network on the one hand and the growing pauperization and marginalization of people and suppression of their dissent and protest.

Imperialism, rapid communication and globalization have brought people into greater contact. Today scholars and activists from around the world are at the forefront of articulating a fresh, global perspective in gender history and gender roles. However, women's mere visibility in both public and private realms should not be mistaken for empowerment as emergence from the periphery to representation needs to create real space for their assertion. Learning to exist and co-exist peacefully in potentially violent religious, political, and psychological contexts is a challenge that perhaps can be faced in a better way through women's traditional wisdom culture and re-imagining the feminine. This can be achieved by critiquing the old and constructing new modes of thinking and being. Individually or collectively, will women be able to act in the world at large? In the pursuit of global peace that should not just remain an unrealized dream. Women's far-reaching wisdom of understanding, acting and conquering out of stillness will be the way out of our worldly impasse.

[1]Purusha and Prakriti: Purusha deals with silence and passivity and looks at Prakriti. It is a form of consciousness that is a silent witness of the actions of Prakriti or in other words, world and nature. Prakriti also deals with thoughts, ideas, desires and the unchangeable laws of physical life whereas in order to find Purusha consciousness, one has to reject everything in the lower plane (Aurobindo, *Evening Talks* 39, 437-438).

REFERENCES

Adi Granth. Compiled by Guru Arjun Dev, 1604. Trans. G. Singh. Sri Guru Granth Sahib, 4 Vol. Delhi, 1962. Print.

Aurobindo. *Evening Talks*. Pondichery, India: Sri Aurobindo Society. 1982. Print.

Aurobindo. *On Women*. Pondichery, India: Sri Aurobindo Society. 1992. Print.

Finn, Geraldine. "Politics of Spirituality." *Shadow of Spirit: Postmodernism and Religion*. Eds. Philippa Berry and Andrew Wernick. London: Routledge, 1992. 111-122. Print.

Giddens, Anthony. *Modernity and Self-Identity: Self and Society in the Late Modern Age*. Cambridge: Polity Press, 1991. Print.

Gross, Rita M. *Buddhism After Patriarchy: A Feminist History, Analysis and Reconstruction of Buddhism*. Albany, NY: State University of New York Press, 1993. Print.

Juschka, Darlene M., ed. *Feminism in the Study of Religion*. London: Continuum, 2001. Print.

McNay, Lois. *Foucault and Feminism*. Cambridge: Polity Press, 1992.

Nesbitt, Eleanor.1996. "Sikhism." *Ethical Issues in Six Religious Traditions*. Ed. Peggy Morgan and Clive Lawton. Edinburgh: Edinburgh University Press, 1996 .99-134. Print.

Singh, Renuka. *Women Reborn*. Delhi: Penguin, 1997. Print.

"Towards Equality: Report of the Committee on Status of Women in India." New Delhi: ICSSR, Department of Human Welfare, 1994. Print.

United Nations Populations Fund (UNFPA). "Introduction." *The State of World Population, 1994: The Cairo Consensus at Ten: Population, Reproductive Health and the Global Effort to End Povery*. New York: UNFPA, 1994. 1-9. Web.

Wyschogrod, Edith. *Saints and Postmodernism*. Chicago: University of Chicago Press, 1990. Print.

12.
Feminine Democratization
of the Iranian Society

PARVIN ARDALAN, IRAN

T HIS CHAPTER PRESENTS THE HISTORY of Iranian women's movements, especially during the three decades following the Islamic revolution, including their demands, struggles and the obstacles they had to overcome. It discusses the development of the Women's Cultural Center, one of the well-known non-governmental organizations (NGOs) after the revolution to advocate women's rights, along with the growing movement known as the "One Million Signature Campaign to Change Discriminating Laws" (OMSC). I will analyze the impact of women's movement on an everyday society, as well as on the interrelations among activists, our struggle and our successes as they have become known in much of the world. My experience and analysis are based upon my field work in the women's movement as an activist and a journalist.

HISTORICAL BACKGROUND

Thirty-four years have passed since the brief period of exhilaration that Iranian women felt about the Revolution, and their subsequent widespread protests. Thirty-four years have passed since we came to understand and recognize the tragedy of defeat on the brink of victory when the *Family Protection Act* was repealed, the forced veiling was introduced and our cries were silenced.

In 1979, Mohammad Reza Pahlavi,[1] the Shah of Iran, was overthrown and replaced with an Islamic Republic. The Shah and Shi'a clerics had gone head-to-head for decades over certain modernization plans implemented by the Shah. The Shah's influence was secular and he had a lot of support from the West, while the clerics advocated more Islamic traditions.

In 1967, by the efforts of women's organizations and members of the

parliament, new laws were established with more rights for women—
The Family Protection Act. For example that law gave women the right
to divorce without the permission of the husband. Also the consent of
the first wife was necessary if a man desired a second wife. Legal issues
related to familial disputes were taken to secular jurisdictions, whereas
this had been previously the domain of Muslim law, and in particular,
the more patriarchal interpretation of Shari'a, Islamic law. Those
reforms in addition with growing more liberal and western attitudes
were in contrast with extremist religious perspectives. The governmental
suppression against the left groups and other opposition groups led to
increasing conflict between the Shah, the opposition groups and the
leading Shi'a cleric, Ayatollah Khomeini.[2]

Thus, during my early years, there were continual conflicts between
those following the ways of the Shah and those promoting his overthrow
and replacement with Ayatollah Khomeini. The Shah was a Muslim
but his secular tendencies gave women far more freedom than would
be allowed under a rigid interpretations of Islamic jurisprudence. But,
although Ayatollah Khomeini lived in exile in Iraq and later in France,
he continued to exert influence. Many intellectuals both feared and
opposed his views, preferring a more modern direction for Iran.

During the process of the Shah's modernization inside Iran, and as a
result of women's movements around the world, and their demand for
equal rights, especially among middle-class women in Iran, the Shah
appointed a few women to top posts, including the appointment of
Mehrangiz Manouchehrian as the first female senator in the Iranian
parliament (September 1963). Manouchehrian, a lawyer who had a
tremendous command of the law, was well respected during her tenure
as a senator for her activism for women's rights. She introduced the
Family Protection Act (February 1964), which was unique and radical
in Iran for its time. She was both a feminist and a conscientious
opponent of legal discrimination against women. During her time in the
senate, she founded the Association for Women Lawyers, an NGO to
further social activism, for which she earned international recognition,
including winning the International Prize for Human Rights (March
1968). It was a time when Iranian women first experienced what it was
like to enter the political arena such as the parliament.

This, however, was not enough. On the one hand, religious authorities
did not approve of Manouchehrian's outline for the proposed family bill,
and her bill was not publicly debated by parliament; on the other hand,
the modern religious state, which was also engaged in confrontation
with the religious authorities, was bent on a show of force even as

it lacked the requisite courage to stand up to the religious jurists. Manouchehrian's project was therefore set aside; ultimately through another effort, in 1967 women managed to get the government to consider the bill in parliament, and by taking into account the views of modernist religious jurists, the *Family Protection Act* was promulgated. In any case, a step forward had been taken. Meanwhile the discourse on women's rights was only at the beginning of its transformation into a public and socially broad discourse.

The fact that the law was more advanced as compared with the culture of the society, meant that it was still possible to make further progressive adjustments. Thus, five years later (1972), a number of amendments were made to the law; for example, although it appeared to be impossible to abolish polygamy despite all the various pressures to remove the man's right to take an additional wife, it was nonetheless possible to make this right conditional upon the first wife's permission. This progressive trend came to a halt with the Islamic Revolution of 1979. The *Family Protection Act* was rescinded and women's situation returned to the way it had been some 40 years earlier.

The 1960s and '70s saw the entry of women into the public sphere and their achievement of some basic rights; the end of the 1970s and '80s were the years in which these rights were once again taken from them. Since the 1990s, women have fought to find their way back into the highest level of public sphere, to bring their own demands to the fore, and impose themselves on patriarchal structures. The decade of the '90s can also be termed the years of the rational, active, methodical presence of women in the public sphere specifying and pressing their demands.

Only a month into the 1979 Revolution (March 1979), Iranian women began grasping the real intentions of the new Islamic leaders. Protests and marches began against the forced veil and the rescinding of the *Family Protection Act*. The women, who saw the two faces of the Ayatollah Khomeini and heard his double-talk in Paris and Tehran, understood the true meaning of "Islamic Expediency," a baton held over our heads for the past 34 years. As the most informed elements of the revolutionary society, women have coined an image in the history of Iran that is also the narrator of the upheavals of women's history in the last one hundred years.

The Iranian revolution of 1979 was quickly kidnapped by the clerics, who were more organized in the vacuum created by an absence of a civic society and unity among progressive and the leftist oppositions. This occurred in February 1979; in the first week of March 1979, it was announced that the Family bill was repealed, no woman could be a judge in a court of law, and women must wear *hijab*,[3] or head-covering, in public. Gradually, in the following years, alcohol, gambling and nightclubs where banned. Women and men were segregated in public arenas. Music was not allowed in the media and many newspapers were terminated for advocating opposing views etc. A huge number of the opposition were arrested, executed or had to leave the country.

The strife continued and further limitations were forced upon the Iranian people—both males and females. Women were losing many of the rights they had achieved, such as the simple right of women to cover the heads or not. Polygamy became easier once again—biasing the rights of the male side of humanity. Women were faced with a choice: to accept this version of Islam, or work to change this increasingly oppressive situation. Many women made the choice to fight back.

Recognizing the mass involvement of the Iranian women in the ousting of the Shah, the Islamic regime decided to leave in place some of the rights granted to women during the Shah's regime. After the revolution, for example, women's right to vote was not taken away, but was even ratified. This was because the women's vote, as half of the population (18.5 million) of the country, was effective in legitimizing a government that Ayatollah Khomeini was assembling.

However, if we believe the women's political participation goes beyond the right to vote, this participation took a different form after the revolution and it included a large number of religious and traditional women. In the male-dominated construct of power in Iran, in addition to the fully consolidated religious government, women's participation adopted an Islamic colour. The goal was to organize an Islamic society against the West and to wipe out western symbols from the women's lives, all but the "Shah's gift to women—the right to vote." The right to vote was not taken away but women's ministerial posts, established during the Shah's regime, were ignored. Further, Farrokhrou Parsa, the first female minister in Iran, was executed in a horrific manner. Ayatollah Khomeini's government did not take away women's right to vote, but eliminated female judges and prevented them from holding judicial posts.

Meanwhile, the meaning of women's political participation was defined by combining Islamic ideology with values such as "Muslim women," "duty," "obligation," and by presenting the inequality of the sexes as a natural phenomenon. In this way, Islam was used as a political tool against women. At the same time, women were called upon to participate politically in prescribed areas. Muslim women were organized in religious campaigns and gatherings, networking, walks and demonstrations, and attending Friday prayers.

Contradictions prevailed again! The masses of women who were defined as "dutiful Muslim women" and were used as a political force, had no political role in decision-making and were eliminated in this ideological male-dominated construct. They were denied Islamic jurisprudence and religious leadership. Even today, they cannot head the three branches of the government or even be a member of the Guardian Council,[4] Expediency Council,[5] Assembly of Experts,[6] foreign affairs etc. Thirty-four years after the revolution, women can become ministers only for propaganda purposes. The interesting thing is that a majority of "Muslim" women who were at the heart of these valued placements at the beginning and acted upon them, have distanced themselves from the power, seeking more secular pursuits.

FROM WITNESSING TO ACTION

The role of the Iranian women's movement three decades after the victory of the Islamic Revolution in Iran is above all, focused on increasing gender awareness, constructing discourse, and mobilizing women in a path not so smooth. We owe this to the movement's elders and to the new generation with a passion for wanting more than they were given. These young activists know how to break the barriers; they are trail-blazers in their own right who came about after the revolution. After the revolution the movement started from individual actions in the form of published essays and group gatherings and expanded by women's empowerment in literary circles, media, and collective actions. In the process, we broke the traditional framework and unidirectional education; we learned from each other and taught one another.

The experience of gender awareness was a gradual development. Some in my generation were witnesses and observers to the first years of the victory of the Islamic Revolution in Iran, with no power in its changes. As a woman, no one saw you—but you saw the others. We were observers of the prejudice perpetrated against our mothers and against women in general, and it chained our feet as well. In contrast to the motherly anecdotes that "You become a real woman when you start your period," my generation and I had crossed the age of nine reaching the reality of womanhood. I despised womanhood because it challenged my childhood freedoms. Before I could live out my childhood, I became an adult. I saw my classmates getting married at an early age under the newly-implemented laws; my womanhood in the ruler's narrative had become faceless and without identity.

Rebellion against lack of identity was once again a pronouncement of "womanhood" and this time by our own definition. We decisively stamped our feet and proclaimed that "we are women" according to our own definition, not the one the rulers had constructed. We unleashed our protests onto a male-dominated society that either made women obscure or put them on the pedestal as sacred. We proclaimed that "we are feminists" who we will not be silenced before prejudice and indignation, that we shall critique, challenge, and take steps to implement change.

The consciousness we had developed took root in our individual and collective actions, each process involving an effort to prompt discussion and to move on, to prepare the ground for change. As semi-civil spaces were opened up, our small circle gatherings evolved into official and unofficial groups, either aligned with government institutions or non-aligned and independent of the government. Gradually, we pooled our forces to establish collective organizational structures for holding meetings and launching campaigns against sexual and domestic violence, speaking out against militarism and in support of peace, combating legal discrimination and striving to change discriminatory conditions in the areas of legislation, ethnicity and nationality, religion and gender, and celebrating the 8th of March as a traditional day of protest.

Thus, we proceeded from the stage of building individual consciousness to building collective consciousness, and subsequently to taking collective action to push for change and, despite the limited tools at our disposal for prompting discussion, we managed to generate an influential discourse on subjects such as resisting violence, striving for gender equality and communicating with other social movements.

In our struggle for equality we have had some high points; the selection of an Iranian woman, Shirin Ebadi, to win the 2008 Nobel Peace Prize brought us all to the streets. With placards in our hands we all became Shirin Ebadi,[7] Mehrangiz Kar,[8] Parvaneh Forouhar,[9] and Zahra Kazemi.[10]

In 2005, in the transition phase between two governments, we soared to even greater heights, crying out that we opposed the discrimination against women entrenched in the constitution, and closing ranks with our friends of the labour, students' and ethnic minority movements. In doing so, we were focused on demands, not on candidates.

The presidency of Mahmoud Ahmadinejad brought a consolidation of power that increased repression. During a gathering in Daneshjoo

Park in Tehran, on March 8, 2006, the government forces did not spare even the first lady of the women's movement, 80-year-old poet and activist Simin Behbahani[11]—attacking and beating her.

After the announcement of the election results and the formation and expansion of the Green Movement centering around the slogan "Where is my vote?," many people wrongly claimed that the Iranian women's movement had not managed to adjust itself to the Green Movement. Of course, this is a misleading analogy; that is to say, a civil society movement that grew slowly on a "qualitative" level cannot be compared with a protest movement calling for the right to vote that emerged suddenly on a mass scale. However, it can be said that the achievements, experiences, and teachings of the women's movement were used on a larger scale by the Iranian Green Movement, for example, discussions on networking, multiple leadership and horizontal organization. All these were, in fact, solid achievements and methods that we had already thoroughly tried and tested.

Tying up different social movements with each other, or subordinating one movement to another, is a dangerous thing. It promotes the increasing hegemony of a movement like the Green Movement, while it deprives the other movements of their independence, and it makes them all indistinguishable from one another. It also has the dangerous potential, on the one hand, of overlooking the numerous accomplishments of the women's movement resulting from the One Million Signatures Campaign, and on the other hand, shifting the responsibility for the campaign to one movement that is now expected to take care of everything.

However, after the 2009 presidential election and horizontal suppression in Iran, there is continuous discussion and conflict within the women right's movement about the role and positioning of the movement. In my opinion, our movements can learn from each other, we can critique one another, at certain points we can go along and self-replicate and align or we can become distanced. But we only walk beside each other when we are equals.

THE DISCOURSE OF HIJAB IN IRAN, WOMEN'S REACTION AND RESISTANCE

The Iranian revolution in 1979 was not only kidnapped by the Islamic authority. In another sense, the revolution was against the Iranian women's situation. Both within and outside Iran the women opposed the *hijab* but by different means.

In 1980, as women were preparing to celebrate International Women's Day, Ayatollah Khomeini transformed the celebration to a protest by ordering women to wear *hijab* in the public sphere. Iranian women held the largest and the first demonstration against the Islamic Republic in March 1980. The discussion about women's *hijab* took various turns as different religious leaders tried to give their own interpretation of what Khomeini had said and what Islam demanded. Women were invited by some to "self-cover," "be decent," "be simple," and "be a woman." They were told *hijab* is not really necessary because Islam does not demand it. And with every proclamation came reactions by various groups.

Gradually the "invitation" to wear *hijab* became the law to the point that those women appearing in public without it received 74 lashes. With *hijab* as the law, the extent of control, arrests, and punishments of the "perpetrator "intensified. And then a new crime with no precedent in Iran was established, the crime of "bad-*hijab*." Bad *hijab* refers to the women who did not obey the law of covering ALL their hair.

Activists took to the streets in Tehran and other cities. While women were shouting, "We didn't go through the revolution to return back," the enforcers shouted back, "A scarf or a blow to the head!" At the beginning, the provisional government retreated and announced that there was no mandatory *hijab*-code. But this was only a tactical move.

After these demonstrations, discord grew among women and the political groups and many of them, even the leftist groups, criticized women for holding the demonstration—so much noise for an already resolved issue—as it was considered useless by many. And some, if not overtly disagreeing, did not show support.

From that first demonstration of 30,000 strong women on March 8th of 1980, the term *hijab* has gone deeper in the political discourse. Not only the image of "without *hijab*," but the concepts of "*hijab* demeanor," and "*hijab* in words," were being planted deep in our lives so that we did not blind vulnerable men with our "glow" and "charm!" If during the Pahlavi regime we had become familiarized with "forced *hijab*-removal" as a masculine and royal edict, after the revolution, they were put back on women's bodies by force instead of by choice, as a masculine retaliation. After that, many male-constructed definitions entered our *hijab* lexicon. Terms such as "without-*hijab*," "with-*hijab*," "bad-*hijab*," "street-*hijab*," "exercisable-*hijab*," "*hijab*-overcoat chain-stores" as well as other forms of *hijab* words crept into our dictionary to take away the public sphere from women and insinuate *hijab* into our value system. Other examples of *hijab* expressions were: "free *hijab* education"; "*hijab* is a protection not a limitation"; "*hijab* is a women's most valued ornament"; "your *hijab* is more forceful than my blood," etc.

Public notices and signs such as "enforced Islamic *hijab*" or "we are excused from giving service to bad-*hijabi* women" were placed in different institutions, educational centers, on bus tickets, inside buses, commercial billboards throughout the city, as ubiquitous and commonplace as signs warning that "Parking Your Car in This Spot is Equal to a Flat Tire!" Furthermore, women had to pass through the *hijab* checkpoint at every government institution and organization. All of these controls programmed women to continuously self-correct at the sight of a *Hijab* Search Committee.

The Constitutional Revolution of 1906 was an opportunity for women to be present in the public sphere, even though women did not have as many rights as men according to the Constitution. That was the beginning of women's struggle for the rights of education and equality. It was the presence of women that started the resistance, as women began to emphasize their rights as pioneers of modernity in Iran.

Women's basic challenges against the *status quo* included the demand for equal rights with men, obtaining rights of citizenship such as the right to vote, the right to choose clothing, jobs etc. During the second phase, the forced removal of women's *hijab* (*hijab* discovery) was issued and this motion was interpreted as granting "women's liberty" by the officials of the Pahlavi government.

After the Islamic Revolution, women's forced *hijab* by official institutions was justified as an Islamic requirement, an anti-imperialist statement, and as a show of unity with the revolution. But later on it was expressed as the law, value, dignity and reputation for women. Following women's resistance in the private sector, the significance of *hijab* has changed as well. Perhaps, women having given variety to their scarves and overcoats had a role in changing the definitions of *hijab* or rendering the official values and definitions meaningless. However, the transformation of the women's garments in the public sphere, despite the existence of *hijab* law and the instructions for long overcoats, head scarves, and loose pants with dark colours have evolved to images of short overcoats, colourful and small scarves, shorter pants and extensive make up. These actions do not take place in a vacuum; they are images of individual and collective resistance of women within the society and their effect on the framework of the dominant discourse. These actions are not organized but they paint an image of a collective spirit.

The male-dominated regime with various instruments of control, in its modern or traditional form, simply wants to control women, whether through the modern form of "*hijab*-removal" or by the traditional rule of *hijab* laws rule. And *hijab* in any form has a direct relation with controlling society. It is telling that the majority of the experts and those in charge whose views in this regard have been published are not women, but the male intellectuals and the male clerics who issued a decree for our garments.

Today, women in Iran still have to wear *hijab*. However if the forced *hijab* was the symbol of Islamic country the *hijab* of today is a symbol of secular resistance by women's bodies in the Islamic contest since the form and shape of the *hijab* has been transformed by the women.

THE WOMEN'S CULTURAL CENTER (WCC)

By the end of the 1980s, the Iraq-Iran war ended and Ayatollah Khomeini died. Social freedom and collective activities were once again allowed. By the end of the '90s, the political reformists reigned. Civil society developed and the number of the organizations increased. The Women's Cultural Center (*Markaz-e-Farhangi-ye Zanan*), the first independent and non-governmental organization, was established. The WCC became a center for opinions, analyzing and documenting the increasing issues facing Iranian women. The necessity that gave birth to this organization, surfaced not in the privacy of our homes, but rather as a base for organizing a public demonstration on March 8th, the internationally recognized Woman's Day. It was after this collective effort that we tried to learn from our experiences and become aware of all that was assumed to be "natural" against women in our society.

We became determined to fight against civil injustices and to raise consciousness of our own, as well as that of other women's, feminism through critique of issues concerning the lives of women as a social and public matter. We began with smaller committees, which organized around specific projects. In this way, we could all experience large-scale collective effort and stay focused on, and become active about, what we individually sought. Our diversity in ethnicity, social status, and class brought us a wide range of views but also created a wide range of obstacles and social problems.

In this light, problems such as the massacre of street women, the problems of women workers, women and peace, women of Palestine, violence against women, etc., became the focus of our attention in our seminars and conferences, educational workshops, public meetings, and so on. One of our accomplishments during these years was establishing the Sedigheh Dowlat-Abadi Library, which holds publications by and about women. The library was shut down by the authorities in 2010.

The Women's Cultural Center also had a newsletter, but it too was stopped by the authorities. We determined to continue in another way and the WCC became the birthplace of the *Feminist Tribune* website and the *Zanestan* website, Iran's first online magazine focused on women's rights. At the time, I was the editor of the first site and a member of the editorial board of the latter. I also contributed to one of the most influential women's rights magazines, *Zanan* and the literary monthly journal, *Audineh*. In January 2008, the government suspended *Zanan*, charging it with "painting a gloomy picture of Iran."

The *Feminist Tribune* website[12] was active for two years, publishing the works and the efforts of WCC along with other activists of the women's movement. The *Iranian Feminist Tribune* was shut down by the government in 2004. Our way of dealing with this was to simply return with a new magazine under a different name. This magazine addressed issues such as marriage, education and violence against women, as well as problems related to prostitution and AIDS. Eventually both magazines were shut down by the government in 2007, but we keep their archives online.

WCC's activities were stopped by the Iranian authority in 2005. However the group has continued its work through other venues despite the following years of struggle and censorship.

HAMANDISHI

The year 2003 was an energizing year despite all of its challenges and hurdles. It was the year that the pervasiveness of the women's movement exponentially increased, promising to explode in numbers. By selecting Shirin Ebadi as the winner of the Nobel Peace Prize in 2003, the women's movement became visible. It led us to form a forum and network with women's organizations and women activists called Hamandishi. Through this forum we discussed women's issues.

In 2005, we organized a large demonstration peacefully protesting constitutionally-sanctioned violence against women in front of the University of Tehran. The demonstration received great support from the student movement and workers' syndicates. We called it the day for women's movements' solidarity, or the "Say NO to violence against women in constitutional law" day. Despite our victory, a subsequent women's movement demonstration in March 2006 in Tehran, at the popular Danashjo park, was suppressed by extremists affiliated with the government. Many activists were arrested and received sentences.

After the power grab of the conservative government during the election of 2005, even though conditions were harder on women and despite the fear of an expanding militaristic environment, women's groups were still determined to celebrate International Women's day. A coalition of different groups organized the March 8th gathering. However, lack of coordination by the organizing committee from one side, and extensive police brutality that did not spare anyone, turned that day from celebration to "police brutality against women" day. Extensive violence such as this affected decisions about future peaceful demonstrations. Perpetrating brutal actions for holding a peaceful assembly meant only one thing—that women's gatherings would no longer be tolerated. While we continued to exchange ideas and had discussions on the role of the youth in the movement, the power of the elders, the power relations inside the movement, and the intense pressure we felt from the anti-woman government, as well as weak organizing, resulted in an increase in the differences and conflicts among the activists and organizations. The pressure by the regime and our internal conflicts made the movement weaker and reduced our solidarity.

Given the repressive momentum of 2005's new government, demanding changes to the Constitution became dangerous. There was much disagreement over the manner by which our demands were put forth; some thought issuing a statement would suffice, and some promoted holding indoor programs. We belonged to the side that favoured coordinating peaceful street demonstrations. The most worrisome issue for our critics was the price that would be paid for activism. The critics believed that our peaceful street methods were "revolutionary" and would be repressed. If repression did not completely destroy women's actions, at the least it would greatly limit them. But we believed that all movements must pay the price to advance their goals and they should not lose any opportunities afforded them.

For example, the 2005 presidential election period gave us the opportunity to intensify our protest about prejudicial laws during the election environment when there was less government pressure on people. This experience showed us that understanding the common situation, and being prepared to pay the price for the women's movement to engage in civil peaceful protest, is necessary. Otherwise the danger of sacrificing the interest of the movement for our own benefit will always remain a serious threat. Our protest had another blessing: the unprecedented unity of the public transport syndicate workers with the women's movement.

Finally, in June 2006, some women's rights activists such as myself announced a protest and invited people to show solidarity with women against discriminatory laws. It was intended to be a peaceful demonstration in one of the popular squares (Haft-e Tir) in Tehran. This protest was also suppressed and about 70 persons were arrested. We were not able to stay for even fifteen minutes. The police force included female officers who also attacked protesters and supporters. After this defeat, we needed to rethink our strategy and tactics.

A major development that came out of the WCC, Hamandishi, and the analysis of our activities and the impact of government suppression guided us to form a new strategy: the One Million Signatures Campaign, to demand gender equality and to change the unequal laws through networking and mobilizing.

THE ONE MILLION SIGNATURES CAMPAIGN

In an atmosphere of severe repression after our rally in Haft-e Tir Square was stifled, and several groups and organizations were banned, we began to look at different ways of proceeding. We learned a sweet lesson from the experience of our sisters in Morocco,[13] which taught us not to limit our demands and struggles for change to one or two days of protest. This led to the launch of the One Million Signatures Campaign (OMSC).

It is generally believed that laws should promote social progress by being one step ahead of cultural norms. But in Iran, the law lags behind cultural norms in terms of women's position and status. The Campaign began with the goal of obtaining one million or more signatures advocating for equal rights for women. Activists contacted women where women usually gather—shops, schools, offices, hair salons, or their homes. They creatively combined traditional door-to-door petitioning with modern technology. Members of the Campaign and supporters—most of them young women in their twenties—spread their message through the Internet and print media. They ask the public to sign the petition, but whether they signed or not, they received a booklet explaining how the Iranian legal system denies women full rights.

The booklet, entitled "The Effect of Laws on Women's Lives," discusses some of the legal changes that the campaign seeks, such as equal rights for women, an end to polygamy and temporary marriage, an increase in the age of criminal responsibility to eighteen for both girls and boys, the right for women to pass nationality to their children, equal *dieh* (compensation for bodily injury or death) between women and men, equal inheritance rights, reform of laws reducing punishment for offenders in cases of "honour" killings, equal testimony rights for men and women in courts, and other laws that discriminate against women. In summary, the Campaign seeks to bring Iranian law in line with international human rights standards. Thus, even the women who do not sign the petition will be informed about their second-class status. The strength of the Campaign rested on the bottom-up strategy, the interaction between activists and ordinary women, the peaceful and non-violent approach to legal reform, and on stressing the importance of each woman's agency and choice. The Campaign was built on the belief that dialogue and education helps transform political culture and provides the building blocks of a dynamic social justice movement.

The Campaign's goal was, and remains, a quest for equality for the vast number of men and women influencing the legislative institutions; it is an endeavour that requires our bodies, minds, and souls. The Campaign brought the attention of the populace to the fact that promoting women's rights could well be a part of the wider promotion of democratic values. None of us in the Campaign believed that we could change the discriminating laws anytime soon. Our success would lie in changing the Iranian people's attitude toward such laws.

We poured out into the heart of our society to collect signatures. In the alleys and streets, in cities across the country, we mingled with anyone who was willing to listen to what we had to say. Our efforts to build consciousness made another leap forward. The image of the signature collector began to coincide with the image of the signatory; the image of the women's rights activist grew closer to that of the women of the community, and as a result, we multiplied; we mixed with other social movements and boosted each other's size. We had only one demand: A Change for Equality.

The critics of the Campaign claimed that this was a movement driven by self-interest. However, this Campaign, unlike its opponents, was focused on gaining one single reward only: gender equality. From religious people to secular ones, from women wearing the Islamic veil to those who did not believe in it, from individuals who would seek the channels of *fatwa* to legitimize their demands to those who saw equal rights as not being conditional on religious laws and beliefs—all of them had down-to-earth demands, not irrational desires that were nothing but beautiful rhetoric. These were secular demands that were digestible, but which required discussion and the questioning of basic intellectual assumptions and everyone had to do this in their own way.

The Campaign made the movement more mature, allowing its activists to leave black and white thinking behind and begin to see the shades of grey. It brought us a horizontal movement within a vertical structure: a conduct based on a fundamental doctrine that "movement" implies not standing still or remaining in the same state. In other words, it meant conserving our strength on the one hand and acting strategically on the other hand. If activities in a small circle did not trigger a response, we would move on to forming another group. If we did not have permission to form a group, we would become active in existing groups. If we lacked a publishing license, we would issue a newsletter. If they confiscated the newsletter, we would move on to communicating through websites and virtual networks. If we were prevented from assembling and transmitting our messages to the people, we would switch to face-to-face communication. If we were prevented from forming groups and communicating with other movements inside and outside of Iran, we would engage in forming coalitions and launching campaigns and networks; if these networks were weakened, we would set our sights on the groups that had emerged within these networks. In fact, the only major danger the women's movement faced was that of a complete standstill in our institution-building. Today, this way of moving forward enables us to join with and operate within contemporary movements and may thus even reinvigorate the Campaign itself to bring forth many new forces and groups from within it.

The very obvious presence of the women's movement in Iran and all its activities is reflected to a great degree in the field of journalism by other writers. During these years, in addition to increased numbers of female bloggers, the number of women writers increased exponentially, especially in social and literary fields. The progress of the women's movement and advocacy efforts for women's rights increased criticism of laws that discriminate against women, and continuous awareness-raising activities through face-to-face activist strategies is now intertwined with the increased presence of women in various fields of the media.

This development also increased sensitivities within this sector towards women's issues and infused the media with a feminist perspective, as well as elevated the role of women from mere reporters to professional journalists, even feminist journalists, at the same time significantly increasing the number of the discriminatory subject matters covered by the media. In essence the women's movement imposed itself on the male-dominant structures of the media.

The appeal of the legal demands of the One Million Signatures Campaign on one hand, and the de-centralized structure of the Campaign as a movement on the other hand, allows it to rebuild itself quickly after each crackdown or attack. With each arrest, another activist will emerge. Indeed, these arrests and all the costs imposed on the movement, work to publicize the Campaign and its demands further. Suppressing a movement such as the Campaign was difficult. To crack down against it, one must tear down its continued appeal. The continuity of the Campaign is not reliant on its financial resources because the movement is supported by and with its human resources.

THE RELATIONSHIP BETWEEN TWO MOVEMENTS

As I discussed earlier, the women's rights movement is not new in Iran, but rather has more than 100 years of history. At the beginning, the demand was the right to education, then developed into political participation and to reform civil laws and so on. After the 1979 revolution we lost some of the rights that we had achieved.

Once the religious leaders seized the revolution, their first move was to put limits on the presence of women in the public life. Gradually, the rights that women had fought for were taken away and the new *Shari'a* law took its place. These included the penal code which recognizes the value of women as half that of a man, complete overhaul of the Family Law, enforcement of laws forcing women to cover their body, making polygamy easier and much more. We had to accept that all of these things were happening under the umbrella of Islam, or we had to put effort into changing our situation. And so, once again, we started fighting for these rights even under discriminatory laws.

Since the inception of the Islamic Republic of Iran, women have been able to use a variety of strategies to build a peaceful movement. We have worked hard to ensure the success of these three major elements: to work face-to-face, to make it mainstream, and to raise public awareness. We made every effort to ensure that we concentrated on the grassroots level, building a horizontal movement without a vertical structure.

The Green Movement was shaped after the presidential election of 2009. Those who had voted for two of the candidates, Mir-Hossein Mousavi[14] and Mehdi Karroubi,[15] had objected to the widespread cheating in the elections. Mousavi's campaign colour was green, and so his supporters later called themselves the Green Followers. In the absence of political parties, people at different junctures of the Iranian history have formed various groups to make their voices heard which later evolved into the Green Movement's "Where is my vote?"

The movement for democracy used the strategies of the women's movement—in particular those of the One Million Signatures Campaign in its work. There were many similarities between the two movements: they both were horizontal peaceful movements for freedom, civil and political rights, and both are based on grassroots activism. The women's movement started on a smaller scale but in time grew to cover a larger population across the country.

It was a natural process to see the effect of the One Million Signatures Campaign in the social uprising since many of the activists in the Green Movement were also people from the One Million Signatures Campaign. The Green Movement did not develop as expected because of the horizontal suppression against all movements. This not only stopped the process of peaceful struggling, but also had a backlash effect on the society as a whole.

THE WOMEN'S MOVEMENT AT THIS JUNCTURE

In order to understand Iran and its democratic movements, one needs to analyze it from both external and internal viewpoints. Looked at from outside, considering the development underway in the region against the dictatorships, the repressive Iranian rulers are subject to intensified criticisms and protest: this will create a renewed energy and passion in the region. As the dictators learn from each another so do the movements. The demand for change that has echoed in the Middle East has increased the unity of the people of the world for freedom and democracy against the dictators. In fact, the developments in Egypt and Tunisia are a serious shock for these countries and the region.

The developments of the Arab Spring arouse hope in Iranians, since they have been living in hopelessness after the 2009 suppression. Their hope has changed into fear, and they are suffering from poverty and destruction while witnessing the militarization of the region, especially in the case of Libya and Syria. Women in these countries face great internal fundamentalist forces. A positive result, however, is the higher visibility of these regions among women and thus better communication among movements for solidarity.

Recent events in the Middle East have created an imbalance in the new world order, not only mobilizing the people in these countries, but unifying them. The experience of the Iranian revolution of 1979 and its denigrating effects on women's place in the society must logically have taught nations in North Africa and Middle East to take fundamentalism and political Islam seriously. In 1979, none of us had a complete understanding of this phenomenon. Today, this knowledge has been acquired at a heavy price and we all are sensitive toward the strategies of various Islamist groups in the area.

However, it is we women who must be persistent in reflecting our experiences and in our global struggles for women's rights, reminding them of the reasons Iranian society continues to internally spin within the never-ending wheel of systematic violence. We must keep reminding others of the potential for the repetition of social tragedies in developing countries.

In February of 2011, I was invited to Brazil to participate in the Conectas Human Rights Organization's Conference. In my discussions with my Brazilian counterparts, parliamentarians, human rights attorneys, Brazilian women's groups, journalists, foreign minister and the president advisors, I stated that the only channels of dialogue and relations with the Brazilian society have been official, through the Government of Iran. We were surprised by the silence of the civil society in Brazil in reaction to the pervasive crackdown on the civil and political activists in Iran. We believe that societies must strengthen each other's voices in solidarity.

So, where do we go from here?

In my opinion, we, the Iranian women, must stand in solidarity with women who are awakened in the local struggles and want sustainable change in their political and social lives. In this process we must strengthen the mutual relations with the activists and the challengers of the civil institutions in the Middle East.

The path is not clear but the hope of solidarity will lead us.

I would like to extend my special gratitude to Zarin Shaghaghi whose dedication by volunteering her time and contribution in providing translations, conducting research and editing were crucial in this project and helped me to coordinate writing this chapter.

[1]Mohammad Reza Shah Pahlavi King of Iran, ruled from 1941-1979.
[2]Ayatollah Khomeini was an Iranian religious leader and politician, and leader of the 1979 Iranian Revolution, which saw the overthrow of Mohammad Reza Pahlavi, the Shah of Iran. Following the revolution and a national referendum, Khomeini became the country's Supreme Leader—a position created in the constitution as the highest ranking political and religious authority of the nation—until his death.

[3]*Hijab* refers to both the head covering traditionally worn by Muslim women and modest Muslim styles of dress in general.

[4]The Guardian Council, or Council of Guardians, is an appointed and constitutionally-mandated twelve-member council that wields considerable power and influence in the Islamic Republic of Iran.

[5]The Expediency Council is an administrative assembly appointed by the Supreme Leader Khomeini and was created upon the revision of the Constitution of the Islamic Republic of Iran on 6 February 1988.

[6]Assembly of Experts, also translated as Council of Experts, is a deliberative body of 86 Mujtahids (Islamic scholars) that is charged with electing and removing the Supreme Leader of Iran and supervising his activities. Members of the assembly are elected from a government-screened list of candidates by direct public vote to eight-year terms.

[7]Shirin Ebadi is an Iranian lawyer, a former judge and human rights activist and founder of Defenders of Human Rights Center in Iran. On October 10, 2003, Ebadi was awarded the Nobel Peace Prize for her significant and pioneering efforts for democracy and human rights, especially women's, children's, and refugee rights. She was the first Iranian, and the first Muslim, woman to have received the prize.

[8]Mehrangiz Kar is a prominent Iranian lawyer, human right activist and author. Mehrangiz Kar is one of the most celebrated activists in the history of the women's movement in Iran.

[9]Parvaneh Forouhar, an Iranian dissident and activist who was murdered along with her husband during the Chain murders of Iran in November 1998. The murders, which are believed to have been politically motivated, remain unsolved, although the general belief is that the Iranian Ministry of Intelligence had ordered the killings.

[10]Zahra Kazemi was an Iranian-Canadian freelance photographer, residing in Montreal, Canada, who died in the custody of Iranian officials following her arrest.

[11]Simin Behbahani is a prominent figure of modern Persian literature and one of the most outstanding amongst the contemporary Persian poets. She is considered Iran's national poet and an icon of the Iranian intelligentsia and literati who affectionately refer to her as the "lioness of Iran." She has been nominated twice for the Nobel Prize in literature, and has received many literary accolades around the world.

[12]See www.iftribune.es.

[13]For further information, see Sadiqi and Enaji.

[14]Mir-Hossein Mousavi is best known for holding the premiership between 1981 and 1989, a period of time punctuated by the Iran-Iraq War. After his resignation in 1989, the position of the prime minister

was abolished altogether, and Mousavi vanished from the public eye. He is an Iranian reformist politician who was the Minister of Foreign Affairs. He was also a member of the Expediency Discernment Council and the High Council of Cultural Revolution, though, he has not participated in their meetings for years. Mousavi holds a Master's Degree in Architecture from Shahid Beheshti University, specializing in traditional Islamic architecture. He was a candidate for the 2009 presidential election and served as the president of the Iranian Academy of Arts until 2009 when Conservative authorities removed him. In the early years of the revolution, Mousavi was the editor-in-chief of the official newspaper of the Islamic Republican Party, the *Islamic Republic*. In the 2009 presidential election, Mousavi chose green as his campaign colour, a colour which has since become pervasive in Iran.

[15]Mehdi Karroubi is an influential Iranian reformist politician, democracy activist, clergy and chairman of the National Trust Party. He was Chairman of the parliament from 1989 to 1992 and 2000 to 2004, and a presidential candidate in the 2005 and 2009 presidential elections. He is a founding member and former chairman of the Association of Combatant Clerics party. Karroubi is a critic of the Guardian Council and Iran's Judicial System. By appointment of the Supreme Leader, he was a member of the Expediency Discernment Council and an adviser, posts he held until resigning from all his posts on June 19, 2005 after the first round of the 2005 presidential election.

REFERENCES

Ardalan, Parvan and Nooshin Ahmadi. *Senator.* [Tehran, Towse'e], 2003.

Sadiqi, Fatima and Moha Enaji, "The Feminization of Public Space: Women's Activism, the Family Law, and Social Change in Morocco." *Journal of Middle East Women's Studies* 2.2 (2006): 86-114. Web.

13.
Changing the World from the Kitchen

Tubu-Tubu Peace Food

YUMIKO OTANI (TUBU-TUBU GRANDMA YUMIKO), JAPAN

JAPAN IS TRADITIONALLY a nation of polytheistic animists, who believe in the existence of gods throughout nature. The ancient Japanese believed that they were themselves spirits separated from the gods. Led by the goddess *Ama-terasu*, the source of all creation, culturally isolated by the surrounding seas, they continuously developed their own unique and peaceful civilization, which focused on respecting women and cultivating the spirit.

In an ancient myth, *Ama-terasu* mourned the violent acts of men and the battles they fought, finally hiding herself in a cave. This made the world dark. The myth can be interpreted as a critique of the predominance of patriarchal culture, which began to emerge around 2000 B.C. Although the goddess seemed to have come out of the cave, patriarchal culture has since dominated the world. The traditional Japanese spirit, that had been led by *Ama-terasu* and had remained among ordinary common people, collapsed in the second half of the nineteenth century, when the nation's long seclusion ended. It was said that the loss of *Ama-terasu* diminished the spirit in all living things, including vegetation.

Japan quickly began adopting aspects of Western civilization, leading to rapid modernization and militarization, and culminating in a devastating war. After the Second World War, the country promoted further Westernization of lifestyles and education under the direction of the U.S., and this trend has continued since. As the country was modernized, traditional elements of Japanese culture were lost, and most Japanese have forgotten their ancestors' view of nature and the universe.

The shift from a matriarchal society that respected women as the source of life to a patriarchal society that controlled women as dependants marked the beginning of battles and repression throughout

Japan. As a result, many women have been raised to believe that they are incapable of supporting themselves without depending on men. In addition, women have lost some of their creativity, and men have forgotten how to connect with nature and the universe. Both women and men therefore have difficulty in finding balance in their lives, and they tend to feel unconnected to the universe as a whole. I believe that these are the fundamental issues responsible for many of the planet's current ills.

As a young girl growing up in post-war Japan, I witnessed rapid progression along the path of modernization and Westernization. With the abandonment of the traditional Japanese lifestyle and religious customs, Japan's change was dramatic and frightening. Her social structure, dietary habits and lifestyle were all restructured by placing higher priorities on science, technology and the economy. Prior to this restructuring, the Japanese diet focused on native grains, vegetables and fermented seasonings, such as soy sauce and *miso*. As a result of this change, however, school lunches began including white bread instead of rice, and milk, meat, and eggs. People at that time made this dramatic change with the aim of improving Japanese society, as if they were being tested to survive this rapid change, including a rapid shift in foodways, in traditional culture. As a result of this rapid change, modern Japanese people are facing crises in physical and psychological health, food, and the environment. Today, these issues are all visible at the forefront of Japanese society.

People have experienced an unprecedented collapse of their lifestyles and their minds. Serious diseases are striking people from childhood to adulthood. Men are forced to work for longer hours, often late into the night, under the guise of economic growth. Women also commonly work in order to bring more money into the household. These conditions have eliminated the traditional idea of families having dinner together, and have turned the home into a place only for sleep rather than family. As a result, women can no longer dream of starting a family and raising children, and men fail to grow up and enter the workplace, and have difficultly forming healthy relationships with women.

For as long as I can remember, I have always felt "something is wrong" about the changing world around me. I was curious about what was happening. I found that in a society dependent on material wealth, contrary to the rules of nature, both men and women were afraid of losing wealth and that despite their excess wealth, people were distressed. I wondered how I could solve this problem, and 30 years ago, as I stood in the midst of the Parthenon, I felt that the Earth herself answered my question: "Everyone should rebuild themselves with native grains!" I was in Greece looking for something important. Although I didn't recognize it then, I came to believe that the message came to me from the Earth through the goddess Athena.

Our bodies take in the energy of food to make blood. Blood carries water, oxygen, and nutrients throughout the body, which is capable of producing as many as a trillion cells per day. Eating food that contains vital nutrients leads to healthy cells and has a positive effect on both physical and psychological health. Grains, a common staple food for humans, include numerous essential nutrients in good balance, and are full of life, which fosters a healthy spirit.

In Japanese, gods are referred to as *"kami,"* which means "origin." Japanese people describe the origin of the great energy that created and has been sustaining the universe as *"haha"* (in English, "mother"). The goddess *Ama-terasu* is a symbol of the Sun, which generously pours energy from the root of the universe onto the Earth. The universe was created by *Ama-terasu,* including our bodies, and everything is part of the temple of the gods. That is the basic belief of the Japanese people. Respecting women, who are able to create new life, was a matter of course.

Three years later, when I was thirty years old, I had my first taste of native grains. At that time, I jointly owned a company with five female designers who worked in different areas; we offered our client companies proposals for product development and design that would appeal to women. I had hoped to perform sophisticated work with a high level of knowledge, make money quickly, and spend my free time traveling around the world to seek the meaning of life. I used to like so-called "delicious" foods, and regarded eating as either "refueling" or pleasure. However, when I first ate native grains, I was overwhelmed by their flavour, which seemed to permeate every cell in my body. At the same time, I came across the idea that human beings can survive on just 60 kilograms of unpolished grains, natural salt, and a small amount of vegetables annually. This idea was shocking to me because I had always accepted what I learned about nutrition in school: that rice has no nutritional value, and that it is better to eat bread instead of rice, with a lot of side dishes made from meat, eggs and dairy products.

As a result of the nutrition education at that time, native grains were not common in most people's daily diets. Most people weren't even aware that Japanese people had traditionally eaten native grains on a daily basis. I also had not eaten them—nor learned about them—until

I was 30 years old. My desire to learn grew, and I began to wonder how and why such delicious foods had disappeared from the traditional Japanese diet, the staple of which has always been grains. I began to learn the history of Japanese food with the keyword "native grains." I also studied the origins of traditional foods of native tribes around the world.

I found that Japanese food historically differed from the diet that spread in the postwar years; the traditional Japanese diet is based on plant foods, has grains as its staple, and is in harmony with natural cycles. I also understood the fact that, as a result of this diet, the Japanese had lived in good health until only a few decades ago. I was particularly moved when I learned that my Japanese ancestors called the staple grains "*ine*," which means "the root of life." As I studied, I also found that both Japanese and native peoples from around the world held their staple grains in high regard, regarding them as food to nurture the spirit given by the gods worshipped since ancient times.

Hoping to find the answers I had been seeking for so long, I began growing grains and cooking them with traditional seasonings centered on natural salt, vegetables and sea weeds. At the same time, I began to organize seminars and manage a restaurant. My attempts at cooking were surprising. The dishes I cooked with traditional food materials were far from what I had first imagined. I had thought they would be bland and tasteless. However, the flavours were wonderful. These foods, which are full of energy, can create a variety of flavours by using simple cooking methods. My experience led me to increasingly enjoy cooking.

Despite using traditional cooking methods with native grains and vegetables, I found the flavours to be very modern. As I continued to eat such meals, I came to think of the Earth as human beings' mother and the grains as her "milk." I also found that I became healthier in my body and more at peace in my mind. This is where I got the idea for the name "Tubu-Tubu Peace Food." I felt that the Earth was trying to tell me that her breasts were overflowing with milk and that she was concerned at our becoming weaker and weaker without her bounty.

In modern Japan, many women have begun working to answer questions such as "What is the meaning of my existence?" and "What is real happiness?" The Tubu-Tubu Peace Food endeavour began to play a great role in helping such women find the answers they are now seeking. Women have begun seeking safe, organic foods, and a return to traditional Japanese dishes. By rebuilding their bodies through the consumption of native grains, they are potentially becoming aware that ancient women flourished. As a result of this trend, the activities of Tubu-Tubu are drawing much attention.

I believe that when people bring back essential foods to their daily lives, fear, anxiety and anger will fade away, and courage and wisdom will blossom. People may also feel a sense of unity with the Earth and the universe, and begin to feel more positive energies. Women will become more aware of their own ability to empower themselves, while men will be able to awaken their own femininity, balance their minds, and develop better dispositions. Cooking and eating traditional native grains with belief and appreciation, and maintaining a diet based on plants in accordance with universal harmony can bring peace and balance to the mind and body and awaken one's dormant femininity.

The patriarchal nature of Japanese society comes from reduced self-confidence caused by the loss of our connection with nature, as well as the fears and anxieties associated with economic independence caused by inequality in wages and employment opportunities, marriage, and the bearing and raising of children. I have tried to offer women opportunities to build confidence through Tubu-Tubu Peace Food. Women learning and practicing the diet can awake themselves and connect to real wealth of the Earth, improving their sensitivity to the universe, and fostering their minds to respect the Earth and the Sun. With such food, they can arouse the spirit to respect the peace and nature once enjoyed by the ancient Japanese. I believe that these processes bring the women confidence. The empowered women can make a resurgence of a peaceful world. I also believe that by thoroughly pouring their energy into it, great changes can be achieved.

It is difficult to change dietary habits with logic alone. However, if the food is more attractive and delicious than other foods, everyone will desire it. Appearance is important, as people are interested in something beautiful, attractive, modern and unique. But even when food is fascinating, nobody wants to spend excessive amounts of time preparing complicated dishes. It is more important that food is simple, honest, and flavourful. We developed a clear plan to communicate the simple relationship between life and food, and the simple skills needed to cook foods that are full of vitality and in harmony with the universe. Having worked as a designer at a stationary maker after studying industrial design at university, I had obtained skills in marketing, and produced many popular products. I took advantage of those experiences and skills to design attractive foods and create systematic recipes.

Japanese grains are the most diverse in the world. Surprisingly, each has a unique flavour, calling to mind ground meat, eggs, cheese, chicken, and fish. This was something I discovered in the early days of Tubu-Tubu cooking. Because of this range of flavours, it is possible to make hamburgers, nuggets, pizzas, fish and chips, sausages, mayonnaise, and even non-sugar pastry cream from grains and vegetables. More and more people are discovering how to make healthy dishes, as the flavours are often more enjoyable than in meat-based dishes. People are able to digest high levels of micronutrients, lose weight, and overcome conditions such as constipation, anemia, sensitivity to cold, and allergies. This way of eating, such as that demonstrated in Tubu-Tubu Peace Food, is miraculous in that it restores healthy *kami* (spirit and energy).

Grains are like crystals of the Sun's energy; by taking the natural energy of native grains into the body, the ancient mind of *Ama-terasu* is aroused, the body is revived, and the *Ama-terasu* within each woman figuratively leaves the cave. I name such women "Tubu-Tubu Ten-nyo." In Japanese, *Ten-nyo* refers to a female angel who comes down to earth with a feathered robe in a folk tale. "Tubu-Tubu Ten-nyo" is a woman who daily cooks and eats Tubu-Tubu Peace Food and is awakened to her authentic nature, the mind of *Ama-terasu*. I believe the more "Tubu-Tubu Ten-nyo" increases, the more we can create a peaceful world.

I have been working on Tubu-Tubu activities with the aim of developing the global market. My dream is to take the term "Tubu-Tubu" global. I coined the term to describe native grains here in Japan, but I hope that it will spread worldwide. Another meaning of Tubu-Tubu is the knowledge that each of us enshrines the creativity of the universe inside our mind. By restoring our connection with native grains, the entire world can re-unite with the Great Mother-Sun, *Ama-terasu Omikami*. We are bringing the Great Mother out of her cave and back into the fullness of life.

Tubu-Tubu Peace Food and similar ways of eating can change societies, creating a world without wars. Fighting cannot lead to peace. Enjoying the act of cooking and eating dishes based on native grains will both encourage and spread happiness. Our diet changes how we feel, and with improvements in how we feel, our behaviours change accordingly. Such simple acts can change the world, and can stop the current health, food and environmental crises, and possibly even go some way to prevent larger battles.

This work has also supported women in their economic independence. When women learn about how I started Tubu-Tubu Peace Food, they often gain the confidence to take the initiative to make their own mark in the workplace, for example, by managing restaurants, holding lectures, and teaching Tubu-Tubu cooking techniques. Many women are becoming aware of their potential. Every day, I see that more and more women are trying to cultivate themselves and better the way they live. I think it is important for women to enhance their sense of control and to improve their economic status. In order to support those women and work together to spread Tubu-Tubu worldwide, I started a training program in 2011 for "Tubu-Tubu Mothers." A Tubu-Tubu Mother is a "Tubu-Tubu Ten-nyo" whose mission is to guide people to cook and eat Tubu-Tubu Peace Food. My dream is to create a global network of Tubu-Tubu Mothers.

Currently, I employ fifteen staff members to support my work, and of these, twelve are women. All of my staff members, including the men, are people who have become aware of and embraced their own femininity. I have incorporated a new approach to work, which strengthens teamwork in accordance with everyone's unique characteristics and lifestyle. I always try not to separate work, play and life. Work hours are flexibly set on each staff member's responsibility. For lunch, in Tubu-Tubu restaurants, they have the same dishes as they serve to customers. Their children are welcome in the workplaces anytime, and can help the members according to their personal interests. As a result, all the staff members are involved in raising the children. Our events are planned so that the staff and their children can enjoy them together. In order to keep everything in balance, I hold a meeting every Tuesday for all the staff members. By exchanging opinions, each member improves the spirituality and the skill to act, and also learns how other members feel about their work environment. There are approximately 1,000 members of the Tubu-Tubu Peace Food organization, and I accept a wide range of involvements, respecting their roles such as volunteers, part-timers, lecturers, trainees, and native-grain producers.

The delicious Tubu-Tubu recipes are now becoming the standard for natural food cooking in Japan, and are beginning to take root in the daily lives of many people. I hope to tell women around the world how enjoyable it is to connect with the universe through cooking, how delicious foods cooked in harmony with nature can be, and of the immense power of Mother Earth's natural grains; this healthy way of biologically and emotionally connecting with life will release the hidden Ama-terasu from her cave.

On March 11, 2011, an unprecedented earthquake and tsunami hit Japan. At the same time, a terrible nuclear accident occurred, and as the situation continues, the severity of the crisis has now exceeded the accident at Chernobyl both in duration and in radioactive materials released. The entire country has been covered with radiation. In the aftermath of this earth-shattering catastrophe, German Chancellor Angela Merkel decided to scale back operations at nuclear power plants in Germany, with the aim of ultimately eliminating its dependence on nuclear energy. Runaway patriarchal culture has led to the dependence on nuclear energy, and the abuse of this dangerous source of energy has become a symbol of that culture. The rapid declaration of the intention to eliminate nuclear power by a female leader is now a symbol marking a time for women to change the world. Japan is the only nation ever to have suffered a nuclear attack. Diet was then shown to be a factor in warding off the harmful effects of radiation; in Nagasaki, a 29-year-old doctor, Tatsuichiro Akizuki, was 1.4 kilometers from ground zero at the time of the nuclear blast. Refusing to leave, he devoted himself to treating the victims. His tireless efforts saved many lives, including medical staff, by helping their bodies recover from radiation injury through proper diet, upon which Tubu-Tubu is based. Dr. Akizuki continued his work until his death at the age of 89. Because we feel that it is important to hand down his legacy to as many people as possible, Tubu Tubu continues to play an active role. As more information comes to light about this situation, people have been feeling greater anxiety, fear and anger. This negativity will attract more negative reality.

Switching our diet to Tubu-Tubu Peace Food awakens the body's full potential, which greatly prevents the harm of radiation. It is important to rebuild our lives by enjoying our daily food in a bright, positive and thankful spirit. Tubu Tubu has been making efforts to convey this message. *The Kami from the Great Mother Sun in all of us must be protected!*

14.
The Feminine Social Enzyme

An Italian Story

PAOLA CONTI, ITALY

MY MOTHER'S SIDE OF THE FAMILY is a family of women. She comes from the innermost part of Sardinia, a resplendent island, hard, and with a strong character, at the centre of the Mediterranean, and at the centre of the cult of the "mother goddess."[1] My aunts, now fat and elderly matrons, have taught me to know their rather odd powers: all are tied to insignificant husbands, whom they tolerate with apparent self-abnegation and quietly rule with an iron will in all daily affairs. They are wise, tenacious, stubborn and vexatious. With them, every meeting is an intimate, joyous occasion to tell true stories and romances from their own young lives and from the wider family, stories of weddings, of deaths, of births, of misfortunes and strokes of luck. They speak about how, when they were young, they lived in places with very little crop farming, a lot of sheep and poverty, and ancient traditions, hundreds if not thousands of years old: at the full moon, women still went to a spring at night to undertake rituals which are fading from living memory.

Later, some of them emigrated to continental Italy. They began to work outside the home, taking low status jobs, with an inferiority complex from not being schooled, and barely knowing how to read and write, as with many women in those years.

I am the first woman in the history of my family to have a university degree, and I belong to the first generation for which it is natural and essential not just to work, but to "have a profession." My generation has measured itself and struggled against the role men play, with masculine power dominating both culturally and politically. In its first phase, the feminist movement competed with men: the fight then was for the right to speak. The first feminist struggle was to win public rights, and it produced laws, journeys and experiences that seemed for a brief moment to have changed Italian society forever.

162

And yet, the women of my son's generation, who are still studying, seem to have no memory of "before." They state that equal opportunities between men and women are a fact, and that there is no such thing as gender discrimination. These same young women, stepping out into the world of work—bright, ambitious, clutching degrees and specialized qualifications—find that their careers stall, that their pay packets are smaller than those of their male colleagues', that on reaching the limits of child-bearing age they must choose between work and family. Or they choose both with unspeakable effort, and struggle through their days with a thousand obligations and not even a memory of time to themselves.

Personally, I find it harder and harder to talk about "Women": visible and invisible, strong and vulnerable. Different, while still brought together by taking on a feminine social role that can be culturally shared, or interpreted subjectively. They work and study with some success, but the data show that they still find it hard to climb the career ladder and make their way to the top of institutions: on one hand they step away, preferring to pour their energies into emotional and interpersonal relationships instead of competitive dynamics, on the other hand they are still discriminated against, or they abdicate their own characteristics, taking on "successful" classical masculine models.

In any case, my personal way of taking on the male domination of the sites of power was, for a long stretch of my professional career, to achieve positions of responsibility (for example, I spent twelve years as a leader in the most prominent Italian trade union). From that position, I have attempted to bring other women up with me, and to take my place after me. Today, as a manager and entrepreneur, I surround myself with professional women, and I employ young women who have just graduated: they learn, grow, and move on.

...TO "BIG BROTHER"

Pleasant, co-operative, positive. The Italian woman shown on television is portrayed positively as a protagonist, but generally the space she is offered is controlled by an "ordering" male figure. She is beautiful, glossy and, crucially, young. The media image of women is polarized between the world of show business and that of violent crime reporting. It is a distortion compared to real women's worlds: older women are invisible, the perceived socio-economic status is medium to high, and disabled women never appear at all. Themes which women are associated with most often are show business and fashion, physical violence and justice: hardly ever politics, professional success or "high" cultural activity.

In entertainment the presenter is male, the presenting style is witty, snide and a little aggressive; costumes are daring, camera shots are voyeuristic and only 15.7 percent of coverage focus on the artistic abilities of women shown ("Women and Media"). The general esthetic is that of a somewhat tawdry, mediocre piece of vaudeville. In Reality shows especially, women are praised for adaptability, cunning, and lack of inhibition.

In news, women are mostly shown as part of crime reporting, where they appear as victims of violence, rape, and all other kinds of abuse. In 45.2 percent of occasions, their voices are heard as part of a television report for under 20 seconds. In factual programming there is a male hand on the presenting tiller (63 percent) ("Women and Media"). If women are brought in as "experts" it is usually on "soft" topics such as astrology, nature, crafts and literature.

Women, then, have the spotlight thrown on them principally in the polarized contexts of fashion, entertainment, esthetics and beauty, or violence, criminality, and victimhood. Very little attention is given to women involved in culture, research, schools or social engagement.

Day after day, the media-reinforced image of women is essentially that of young women willing to do anything to climb, if not onto the stage of a TV studio, then into the halls of councils and parliaments; of women with nice bodies, ready to offer themselves to leading businessmen and politicians to earn direct and indirect advantages (an institutional position, a leading role in a mixed society, a loan or grant, a useful legal codicil). This image portrays just a fragment of reality, even if it is backed up by the bodies that ubiquitously fill the pages of high-circulation publications and the screens of the most-viewed programs. But it is a portrayal which does not do justice to the thousands of women who dedicate themselves to politics with authority and passion. Recently, female academics and public servants have opened up a public debate to react to what the press has been calling "the silence of women" on political events, and the relationship between gender and power. They are looking for alternative examples.

Until ten years ago many of the women engaged in the politics of social change hoped to be able to change the rules, content and values of the job market, of politics and of personal relationships through the strength of their "difference." Now, however, the effort of elbowing their way through a world which remains perniciously masculine, and the requirement, in order to get a say, to become the same as everyone else, have even brought many women to give up what was considered their principal competitive advantage of *emotional intelligence*.

Many women have abandoned vengeful attitudes, or even just defensive ones. On one hand this is because intellectual and professional women prefer a strategy of "contamination," opening up a dialogue with men, encouraging them to reflect on their peculiar position of men "constricted" by a model of masculinity which is no longer satisfying. On the other hand, it is because we are now seeing women withdrawing into themselves, closing themselves into their private lives where competition for survival in work and social roles is heavily affected by the economic crisis, by the persistence of gender stereotyping, by discrimination and by the rise in violence against women perpetrated by men.

Culture is the hinge between organizations' formal/rational variables and social/relational variables and it defines coherence, equilibrium, comparisons and clashes between them. Both for organizations and individuals culture—whichever culture it is—determines the values which guide the making of decisions and permeate their implementation, frequently entirely unconsciously for the decision makers.

GENDER GAP

Italy is at the tail end of the European Union for equal opportunities: according to 2012's Global Gender Gap Report—the World Economic Forum's study on the differences between men and women in the workplace—Italy ranks 77th (see Hausmann, Tyson and Zahidi) with women's wages lower than men's, and few women in positions of power.

One of the factors that has the greatest effect on gender differences is still the caring role taken on by women within the family, and the difficulties in redistributing domestic labour and the isolation that often results. Women's reproductive role and periods spent away from paid work for maternity and childrearing duties are still shown to be among the principal causes of direct and indirect discrimination against Italian women, even at this time when the birth rate has dropped to a historic low: Italy ties for second place with one of the lowest birthrates (9,30) (WB), but women's trajectories through life and work (and their consequential income) are uncertain and poorly protected. Women are demonstrably more heavily affected by family events and are also more exposed to health risks correlated with the extended and severe stresses of having multiple responsibilities. This underlines how this role, traditionally given to women, still exerts a substantial pressure on health, and on the significance that deprivation or illness takes on for individual people.

According to the 2011 census (ISTAT), the population of Italy is approximately 60 million people, with slightly less than two million more women than men. This demographic difference can be ascribed to several factors, including the aging population and women's longer lifespan. Despite the fact that more males are born than females, higher male mortality right from youngest age group means that women outnumber men in the overall population. Data confirm that in Italy the burden of care for the aging population falls almost entirely onto families—or rather, onto women, especially adult daughters, who in turn resort ever more frequently to the caregiving services of immigrant women.

So are we, in Italy, looking at a culture affected by misogyny? Probably yes, but we are also looking at an aging nation, and a nation that is aging in part because it has not solved the dilemmas of the social role of maternity. Childbearing has become a dramatic conflict in the lives of both women and men, and nature seems to be acquiescing to this new fearfulness with rising sterility and infertility problems.

Compared to the statistics for Europe, Italy's ISTAT data shows a perceptible growth in female presence in various social contexts, but also comes with contradictory data showing social and workplace exclusion damaging women, especially in the fields of political representation and economic governance, as well as in fields with a strong technological bent (see Censis). Nonetheless, several positive changes are occurring, especially in some sectors: women's presence is continuing to increase in intellectual professions, in medicine, the judiciary, public administration, research and development, estate agency, and in business services.

The low female participation rate in the workforce in Italy is due to factors such as the poor availability of daycares or nursery schools, of structures supporting the family, insufficient tax benefits for dual income couples, but also and crucially to discriminatory employment and salary expectations, which discourage women to the point where some will leave the work force and enter the category of so-called "inactive persons." No wonder, then, that there is a huge gap between our country and the European Union on inactivity rates.

ENZYME "FEMALE"

Italian women, as can be seen, are a varied and strongly dynamic universe: they invest more in culture than men do, do better in their studies, give more importance to work, experiment with new forms of production and reproduction, and take on a multitude of roles in the various phases of life. A network of transformations, aspirations and behaviours redefines their biographic journeys (through schooling, work, relationships, marriage and parenthood), modifying length and content of the various phases of the cycle of individual and family life. In a lifespan which reaches ever greater ages, the calendar of key events tends to shift forwards in time for the most important life transitions: women take on longer educational careers than their male contemporaries, the age at which they leave home tends to get closer to the age at which men do, they have ever fewer children and later, they live together with them for longer, they have an average life span which is longer than men's, but the number of years in which they enjoy "good health" is lower than for men. Women experiment with cohabitation more often than their male contemporaries, they question life choices in ways which can lead to breaking up marital unions, and their increasing participation in the work force contributes to defining new roles and relationships within the family.

These changes, admittedly in different ways and to different extents, affect women of every social class in every part of the country. They may appear most relevant to the younger generations, but do not spare adult or older generations either. Therefore, I believe that, despite traveling at different speeds, despite taking a few steps forward in some arenas and a few back in others, women in Italy, as in the rest of the world, remain the *essential enzyme* to mobilize society and culture through their resilience and their desire to keep on asking questions of themselves and others in a world which is so very disposed to provide one answer that is supposed to be the best for everyone.

A time came in my professional practice, a few years ago, when I realized that the words "equal opportunity and gender politics" no longer spoke to women; men had always heard these words only distantly, as if they had nothing to do with them. "Women's stuff!" These words also sounded far away to women who were busily trying to get through their day-to-day lives, they sounded irritating to women climbing the career ladder, and irrelevant to those who had never thought about the daily negotiations between genders. The words had become, in the end, jargon for experts, used by professionals who, working on gender politics, and politics from a gender point of view, stood for a sort of professional group, elitist on the one hand (or considered such), underpaid on the other, in proportion to the cultural, social and economic weight given to women's rights and to equality themes more generally.

Asking myself what it means, for professionals, to know how to do their work taking account of gender, I abandoned the debates on what women or men were better at: it was all too easy to slip into a vicious circle of banalities and stereotypes. With a sense of frustration and irritation at first, and later with a growing passion, I began to involve men in "gender" reflections, seeing that some of them are interested in discussion and elaboration. Initial adversarial feelings (which I still feel from time to time) came from the thought that whilst women had been examining themselves and the world starting from themselves, creating voices, ideas, experiences, original and multiplicitous knowledge, men had taken for granted that they represented the universe in a one-to-one relationship, without on the other hand knowing anything about their own specificity. Must we ever be midwives, this time in birthing male self-awareness? The lack of active participation from men in the struggle for a greater equality between the sexes is now universally acknowledged as an obstacle to be overcome through their active involvement, identifying specific advantages and objectives for men and for a new role for "masculinity" in a more equal society, as pointed out by the European Commission's Advisory Committee on Equal Opportunities for Women and Men.

FROM GENDER DEBATE TO GENDER DIALOGUE

As we know, "gender" represents an interpretative paradigm and constitutes, within social sciences, a synthesis of the process through which individuals who are born female or male enter into the categories of women or men. Viewing health through a "gender lens" permits one, for example, to predict, evaluate and, possibly, measure the varied impacts of social-economic and cultural deprivation on women and men. This is only possible by identifying specificities, variables, differences and differentials. And yet gender is a pervasive concept that acts across all political targets and implies an intersectional approach to the analysis and impact evaluation needed to read the peculiarities *of individuals* correctly, so as to be able to understand the differences *between individuals* in context.

"Gender" is, more than any other, an "embodied" concept in that it cannot be disentangled from the bodies of the observer or the observed; entering a workplace, for example, we observe and act from our positions as women or men: being "neutral" is not an option, whereas the studies, analysis and actions are represented as if that neutrality were perfectly possible" (Conti). What is interesting in the culture of gender difference is not so much the emergence of the difference itself, but rather its emergence as a positive thing, a difference without inferiority and characterized by a form of complementarity. How is it possible not to agree that women's bodies, minds, sensibilities express a different view of the world? These are riches. In the relationship between men and women there is something irreducible, which cannot be synthesized. The thing to avoid is transforming the apparition, the un-exhaustableness of the other, into a closure. Then, difference becomes separation and, instead of an openness to the signs, the messages and consequentially sinking into the otherness in order to explore it (the exploration of the feminine on the part of the masculine, and of the masculine on the part of the feminine), difference is reduced to a resistance which separates. Difference understood in this sense is traduced from exploration of the other to absolute enmity. This transformation of difference into schism and separation has come to pass, in my opinion, because of a politicization of difference. To postulate difference not as a dimension of reciprocal exploration of signs and senses, but as something absolutely irreconcilable seems to me to be a genuine loss.

Gender difference, then, sits in the general picture of relational ethics. To relate to the other without reducing it to the self, to allow the other to be, with all their characteristics, with their corporeality: beautiful and ugly, young and old, rich and poor: as soon as the other presents itself to you it immediately places you into an ethical relationship by the simple fact of being there.

The "other" is an open dimension: presence and opening. This is true in general for relationships of otherness. The feminine presents itself with those characteristics of difference like body, sensibility, gesture, way of being and of expressing which makes it a part of the world. If you are a man, in femininity you reveal something which you are not. Something else is added to the difference of otherness: femininity, another world—another part of the world, which cannot be understood through generic otherness. You are called to relate to one who is other to yourself. The problem is in making contact, resonances and therefore to dip into the richness of those who see the world differently from how you could ever see it, not just emotionally or existentially, but even cognitively. The perception of this difference makes you grow.

I have observed that time is perceived and used differently by men and women. For men life generally runs through a kind of inexorable hourglass, with obstacles to be overcome and aims to reach, but in a linear fashion. For women, instead, we would have to invent a circular timer, with variations from the main path, pauses, and diagonal shortcuts.

Women, more than men, preserve a feeling of what they have lived through and an ability, crucially, to express it, that is to describe the passage from an outward-facing culture of conquest to one facing inwards towards self-knowledge. Every woman walks through a sensory world built from her culture and her own personal history, but the body is none the less the filter through which she takes in the substance of the world.

Men more often construct their individual identity outside themselves, through work and their external environment. This separation from their own bodies means that they can rarely make them a site of healing and relationship, and achieve intimacy with other bodies: with the young, that is with children and infants, intimacy with women, intimacy with the bodies of other men, with other generations. In my work I often meet men who are trying to live their masculinity according to a different model and are therefore discriminated against. I see more and more often how discrimination hits against *the behaviours* of women and men, particularly those that evoke freedom of choice, individual options for change and affirmation of values of solidarity rather than competitiveness.

The dichotomy between male and female roles has been a heavy weight for millennia, and has now cracked in the face of the chance to build a new symbolic order in which men and women are three-dimensional subjects, with access to the same spheres of politics, sciences, arts. This change affects public life and creates the possibility of building a different imagination which deconstructs the monolithic image of womanhood, with its fixed identity, standardized and incapable of being able to embrace human activities in all their complexity.

A RETURN TO THE GODDESS

Perhaps it is no accident that lately opportunities are springing up for a debate, which in Italy is "culturally difficult"—the debate around the feminine of the divine, or of divinity in the feminine. The Feminine Divine underlines a particular sensibility, a gaze which seeks out and translates the experience of the sacred, in the same way as the expression God is a masculine gaze and translation and not the experience itself. This search for the Feminine Divine has come from and is fed by women, a sensibility which, luckily, is also shared by many men.

An inner search for the Feminine Divine must take into account that it is not a pure abstracted search for the divine, or the sacred, or of transcendence. An example which really struck me of a "feminine" way to rediscover the shared human spirituality that can change the world is that of "The Fruit Salad Tree," a family-based community. They are a Muslim couple and a Catholic couple, two families who have agreed to share a lifestyle, partly to prove that "it is possible for Christians and Muslims to live together," even in the minefield of every day life, with the shopping to do, the children to take to school, the bills to be paid and the daily problems with work, money, plans to be made. "I thank God for the fact that I feel no different from you Christians: our ethical and moral principles are the same," explains Fatima Eddahbi, 36, with a beautiful smile. With her husband, Mustapha Hanich, age 44, also Moroccan, she is planning to move in with Margherita Valentini, age 48, and Margherita's husband, Beppe Casolo, who is 47. Alongside the adults is a great tribe of children. The community is growing and will soon be welcoming two more family units.

A few years ago, in 2009 in Rome, an event was organized called "A New World is Possible: An intercultural and inter-religious meeting to discover the feminine face of the divine, for a peaceful future." Men and women from many different religions and spiritual movements came together to build an important moment of shared reflection, and a bridge of understanding. And yet, the men were much more focused on speaking than listening. I was very struck by this attitude, which was sadly not new to me. Two women, Rabbi Barbara Aiello and Shahrzad Houshmand Zadeh, on the other hand, truly dialogued, turning to representatives of other faiths, and to the audience, working hard to make their point of view comprehensible to everyone, as they worked on this ancient and yet modern topic. This confirmed to me that this is still a completely feminine challenge. Yet again the woman's way is that of cross-fertilization, of meeting and discovering the other.

Rabbi Barbara Aiello is the first and only Italian female Rabbi. She comes from the Beth El Temple in Bradenton, in Florida, and has been a Rabbi since 1999, after studying at the Rabbinical Seminary International in New York. Rabbi Aiello defines herself as progressive, keeping faith with Jewish traditions and culture, and simultaneously welcoming instances of contemporary conscience. At the public talk in Rome in 2009 she stated: "In the Bible we read that when Adam and Eve left Eden, God's heart, Shakinah, went with them. In the Bible there are 26 names for God, the only feminine one is Shakinah. God gave his heart, his feminine part, to humanity to make the world a better place, with the labour, the strength, the courage that women possess and demonstrate." Since 2007, Barbara Aiello has been ministering in the Ner Tamid synagogue in southern Italy, at Serrastretta (Catanzaro).

Shahrzad Houshmand Zadeh is an Iranian theologian. She studied Islamic Theology in Iran; in Italy she took a diploma in Catholic Theology at the Faculty of Theology in Reggio Calabria. She is a mother of three, a girl and two boys. She has always worked on Islamic-Christian dialogue, and has been collaborating with Cipax (Centro Interconfessionale per la Pace) since June 2005.

FROM SPIRITUALITY TO ECONOMICS

In a recent study, thirty Italian female managers were interviewed. They spoke about how, for them, a successful career is one that leads to a good balance between family, personal and working life. In summary, "the aim is a satisfying life overall, where work has an essential place, but is not the centre of everything, to the exclusion of everything else." The idea of career as an objective above all others reflects a masculine view of work which colours the rest, as it puts in place, in business, a mechanism which is "often invisible and intangible." The researchers (Pogliana) found that women "are held back by male beliefs about them, and by the singular management model."

The prevalent "feminine" conception of power is different: "freedom and not domination, authoritative and not authoritarian, guidance and not control" (Pogliana). Equally, in the workplace, relationships and emotions are fundamental, taken as factors which help us reach our stated aims. But, is something changing? Yes, unfortunately—research conducted on 1,200 people in 2009 by Cofimp, the business school of Unindustria Bologna, revealed that the differences between women's and men's workplace behaviour have narrowed as women are starting to act more like men and, the contrary, men are starting to act more like women.

In contrast to the myth of "presentism," which penalizes women, female workers believe in flexibility, in productive work which does not necessarily mean standardized hours in the office—far from it. And they believe this not because they have trouble juggling their varying roles, as some corporate managers believe. Women see no "either/or" between work and motherhood, as they have complex ambitions, a "self-realization that is not linear": they want to move forwards in projects where there is no separation or hierarchy between the individual parts.

They take a "small steps" policy, because there are "a thousand micro-solutions" possible every day, and waiting for a change from on high would be a pointless waste of time. In some cases they are aware of how a reciprocal support network can be a "strength multiplier, an instrument of change for all" women who are struggling with the same problems. Women in business, and many others, have reached this phase: they accept the implicit risk in leaving behind shells which do not fit them, to grow new shells which will allow them a life, and work, made to their measure.

ENDLESS COMPLEXITY

A mosaic is a form of art in which pictures are produced by joining together many minute pieces of glass, stones and other materials of different colours. In a different context, mosaicism may also result from the abnormal behaviours of chromosomes during the cell division in the fetus. A female is a mosaic because she consists of a mixture of two kinds of cells: each with different functional chromosomes. Because X Y males have a single X chromosome, while X X females have two of them, some kind of adjustment is needed: the X chromosome inactivation. Because of this X inactivation, all women are natural mosaics: although all their cells have the same two chromosomes, one from each parent, the mother's copy works in some cells, while the father's works in the others. The two kinds of cells often function differently, especially if one of the chromosomes carries a defective gene: for this reason, Barbara Migeon underlines women's superiority to men in coping with disease and the environment: "...females are mosaic because X inactivation creates two populations of cells that differ regarding their active X, and because the same X chromosome is not expressed in every cells. In all her somatic tissues, she has mixture of cells, some expressing her maternal alleles, the others expressing the paternal ones."

Women's lives, both culturally and physically, are a mosaic in which the whole is bigger than the parts. In our endless complexity, personal responsibility becomes important. How much we care for and cultivate our qualities, and with how much love we look after the masculine and feminine sides which characterize us, will in turn determine the shape and form of our society's mosaic, for the betterment of all.

[1]The Great Mother is a primordial female divinity, present in almost all known mythologies. In her are manifestations of the earth, of fertility

and of femininity as mediator between the human and the divine. The archeologist Marija Gimbutas (1921-1994) is largely responsible for the renewed interest in religions oriented towards the cult of the Goddess. For fifteen years, Gimbutas was active at digs in South-Eastern and Mediterranean Europe, which have brought to light the existence of a prehistoric culture which venerated the goddess. For at least 25,000 years this peaceful civilization clearly practiced absolutely equal rights between the genders—socially, politically, and with regards to religion.

REFERENCES

Advisory Committee on Equal Opportunities for Women and Men. "Opinion on Men in Gender Equality." European Commission, 2006-2007. Web.

Censis. 46° *Rapporto Censis sulla situazione sociale del Paese 2012*. Milano: Franco Angeli, 2012. Print.

Cofimp. Società di Formazione e Consulenza di Unindustria Bologna. Web.

Conti, Paola. *Genere e stress lavoro correlato, due opportunità per il Testo Unico*. Roma: INAIL, 2009. Print.

Gimbutas, Marija. *Il linguaggio della dea*. 1989. Roma: Venexia, 2008. Print.

Hausmann, Ricardo, Laura D. Tyson and Saadia Zahidi. "The Global Gender Gap Report 2012." Geneva: World Economic Forum, 2012. Print.

Istituto Nazionale di Statistica (ISTAT) (National Statistics Institute). Population Census, Italy, 2011. Web.

Migeon, Barbara. *Females Are Mosaics: X Inactivation and Sex Differences in Disease*. New York: Oxford University Press, 2007. Print.

Pogliana, Luisa. *Donne senza guscio*. Milano: Guerini e Associati, 2009. Print.

"Women and Media in Europe." Report of the European Commission, Rome, February 13, 2006. Web.

World Bank (WB). "Birth rate, crude (per 1,000 people): Italy 2010." World Development Indicators. World Bank, 2012. Web.

15.
The Long and Winding Road
to Reproductive Rights in Mexico

MARIA LUISA SÁNCHEZ-FUENTES, MEXICO

IN RECENT YEARS, a significant democratic space has opened for the women of Mexico, within a national context of social, political, and economic crisis, a biased justice system and gross gender inequalities. On April 24, 2007, Mexico City's Legislature approved a law that decriminalized abortion up to twelve weeks of gestation[1]; the same law also required the Secretariat of Health to design a comprehensive program that would provide sexual and reproductive health services for women.[2]

Unexpectedly, after more than three decades of struggle, with the government of Mexico City's full support, women have the right to interrupt a pregnancy under legal and safe conditions in public city hospitals, free of charge. As would be expected, the new law ushered in significant change for women. This is evidenced by the fact that as of April 2013, according to the Mexican Secretariat of Health, approximately 95,000 women had terminated their pregnancies with the use of modern surgical techniques, with women experiencing neither major health complications nor barriers.[3]

Mexico is recognized as a secular state, with a very clear separation of church and state articulated in its Constitution. This means that the Catholic church should have no power to intervene in public policy nor in legislation—but it does.

The influence of the Catholic hierarchy is huge, as is true virtually all through Latin America. Still, a large percentage of the Mexican population considers itself to be culturally Catholic, rather than religious. This means that although more than 80 percent of the people were raised Catholic, they do not follow church dogma, and believe that the church should keep out of politics and public policy. The Catholicism they believe in is a community and social force, rather than a religious force.[4]

MARIA LUISA SÁNCHEZ-FUENTES

MILESTONES THAT PLACED ABORTION RIGHTS
ON THE PUBLIC AGENDA

This momentous societal and cultural shift was tremendously influenced by the discourse about abortion catalyzed by the case of Paulina Ramirez Jacinto, a then thirteen-year-old rape victim, who in 1999, was denied a legal abortion despite her repeated requests and the support of her mother and family for this medical service. She was deceived and denied by the director of medical services in the Secretariat of Health of Baja California from exercising her right to terminate her pregnancy (Barzelatto). Abortion in cases of rape is a legal right throughout Mexico; this denial of a safe abortion was a gross violation of Paulina's rights. Her shocking treatment was widely known and discussed in the Mexican media, as well as academic, medical, legal, and political circles.

The case of this young, poverty-stricken, Indigenous and immigrant child/woman, forced to have a child she did not want at age 13, became internationally known, emblematic for Mexico and the Latin American region. Paulina became outspoken about what had happened to her and she came to represent the lives of numerous marginalized women, with a unifying theme: the lack of justice when violations of human rights occur, especially when it relates to situations of abortion.

Under these circumstances and once it became impossible to resolve the Paulina case in Mexico, NGOs came to support her legal case. These included *Alaide Foppa* from Baja California, the Center for Reproductive Rights based in New York, and the *Grupo de Información en Reproducción Elegida* or GIRE (Information Group on Reproductive Health) in Mexico City. Paulina was able to fight back at the Inter-American Commission of Human Rights, and was ultimately granted reparations with the signing of a friendly agreement between the State and the local government of Baja California. Her story became an inspiring symbol of empowerment for women throughout the world and set the tone for much of the debate on abortion. The flaws and violations of the abortion laws in the states of Mexico were widely revealed and the biases of public officials were discussed throughout Mexican society.

But even before the significant catalyzing impact of what became known as the "Paulina Case," abortion had gradually become an issue in Mexican society during the early 1990s. Significant milestones contributed to an in-depth discussion beyond the feminist movement, involving public agencies and NGOs. Indeed, GIRE was founded in 1992 to become a key source of accurate information to policy- and decision-makers on the issues of reproductive rights, including the critical importance of safe and legal abortion in women's lives. Many other NGOs, as well as the feminist movement at large, were also influential in keeping the topic in the public arena and for the discussion of abortion to remain front and center in Mexican society, creating the possibility of a societal shift on the topic.

In July 1998, Juan Ramon de la Fuente, dean of the National University of Mexico (UNAM), then Secretary of Health, and future federal Minister of Health (1999-2003), took a public stance on abortion:

> Mexican society cannot continue thinking that abortion doesn't exist. It is a severe public health problem and contributes importantly to maternal mortality. We have a significant deflation of numbers, precisely because the current legislation, invites, in some degree, to secrecy that leads to underground abortions. (see Chacon)

International factors were also at work in bringing abortion rights to the foreground. The United Nations International Conference on Population and Development in Cairo (1994) and the Fourth World Conference on Women in Beijing (1995) also became critical milestones in the efforts to push governments to recognize reproductive rights as human rights and to ultimately review their restrictive abortion laws. One hundred seventy-two nations signed agreements that placed the empowerment of women at the center of development in order to reduce poverty. The core themes that emerged included the need to address sexual and reproductive health, education, health services and information, as well as the availability of contraception to prevent unwanted pregnancies, and the provision of maternal health care, in order to facilitate informed choices on sexuality and childbearing. The implementation of the Cairo agreements and the Beijing platform of action became essential in this cultural shift. Public officials and decision makers were keen to know the meaning and reality of sexual and reproductive health and rights, which also ensured that the discussion of abortion was kept on the agenda. This presented an opportunity to incorporate a feminist perspective and women's empowerment analysis into the dialogue.

The 2006 presidential election in Mexico, which resulted in a parliamentary majority for the left-wing political parties in the house assembly of Mexico City, presented a significant opportunity for the various left wing political parties to take a stand on the issue. This was one of the most important reasons that the decriminalization of abortion occurred, despite the aggressive opposition of the Catholic church hierarchy.

And last but not least, the National Alliance for the Right to Decide was at the right place, at the right time, and well prepared to seize the opportunity that was placed in its path and achieve a momentous victory that had been building for more than 30 years.

NGOS MONITORING THE QUALITY CARE OF ABORTION SERVICES

As is true of all women who live in countries where abortion is illegal, Mexican women have risked their health and lives seeking out unsafe, clandestine abortions to terminate unwanted or unplanned pregnancies.[5] The fundamental difference is that today the women of Mexico City are recognized as full citizens—indeed, as moral and ethical agents who can be trusted to make decisions that affect their lives, their health, their families and their futures.

A great deal of research and analysis is now being developed with different interpretations and approaches to document and understand women's experiences with abortion on the one hand, and on the other, to monitor the clinics and hospitals so that they are providing professional services and quality nonjudgmental care. Nonprofit organizations, such as the National Alliance for the Right to Decide (comprised of five NGOs working since 2000 to decriminalize abortion in Mexico including *Catolicas por el Derecho a Decidir, Equidad de Genero, Familia, Trabajo y Sociedad*, and GIRE),[6] have played a critical role in ensuring that women are treated with dignity and respect, and have worked to institutionalize the program of quality abortion services in coordination with the Secretariat of Health in order to guarantee its continuity. Training health personnel on sexual and reproductive health and rights has been a priority encouraged by the Secretariat of Health itself. As a result, the perceptions of health staff have changed throughout these four years of legalization, since they feel more confident and have the support they need to provide these services. The Alliance, and a newly created program which it supports, *Fondo Maria*, are escorting women who seek abortions from other states of the country. The number of women who travel to Mexico City shows the overwhelming need for women from throughout the country for access to safe, legal abortions, and demonstrates the striking inequalities and the impact of abortion restrictions from state to state. This is reflected in women's abortion experiences, as seen in the next section of this paper.

SHIFTING SOCIAL NARRATIVES AND THE ATTEMPT
TO NORMALIZE ABORTION[7]

Certainly, the law on abortion in Mexico City has set new and different coordinates for women, culturally, politically, and in practical terms for their personal abortion experiences. Thus, a dramatic and life-changing social and institutional transition has occurred and abruptly transformed the choice of abortion from illegal to legal, from dangerous to safe, from gender discrimination to acceptance.[8]

What effects has the legalization of abortion had on the experience of voluntary abortion? How has this change affected Mexican women's perceptions or notions of rights? Has this shift facilitated notions and practices of citizenship? How has the concept of empowerment been integrated?

Women's abortion experiences in Mexico City's government health services have been illustrated by a qualitative analysis, conducted by Ana Amuchástegui and her colleagues.[9] Although induced abortion as a physical, psychological, and emotional event is strictly an individual experience, it is marked by a series of social processes. First, in addition to the fact that all pregnancies or abortions take place in the context of varying and numerous personal and societal relations, the experience of legal abortion occurs within the framework of significant structural changes in women's social conditions. There are many factors that frame women's experiences of abortion: the artificial decrease of fertility and its impact on the family-making process; the delay and increasing dissolution of marriage and a subsequent trend towards dissociating sexuality, marital and reproductive life; a growing presence of women in the workplace; increased educational opportunities for women and men which has led to a higher level of schooling among young people; as well as a steady decline of income which has forced other family members to join the labour market (INEGI). On the other hand, the current raging political debate regarding the right to abortion in Mexico eloquently shows that women's autonomy to choose an abortion as an aspect of reproductive freedom is entangled in a vicious tug-of-war between social discourses that fight for the hegemony over its control and production. Catholic morality and population control policies are very powerful and pervasive and they are fighting against modern conceptions of freedom, equality, and self-determination held not only by feminist movements, but by the international human rights framework that acknowledges these fundamental rights as core to gender justice and liberty.

The first effect that is clearly derived from women's narratives regarding their legal abortions is a shift in attitudes and a very strong sense of physical and legal safety, since most knew (either from their own experiences or those of other women's) about the many risks of having an illegal abortion, such as irreversible physical and emotional damage, sterility, and even death. Even the possible psychological aftermath of abortion is lessened because of legality. One woman, Lucila, describes her thoughts:

> Before [the law] I felt a lot worse, because I would think: "abortion is illegal, there must be a reason," right, "there must be a reason for abortion to be illegal and I am doing something illegal." I felt guiltier. Now there is guilt also because whatever it is, the pregnancy is yours. But it's never as strong as it was. (Lucila, 19, two children, housewife)

The fact that *government* clinics are providing the service holds authorities accountable, in tremendous contrast to the fear, defenselessness, and powerlessness which women previously felt when having to resort to clandestine and illegal providers. Not only do women feel safer, they also feel that their health will be taken care of by professional doctors and preserved within the hospital context in the rare case of a complication. This feeling of relief and trust is now brought about by the state:

> If it is legal now and they are going to do it in a hospital you can trust them, there are doctors here, and it is safer. I don't think they will put your life at risk by doing it wrong. Here they will have you in observation and any complication can be resolved right here. (María, 25, single, childless, professional)

MARIANISM, MORALITY, AND MOTHERHOOD

Beyond discourses uttered by the Catholic hierarchy, the strong presence of its narrow and oppressive morality and its emphasis on Marianism, or worship of Mary (represented in Mexico by the deep veneration of the Virgin of Guadalupe), the experiences of motherhood, and consequently of abortion, is clearly marked as a choice. In the Marianist context, motherhood has historically been constructed as women's ultimate and only destiny, which likely explains why the women who were interviewed didn't feel as much entitled to decide as to *whether* to have children, but rather *when* to do so and *how many*. Paradoxically, motherhood is also the reason most argued by them to interrupt a pregnancy, as women often decide not to have another child at a particular time to be better mothers for their present or future children.

Yet another major symbolic shift is unfolding in Mexico as a result of the legalization of abortion in Mexico City. Even before the 2007 amendment took place, there was a conflation of morality with the law, since women who had an abortion defined it *both* as a personal sin *and* as a secular crime. However, after the law was passed, women were empowered by the ability to separate these spheres by individually assessing abortion's moral considerations for themselves, as they were clearly recognizing their *entitlement* to safe abortion services. The evolving perception is that abortion is no longer considered a crime; at least, the legality of abortion allows women to feel a *reduction* of remorse, stigma, and guilt, and gives them "permission" and empowerment to be better prepared to make this choice.

In this sense, abortion is slowly becoming normalized and women are moving from being viewed as societal offenders and outlaws to becoming the subjects of rights. The fact that the government itself provides the abortion service implies recognition not only of the legitimacy of the decision to terminate a pregnancy, but also recognition of the subjects of such decisions, that is, of the women themselves.

> *If it weren't legal I would have felt a lot worse, just imagine! What would I have done without money? In these clinics there are good doctors and they give good service and everything.... Many horrible things happen out there. How many women die? The truth is that it hurts as a human being that I am, but thanks to the government and how they are supporting us now, it is much better.* (Isabel, 47 cook, mother and grandmother)

THE PUBLIC SPHERE ENABLES THE PRIVATE SPHERE

Within this process of legal abortion, it is important to speak of a subjective experience of the Mexican secular state, because it is the *public* sphere—the Mexican state—that provides the enabling conditions for women's decisions within the *private* sphere.

> *It's good that it's legal because then every woman can make her decision. It's not up to anybody else, not your parents, nor your*

friends or boyfriend, it's up to oneself. And even better that it's legal and you don't have to hide or to take risks, because when it was illegal there were a lot more risks, a lot more deaths.
(Liz, single, 21)

The legalization of abortion is thus understood by women as a social and institutional endorsement of their right to decide over their reproduction, to use contraception, to possess the choice of abortion, and to space their children. This, then, precipitates the conditions to enable a sense of autonomy and self-determination, as well as feelings of empowerment. Even with women's sexuality and reproduction still controversial and still under fierce debate in Mexico, the experience of legal abortion appears to create and inflict on an incipient sense of citizenship, equality, and rights. That is why this law mandating the legalization of abortion, carries with it social conditions for new meanings and definitions of femininity, motherhood, sexuality and reproduction, personal and familial relationships, women's role in society, and women's perceptions of their bodies. Further, far more powerful notions and practices of sexual and reproductive rights for women are gradually being recognized.

Women's experiences of abortion will always vary and not all women who choose legal abortion will feel empowered, even when they know that the abortion is the best and most ethical choice. This is because a sense of empowerment depends on a myriad of factors, specifically the material and social conditions of a woman's life. However, what *is* clearly empowering for all women is the *human right to choose a safe and legal abortion*, since the legality of abortion endorses, recognizes, and respects the complexities and realities of women's lives.

COUNTERACTIONS FROM THE ANTI-CHOICE MOVEMENT

As was expected, numerous counteroffensive actions rapidly occurred after abortion was decriminalized in Mexico City. The most onerous tactics enacted to restrict sexual and reproductive rights were sixteen constitutional laws that were written to protect life from the moment of conception and, in some cases, until natural death. The content of this organized and oppressive backlash is both anti-abortion and anti-human rights as they place several fundamental rights at risk. These include the right to choose a legal abortion, the right to access emergency contraception (included in the National Family Planning Norm) and the use of intra-uterine contraceptive devices, or IUDs.

These severe restrictions also limit stem cell research and reproductive assistance, which further results in the restraining of the fundamental right to enjoy the benefits of science and reproductive technologies. The constitutionality of these laws was quickly challenged in the National Supreme Court; legal stays[10] were also presented by Mexican women before tribunals in order to protect themselves from these harmful laws that limit their access to sexual and reproductive health services. Several cases of women's incarceration due to *alleged* abortions have also occurred (most of these women state that they have had miscarriages), demonstrating the social determinants that especially poor women face, the lack of gender justice, and the severe disparities within each state of Mexico and throughout the entire country.

Another barrier that impacts the provision of safe abortion care is the concept of conscientious *objectors*, where physicians (and only physicians) can opt out of participating in abortion services. This balance of rights and needs is challenging, as there continue to be on-going attempts to achieve acceptance for both those doctors who refuse to provide this care and for those who currently perform safe abortions. These abortion providers are known as the conscientious *providers*. Both providers and objectors have been urged to be respectful of women's rights and choices; this is key to women's empowerment, as is the concept of informed consent, where women who present for abortion care are given factual information, free of ideological and religious deception, and are trusted to make their own decisions about their pregnancies free of the medical staff's possible biases.

FINAL THOUGHTS

The decriminalization of abortion is transforming the social, cultural and political context in which women experience an abortion. As previously noted, although this change particularly serves and benefits the women of Mexico City, it has opened a fundamental break for all women throughout the country. The breakthroughs are enormous, as is women's transformation and their self-perception as being entitled to rights. Simultaneously, society, with its laws and regulations, as well as the discourse on abortion, has also shifted. Unfortunately, the reaction of the anti-choice movement to this tremendous victory to advance women's fundamental and human rights is inversely proportional to its size. With the huge power of the right-wing and the seemingly ceaseless influence of the Catholic church hierarchy, there is little hope at this time that abortion can be decriminalized in other states of the country.

However, because the ceiling has been raised due to the Mexico City victory, we have had some progress in amending laws and putting procedures in place for abortion in cases of rape, which is *theoretically* allowed throughout the country.[11] In many states it remains extremely difficult for women to obtain safe abortions, even when permitted under the law. Women have chosen to travel to Mexico City for safe and legal abortions.

The work goes on and the deep commitment to women's empowerment is never ending. The tiring battles will continue for women's rights, respect, recognition, and the right to choose a safe and legal abortion so that women are able to freely determine the direction of their lives.

Many thanks to Marcy Bloom and Domenick Dellino for their outstanding and thoughtful review of this chapter.

[1]The reform to the Mexico City Penal Code establishes that abortion is *"the termination of pregnancy after 12 weeks of gestation."* The code establishes that pregnancy is "the part of the process of human reproduction that starts with the implantation of the embryo in the endometrium" (Article 144, Mexico City's Penal Code, *my emphasis*).
[2]Mexico has a Federal system and each state has its own penal code. Therefore, the decriminalization of abortion applies only to the women of Mexico City. Abortion continues to be a crime, and is therefore severely restricted for most indications in the rest of the country, with differences in constraints in each state.
[3]The exception was a maternal death due to medical negligence. The doctor was removed from his position.
[4]Eighty-one percent of Catholics are against the Catholic church expulsion of women for having an abortion. Seventy percent are in favour that women should be allowed to have an abortion under certain circumstances (*Encuesta de opinión Católica en México*).
[5]According to data disseminated by the Grupo de Información en Reproducción Elegida (GIRE) (The Information Group on Reproductive Choice), in 2006, well over 800,000 abortions were carried out in Mexico (Guttmacher Institute, Population Council and the Colegio de México [2008] cited in GIRE).
[6]The five NGOs are: *Catolicas por el Derecho a Decidir* (Catholics for the Right to Decide), *Equidad de Genero, Familia, Trabajo y Sociedad* (Gender Equity, Family, Work and Society), *Grupo de Información en Reproducción Elegida* (GIRE).

[7]This section was adapted from the work of Ana Amuchástegui, who kindly shared part of a collaborative research project and analysis with the author (see Amuchástegui, Cruz, Aldaz and Mejía).

[8]Some 1,010 Mexico City residents aged fifteen and older participated in a poll conducted by the Population Council of Mexico. Knowledge of the new law increased significantly one year post-reform (72 percent to 84 percent). Support for legal abortion also increased significantly from 38 percent to 63 percent (26 percent opposed and 11 percent no opinion). Most (69 percent) wanted the law extended throughout Mexico. Multivariate analysis showed that higher education, male sex, and less-frequent religious services attendance were significantly associated with more favourable opinion about the new abortion law (see Wilson et al.).

[9]Between February 2008 and February 2009, as part of a broader research study to determine the subjective effects of the legalization of abortion, nineteen women were interviewed at two public hospitals immediately after health providers had confirmed the abortion had been completed (Amuchástegui, Cruz, Aldaz and Mejía).

[10]Legal stays, or *amparos* in Spanish, refer to a legal action, similar to a lawsuit that protects an individual from laws that violate their human rights. They apply only to individual cases and not collectively, should there be a favourable outcome.

[11]Seven states have approved procedures for abortion in cases of rape after the decriminalization of abortion in Mexico City.

REFERENCES

Amuchástegui, Ana, Guadalupe Cruz, Evelyn Aldaz and María Consuelo Mejía. "The Complexities of the Mexican Secular State and the Rights of Women: Final Research Report." Geneva: United Nations Research Institute for Social Development (UNRISD), July 2010. Web.

Barzelatto, José. *Paulina: In the Name of the Law.* Coyoacán, Mexico: GIRE, 2000.

Chacon, Richard. "Mexican health official urges debate on legalizing abortion." *The Boston Globe* July 29, 1998. Web.

Encuesta de opinión Católica en México. Católicas por el Derecho a Decidir, con la colaboración del Population Council, Mexico, July 2003. Web.

Grupo de Información en Reproducción Elegida (GIRE) (Information Group on Reproductive Choice) "Facts and Figures: Data on Induced

Abortions in Mexico." Web.

Instituto Nacional de Estadistica, Geografia e Informatica (INEGI) (National Institute of Statistics, Geography and Information), 2009. Web.

Wilson, Kate S., Sandra G. García, Claudia Díaz Olavarrieta, Aremis Villalobos Hernández, Jorge Valencia Rodríguez, Patricio Sanhueza Smith, and Courtney Burks. "Public Opinion on Abortion in Mexico City after the Landmark Reform." *Studies in Family Planning* 42.3 (September 2011): 175-182. Web.

16.
Obedient, Beautiful and Silent

GAL HARMAT, ISRAEL

THERE IS ONE CONCEPT that terrifies peace and anti–occupation activists from both the Israeli and Palestinian side more than any other: normalization. For example, bi-national youth projects that aim to share and recognize the others' narratives are considered dangerous, as almost an act of collaboration with the enemy and sometimes even a threat to the war effort. Both Israelis and Palestinians feel that if their children learn to conceive the "other" narrative as equal to their own story, then their own narrative will be lost as a means for justifying their side's struggle. In addition, they claim that talking as equals in an unequal situation may legitimize the inequality in the occupation. They call it a "normalization" project, meaning that it will make their children forget who and what they are. Their main claim is that normalization should not take place until their own narrative is legitimized and their identity as people, as a nation, is established.

I would like to discuss here the concept of "normality" and distinguish it from "normalization." There is no reason to normalize the existing state of affairs, between men and women or Israelis and Palestinians, and legitimize it. Instead, I would want men and women to be able to sit together in bi-gender settings, whether in a constructed discussion or in an informal meeting, and converse sincerely about their gains and losses from occupation, war and oppression—for Palestinians, for women in general and Palestinian women in particular, and for men and Israelis as well.

We need to see that we might be losing more than we gain when we choose war and domination, whether as occupiers or as freedom fighters, or whether we remain in oblivion, and simply abide by the norms of beauty presented by our media and society, allowing our bodies to be used as a commodity. We need to see that we lose our humanity and our ability to simply enjoy life. Israelis lose their ethics, their values,

187

their 2,000 years of tradition, as well as their personal security when soldiers return home and reproduce the violent behaviour demanded from them at checkpoints within their personal relationships. In many respects, Israelis also lose their international prestige. The occupation has already become almost the only thing they are known for, and the only perspective by which they are judged. And they continue it and reproduce it when abroad. A recent study shows that when post-military service Israeli men (and women) travel abroad they continue to behave like occupiers wherever they go—India, Thailand or South America—treating and especially perceiving the locals in the same way as they did treated and perceived Palestinians during their military service.

I would like to parallel this loss of Israelis' humanity and ability to enjoy life due to militarization and the loss experienced by men (and women) due to patriarchy: the occupation of the feminine and the domination of women's bodies. Much like the loss experienced by Israeli society as a whole, men also lose their morality, their values, their humanity, their ability to feel pain, to cry, to love their children, and to be with their children. They also may lose their lives with their readiness to die in the name of protection and patriarchy, whether protecting women or protecting the homeland.

Following the idea that the personal is the political, normality refers to the interpersonal level in the sense that it is worthwhile for Israelis to make justice with the Palestinians because it will allow them to return to be what they want, whether as individuals or as a nation, rather then what they are forced to be by fear and hatred. And on a deeper level normality refers to the interpersonal level in the sense that it is worthwhile for men to be just with women, to win back and not give up what they are, what they want to be and what they hope for, not to be forced to define themselves by their domination over women.

There is a connection between the need to be free from war and conflict, and the need to be free from patriarchy and its control over women's bodies. For example, women's bodies are being used and exploited on all levels: cultural, political, commercial, social, and interpersonal. However, in conflict zones they are exploited particularly for the purpose of escalating conflict and/or enhancing national pride and the division between "us" and "them." The use, control, and domination of women's bodies, based on the Israeli example, occurs on a number of levels. I will deal here with three of them: the perception that women's main role in Israeli society is as "reproducers"; the social norm of nurturing women's bodies; and the idealization of beauty as a means of domination.

I will also present these same means of domination as possible mechanisms for positive transformation by suggesting the concept of "Reclaiming." This means women reclaiming their own bodies— reclaiming the ideas of reproductive health, of nurturing their body and beauty image and using them according to their own will, needs and desires—thus facilitating feminine caring and activism towards creating peace both within ourselves and with our Palestinian neighbours.

REPRODUCERS: WOMB AND OVARIES

Any Jewish woman who does not bring into the world at least four healthy children is comparable to a soldier who evades military service.
—David Ben-Gurion (qtd. in Sharoni)[1]

A woman is a womb.
—Simone de Beauvoir, *The Second Sex* (95)[2]

I have experienced this reduction of womanhood and femininity to reproduction much like other Israeli women. My own womb and its capacity to produce began to be the focus of growing attention by my close and far social circles as I entered adulthood. People have been asking me if I am married and how many children I have since I was 21 years old. "How come you do not have children?" or "Why only one?" were and still are frequent comments in both social and professional settings.

According to Nira Yuval Davis, Israel puts an emphasis on giving birth and motherhood, presenting it to women and men as a national duty and task. Similarly, Uta Klein notes how the Israeli media widely discusses the Jewish Israeli birth rate, mainly in relation to geographic areas where Israeli Jews are not in the majority, like the Negev and the Galilee areas. Israeli officials and the Israeli media categorize these parts of the country as being "under a demographic threat," and encourage young Jewish couples to move to these areas, live, and reproduce there. The government encourages immigration by reducing taxes and by providing cheaper social services. Child support through a monthly minimum wage is given to families with more than four children, whether they financially need it or not.

Women in Israel are expected to give birth as soon as they get married. Lilach, a 27-year-old woman, shares her story:

As soon as we got married, everybody started to bless me to have a first-born boy. After a few months, my family and friends started to wonder what was going on with us, and after a year, relatives and even people I hardly knew were asking what's wrong with me and whether I have a problem. When I gave birth to Yuval I thought it would all stop, but No! I am now being asked constantly when will I give her a brother. I feel as if people around me only see me as a baby-producing machine and not as an autonomous woman with needs and wants. The fact that we are living in the Galilee makes it even harder and puts more pressure on me to give birth to many children.

In Israel as of 2009, women have more fertility treatments at the expense of the government than any other country in the world. Israel's allocated budget for this purpose is the highest in the world, and so is the number of patients (Lindar-Gantz and Darom). Except in very rare cases, treatments are never terminated; cost is not an issue. Women can repeat the process as often as desired, "as much as you can tolerate," as my numerous gynecologists and fertility experts stated.

Despite the enormous dangers to their bodies and minds, women sacrifice themselves on the altar of hope for a biological child. Some women in Israel even put their lives at risk, choosing to go through up to fifteen rounds of treatments, in order to fulfill the socially-constructed "national duty" of providing more soldiers and fighting the "demographic threat."

To emphasize that this is a symptom of women's role as "reproducers" in Israel, it is worth comparing state support provided in the case of a woman's need for an abortion. A woman can not have an abortion at the expense of the state (or even through her private medical insurance) without the approval of a "termination committee" composed of a rabbi, a social worker and a psychologist. Fertility treatments, on the other hand, are considered a regular state medical procedure. There is no need for a special approval, medical or psycho-socio-religious, although it is at least as risky a procedure as an abortion.

NURTURING AS MEANS FOR DOMINATION AND MILITARIZATION

It is common knowledge that new male recruits are called fresh beef or meat and new female recruits fresh mattresses.
—Shlomo Benizri ("Editorial")[3]

As a little girl I didn't want to cut my hair—ever. I hoped that when I reached eighteen and joined the army I would have knee-length hair. Our homeroom teacher in elementary school used to say to the boys: "when you grow up you'll be a brave soldier," and to the girls: "when you grow up you'll be a beautiful soldier." I really wanted to be a beautiful soldier. I wanted to have the longest hair. I saw female soldiers with long hair on the streets and envied them.

A woman's body is perceived as the antithesis to a man's body, the warrior's body (Ben-Ari). Even when women are included in army training, as in Israel, they are assigned roles that reinforce these dichotomies. Women who are professional athletes often participate in the men's fitness trainings as *Madrichot kosher kravi*—combat fitness instructors. The female instructors' role is to prepare male soldiers for combat training and to encourage greater efforts by instilling a sense of shame at being physically inferior to a woman. Neta, one such combat fitness instructor, explains this process:

> As [the freshly recruited soldiers'] fitness trainer, I was in very good shape. I taught them to compete with me, as they felt that if I can do it they could do it.... If I, a girl, can run six km, if a good-looking woman can do 100 push ups, so can a male soldier ... They feel as if it is an insult to lose to a girl, so they train harder and harder. I saw men who didn't sleep at night out of shame, training in their free time in order to beat me in a sport competition. It was very funny to see how those boys, totally new soldiers, who were just conscripted, played the game that I had set for them. They felt and did everything I wanted them to do as long as I could do it too.

Military fitness courses for women, on the other hand, only require them to achieve a basic lowest standard of fitness. Women in the army, it seems, do not need physical fitness, according to this theory, as they are simply there for the sake of appearance.

The military thus educates and assists men in constructing themselves as the warrior or soldier, as *the protector*—the antithesis to women, who are perceived as the *protected*. This builds on and reinforces dichotomies such as weak vs. strong, good vs. evil, us vs. them, capable vs. incapable, protector vs. protected, men vs. *women and children*. Galit, a 28-year-old woman, notes:

> During my military service I felt that everything about womanhood and femininity was wrong and ugly, while

everything concerning masculinity and manhood was great, something that the army and the state were proud of. I felt sometimes that if the word gever [the Hebrew word for man, literally meaning to overcome and considered a compliment] captures all that is good and positive in the army, then the word nekeva [the Hebrew word for female, literally meaning a cavity or perforation] describes only a hole, a genital organ that is only good for sex and giving birth.

In short, the Israel Defense Forces (IDF) Treats the female and the male body differently. There are completely different discourses concerning corporeal projects for men and women (Sered). Men are usually advised to focus on their physical fitness, while for women the focus is on their appearance, since they represent the IDF and so are required to look nice.

Women soldiers' uniforms and appearance take a major amount of the time, money, energy, and trainings in Israeli society, in general, and in the IDF in particular. The women's corps is called *Chen* in Hebrew, which literally means *beauty* and *grace*. The women's corps does not have any practical nor particular responsibility in the IDF; it is simply responsible for the women who join the military.

Finally, women are routinely used by the IDF in promotional posters as a "morale"-raising tool. It is not rare to see a picture of a woman soldier with a wet T-shirt and uniform trousers holding or sometimes hugging an M16 rifle. Pictures of these beautiful, smiling soldiers appear often in daily newspapers in Israel and are considered by many as a way to raise the national moral and the pride of the IDF. Some of these photos invoke the tropes of "soft" pornography, showing images such as a female soldier with full makeup and a white, wet T-shirt, nipples showing, with an M16 rifle held between her legs; these can even be found occasionally on the front pages of daily newspapers. Images of sexy female soldiers decorate Ministry of Tourism-sponsored posters inviting tourists for a unique visit to Israel. The implicit message is that they will do everything for you, everything you want, if you just ask for it. They are depicted disarming a weapon and holding it between their legs, their faces expressing pleasure. Or, they lie on their backs wearing a camouflage-patterned bikini, just waiting for the opportunity to advance and promote Israel's affairs. Sometimes they just lie on the floor in their wet T-shirts, bending around a machine gun—just come! It is often easy to confuse these ads and commercials for sex tourism.

PLAYING "BITCH" GAMES—NOT ONLY IN THE MILITARY

This does not remain confined to the militaristic (and sexist) discourse and international image of Israel. A recent Internet and television advertising campaign meant to "sex-up" Israel's image portrays women on the beach wearing bikinis and G-strings, moving erotically around, playing beach games, while two male tourists "check them out," saying "holy shit," "holy f@!#[expletive]," "holy cow" only to introduce the slogans "Israel—no wonder they call it the holy land!" and "the holy land, not what you thought."[4] What were they thinking? What do the leaders of my country think? I don't look like that; I don't want to be expected to have random sex with male tourists in order to advance tourism to Israel. I don't want this not only because I am not a piece of meat, I do not want it because it is well known that this kind of targeted tourism increases the rate of sexual assault of local women by tourists. As a woman, I had hoped that my country would protect me from such a vicious prospect, not pimp me. I had learned throughout my life how to represent Israel with dignity—I have always been told that when abroad, I am "the face of the country," that I am the state. So I thought the reverse was true: that on the international stage, the face of the state is me, that the state represents me. Well, apparently, it is not!

Women in Israel have achieved great successes—including Ada Yonat, a recent Nobel Prize Laureate for Chemistry—yet media and public attention is predominantly focused on promoting Israel women in bikinis, who move around erotically while holding phallic-symbol weapons between their legs.

Furthermore, the use by the government of women's bodies to connect sex and militarism, in order to advertise Israel, is a testament to the government's hypocrisy regarding women. On the one hand, it says it wants to include women in decision-making and the peace process by signing the Peacewomen Project's 1325 resolution (passed unanimously by the UN Security Council on 31 October 2000)[5]; on the other hand, when a woman runs for prime minister, whatever her political stance, she is literally belittled by her opponents: "it's too big for her." She is always placed with the little, the small, in need of protection.

DOMINATION OF THE BODY, HEART AND SOUL

"You become prettier every time I see you," a senior manager of a peace organization told me just before I delivered a presentation. "It's so pretty to look at you when you teach," said the chairperson of the college I teach at. "You don't really look like a professor of gender studies, you are beautiful, thin and feminine, you dress fashionably" is what many of my students tell me. "The high grades your students give you for your teaching qualifications are only due of the way you look, dress and get around," said one of my colleagues. "What is a beautiful flower like you doing alone on the beach/coffee shop/street/university library/office?"

As a woman, I assimilate and reinforce this beauty image. I wear red high heels when I want to get an interesting research position; I put on red lipstick as a way of highlighting my academic skills. I am aware that my body is being used, that I use my body, but experience has taught me that there are only two options for me to get a job in Israel—to behave in a more masculine and patriarchal manner then men (and be ridiculed for it by both men and women) or to adopt ultra-feminine western stereotypes of womanhood that signify me as subordinate, weak, and easy to control.

Still, even though I play the game of how a "good" woman behaves, my voice is not being heard; my interests are not represented or taken into account on the decision-making level. Whether it is the peace process with the Palestinians or the need to reform the education system, my needs are not mapped, my interests are not counted. I do not count. I am transparent. Discourse and practice are patriarchal in the classic notion of control and domination, while excluding women (and men) who do not abide by its rules and norms.

One of patriarchy's strongest tactics of domination is through physical fear and intimidation, by connecting the personal and the public. This way the controlling narrative, the "strategic" or "enemy threat," is also the threat over one's own body. Both Israelis and Palestinians base their control through the use of fear. The discourse of protection in Israel—whether it is the anti-missile "shield dome" or the separation barrier—always refers to the fear of an outside enemy. The dominating fear in women's lives is the fear of losing the lives of their loved ones, of their children and spouses, and their own lives and bodies, in war or "terrorist attacks," or by rape by an Arab or a migrant worker— the "outsider." This fear is pumped through media, society and family and it blinds women from seeing the alternatives or the possibility of an alternative. However, almost ironically, as a woman in Israel those who are most likely to hurt me—physically, mentally, historically and geographically—are, statistically, my husband, my father, or my next door male neighbour, not an "outsider" enemy or foreigner. The demand and pressure to risk and subordinate my life to giving birth to as many children as possible and raising them in the name of the continuation of the Jewish race will come from my nuclear and distant family. If I choose not to enlist to the army to play the role of the protected or the supporter and morale raiser of male soldiers, the saint or the whore, I will be socially punished by my very close social circles—my community, society, family. And finally, I am virtually pimped, as a sexual attraction, in order to advance tourism for my government.

NORMALITY, PEACE AND RECLAIMING

Should women "give up" on reproduction, nurturing their bodies, and beauty? Is "giving up" on feminine norms the only way for women to free themselves from domination and gain peace, build peace? No, we should not, for as the numerous chapters in this book suggest, it is a feminine way that will bring true peace to our humanity and the planet we all share. We need to understand what peace means to each of us.

By peace, I refer to the concept of a culture of peace, specifically to the gender aspect of culture of peace. In this respect, women who live in peace do not have to worry about having someone to protect them; they are able to protect themselves and do not need to use their body and subordinate it to seek protection by marriage, child-bearing and home-making. Women could choose how many, if any, children they would like to birth. They could decide whether they would like to cultivate and nurture their bodies (and according to whose ideal of beauty), since they are not obliged to do so in order to attract potential protectors in a manner that fits men's desires. They will not feel the need to give birth to many children for fear of losing them to wars and violence.

My peace does not rely on an "outside" enemy, but on my close and distant family, social circles, community and government, who use this "outside enemy" as a way to block me from even considering the possibility of peace—a peace which will benefit me. The chances that my child will die in a traffic accident are much higher than those of dying in a war, to which he will be sent to in order to propagate and continue fear. Nevertheless, the latter fear is continually invoked. Thus, to be afraid that my child will die in war is just another way of influencing me to give birth to more children in order to safeguard myself, my people and my country. It is a vicious circle, which includes military as much as paramilitary actions like suicide bombings. It is a circle of revenge that keeps the fear alive and keeps women under the rule of domination.

RECLAIMING THE BODY, RECLAIMING PEACE

The notion of reclaiming is based on the idea that the mechanisms for changing reality can be found within present reality. Hegemony tends to expand its legitimacy by co-opting social, cultural and ethical norms. In this sense, reclaiming means re-interpreting and freeing these mechanisms from the domination of hegemony, that is, by "taking" them back and using them instead of abandoning them. In the recent Iraq war, for example, many American veterans reclaimed the notion of patriotism and called for an end to the war instead of its continuation as the most patriotic act—protecting the nation and its future.

Thus, in Israeli-Palestinian, Jewish and Arabic cultures and societies themselves we can find the mechanisms for resolving these conflicts. Muslim and Jewish, Arabic and Israeli, cultures can suggest their values and ethos as a base for resolution. This is said with respect to the concepts of peace studies theory which on many occasion were formed in different cultural settings. Although they suggest strong insights, they do not always fit culturally with the Israeli-Palestinian context. It is important to see that our own cultures suggest similar concepts for peace building, only articulated differently. Jewish/Israeli and Arabic/Islamic traditions and culture include mechanisms for resolution, reconciliation and dialog. For example, in Jewish culture there is the notion of *slichot*, which places emphasis on the gravity of inter-personal offenses rather than offenses against god. It stresses the importance of being able to forgive crimes against us, not only the ability to ask for forgiveness for what we have done to one another.

Dialogue is another fundamental aspect of both Jewish and Arabic culture. In Judaism, lengthy debate and casuistry are highly valued, almost to the degree of sanctity. Controversy over competing Biblical and Talmudic interpretations becomes a debate of different views. It is not a classic negotiation of interests where there is a need for compromise or persuasion, or for a winner and a loser, but an understanding that the intersection of two ideas sometimes creates new ideas—a creative resolution of a conflict where everybody wins.

Current Israeli culture itself includes processes for accepting the other and otherness in an honest and creative manner. It happened, for example, when homosexuality stopped being seen as a perversion and instead became normalized. In a very similar fashion, talking with Palestinians was considered to be a perversion and yet has become normalized, and there are now, besides the official and unofficial talks between Israeli and Palestinian governments on all levels, numerous, mainly small and grassroots, bi-national dialogue groups and projects (like the Combatants for Peace or the Bereaved Parents Forum). Both transformations are taking place thanks to the mechanism of reclaiming one's human validity. For example, when homosexuals reclaimed "gay," taking back the same word/terminology which had been used in order to oppress them, and using it as a positive identify element—when they answered their offenders "yes, I am gay, so what?" then "homo" stopped being used as a swear word and homosexuals stopped being something to be scared of. In a similar fashion, when Abby Natan[6] broke the silence around the secret talks with Palestinians, the taboo of talking with Palestinians collapsed. Organizations like Combatants for Peace are now reclaiming the notion of "combatant" saying that only peace is worth "combating" for and acknowledging that the culture of peace means abandoning the whole discourse of fighting, the discourse of *us* (soldiers) and *them* (civilians, and those we see as combatants).

However, women and men, Israelis and Palestinians ignore these mechanisms of dialogue, creativity, normality and reclaiming because they are focused on their gains from control and domination and are blinded, by fear, to their loss. These fears and gains are constantly pumped by the media and the education system. To demonstrate this, let me tell you about my first visit to the deep areas of the Occupied Palestinian Territories. By then, I was no longer dominated by stereotypes as most of them had dissolved. I now had many friends in Palestine (in fact, that time I went to visit them). I even had already been to the border areas. But, when visiting the deep areas of Palestine I was still afraid that the men there might harm me. I was not afraid of my friends, but of other people. Throughout my life I had been told that Palestinians could kidnap me, rape me, kill me, and that this was and is their main concern in life, the only thing that mattered for them. Having internalized this fear, it caused me to be afraid to walk around in a Palestinian city. I was not afraid of my friends but I still walked around with a deep, non-specific and general feeling of fear, without any real reference.

I still feel this general sense of fear when it comes to traveling to the Gaza Strip. Israeli media, culture, friends and family constantly encourage the Israeli's fear of "Hamastan." I am afraid because it is the "Hamas" over there, much as Israel is seen around the world as "the occupiers." In actual fact, "over there" are people—some voted for Hamas and others did not, some are nice and others are not, some are religious and others are not. But this fear, the separation and the colouring of everyone there in the same colours, as the "Hamastan," prevents and denies normality.

What do Israelis gain by this fear, by its reproduction? We gain the ability to not see with our own eyes that Gaza is one of the poorest and most-crowded places in the world, and that we, as Israelis, bear responsibility for this situation.

This sense of general and constant fear, a feeling of mental terror, is expressed by the body as well, when the domination of my consciousness creates the conditions for the domination of my body. My deep fear of Palestinians leaves my body exactly where the Israeli government wants it to be—in Tel Aviv—without even having to use force. The control over consciousness by fear eliminates the body's freedom to move freely. There is no need for any physical or legal threat and prohibition—I create them myself on the basis of my fear.

At the same time, I, as a woman, can recognize that Palestinians experience this same fear every time they see an Israeli uniform, or military vehicle as it also represents suppression of mind, spirit and body for them.

ON A POSITIVE NOTE

I would like to conclude with a recent example of Palestinian women reclaiming the notions of motherhood and womanhood, not allowing themselves to be used for nationalistic purposes, but rather for their own need and desire for normality. As reported, when the group of female Palestinian prisoners were released against the video tape of the poisoned Israeli soldier, Gilaad Shalit in September 2009, the mothers in the group of released prisoners, and the mothers of the young girls in the group, issued a declaration wishing and hoping that Shalit's mother will see him soon, and that she deserved for him to soon be released as well (*Haaretz*). They used this indoctrinated equation of woman=mother in a way that created and called for unity and solidarity rather than for war, for peace building rather then revenge. In this way they have reclaimed it and used it for their own needs, rather than as nationalistic propaganda. They have reclaimed the power of their motherhood and used it as a call for peace. Meanwhile, Hamas, the masculine leadership, was trying to use motherhood as propaganda for the escalation of conflict and as a means of supporting the claim that Hamas "won" in this case, and issued a war-like statement saying that Israel was "bent down" to her knees. For me, this mothers' declaration echoes the Israeli "4 mothers" movement when they resisted the use of the Israeli government of motherhood as a motivation to increase support of the 1984 Lebanon war. Rather, these mothers used the notion of motherhood as a way to protest war, as a way to say "we do not want to send and lose our children and husbands to such an unjust and unjustified war." The words of Kofi Annan, Secretary General of the United Nations, on October 24, 2000 (cited in the Introduction to this book) underpin this understanding, "*For generations, women have served as peace educators, both in their families and in their societies. They have proved instrumental in building bridges rather than walls.*"

In this respect, I would suggest that any dialogue group, any bi-national peace organization or activity in our nation, should include the gender aspect, not only in the sense of equality or of counter-balancing gendered social constructions, but in the sense of understanding that peace will not only free the Palestinians (and Israelis as occupiers) from occupation and war, but also it should free women, on both sides, from their subjection to the patriarchal war machine, the same way these brave Palestinian women have freed themselves from the Hamas propaganda machine, and the *Machsom* Watch protect our neighbours. Putting gender as a central element of peace building would mean that the builders must address the similarities of both people— those same struggles which unite them, rather than differentiate them, like the struggle against patriarchy's domination and subordination of women's bodies and minds. I suggest here gender, the observation and then transformation of the power relations between men and women, as a unifying platform for peace building between Israelis and Palestinians. I see gender mainstreaming—women's (and men's) efforts to create change—as a struggle that will open the road for a joint bi-national struggle, which will transcend the conflict, and transform it into a joint struggle instead of a struggle between the two nations.

[1]The first prime minister and founder of the state of Israel.
[2]Simone de Beauvoir asks "What is a woman?"
[3]Israeli Parliament member at the time and current government minister.
[4]See "Hot Israel." YouTube September 17, 2007. See http://youtu.be/fa1LwuS4lhw.
[5]For further information, see http://www.peacewomen.org/un/sc/1325.html.
[6]Aby Nattan, a well known persona in Israel and former IDF pilot, was the first Israeli to break the strong taboo against talking with the Palestinian leadership. He just went abroad and met Palestinians publicly; although

he was imprisoned for this behaviour when he returned to Israel, the taboo had been broken.

REFERENCES

Ben-Ari, Eyel."The Military and Militarism in Israeli Society." New York: SUNY Series in Israeli Studies, 2000. Print.

Davis, Nira Yuval. "National Reproduction and the Demographic Race in Israel." *Women, Nation, State*. Ed. Nira Yuval Davis and Floya Anthias Houndsmills. Basingstoke: The Macmillan Press, 1989. Print.

"Editorial." *Jerusalem Post* February 3, 1995. Print.

De Beauvoir, Simone. *Hamin Hasheni (The Second Sex)*. Trans. Sharon Preminger. Tel Aviv, Israel: Babel Publications, 2001. Print.

Galit. Personal interview. 28 April 2004.

Haaretz 14 November 2009. Print.

Klein, Uta. "The Contribution of the Military and Military Discourse to the Construction of Masculinity in Society." Paper delivered at the seminar Men and Violence Against Women. Strasbourg, 7-8 October 1999.

Lilach. Personal interview. 5 March 2004.

Lindar-Gantz, Roni and Naomi Darom. "Professor Aviram: 'Israel has the largest number of fertility treatment units per population – it is a wild exaggeration'." *The Marker* July 7, 2008. Web.

Neta. Personal interview. 23 December 2003.

Sered, Susan. *What Make Women Sick?* Hanover, NH: Brandeis University Press, 2000. Print.

Sharoni, Simona. *Gender and the Israeli-Palestinian Conflict: The Politics of Women's Resistance*. Syracuse: Syracuse University Press, 1995. Print.

17.
Inter-religious and Intercultural Dialogue

Supporting the Human Rights of Women and Children

ANNIE IMBENS-FRANSEN, NETHERLANDS

As in any society, the best goals emerge from the dreams of men and women together.
                                    —Margaret Wertheim (252)

LTHOUGH THE MONOTHEISTIC RELIGIONS Judaism, Christianity, and Islam all stress the importance of justice and truth, as well as love and respect for one's neighbour, they have traditionally been dominated by patriarchal leaders, whose religious views reflect androcentric perceptions of reality. The views and spirituality in these religions are based on the experiences, problems, questions, feelings, insights, and interests of men and on men's desires, fears, dreams, and fantasies. In the age-old practice of male domination in these religions, men with such androcentric, patriarchal views consider themselves as superior to women. They claim exclusive authority to determine how God must be viewed, what is human, male, and female, and to identify God's allocation of roles and responsibilities among men and women. Accordingly, women's experiences and views on religion and spirituality have been ignored and excluded from the discourse in patriarchal religious and academic circuits.

This chapter discusses many of the values expressed in our religious ideals and declarations related to human rights. It exemplifies the many communications, actions and networks emerging and working towards a more egalitarian world. I also illustrate the obstacles we are facing as we move towards gender balance. In examining the following declarations, we have to ask: what prevents these ideals from being fully realized?

DECLARATIONS ON WOMEN'S AND CHILDREN'S HUMAN RIGHTS

The *Universal Declaration of Human Rights* of December 10, 1948, recognizes in its preamble the inherent dignity and the equal and inalienable rights of all members of the human family as the foundation of freedom, justice, and peace in the world:

> •Article 2.1 Everyone is entitled to all the rights and freedoms set forth in this Declaration, without distinction of any kind, such as race, colour, sex, language, religion, political or other opinion, national or social origin, property, birth or other status.
> •Article 18 The right to freedom of thought, conscience and religion, is one of the fundamental Human Rights. It includes freedom to change his/her religion and the freedom to manifest his/her religion, either alone or in community with others and in public or private, and to manifest his/her religion or belief in teaching, worship, and observance.

Recognition of the right to freedom of thought, conscience and religion as a fundamental human right implies that nobody has the right of imposing his/her beliefs on others, nor to force others to his/her beliefs. However, the right to freedom of thought, conscience and religion is frequently abused by patriarchal, religious leaders to dominate women and children and to deprive them of their human rights. Since the initial declaration in1948, numerous declarations and resolutions have been adopted to eliminate discrimination against women and children and to protect their human rights. For example:

> •June 1993. In Article 18, the *Vienna Declaration and Programme of Action* expresses, "The human rights of women and of the girl-child are an inalienable, integral and indivisible part of universal human rights."
> • September 1995. The *Beijing Declaration and Platform for Action*, which contains 361 articles for the protection and implementation of the human rights of women and the girl child, in order to ensure the full implementation of the human rights of women and of the girl child as an inalienable, integral and indivisible part of all human rights and fundamental freedoms, declared, "Governments must not only refrain from violating the human rights of all women, but must work actively to promote and protect these rights"(UN Article 214, Annex II).
> •March 2002. The European Parliament's Committee on Women's Rights and Equal Opportunities drafted the

"Resolution Women and Fundamentalism." The resolution addresses different kinds of religiously-motivated violations of the human rights of women and girls, and indicates that throughout history women have been and are among the main victims of religious fundamentalism. The day before this resolution was on the agenda of the European Parliament, different Christian denominations and organizations argued against this "secular confession of faith" and pleaded strongly against it.

•June 2008. The UN Security Council adopted Resolution 1820: Article 2 demands the immediate and complete cessation by all parties to armed conflict of all acts of sexual violence against civilians with immediate effect; Article 7 requests continuing and strengthened efforts to implement the policy of zero tolerance of sexual exploitation and abuse in United Nations Peacekeeping operations, and urges troop- and police-contributing countries to take appropriate preventative and other actions to ensure full accountability in cases of such conduct involving their personnel; Article 12 urgently appeals to women to participate in discussions pertinent to the prevention and resolution of conflict, the maintenance of peace and security, and post-conflict peace building. It encourages all parties to such talks to facilitate the equal and full participation of women at decision-making levels.

CELEBRATING THE SIXTIETH ANNIVERSARY
OF THE UNIVERSAL DECLARATION OF HUMAN RIGHTS

During September 2008, I participated on behalf of United Religions Initiative (URI) at a UN conference to celebrate the 60th anniversary of this Declaration. A few days before the conference started, a Dutch newspaper had published an article alleging that UN peacekeepers often sexually abuse children. I decided to address these crimes against children during the conference, which I did at a plenary session.

The next day, I participated in a workshop about resolutions 1325 and 1820. Near the end of this workshop, an ambassador recommended writing an Open Letter to the UN Secretary General. We drafted the letter "Making Senior UN Leadership accountable for sexual abuse/exploitation by UN personnel in Peace Operations." By November 2008, the letter had been signed and forwarded to the Secretary General by 180 international non-governmental organizations and

84 public figures, including academics, writers, government officials, peace advocates, human rights activists, and former UN officials. This was a group of non-political and non-patriarchally motivated men and women, engaged in serious humanitarian work.

RELIGIOUSLY MOTIVATED VIOLENCE
AGAINST WOMEN AND CHILDREN

Until now, the UN declarations have not motivated patriarchal, religious leaders to take the necessary steps to eliminate religiously motivated violence against women and children. They continue to abuse the right to freedom of thought, conscience and religion to deprive women and children of their human rights.

The story of a thirteen-year old Somali girl is a cruel example of this fact. In October 2008, the media reported that Aisha Ibrahim Duhulow—who told her father that three men had raped her—was accused of adultery and stoned to death by dozens of men in a stadium, packed with 1,000 spectators. They said they were carrying out this punishment "in the name of Allah." The brutal killing of Aisha stresses the importance of addressing and stopping religiously motivated violence against women and children. It is also an urgent appeal to transform our religions into instrument of peace, justice and healing. Women and men, as parents of the human race, cannot allow such injustices to take place. Patriarchy needs to be replaced by a gender-balanced, egalitarian model—worldwide.

DIFFERENT SIDES TO SPIRITUALITY

After considering many women's stories about their daily lives and reflecting on my experiences—especially during my study of theology and my activities in pastoral care for sexually abused women—I discovered two different sides to spirituality.

First, spirituality is a stimulating and empowering source of strength and insight that grows as we become more receptive and realize our abilities and limitations. Inner strength stimulates us to open our eyes to the structures, mechanisms, and limitations in our society that support unjust practices and relations, and to the suffering, they cause.

Spirituality also cultivates our insight, self-esteem, strength, courage, creativity, and sensitivity to truth, justice, beauty, and love, which are the necessary instruments or attributes for transforming ourselves and our societies and for creating a better life for all beings. This view on spirituality emanates from texts and stories from my Christian heritage, and also from many women's stories.

Two biblical texts have acquired a special meaning to me, both in my personal life and in working for justice for all. The first text asks the question, what is needed to inherit eternal life or enjoy the fullest possible existence? We should love God, wholeheartedly, with all our soul, all our strength, and all our mind, and we should love our neighbour as we love ourselves (Luke 10:27). The second text is a story of a widow who was involved in a lawsuit. The judge who heard her case neither feared God nor respected people. After refusing for a while, he finally granted her justice. The widow succeeded in convincing this judge of his obligation to dispense justice by repeatedly telling him, "Provide me justice against my opponent." She persisted until the judge sighed, "I have no fear of God and no respect for anyone, yet because this widow keeps bothering me, I will see to it that she gets her rights. If I do not, she will keep on coming and finally wear me out." This story advises us how we should believe and pray, and the value of persistence. It also expresses the power of justice and the wisdom and strength of a woman who knew how to obtain her rights before an unjust or corrupt judge (Luke 18:1-8).

However, when examining these issues, we also need to recognize that there is also another destructive side to spirituality. In the 1980s, when I was teaching a course called "Reading the Bible through Women's Eyes," women started telling me their stories of rape and incest. At first, I wondered about the correlation with the contents of my lectures and courses, and the women's reasons for sharing these experiences with me. Later, I began to understand the connection between my approach to theological themes and these stories of sexually-abused women.

As a feminist theologian, I stimulated women to view reality and to interpret biblical texts from our own perspective and with our insights, based on our questions, experiences, feelings, interests, and desires. For the first time these women learned to interpret their experiences with sexual violence from their own perspective. They started to realize they had not brought the assault on themselves through tempting female behaviour, as the androcentric view alleges. They became aware they had been confronted with sexual violence because of male aggressive behaviour toward them. Becoming aware of this fact changed the survivor's attitude toward their experience with sexual violence. Their silence, out of a sense of guilt imposed by others, made way for expression of the sense that they had been wronged. Hearing these women's stories increased my awareness of the negative and harmful spiritual contents for women of mainstream androcentric religion, theology and spirituality.

Several research projects revealed how oppressive and destructive androcentric, patriarchal Christian thought and spirituality can be to women. Annie Imbens' and Ineke Jonker's study *Christianity and Incest* concludes, "When Christian upbringing is seen from the perspective of patriarchal premises, the experience and teaching of Christianity makes girls easy prey for male family members. This religious education complicates the woman's or girl's ability to overcome the effects of sexual abuse."[1]

WOMEN'S PARTICIPATION IN INTER-RELIGIOUS DIALOGUE

It has been a long journey for women to receive recognition in any religious discussion, let alone inter-religious dialogue. The September 1893 Parliament of the World's Religions (PWR) Conference in Chicago is remembered as the birth of the interfaith dialogue. Main objectives of this conference were:

- •to show the importance of religion,
- •to promote and deepen cooperation and understanding among people from different traditions,
- •to discover what and how religions could contribute to solve the problems of that time, particularly those connected with temperance, labour, education, wealth and poverty, and peace among nations.

The objectives of the women who assured that women could participate, and the women who actually participated were different. Hannah Greenebaum Solomon[2] and Augusta J. Chapin[3] took care that women could participate and were among the speakers. Antoinette Brown Blackwell, Elizabeth Cady Stanton,[4] Susan B. Anthony, Lucy Stone, Julia Ward Howe, Frances E. Willard were among the speakers. They were active in anti-slavery, temperance, education, suffrage, peace, women's human rights, biblical studies, and politics. They appealed to women to continue to speak the truth fearlessly, to obtain equal and full justice for women in all aspects.

More than a century years later, at the PWR Assembly of 2004, equal participation and contribution of women was still problematic. During the Assembly, both female and male participants expressed their disappointment and anger about the male dominance, and the lack of respect for the minority of women who participated in panels. After discovering two young female students crying in the hall near the ladies' room because of this oppressive atmosphere, I organized an Open Space Gathering, "Listening to the Voices of Women in the Parliament of the World's Religions." More than 100 women and men participated. We formed a committee of twelve volunteers to prepare a Petition including recommendations to the PWR.

In 2009, when asking for a response to this Petition, I was informed that the issues as addressed have been taken up in its program and its processes and structures. The PWR continues to recruit women of great spiritual power to their Board of Trustees, particularly women who speak out clearly and with great passion and compassion for the issues of women, children and the oppressed, locally and around the world. Sometimes slowly, but certainly steadily, changes in power structures are being realized.

PARTICIPATING IN THE FOUNDING OF
A NEW INTER-RELIGIOUS ORGANIZATION

In the spring of 1997, I received an invitation from United Religions Initiative (URI) for one of their regional consultation conferences at the Brahma Kumaris Retreat Centre in Oxford. The included papers indicated that URI was in its founding stage. The idea was born in 1993, when Anglican bishop, William E. Swing of California, was preparing a worship service for the celebration of the 50th anniversary of the signing of the United Nations Charter. URI aimed to be a forum for dialogue and co-operation among religions and peace among nations, and "to address urgent human need, to support freedom of religion or belief and the rights of all individuals, as set forth in international law, and to provide an opportunity for participation by all people, especially by those whose voices are not often heard." Reading this invitation, I expected URI would be the right place to communicate women's experiences and views on religion and spirituality and to address the worldwide mental, physical and sexual abuse against women and children (see Imbens-Fransen).

At this first regional conference, one third of the participants were women. While being asked for topics we thought important for URI, I proposed "Women's Experiences and Views on Religion and Spirituality." We started a group with twelve women and men from different countries and religious backgrounds, including priests and an imam. We spoke honestly to each other, and asked each other sometimes-difficult questions. This open atmosphere enabled a Christian woman to say to the imam, "I have never been in a women's group with an imam, and honestly said, I am afraid of you. It makes me try to behave nice to you, but I also want to express my anger about the oppression of women in religions." Her words created an opening to go deeper into women's concerns about the impact of religion on women's lives. The imam explained that Muslim men feel the need to protect women. When asked how he would feel if women were to protect men in the same way, he responded, "You are right, it is patronizing women."

We also shared favourite texts from our religious and cultural traditions. We took care that the wife of the imam, who did not speak English, but could understand it enough to follow the conversation, could participate. We asked her for her opinion, and asked her husband to translate her words. Near the end of our dialogue, she asked her husband to translate, "In religions, there is no justice for women. That is the same in all religions. In all religions women are oppressed." Later, the imam told us that his wife was going to learn to speak English, he explained, "So that she can speak for herself at conferences."

After three sessions, we agreed that,

- •URI should be based on equal representation of women and men and full participation of women in decision-making,
- •URI needs to be a space for women to develop and exchange our views on religion and spirituality,
- •Women's experiences and views are needed to enable the full humanity of humankind and to advance the well-being of all beings, and the Earth.

I became deeply involved in URI. I participated in the global conferences to prepare the Charter. When participating in the group *Defending Religious Rights,* with a Buddhist, a Christian and two Muslim men, I stressed the importance of respecting women's human rights in religions. They responded by discussing whether it would be wise for URI to address respect for women's human rights within religions from the beginning on. They asked me for examples of religiously-motivated violence against women and children. I showed them my copy of *Christianity and Incest,* and informed them about the violence against women and children in other traditions. The stories Christian, Jewish and Muslim woman had shared with me helped me to convince participants in this group that in these religions women are still oppressed.

Later, I was asked to become the convener of this group, to prepare a paper on this topic. Together with two Muslim men, I wrote the text "Religious Rights and Responsibilities," in which we focused on these themes:

- •Interdependence of religious rights and responsibilities;
- •The reality of poverty and inequality;
- •Proposals to change in the gap between the rich and the poor;
- •The reality that woman are worldwide subjected to inequalities;[5]
- •Proposals for URI actions to promote religious rights and responsibilities;
- •Proposals to promote, protect, and implement women's human rights;
- •Some religious, spiritual, and ethical texts that promote equality, justice, respect, solidarity, and peace among people and to preserve the earth.

Responses to this paper indicated that many women and men were not aware of worldwide violations of women's human rights. I shared my concern about this lack of information at a URI conference with Sharon Franquemont, and we decided to include statistics about violations of women's and children's human rights in a ceremony.

We started with a prayer, then seven women and six men from different religious and cultural traditions read, in turn, 25 statistics. We ended with a prayer. During this ceremony, there was a deep silence. Later male and female participants expressed not being aware of the amount of violence against women and children in their own country. Some of them asked for permission to read this prayer in their own religious communities.

From 1997–2000, I participated in global summits to prepare the URI Charter and its organizational structure. We had an intense dialogue about the Purpose Statement, particularly on the terms *religiously motivated violence, justice,* and *healing for the Earth and all living beings.*

We finally unanimously agreed on a text:

> *The purpose of the United Religions Initiative is to promote enduring, daily interfaith co-operation, to end religiously*

motivated violence and to create cultures of peace, justice and healing for the Earth and all living beings.[6]

To include a principle about equal participation of women and men in the Charter continued to be problematic. When requesting the staff to include this topic in the agenda of the telephone conference for the final draft of the Charter, I was told this topic would not be included, because they expected it would not be accepted.

The only possibility to have this principle included was to propose it at the start of the telephone conference. At the moment the chair asked, whether we had a question or a remark, I proposed to include this principle. I am still grateful for Mohinder Singh's support. He explained that we had agreed about it from the beginning, and stressed the importance of this principle for the women in India, because of the continuing violations of their human rights. After his explanation, Principle 8 of the URI Charter, "*We practice equitable participation of women and men in all aspects of URI*" was unanimously accepted.

From 1999-2005, I was a member of the URI Interim Global Council, the URI Global Council and URI Europe. Since 1999, I have been initiator and co-coordinator of the URI Council for Women. It is worthwhile for women to spend time and energy in the Inter-religious Dialogue. Feminist theologians have an important role in developing ideas and ways to make the Inter-religious Dialogue an effective tool to promote and implement the human rights of women, children and other "outsiders."[7]

INTERPRETING RELIGIOUS TEXTS FROM THE PERSPECTIVE OF WOMEN'S AND CHILDREN'S HUMAN RIGHTS

On December 10, 2003, the Iranian lawyer Shirin Ebadi—a human rights activist for refugees, women and children, and founder and leader of the Association for Support of Children's Rights in Iran—received the Nobel Peace Prize. The Nobel Committee described her as a representative of the Reformed Islam, which argues for a new interpretation of Islamic law in harmony with vital human rights such as democracy, equality before the law, religious freedom, and freedom of speech.

In her Nobel Lecture Shirin Ebadi said, "Some Muslims, under the pretext that democracy and human rights are not compatible with Islamic teachings and the traditional structure of Islamic societies, have justified despotic governments, and continue to do so. In fact, it is not so easy to rule over a people who are aware of their rights, using traditional, patriarchal and paternalistic methods." The decision to honour Shirin Ebadi with the Nobel Peace Prize is an important contribution to stop religiously-motivated violations of children's and women's human rights. Her voice represents a worldwide choir of feminist scholars from different traditions—like Athalya Brenner, Fokkelien van Dijk-Hemmes, Catharina Halkes, Riffat Hassan, Elisabeth Schüssler Fiorenza, Zeenat Shaukat Ali—who have developed and applied methods to interpret sacred text from the perspective of women and our human rights.

VIOLENCE AGAINST WOMEN AND GIRLS

As noted at the beginning of this chapter, despite all of our religious ideals and humanitarian declarations, on a global level approximately six out of every ten women experience physical and/or sexual violence in their lifetime. Violence against women and girls continues to be one of the most widespread violations of human rights. A *World Health Organization* study of 24,000 women in ten countries found that the prevalence of physical and/or sexual violence by a partner varied from 15 percent in urban Japan to 71 percent in rural Ethiopia, with most areas being in the 30-60 percent range.

For women and girls between 16-44 years old, violence is a major cause of death and disability. In 1994, a World Bank study on ten selected risk factors facing girls and women in this age group found rape and domestic violence more dangerous than cancer, motor vehicle accidents, war and malaria. Studies also reveal increasing links between violence against women and HIV and AIDS. A survey among 1,366 South African women showed that women who were beaten by their partners were 48 percent more likely to be infected with HIV than those who were not (UN Women).

On November 6, 2009, UNIFEM launched its new platform for action: "Say NO—UNITE to End Violence against Women." One of these programs focuses on reducing sexual harassment and violence in urban public spaces. UNIFEM indicates that worldwide, millions of girls and women are subjected to harassment and abuse when they use public transport, fetch water or go to work. Despite this widespread phenomenon, this violence is often neglected by laws, policies and society at large. The Safe Cities program is the first global effort to develop an intervention model that can result in preventing violence against women. Again, this is evidence of women working not only to help other women, but to create a better world.

THE EMILY FUND RAISES AWARENESS ABOUT DATING VIOLENCE

When working on this chapter, I received an e-mail from a URI member about dating violence. A talented nineteen-year-old student, Emily Rachel Silverstein, was murdered by her ex-boyfriend at Gettysburg College after she had ended her relationship with him. Her father founded the *Emily Fund* to raise awareness about dating violence. His research and consequent writings note that this abuse is very common. For example, one in three teenagers report they have experienced physical, verbal, emotional, or sexual abuse in a relationship. The website stopdatingviolence.org gives valuable information about how to address and prevent this violence. It also gives information about the signs of an abusive relationship, and about how to protect oneself in such a relationship. This is where religious and humanitarian ideals can unite to ensure such violations no longer occur.

Many inspiring international organizations cross the lines separating people of different faiths. Examples include:

- Brahma Kumaris, because of its inspiring spirituality and their conferences, such as "The Four Faces of Women" and "Beyond Leadership."
- The World March of Women, because its activities on women's human rights and their "Women's Global Charter for Humanity."
- The European Society of Women in Theological Research, because its research and conferences.
- Women's World Summit Foundation (WWSF).
- The Association for Women's Rights in Development (AWID).
- United Religions Initiative (URI).
- The Parliament of the World's Religions.

In closing this story of my work in the inter-religious dialogue I want to emphasize the importance of communication across faiths, and also the necessity of working together—both women and men—on behalf of the protection of women's and children's full human rights.

[1]For an extensive summary of *Christianity and Incest,* see Imbens and Jonker.
[2]The leader of the Jewish women.
[3]Founding member of the American Woman Suffrage Association and

member of the first executive committee of the Association for the Advancement of Women.

[4]Ken Burns, who made the documentary *Not for Ourselves Alone: The Story of Elizabeth Cady Stanton & Susan B. Anthon,* describes Elizabeth Cady Stanton in an interview as, "The author, in essence, of the largest social transformation that has ever taken place in the United States." He states that Stanton and Susan B. Anthony set the women's movement in motion and describes them as the two most important women in American history from a social and political perspective (cited in the *Examiner*, Sunday, November 7, 1999).

[5]Based on the United Nations paper, *Women's Rights: The Responsibility of All.*

[6]In 2007, a member of the European Commission for Education and Culture expressed being impressed by this strong Purpose Statement.

[7]Michael Gillgannon and James Breeden used the word *outsiders,* when responding to my presentation "Digging Up Women's Sources of Wisdom and Strength in the Quest for Women's True Spirituality" at the 1996 Coolidge Research Colloquium. They both explained the importance of my research and analyses for all people excluded from mainstream discourse in theology and philosophy, including people of colour.

REFERENCES

Imbens-Fransen, Annie. "Digging Up Women's Sources of Wisdom and Strength in the Quest for Women's True Spirituality." *Re-Visioning Our Sources: Women's Spirituality in European Perspectives.* Eds. Annette Esser, Anne Hunt Overzee and Susan Roll. Kampen: Kok Pharos, 1997. Print.

Imbens, Annie and Ineke Jonker. *Christianity and Incest.* Amersfoort: De Horstink, 1985. Print. [4]

Not for Ourselves Alone: The Story of Elizabeth Cady Stanton & Susan B. Anthony. Dir. Ken Burns. Prod. Paul Burns and Ken Burns. Florentine Films. 210 min. November 7, 1999.

Stop Dating Violence. Web.

UNIFEM. "Gender Issues." Web.

United Nations (UN). Fourth World Conference on Women. *Beijing Declaration and Platform for Action.* September 1995. Web.

United Nations (UN). Office of the High Commissioner for Human Rights. *Vienna Declaration and Programme of Action.* June 25, 1993. Web.

United Nations (UN). *Universal Declaration of Human Rights.*

December 10, 1948. Web.

United Nations (UN). *Women's Rights: The Responsibility of All.* United Nations Office of the High Commissioner for Human Rights, 1997. Print.

UN Women: United Nations Entity for Gender Equality and the Empowerment of Women. "Violence Against Women." Web.

Wertheim, Margaret. *Pythagoras' Trousers: God Physics, and the Gender War.* New York: W.W. Norton & Company. 1997. Print.

18.
The Strength of Our Nations Lies in the Hearts of Our Native Women

SUSAN MASTEN, YUROK NATION/NORTH AMERICA

A WOMAN ONCE TOLD ME, "you are like the salmon, you are always swimming against the current." It is true that I have a tendency to tackle impossible tasks. I have always felt a higher calling to make a difference for my family and community, and I firmly believe that when you have capabilities you also have responsibilities. I have a great deal of compassion and dedication to this end, and it has taken me on a wonderful but difficult path.

I come from what my grandmother referred to as "good people," meaning that I descend from the leaders of our Yurok village, Reqwoi, located where the majestic Klamath River meets the Pacific Ocean, a rich and abundant land where the Creator placed our people so that we would never want for anything. Unlike other tribes, we did not have to move around to follow food sources, but lived year round in redwood plank homes in villages along the coast and river. I also come from feather people—the ceremonial keepers and medicine people. My grandmother would never have said all this, as it is not our way. She would simply say we come from "good people—no slouches."

Role models are critical in developing expectations, dreams, and hopes, and key to providing support and encouragement to our youth. I have been blessed by having wonderful, strong Native American women as role models in my family: my grandmother, Geneva Mattz, and my mother, Lavina Bowers. Through their actions and words, I have gained a wealth of knowledge and strength of character that form the foundation of my very being. They fostered in me a strong cultural identity, work ethic, sense of self-worth, perseverance, integrity, tenacity, and honesty in all of my actions. Further, they stressed the importance of our ceremonies and prayer to keep us on the right path and in balance with all other creatures and mother earth. These women erected the foundation that empowered me to persevere through many challenging tasks that otherwise could have derailed me before I even started. It is through their teachings that I have a strong identity as a Yurok woman, and my culture and traditions are at the heart of my choices and decision-making.

One government policy of the United States that had a profound impact on our people and my family was the concerted effort to assimilate Native Americans into mainstream society by "erasing the Indian" in our children. Under this forced policy, my grandmother was taken from her home and family in 1908, when she was only six years old, and placed in a U.S. Bureau of Indian Affairs boarding school some 400 miles to the north in the state of Oregon. At this school she was forbidden to speak her native Yurok language and, if caught doing so, was punished physically and emotionally. This federal Indian policy and others that followed played a major role in how Native women adapted to survive and how we found our way back to serve as contemporary leaders. Young adults were relocated in urban areas to break up our family structures and assimilate our people. These displacement tactics resulted in the loss of language, life skills, and parenting skills, as well as the loss of positive Native role models.

When my grandmother, Geneva Mattz, returned home in her teens she worked as a housekeeper. Despite the boarding school's efforts, she still spoke Yurok with her grandparents, and assisted one of the last medicine women in our family during healing ceremonies. Through her daily actions she stressed the importance of prayer; she would go to the places that were known for returning a loved one lost in the river or ocean for protection, so you could travel without being seen, for medicine for healing and to find your own healing powers, or for wealth to be the best singer, dancer or basket-maker. She was fluent in our language, a basket-maker, singer, and healer, but sadly because of her boarding school experience she did not teach her children our language: we know only the names of some birds, fish, game and commonly used phrases. It is our generation's responsibility to learn our language or risk losing it forever.

My journey to becoming a leader of the Yurok Nation was fostered by generations of my family who instilled a strong cultural foundation and good values that inspired service to Native peoples broadly, and to my own tribe in particular. I have been fighting for the basic rights of Native peoples and serving in tribal governance, including as Tribal Chairperson, for more than 30 years, and will continue to until I am able to do no more.

With more than 5,500 members, the Yurok is the largest tribe in California. Our beautiful territory spans over 580,000 acres and is located in the heart of redwood forests from the mouth of the Klamath River to just above the confluences of the Klamath and Trinity Rivers, and from just north of Klamath to Little River just south of Trinidad on the coast. We still fight to this day to exercise our sovereign rights as a nation, including fishing, gathering and hunting rights, and the right to perpetuate our sacred culture and language.

As a people who were hunted down and ruthlessly killed by the thousands during the land grab that became the California Gold Rush in the 1860s, we struggled to survive not only blatant genocide, but also the theft by settlers and the United States government of thousands of acres of rich forests, rivers, and sacred sites that are culturally important to our way of life. Despite deliberate acts of genocide against us and other tribes, both in California and throughout United States, we still maintained our Yurok identity and core values: our spirituality, roles and responsibilities, and obligation to preserving and protecting our resources for future generations.

I began my leadership career early, at 27, when I served as the lead negotiator for my people during the Salmon Wars which ignited yet another historical round of racist attacks against the Yurok people. During this time, we organized our government, developed our constitution, and elected our first Tribal governmental officials. Throughout those turbulent times, I carried the strength and wisdom of generations of leaders who came before me, using ceremony and prayer to sustain us. I was most honored to serve Native people as the Chairperson of the Yurok Tribe for six years, shouldering the responsibility to guide negotiations for the return of land, salmon, timber and our right to self-determination.

Today, there is a pervasive lack of infrastructure, roads, electricity, telephone lines, and housing on the Yurok Reservation. We have an unemployment rate of more than 75 percent, and, appallingly, more than 90 percent of our people live below the poverty level. There is a desperate need to regain an adequate land base from what was illegally taken, particularly lands that can provide economic development opportunities. I have long worked to achieve this cause alongside other Yurok leaders.

I am very proud to say that in April 2011, we acquired 22,237 acres of ancestral lands around the lower Klamath River in Humboldt County. This is the culmination of twenty-three years of collective hard work to regain and restore part of our homelands that began with the passage of the *Hoopa/Yurok Settlement Act* of 1988. The recovered land will be set aside as a Yurok Tribal Community Forest and more than doubles the tribe's land base. We will use a sustainable forestry management approach to protect salmon, clean up the water, and restore meadows for traditional subsistence hunting and gathering.

But the journey to leadership, and the recovery of our homelands the Creator blessed us with, was fraught with unimaginable challenges to overcome. How could I not be driven when the needs of our people on the Yurok Reservation are so great? Throughout Indian Country—where Third World conditions still widely exist—Native people lead in all negative statistics nationally with skyrocketing rates of unemployment, poverty, suicide, diabetes, stroke, cancer, substance abuse, domestic violence, and drop-out rates. I was compelled to seek solutions to these daunting challenges.

My grandparents worked from the time they got up until the time they went to bed. My grandmother was always telling us to be sure our house was clean as guests may come, and even if we could only afford one good outfit, we were taught to always wash and iron it in order to present ourselves well for work and community. They taught us that we should always do our best. These teachings were directly related to the era in which she grew up, where the stereotype was that of the "dirty, lazy Indian." The stigma was, of course, directly opposite to reality: Yuroks bathed daily and shared the ethic that it was important to work hard and pray so that we would have success, be the best at whatever we did and gain wealth, all important characteristics in our Yurok world. My grandmother made sure we knew what her grandmother had told her of the first European boat that landed at the mouth of the Klamath River. The Yurok people then were concerned that the explorers were dirty and had bugs in their eyebrows. Using sign language, they encouraged the settlers to bathe. In our culture, stories are always used to demonstrate life lessons, and my grandmother told another story to make sure that we would not be lazy or dirty. The story was about a young woman called Keemha. Every time Keemha went to visit someone she would always bring her dirty clothes with her to wash when she got there because she was never ready to travel. Her lack of preparation held her back. No one wanted to be Keemha.

My grandparents lived through the Depression, so they always talked about putting a little money away for a rainy day. They taught us to plant a garden and to raise a few cattle so that we would always have food and a little money when we needed it. In their own humble way, they stressed self-sufficiency and preparedness. My mother always told us that we were as good as anyone else—no one was better then we were. She also told us we could be whoever we wanted to be if we worked hard and got an education.

I always felt loved and supported because my mother and grandparents participated in every important event in my life. They wanted us to have a better and easier life then they had, so they stressed the importance of getting an education in order to obtain good paying jobs. They always stressed the importance of working hard and doing the best we could, instilling expectations that we should strive for excellence.

My mother also taught us strong work ethics as she worked two jobs so we could have what we needed, and yet she still found time to spend with us. As children, we worked every summer picking strawberries, cherries, and beans to make extra money for school clothes. This proved to be a great way to learn work ethics and the value of money. Having strong role models and having support was key in my life for making healthy choices.

I fundamentally believe that education is the key for social and economic change. My immediate family is an example of this. My role models made the difference for me because they expected me to go to college, and because of them I had hopes and dreams. Because of their support and encouragement, I also had the confidence and self-esteem I needed to follow my dream to attain higher education.

The oldest of five children, I was the first to graduate from college in both my father and mother's families. All four of my siblings also graduated from college, a testament to my family's commitment to improve our lives using education as a tool. I recently asked my sister, Diane, what made her go to college. She laughed and said, "Are you kidding me? You took each of us to register for college and helped us make class selections." Ironically, I did not remember this.

But we are the evidence that change can come in just one generation. Today, we are all professionals and leaders in our fields, and now the role models in our family. I'm so proud to say the next generation has outdone us. Besides getting their college degrees, I have one niece who is now a Master of Public Policy, and another who graduated from law school and is working for the Native American Rights Fund as an attorney. We have worked hard and changed our social economic standing in one generation using the cultural values instilled in us.

After graduating from Oregon State University, where I served as president of the Native American Student Association, I moved to San Francisco to work as a marketing specialist and gained valuable private sector experience working for the United Indian Development

Association, a Native American business development organization in the mid 1970s.

In the 1930s, the State of California closed the Indian fishery on the Klamath River. At that time the Yurok Tribe was not organized as a Tribal government to defend our rights, and the Bureau of Indian Affairs as our trustee did not step forward to protect our federally reserved fishing rights. This action did not stop my family from exercising their right to fish as they always had for generations, but it did force them to fish at night to avoid being caught by State Fish and Game agents. My mother's brother, Raymond Mattz, was sixteen years old when he was fishing for salmon with a gill net one night on the Klamath River, next to our mother's allotted land in our family's traditional fishing hole. He was with his brother Emery and a friend, at a place where my ancestors have fished since the beginning of time. That night, the agents came. My uncles hid from them, but the agents confiscated their fishing nets. When they went to claim their fishing gear, they were told they had to plead guilty to get their equipment back. They said no—that it was their right to fish and they would go to court instead. My grandparents had little money but because this was so important to us they used what they had to fight the State of California in a case known as *Mattz vs. Arnett* or *Arnett vs. Five Gill Nets*. This difficult battle resulted in the Supreme Court decision reaffirming our fishing rights on the Klamath River basin in mid-1970s. Sadly, my uncle Emery never saw this victory—he died in a car accident during the case.

Our fishermen were just beginning to feel whole again—they were finally back on the water making a modest living and putting food on the table for their families—when fish populations started to decline. In the interest of fisheries conservation, the federal government called a moratorium on fishing—specifically, Native fishing. At the same time, the Klamath River sport fishermen were still allowed to fish on the Klamath River and the commercial and sport fishermen were still fishing in the Pacific Ocean. In fact, *everyone* else was still fishing—the only people not permitted to fish were tribal people—the only ones who held federally-reserved fishing rights. Where is the justice? Should not all other burdens of conservation be implemented before tribal fishing, an inherited right of generations, is impacted?

So the Yurok people, with my family at the forefront, decided to protest this unjust moratorium. In response, the federal government called in federal law enforcement agents in full riot gear, including helmets, shields, bulletproof vests, and M16 rifles, who came to "protect and save the salmon." Tensions ran high and our family was fearful that someone would be killed during confrontations that came to be known as the "salmon wars" on the Klamath River. In fact, it was so intense that when my small cousins, who were six- and eight-years old at the time, heard the large inboard boats that the federal agents drove coming down the river, they came running down the driveway hollering "the feds are coming! the feds are coming!" My family, afraid that something bad would happen, hurriedly jumped into our car and headed down to the river where my uncle was fishing, so that there would be witnesses on hand to protect him.

Many fishermen were charged with felony counts and imprisoned, all because they were preserving their fishing rights. Women were dragged across the sand bar by their hair and even my 78-year-old grandfather was hauled off to jail because he went out on his own property to see why the federal agents were present. His arm was hurt in the arrest process; my grandparents tried to file suit against the agents but were told it wouldn't go anywhere.

One day, my uncle and other relatives were on the water when several boats full of agents arrived. My 76-year-old grandmother was very concerned for her family's safety, so she wanted my mother to take her to where they were in the rowboat. They went out in the middle of the river in the estuary were it was very swift and rough. The agents were circling my uncle's boat and my grandmother was worried that they would swamp his much smaller craft and capsize it. She stood up in the rowboat, raised her arms to the sky, and began loudly and clearly to sing a prayer song. Several birds began to circle around her. The agents were not sure what to do and it was obvious that this made them very uncomfortable. Finally, one of them said, "let's get the hell out of here."

The Salmon Wars left most of the Native fishermen who participated in this peaceful protest with a deep-seated fear and hatred of the federal and state government officials. This added yet another generation of trauma to those suffered by my people.

I returned to the Reservation in 1978 when my family called me home, a confident young woman—naïve enough to believe if you just followed the law nothing bad would happen. That is when my mother told me "not all laws are created justly," and that was the beginning of my life's journey: to fight for protection of our people's natural resources, cultural identity, traditions, and fishing rights. I found myself on the front lines of the salmon wars. But the racial tensions and political strife lead to intense times. There was even a common local attitude imprinted on a bumper sticker: "Can an Indian, Save a Salmon."

I began to organize the fishermen into the Traditional Indian Fishermen's Association, and was selected as their chair, becoming the representative to negotiate our allocation at the fishery management forums where decisions about our fishery were made. These forums were male dominated—only three women including me participated at this level. We began to develop regulations for our fishery that provided for protection of our salmon and management zones between villages to allow fish to be taken throughout the Reservation. I had to learn about fish biology, politics, and develop negotiation skills all at the same time while laying the ground work for our day in court, at which time we asserted our entitlement for not less than 50 percent of the fishery allocation. We knew this would be challenged by non-Indian fishermen in court. The court upheld the decision that the tribes of the Klamath River Basin were entitled to "not less than 50 percent" of the available fishery harvest, a major victory in the face of discrimination and inequality.

At the same time, I began to work to change the public opinion of the day by becoming a Klamath Chamber of Commerce member and eventually the President and a member of the Del Norte County Chamber. I started attending Del Norte County Democratic Central Committee, becoming the Chair and a National Delegate to the Democratic Convention. This was critical at this time as our State Senator was a Democrat and our Congressman was a Democrat and they were jointly sponsoring anti-Indian fishing legislation. By becoming a leader in the non-Indian community—becoming a peer—I effected a gradual change in attitude toward our people and our fishery.

After 23 years of serving in Tribal government , I decided not to seek re-election—not an easy decision for me, but with no retirement plan and an income of only $35,000 per year as the Tribal Chairperson, I decided that I could no longer afford to stay in that position. It took me a year to decide that it was okay for me to make money, but the bigger question was how could I fulfill my calling and still be able to contribute to making a difference for my community at home and nationally, particularly since my whole self worth and identity revolved around working for a better life for Yurok people. I made a promise to myself that I would create a Charter School locally and a National Native Women's organization. I was recruited by a bank ... but I had no idea what my worth was in dollars—how could I negotiate employment terms when I didn't know the banking business? So I called on my friends in banking to find out salary range and benefits. Then I called a lawyer friend to determine what salary range I should seek given my experience and knowledge. Armed with this I asked for more. After all, they could only say no and nothing would be lost. I had to negotiate the best terms I could. Therefore, I asked for a title of Vice President, a salary, a signing bonus (didn't even know if that could happen) and five weeks off in my first year on the job. I got everything I asked for except for four weeks instead of five, because the policies didn't allow for more. This led to a job in the banking world that I enjoyed for several years.

Once engaged in private-sector banking, I began to work on my promises to myself to create an early college charter high school. I did this by meeting with the vice president of our local community college and my niece who works in public policy. She had worked for an early college initiative that was being piloted in Washington State to discuss the creation of a new charter school. Our students historically have not succeeded in the public school system, with a very high drop-out rate. Most students left school in the ninth grade.

The three of us made a commitment that day to become the founders of this new school and we immediately called a meeting of parents, students, college professors, and community leaders to develop a vision: what we wanted our school to look like, what and how we wanted our students to learn, while providing an environment that was safe, nurturing, supportive, and encouraging.

Our charter school, the Klamath River Early College of the Redwoods, opened its doors in the fall of 2005. We are an independent school district charter that has its own school board; our curriculum is based on the standard one, but incorporates Yurok culture. Students have the opportunity to earn an Associates of Arts degree at the same time as they receive their high school diploma. By our second year, we had 20 students who were Yurok, Tolowa, or Resigini tribal members, as well as Hispanic, Hawaiian, and Caucasian students attending our school. What these young people had in common was that most were "high-risk," and ninety percent were dropout students from the public school system.

In our third year, we had a 97 percent attendance rate at our school, and one student passed into college classes. The following year, 42 percent of our students were eligible for college classes. Students are involved in the community in real-life projects, defined by the Tribal government, making them "rising leaders" and "positive community contributors." Today, 100 percent of our students are enrolled at College of the Redwoods, changing expectations and self-identities, and six students are taking two or more college classes. We will be adding an adult education component to our school this year that will allow many of the student's parents to work on Associates of Arts degrees and high school diplomas. We expect that this will create major change in the social and economic stability of families and our community.

WOMEN EMPOWERING WOMEN

The other promise I made to myself and my family was to contribute to the greater good by creating a national Native American women's leadership organization. During the time that I served as the elected chair of the Yurok Tribe of Northern California. I was also elected to the office of President of the National Congress of American Indians, the oldest and largest organization representing more than 230 of the 565 Tribal governments in America. I am only the second woman to hold this position. Historically, since many of our Indian nations are matriarchal, it was not uncommon for women to be in leadership roles. But the model of government imposed on Indian tribes beginning in the 1930s was a smaller version of what the federal government looked like, although this did not work in diverse Native communities where leadership is not organized in linear hierarchies. Under the U.S. government's 1934 *Indian Reorganization Act,* almost exclusively male tribal leaders operated these fledging new Tribal governments. This created a void, and the important voices of women were muted for several decades until more Native women were eventually elected.

While I sometimes faced anger, skepticism, and gender-based resistance in my leadership roles, I was surprised to find that it was women who were the most critical and vicious in their political attacks. I also noticed that as women we did not have a network of other women decision-makers who actively supported and promoted women, something men do very well through the "old boy network." I observed that men are very good at supporting their colleagues and at bringing business and job opportunities to each other. They are accustomed to being team players because, from early childhood, so much of male socialization revolves around team sports. I wanted this kind of network of support for Native women. I see women daily who are caught in domestic violence, substance abuse, single-parenting their families in poverty and not knowing how to change their situations. Women are very good at taking care of everyone else's needs, but we are often terrible at taking care of ourselves. We need to find ways to balance our lives.

I wanted to find a way to provide resources, training, role models, mentors, and a forum for networking. For all of these reasons and many more, I founded Women Empowering Women for Indian Nations

(WEWIN). With nine of my Native women friends who are tribal leaders, former tribal leaders and business owners, we became the founding board members[1] and began to create our vision for WEWIN. To date, we have held six national conferences attended by thousands of Native women.

WEWIN's focus is to empower women through personal and professional development, by providing networking opportunities, offering support and encouragement to women to run for public and tribal elected offices, as well as promoting buying goods and services from women. At the foundation of this organization is the importance of our cultural values at the heart of all our actions. We know that it is working because women have found job opportunities and business contracts during our annual meetings. Women tell us that they have life-changing experiences at our conferences because of contacts they have made or something that they learned while attending our conferences. We also know that women are feeling empowered through the love and support we offer to help our women heal from everyday injustices and profound losses.

I'm a firm believer that when you have capabilities as individuals, you have the responsibility to be a part of change, making your communities healthier and more prosperous. I truly believe that we are created for a purpose and that we are each given unique talents to use to contribute to the greater good. We continue to learn new skills and fine-tune our gifts through our life experiences. I also think that knowledge and leadership qualities are transferred and inherited from our ancestors.

Given all this, I believe I was born to serve my people and to contribute to the greater good for all Native peoples. Therefore, I have made a conscious effort in my decision-making to provide for positive change. In doing so, I created opportunities to uplift, encourage, and prepare other Native women to become role models and leaders in their families, communities, Nations, and at the work place. During this wonderful and very challenging journey I have been fortunate to witness first-hand an increase in the number and quality of women leaders within my own Tribe, other California Tribes and throughout "Indian Country." I hope that I have been a positive influence in this change in leadership.

Life is a kind of ceremony. We continue to seek balance for our people and a stable future for our children. At home, our people are preparing for our most sacred ceremonies, the White Deer Skin dance and the Jump dance. These ceremonies are prayers to the Creator to keep balance in our Yurok world. When our people are in balance, we are strong, our children's futures are bright, and life is as it should be: good.

When our people are not in balance, we are weakened, our people are disheartened, and we worry about what will become of our children.

Women are the givers of life, the caretakers and the peacemakers. We are mothers, aunties, grandmothers, and sisters. As women, we have the power to create major change to balance the world again. By coming together for the common good, we can make a difference in our communities and the world at large. With global warming and the mass loss of species, and war, we as women must step forward as leaders and join hands as we hold the key to solutions—to create world change.

[1]The WEWIN Founding Board Members include: Veronica Homer, former Vice Chair of Colorado Indian Reservation; Nora McDowell Antone, former Fort Mohave Tribe Chairwoman; Geri Small, the former Chairwoman Northern Cheyenne of Montana; Melanie Benjamin, former Chief Executive of the Mile Lacs Band of Ojibwe Minnesota; Cecelia Fire Thunder former President Oglala Sioux Nation South Dakota; Rachel Joseph, former chair of Lone Pine Paiute Tribe; Sally Smith, former Chairwoman of the Curyung Tribe of Alaska, and Patricia Parker, CEO, Native American Management Services, Inc. and the late Wilma Mankiller, former Chief of the Cherokee Nation.

19.
Costa Rica

A Nation Without a Military

ANA MARCELA GARCIA CHAVEZ, COSTA RICA

COSTA RICAN WOMEN HAVE ALWAYS stood out in important historical events that have defined the Costa Rican character as a nation and consolidated important institutions. The civil rights that we Costa Ricans enjoy at this time are the fruit of women's struggles of the recent past. Considering that our nation does not have a military force—a typically masculine expression—Costa Rica is naturally inclined towards gender balance.

In this chapter, I introduce Costa Rican women who have distinguished themselves and left their seal on the history of my country. I will briefly explain not only what they are doing currently, but also their contributions in the past—especially considering how their teachings in social, cultural, legal and economic fields marked steps forward in the history of our country. Of particular significance is the work being done to reduce some of the obstacles and hardships faced by Indigenous women, as well as imprisoned women, and our efforts to ensure their equal rights.

HISTORICAL CONTRIBUTIONS BY COSTA RICAN WOMEN

When discussing important contributions to the country's legacy by Costa Rican women, I cannot fail to mention Carmen Lyra, the pseudonym by which the influential writer and political activist Maria Isabel Carvajal (1887-1949) was better known. Carmen Lyra was one of the founders of the Communist Party of Costa Rica; she led the fight against the dictatorship of José Federico Alberto de Jesús Tinoco Granados (1870-1931),[1] participating even in an act of public protest that ended in the burning of the offices of the state-run newspaper, *The Information*. As a social activist, she promoted and participated in building schools, in the creation of the National Institute for Children (*Patronato Nacional de la*

Infancia), in the struggle for equal salaries for equal work for men and women, and also for women's right to vote. Because of her revolutionary ideas and criticism of the established government, public institutions and political figures, as well, she constantly faced great personal problems, including the politically-motivated loss of her employment.

In 1948, at age 60, after a short civil war led by José Figueres Ferrer, because of her political and ideological activism, Lyre was wrongly accused as the intellectual author of "war crimes." As a consequence, she and other important members of the Communist Party were forced into Mexican exile. The following year, suffering from serious health problems, she requested to be allowed to spend her last days in her homeland, but the government denied her that right. She died on May 13th, 1949, after only one year in exile. On July 23, 1976, the Legislative Assembly awarded Carmen Lyra the honour of *Benemérita de la Cultura Nacional* (Meritorious Citizenship) posthumously, because she unquestioningly represented the beginning of the struggle for women's rights, and also a strong leadership promoting social changes in Costa Rican society that subsequently would be enshrined in our Constitution. Her image now adorns the twenty thousand *colones* bill.

The feminist struggles of the fifties gave way to the recognition of a series of civil rights granted to Costa Rican women today. The Constitution underwent a series of legislative reforms aimed at creating a more equalitarian and more equitable society. As amended by Law No. 7880, of May 27, 1999, Article 33 of the Constitution represents an essential part of our social economic political and legal system, and states unequivocally: "Everyone is equal before the law and no act of discrimination can be practiced that may be in any way contrary to human dignity." This amendment did not occur by magic;, it represents the hard-won gains of a difficult process led by those who struggled for equal rights under the Constitution for all citizens.

As a result, Costa Rican women are present in virtually every area of the country's life: political, economical, social, cultural, legal, artistic, and intellectual, among others. The Constitution protects every Costa Rican citizen against all forms of discrimination, on grounds of nationality, colour, religion, and of course sex. In this regard, for many other nations Costa Rica is exemplary.

HUMAN RIGHTS AND THE CONTINUED EFFORTS
FOR GENDER EQUALITY

Equality under the law is not only a constitutionally-protected right, but also underpins the legal norms and mechanisms adopted by the State to protect the Constitution itself in the creation of the Constitutional Court (*Sala IV Constitucional*) as a fundamental pillar in the judicial system The sentence is with the correct meaning. This Court is responsible for the effective application and protection of the Costa Rican people's constitutional rights.

Despite being enshrined in law, equality between men and women is far from complete: unfortunately, there are still many instances of notorious discrimination. There is no doubt that the workplace is one of the environments in which discrimination, even in this twenty-first century, can be easily detected. Women in the workplace do not enjoy the same rights and opportunities that men do. Inequalities and prejudices against women are still part of the Costa Rican society. An obvious question can be asked: *Why is it that Costa Rican women do not enjoy the same rights men do?* The answer seems to be that within an ordinary family, a Costa Rican woman plays many roles and is simultaneously a mother, a wife, the head of her household, among others. It seems to be only natural because she is simply ... a woman.

This oversimplification of concepts creates a difficult reality for women in the workplace. Virtually every woman looking for a job is conscious that employers hire women reluctantly, because of the number of additional legal obligations by which they must abide. From this point of view, it is often cheaper to hire men to do a job that a woman can perform just as well. For example, once hired, employers must recognize women's rights under the Labour Code; among other things, under no circumstances can a pregnant woman be fired from her job. This is an achievement of a recent amendment to the Law and sets jurisprudence for the protection of women in the workplace. But, this also creates a dilemma for women as employers may avoid hiring women they perceive as potential new mothers.

Other forms of discrimination can be found, for example, when women compete with men for higher-ranking positions. Experience shows that in a significant number of cases, the best and better-paid jobs are given to men, but not to women.

WOMEN IN THE POLITICAL ARENA

Another area where Costa Rican women are making progress is in the political arena. At this time, Costa Rica proudly boasts of having elected its first female president, Laura Chinchilla Miranda, who came to power February 7, 2010, representing the National Liberation

Party. The 2010 electoral results represented a radical change in the national political scene. Because of these results, prejudices of a highly conservative and patriarchal society collapsed in order to give way and space to the development of a more just and equitable society—one that keeps on striving for more inclusive women's rights.

The still-unanswered question is whether President Chinchilla, a social conservative, will make a difference leading a new kind of government and struggling against the powers that be; or if, on the contrary, the new government will be only more of the same. So far, she still seems to follow the path set before her by her male predecessors. Ultimately, only time will tell and after a good part of her government has elapsed, we will be able to see whether she promoted and implemented the changes needed to allow women to face and solve their problems with dignity— backed up by the women's rights guaranteed by our Constitution.

Other women of the present and former governments have also made a difference, such as the former Health Minister, Maria Luisa Avila Agüero (serving under President Oscar Arias from 2006-2010, and under President Laura Chinchilla until September 1, 2011). Her leadership during the campaign against the 2009 H1N1 pandemic, in which she launched a prevention campaign never seen before in the history of the country, is highly commendable. She also has been concerned and devoted ministerial efforts and resources to the prevention of diseases such as dengue, breast cancer, and AIDS, among others, as well as promoting general participation in campaigns for a healthy and sustainable environment.

Similarly, a great number of women in the Costa Rican Legislature have fought hard for the adoption of laws granting rights to women. One of the most controversial and hard-fought laws is the Law on the Criminalization of Domestic Violence, which finally adopted and defined the crime of *femicide*, that is, "homicide." against women, conceived to protect women who are victims of psychological and physical assault committed by their own husbands or intimate companions. This law was finally enacted after a series of mournful events in the country. Recently, an ever-increasing number of killings have been carried out by the husbands or household companions of victims of emotional and physical domestic violence.[2]

To promote and defend women's rights at the institutional level, Costa Rica created the office of the *Instituto Nacional de las Mujeres* (INAMU, the Women's National Institute), which safeguards women human rights in Costa Rica. INAMU has several branches throughout the country: its main task is to assist victims of physical or emotional violence, and support those who are victims of sexual violence throughout the judicial process, offering them psychological and social assistance by specialists in their respective fields—particularly during the judicial process.

WOMEN CREATING ECONOMIC CHANGE

From an economic point of view, women in Costa Rica are making great progress. As a consequence of their participation in the economy, women entrepreneurs are transforming our country's economic system. Women can be found in both the small and medium-sized enterprises, especially those devoted to the textile industry and handcraft and craftsmanship. Women leaders of large-scale enterprises can also be found. Those women, who at an early age become involved in the business world, have also entered into important international markets.

WOMEN'S IMPACT ON THE MEDIA

One can see an increasing number of Costa Rican women working for the media, including radio, television, and newspapers. From those influential platforms, they send their positive messages to the population, via the news media at national and international levels.

One of the most famous women journalists in our country is Pilar Cisneros, director of *Telenoticias*, a television news program that exerts a great influence on public opinion in Costa Rica. She brings women's issues to viewers and also has introduced them to news of other cultures and lands—an endeavor that expands our awareness. Costa Rican women have also been notably successful in international media. Glenda Umaña, for example, after succeeding in Costa Rica working as a news reporter, has now joined CNN in the U.S.; from there, she broadcasts the news in Spanish—a Costa Rican woman visible to the entire world.

As we can see the media has enabled Costa Rican women to project and express their views on the problems facing the country, and at the same time denounce criminal and corrupt acts, keeping the majority of Costa Rican households informed.

WOMEN TRANSFORMING THE LEGAL SYSTEM

Costa Rican women can also be found in international legal fields. Elizabeth Odio Benito, for example, is currently Vice-President of the International Criminal Court of Justice. Before that, she had been appointed Judge in the International Court for War Crimes committed in the former Yugoslavia. In Costa Rica, she has been appointed Minister of Justice, served office during two government periods, and then became Vice-President of the Republic. Her work in the defence of human rights embraces both academic research and college teaching, and advocacy and protection of fundamental people's rights anywhere in the world. She played an active role in the Human Rights Commission, as Special Ambassador, and the Head of the Mission of the Government of Costa Rica, in preparation for the World Conference on Human Rights held in Vienna in 1993. Her lifelong struggle for women's rights that had begun many years before this international event, greatly influenced the discussions and achievements of this Conference.

Odio's five-year work in the International Court of Justice (1993 to 1998), earned her admiration and respect both from the international legal community, and from civilian groups that work on the promotion and defense of human rights. As an ICJ Judge, she established jurisprudence in various areas of Humanitarian International Law, particularly with regards to crimes committed against women during armed conflicts. Before the War Crimes Tribunal for the former Yugoslavia, sexual violence against women during armed conflicts and wars were not considered war crimes. Her work in this field represented a major change, one that was later substantiated in the Court's rulings, and set essential precedents for the writing of the Statute of Rome that gave birth to the Permanent International Criminal Court.

THE ROLE OF INDIGENOUS WOMEN IN CREATING CHANGE

In this chapter, I cannot fail to mention Costa Rican Indigenous women, who play a very important role in our society. Nowadays, Indigenous women are struggling hard to protect themselves and their loved ones, and still maintain their dignity and cultural identity. Indigenous women face daily hardships in their reserves and the least they ask from the population of the rest of the country is respect to their cultural and family values. INAMU promotes national and specific public policies that will legally protect the identity of these peoples.

In Costa Rican Indigenous culture, the role of women is very different from that of Western society. The Indigenous family is matriarchal in nature; one in which family values and the social network is organized around a strong women's involvement in giving birth, raising and socializing children, and in providing economic support to her family. Thus, the most important social roles of Indigenous women are:

•Social work, community-focused;

•Reproductive, bearing and raising children; and
•Productive, for the extra work they perform at home.

As a good example, we know that in different areas of Talamanca, Costa Rica, Indigenous women bear the burden of maintaining their peoples' cultural traditions, a responsibility that makes them the most important or only bastion at home. They have to build their huts for her family, cultivate the land, take care of children, grind corn and cocoa to prepare food, and sometimes walk for hours or days to take their kids to the doctor, when there is the possibility for it—the child mortality rate among Indigenous populations is high due to lack of access to medical help. It is also their work to go out and get food, a job that will require hours away from their hut across the mountain to get to where the corn, rice, and bean—sometimes an occasional chayote plant—plantations grow.

The great majority of these women cannot read or write, and they live in dire conditions; poverty and strenuous work characterize their daily lives. It is sad that they have to build huts, cultivate the land and take care of children at the same time. They are the true and only responsible members of their families. As a consequence, Indigenous women are heads of their homes and work in "manly jobs" to make ends meet. Men, on the other hand, benefit from this traditional and inequitable distribution of labour. Eventually, greater equality in the distribution of family work and responsibilities between men and women will depend not only on social struggles the Indigenous women might undertake, but on how the reality and the hardships faced by Indigenous peoples of the rest of Latin America evolves, especially in the area of women and children's rights.

HIDDEN BUT NOT FORGOTTEN: THE WOMEN IN JAIL

Costa Rican women stand out in all areas of Costa Rican socio-economic and political life. But, in order to provide a wide view of Costa Rican women, I believe it is important to mention the female population that for various reasons is kept in custody in the jail system. These women undoubtedly play an important role in our society. The fact that they are inmates, and that their civil rights and liberties are therefore limited, does not minimize or take away their vital contribution to the Costa Rican society in general. This has been one of my major concerns as a legal rights attorney. In my own work, I have proposed that imprisoned mothers have separate quarters from the general population, and that they should not be separated from their children. Many of these women are victims of abuse and injustice, which often leads to drug abuse and crime.

Crime and punishment have historically been significantly differentiated by gender. Since laws have generally been created and executed by men, they tend to be primarily centered on men. As a consequence, Costa Rican women have been subject to legislation that has been and remains equal only for men. According to prevailing laws, therefore, people are not judged as individuals but as men and women. Feminist thoughts, such as those discussed earlier in this chapter regarding equal rights for all, have been prevalent in the issue of women sentenced for any type of crime. This also contributed to the development of the recognition of the rights of women subject to criminal sentences.

Women in our country are generally forced to play social roles that cause them to be dependent upon men. This is evidenced in the types of crimes committed by women, which generally fall into the category of offenses against public health, mainly the sale of drugs. In such crimes, it is usually men, their husbands or partners, who influence and convince women to get into the business of selling drugs, either to make a living or to increase family income. Of course, a situation like this cannot be generalized. There are cases in which, due to a change in women's social roles, they may well become the leaders of their own drug business.

Statistics show that women's participation in criminal activities is relatively low in number when compared to men. However, it seems that female heads of household represent the majority of the prison population in our country. One might ask "*Why?*"

In order to address this question, let's examine the most important women's prison in our country, the Institutional Care Center "*El Buen Pastor*," located in Desamparados, a county of Costa Rica's capital city of San Jose.

Throughout history, the recognition of women's rights has marked a fundamental aspect in the treatment given to women in the criminal enforcement programs, especially when addressing the issue of women in the jail system. Data from the Department of Research and Statistics, determined that the inmates of *El Buen Pastor* are usually women immersed in an atmosphere of emotional and material deprivation. Also, many of the studies related to this issue conclude that women deprived of their liberty are victims of violence by their peers. The studies show that the prison population is mostly women with domicile in the capital city, San José, and a reduced number from the provinces. They are usually single, heads of their household, with a low educational level.

Similarly, it was found that the vast majority of women belong to a low social class. All these factors definitively influence the commission of crimes, mainly the commission of crimes against public health, like drug selling, or crimes against private property, such as theft and robbery, among others.

Women inmates find chances inside the facilities to be busy and become productive. Some of the activities inside the prison include courses in sewing, handcrafts, ceramics, office cleaning, maintenance of green areas, cooking, telephone skills, as well as direct paid-work in the center workshops, contracted by private enterprises to produce postal packaging, paper bags, etc. Both enrollment and participation in some of these activities are free, but like the paid jobs, all are taken into account when calculating the time discounted from an inmate's original sentence. The most regrettable thing that was noted in the studies regarding inmates' work inside the prison is that job training programs that might lead to the effective reintegration of women to society are insufficient in number and quality.

The development of sports projects at *El Buen Pastor*, in collaboration with institutions like the University of Costa Rica, are intended to release tensions and strengthen the prisoners' will power to abandon drugs, even though drug withdrawal is also the main cause of problems of coexistence among inmates.

Unlike male prisons, *El Buen Pastor* has a greater number of female security officers. This guarantees the physical safety of prisoners, as well as the security and control of the facilities. Apparently, order and discipline are better kept because female officers are more respected by women inmates. *El Buen Pastor* offers also free formal educational courses, taught by professionals from universities or by volunteers from NGOs. These courses include Basic English, theater, guitar, arts and crafts. There is a special literacy program for prisoners provided by *Alpha Mujer* (Alpha Women), as well as a basic general education program providing high-school equivalency. Among the prisoners of *El Buen Pastor*, a large percentage have not completed elementary or secondary education; a low percentage are illiterate, while a small number possess a college degree.

Sadly, budgetary problems affect a number of aspects that make up for the stark reality of women in prison. In the absence of economic resources, private occupations of freedom are scarce, technical care is insufficient, and a lack of cleanliness and hygiene in the prison jails due to overcrowding is visible.

In spite of the fact that recently additional space has been added to *El Buen Pastor*, there are still many deficiencies in infrastructure. The building lacks an emergency plan in case of earthquake or fire. This situation works against not only the prisoners' safety or the jail personnel, but also against the inmates' children who live in *Casa Cuna*, the children's care center that is located inside the same prison.

Women's issues necessarily generate a need for differentiated treatment between women and men, as well as the need to normalize the treatment of women prisoners, especially when analyzing the situation of inmates who are mothers also, with babies and young children to take care of. Even with its greatest efforts, the jail system has not been able to adequately provide a solution to these mothers.

The need for a real separation of these women from the other inmates remains a great deficiency and an almost insurmountable challenge for authorities at *El Buen Pastor*, one that often exposes children to dangerous situations: A jail is never, and should never be, a place to raise a kid. It goes against Children's Rights and the International Convention on Children. Although we are a country without a military force, we still need to focus on bettering the lives of these women.

This is one of my own largest priorities in my own work.

CONCLUSION

Costa Rican women are definitely transforming the patriarchal model inherited from its past. These women are present in practically all spheres of national life. Their contributions are crucial for the progress of our country; a country recognized worldwide specifically because of its lack of armed forces and its visible promotion of international peace. It can be said that this alone represents an inherent feminine expression within this nation.

I am proud to be a Costa Rican and of the role of Costa Rican women have played both nationally and internationally, but I also know, to be realistic, that we are still far from being a completely egalitarian society. Women need to continue exerting and devoting their best efforts to assure the ideal manifests in positive change. Future generations, our sons and daughters, and theirs as well, will be grateful for our present involvement in the struggle to provide a better quality of life for all— Costa Ricans, and most of all its women, included.

In the stories related in this chapter, I offered some factual evidence on the contribution of Costa Rican women to society, both nationally and internationally, in the hope and intention that after reading this chapter, women and men from other countries will be inspired to join women in their struggles, to back up and promote their human rights for the benefit of all.

[1]José Federico Alberto de Jesús Tinoco Granados (1870-1931), was a general in the Costa Rica military. He was appointed Minister of War in President Alfredo Gonzalez's cabinet. He and his brother Jose Joaquin took advantage of this position and staged a *coup d'état* in which Tinoco seized presidential power. In so doing he established an extremely repressive dictatorship—a militaristic rule that crushed all opposition.

[2]As a side note to this essay, I must emphasize that from my lawyer's point of view, I do not totally agree with the Costa Rican Law on the Criminalization of Domestic Violence, due to a legal analysis that is not relevant here. I must admit, though, that the law represents a giant leap that leads to women' empowerment in the social, cultural and legal fields.

20.
Conscious Mothering

New Routes of Transformation

ELENA TONETTI-VLADIMIROVA, RUSSIA

This is birth: the torture of an innocent. What futility to believe that so great a cataclysm will not leave its mark. Its traces are everywhere—in the skin, in the bones, in the stomach, in the back. In all our human folly, in our madness, our tortures, our prisons. In legends, epics, myths. In the Scriptures.
—Dr. Frederick Leboyer (30)

WHERE I AM FROM, there is a popular saying: "A woman with a child is good, a woman with two children is a hero, a woman with three children is crazy." There is a sad truth to these words. In fact, growing up in Siberia in the 1950s, I did not have a single friend who had siblings.

The housing shortage was a big factor. The Soviet government was busy pretending to be a superpower, conquering both space and nations on Earth. At the same time, it failed to pay attention to its own people's basic needs. Russian winters are not a friendly environment for the homeless, so 60 percent of the nation was crammed three generations in one room in a communal apartment (where each room was occupied by a different family). These were the conditions in which I grew up until I turned thirteen. My mother refused to have another child simply because there was no place in our room to put another bed.

UNCONSCIOUS BIRTHING

The brutality of the Soviet system against its own population initiated a negative population growth. Since the beginning of World War One in Russia, when the Bolsheviks took over and established governmental birth houses in the late 1920s, barbaric attitudes prevailed in them. Women in my mother's generation had an average 23 abortions per woman—all performed without anesthesia. Abortion was the only available form of birth control in this atheistic country; sex education was not provided so there was limited knowledge about sexuality and procreation. Abortions were performed in the same "birth houses" where other women were giving birth, in special rooms that looked like slaughter houses with very long lines of frightened women every morning, waiting for their turn to be tortured.

In spite of the horror of those abortion rooms, women chose to go there, rather than have another child. The thought of giving birth in this environment was even more terrifying. The routine practice was to have all labouring women agonizing all together in the same place—just bare walls and lots of narrow beds. The women were frightened and also separated from their loved ones, with no attention from the staff whatsoever. They were stripped of their identities, badly shaved, given neither water nor food, never mind a friendly smile or advice, while being verbally abused by nurses—basically treated like cattle. Then of course, "when it was time," they were taken to the delivery room to be tied in stirrups, on their backs, crucified to the table, alone, facing the masked doctor and his helpers. No questions or spoken wishes were allowed.

Next the babies were taken away for five days.[1] Let me say it again, to make sure you understand: mothers were finally able to see their babies for the very first time five days after giving birth! During these first five days the newborns were fed sugary water with tranquilizers to keep them from crying. Healthy bonding and a sense of well-being were successfully eliminated in this barren model.

It's still like this in Russia in approximately 70 percent of births. One difference is that at this time, the babies are taken away from their mothers for three days rather than five. The other 30 percent of women are those who can afford a private facility. They are in a much better place as they can choose any type of support or method of delivery they desire. If they can pay, they can have just about anything. But the ability to pay is a huge obstacle among the impoverished population. Women go into enormous debts to be able to go to a private clinic.

THE WINDS OF STORM AND CHANGE

During the 1980s, Russia was boiling with activities, ideas, passions, hopes.... Winds of change were swirling in the air. We *were* the Change! Women were coming out of the dormant state that had kept us submissive for the last millennium and claiming our role in the various arenas of life! What had been suppressed for so long was not willing to be quiet any more. People were snapping out of mass hypnosis and taking charge of their own lives. There had never been a shortage of brilliant, well-educated people in Russia. Unfortunately, there was always a shortage of intelligence in the government itself.

At that time, numerous charismatic leaders emerged locally all over the country. They worked tirelessly in their own communities to make life richer and the future brighter. Life might have drastically improved if they had received some support from the Gorbachev administration. Instead the government conducted a coldhearted sabotage of all grassroots efforts, putting a wet blanket over every initiative, while pocketing billions of dollars of humanitarian aid and taking all of the credit for the positive changes that were happening in spite of the ruling strategies.

In 1982, I met Igor Charkovsky, one of the most complex men I've ever met. This powerful psychic healer, awkward in most social situations, was the beloved Russian water birth pioneer. He, in one breath, (well, it took about four hours), explained to me what is at stake in the process of people-making. He drew a clear picture of the connection between our experience of being born, from the moment of conception through the formative period of the first few years of life. He noted how this experience, along with the quality of our lives, our behavioural patterns and tendencies, influenced our capacity to love, to be kind, healthy, intelligent—or not.

Everything he was saying made sense! He was connecting the dots for me. He explained that it was useless for us to try to improve the quality of our society while ignoring the damaging experience occurring in the very beginning of life. I was learning that we are bound to an experience of misery as a society, unless we alter "the basic settings" in our nervous system, which we acquire in the very beginning of our lives.

When I understood the depth of this implication, I didn't need a second invitation to put all I had—my time and energy—into helping organize young people into what became the "Conscious Procreation" Movement. We organized classes of birth preparation, also attended by future fathers— an entirely new concept in my country! With every new couple that came to the circle, we learned new things, because of the differences each couple brought to the experiences. We noticed that what worked for some people was not necessarily the right thing for others. It was an exciting time of exploring, paying attention, and creating new ways of living! The ultimate culmination of our willingness to be open to this new paradigm included summer birth camps at the

Black Sea, where many babies were born in shallow lagoons, in the presence of wild dolphins.

The idea to have labouring women in water came to Igor in 1962 when he was looking for ways to relieve a baby's brain from the shock of gravity.[2] He considered this to be the main reason why the human brain is not fully available for our use. He explained that whales and dolphins have a much better use of their brains, on levels unreachable for humans, because they are not exposed to gravity shock at birth. As proof of their higher intelligence, Charkovsky pointed out that they were not territorial and did not kill their own. He suggested that the concussion human beings experience as we emerge from the weightless environment of the womb is far more devastating than understood. By the time we grow up and the function of cognitive development and related understanding is available to us, we have no reference point to compare our brain power to what it could have been if we had not been, literally, smacked on the head by the immense pressure of gravity. Many conscious parents were eager to experience a healthier way of birthing their babies—and our program offered a way to do this.

Every couple that came to the birth camp went through the full program of preparation during pregnancy and gained enough confidence and skill to have an amazingly beautiful, empowering experience, delivering their own baby with minimum interference from the outside world. Hundreds of babies were born that way—consciously, gracefully, naturally. This new birthing paradigm stood in stark contrast to the patriarchal paradigm of the past. We were rediscovering our right to take control of the birthing process.

CHANGING PATTERNS—CHANGING OUR FUTURE!

And why is it so critical for us to understand the importance of healthy, happy gestation and birth? Why is it so important to make every effort to eliminate the birth trauma from a delivery? The answer is fairly simple and direct—it impacts our sense of identity and therefore our future in a very big way.

The new baby, long before, during and right after birth, is an extremely sensitive being—in fact, more sensitive than he or she will ever be during adult life. They non-cognitively absorb vast amounts of information in this early stage. But despite having all those sensations and feelings, the baby will not consciously remember them. Those early impressions stay with us for the rest of our lives, for better or worse, on a cellular level, in our deep subconscious. In fact, 25 years of research in the field of perinatal psychology reveals, without doubt, a direct correlation between the conditions of birth and our later behavioural and emotional patterns during adulthood (see APPPAH). This mechanism is called the "limbic imprint."

Limbic imprinting can be likened to the following example. Every computer, TV, camera, etc. has basic settings. Imagine that your TV is set on the maximum blue tone, then, no matter what movie is shown on the screen, everything will be blue! Or if the brightness is set on "dim," then no matter how bright the image is, you will see a dark picture.

This exact mechanism is at work with all mammals. It has been used for thousands of years to train animals to serve people in hard labour and wars—elephants, camels, horses, circus bears. For example, a baby elephant is routinely tied in the yard on a chain. The young elephant rages all his might for a few days and then stops. When he grows up and has enough strength to break the chain, he will no longer make the attempt.

The basic structure of our brain contains three parts. The reptilian brain, located in the stem of the brain,[3] is responsible for our physiology—breathing, flow of fluids, survival, instinctual function. This is the part of the brain that remains functional even when a person is in a coma. For example, the comatose person is still considered alive, women continue to menstruate and continue with gestation if pregnant, because the reptilian brain is still functioning in an attempt to survive.

The cortex, usually referred to as the "gray matter" portion of the brain, is related to our higher mental activity, for example, cognitive functions such as logic, memory; calculating, etc. (This development also allows a woman to make choices for healthier birthing processes when circumstances permit such choices.)

The limbic system is located between the cerebral cortex and the reptilian brain. The limbic system is associated with our emotions, sensations and feelings. Limbic imprinting happens in this section of the brain, a development that is not directly connected with our rational cortex, responsible for cognitive memory. During gestation, birth and early childhood, the limbic system registers all of our sensations and feelings without translating it into the language of the cortex, simply because the cerebral cortex is undeveloped yet. *But,* it is important to recognize that memory of the limbic experiences will continue in the body whether we are aware of it or not. Instinctual fear and related aggression, emotional body memories and later cognitive abilities are all impacted by our emotional experiences during the formative period.

When our early primal experience is tender and loving, our nervous system is imprinted with a deep sense of wellbeing. Being held in the mother's loving arms, feeding from her breast and seeing great joy in her eyes, provides us with a natural sense of bliss and security; it sets the world as the right place for us to be. If our first impressions are less than loving, then *that* imprints as our basic mode of operation. It will be recognized by our nervous system as "comfort zone," regardless of how painful, frustrating and undesirable the experience actually was.

As adults, we will unconsciously re-create those feelings and tend to attract similar circumstances. Research conducted by the pioneers of perinatal psychology, such as David Chamberlain, Thomas Verny, and William Emerson revealed an overwhelming amount of physical and behavioural disorders during adult life are the direct result of traumatic experiences during our formative period, including unnecessary medical interventions, chemical stimulation, elective cesareans, circumcision, injections, separation from mother right after birth, lack of breastfeeding, loud noises, bright lights, etc.

We are all subject to the responses related to excruciating labour pains or into the numbness and toxicity of anesthesia, and thereby imprinted for suffering and/or numbness. Traumatic birth strips us of our power and impairs our capacity to love, trust, be intimate and experience our true potential. Addictions, aggression, poor problem-solving skills, low self-esteem, inability to be compassionate and responsible—all these problems have been linked to birth trauma. This is vitally important to all women, as we are the mothers of the human race.

It is easy to observe this imprint of separation and loneliness is at work in Russia. People are rarely able to support and acknowledge one another, to work harmoniously on a project. The imprint of being alone was embedded in the limbic system by the end of the fifth day in the birth house, as newborns gave up the expectation of somebody out there, in this universe, being there for them. That's why it's so difficult for people to hear each other or to form healthy, committed relationships.

CONSCIOUS BIRTHING

But it doesn't have to be this way. Giving birth can be a huge opportunity for healing, a rite of passage, and an initiation into Motherhood. So much can be done to prepare for a dignified delivery! It is really worth it to invest our time and attention into learning how to give birth without suffering. Birth is never just about birth. It reflects our *past* and defines our *future*. We owe it to our children to do what we can to provide them with a safe world.

Normally, a woman gives birth the way she herself was born, due to the same mechanism of limbic imprint. In my own story, I was helping many others to birth their babies in natural ways, but never planned to have children of my own. My excuse was overpopulation, that it's better to take care of those children that are already here, instead of making more. Although these are valid concerns, at some point I realized that my excuses were covering up my own sheer terror of giving birth. It was impossible for me to even imagine surviving the process. This had been a very deep blind spot in my psyche. As dedicated as I was to helping others, I never experienced the program of healing for myself until this realization.

I still consider a woman's conscious decision to not have a child and, instead, to dedicate her creative energy to other valuable endeavors to be a valid, respectable choice. But that decision needs to be made from the place of power, not because of her fear of giving birth. Like any other important decision in life, the choice should be made *towards* the desirable outcome, and not out of need to run *away* from something.

It took many years for me to even start wanting *to want* a baby. With my own birth trauma, from being born so poorly, I had a lot of ground to cover. So, I had to start my life from scratch, this time consciously. I succeeded, apparently, and my daughter was born in 1990. In this process, I truly felt myself entering into full womanhood.

A NEW PARADIGM FOR BIRTHING

Since 1982, I have been attentively observing children who were unharmed during gestation and birth. They had dedicated parents who were honestly doing their best to raise them. Of course, growing up they experienced their share of challenges—it is a harsh environment in Russia. But these young people born in healthy and loving conditions are gifted with an amazing and soulful strength, which allows them to meet their challenges. I believe the future of Russia belongs to these kids. Yet, in spite of all of our advanced understanding, a few years ago the Russian government issued a decree prohibiting home births—robbing women of the choice for peaceful, dignified delivery. Our early work has had a huge impact on other nations though.

In the four countries with the best birth practices in the world, Netherlands, Sweden, Finland, and Switzerland, 70 percent of all births are natural. These are also the four countries with the highest standards of living and the lowest rates of crime and poverty. And the worst few countries in the world in maternity care scores are the same countries

244

with the worst standards of living and the worst crime rates. Is it a coincidence?

It used to be thought that the baby did not have any senses and memory and for many doctors this still remains a major debate. As a result of these limited beliefs, surgeries on infants were done without anesthesia, performed with paralyzing agents to keep the newborn quiet. Circumcision is a primary example of this offence to the newborn infant. Even though research results have been available for fifteen years, supporting the sensitivity of this new and developing human being, in most places in the world, babies are still treated inappropriately harshly. A traumatic beginning in life can influence self-destructive tendencies and a tendency towards addictions and violence in general. As women rise to our motherly tasks of protecting the lives that are being born, this will change.

The good news is that we can recognize that however tragic our own beginnings, we do have a choice as adults to transmute our suffering and helplessness during birth into the love and joy of being born on this planet. I invite readers to envision the possibilities that would open up for humankind if women fully claimed their birthright as mothers, human mammals, with the capacity to give birth and raise our young without trauma.

I have been teaching seminars about neutralizing our own birth trauma and healthy, Conscious Procreation throughout the world and now have apprentices in 22 countries. I see the results first-hand. For instance, I recently received an email from Costa Rica where a young mother and father described the following experience (one of thousands emails I receive from all over the world):

"Our son arrived following a magical night of labour, low light of the candles, silence and the rhythm of my respiration. It was intense pain yet without suffering, similar to any other process of purification.

"Sensibility and awareness were higher than I have ever experienced before. I felt at one with my body, my spirit, and so far away from my mind. There was no space for "thinking" as, intuition was my guide, as well as the knowledge I was experiencing from my own body. Each contraction drew the way in which we will meet our baby—going back to the primal state of my mamiferal nature.

"This newborn opened his eyes, for the first time, when the head was out of my body but his own body was still inside of me. The first minute of his life in this world was under the vital liquid water!

"Gustavo, my partner, who has always supported me, received the baby into his arms while he was still under water. He took the baby from under my legs and I embraced him. I showed him the sky over the place we were in as he heard the river flowing and the bamboo singing. I gave him thanks for choosing us as his family, and as well I gave thanks to the Great Mother and Great Spirit father for this beautiful gift! Finally, I asked the baby about his sex as I gently pulled up one of his little legs ... and he showed us after all these months of wondering that this new being is a boy!

"His eyes are grey and [he has] light brown hair.... We are in love. There is no space for anything but love in this family. This is our nourishment.

"We are already learning from him. Now, we are his guides and guardians, and he is ours."

I learned that this Costa Rican young couple had seen my video, *Birth As We Know It,* and that this had a big impact on their preparation for this natural, underwater birth.

We made ourselves believe that birthing is a medical emergency; but now we are paying dearly for that concept. Technological birth, mechanical or chemical extraction of the baby's body from the mother's body creates a technocratic view of life, removed from the capacity to allow a deep sense of wellbeing within our souls. In many places on Earth, birth by Caesarean-section has now reached 95 percent. It is believed to be a norm. This is something very different than genuine medical emergencies, when it's a blessing that these doctors are well-trained and available. When that is the case, then C-section actually becomes a positive imprint—"help comes when you really need it!"

OBSTACLES AND POSSIBILITIES:
MOVING TOWARD A PARADIGM OF NATURAL BIRTH

Natural birth does require some preparation nowadays, because the art of birthing is almost lost. Only a hundred years ago the male medical model took over the art that had previously belonged to the midwives. In tribal life it was supposed to be a mother's gift to her daughter—an obvious transmission. But with modern-day stress levels and easy access to drugs, the birthing process has basically become a form of genocide against the human race. This may read like a harsh judgment, but I have noticed that there exists an enormous resentment towards a blissful, happy birth, almost on every level—religious, social, financial, economic, political, mental, and emotional—for as a society, we fear birth and believe that it is the most terrifying event. It can only occur with proper suffering (a model often perpetuated by fundamentalist religious beliefs that women are being punished for "Eve's sin"). Birth is viewed as a state of medical emergency that places new parent(s) in debt.

But women are waking up. We now have hundreds of thousands of women who did not buy into this mass hypnosis. They have broken the spell, for themselves and for their children. They have found what it takes to prepare for dignified, empowering ways of giving birth and raising their children free from being programmed that life begins and continues with pain.

The art of *people-making* should be taught in schools! It is maybe one of the most important skills we need. If women learn to procreate consciously, the following generations will not repeat our mistakes, and a healthier society will be the result—a humanity at peace with itself and therefore with others. Educating children about their future role as parents is critical in raising a healthy, harmonious society.

One of the most important things to remember about birth is that it is not a mechanical event, but a major spiritual experience. A new human being, who did not exist before, coming into existence—it is a major miraculous event. We know nothing about it, really. We can observe stages of gestation and feel that we are somehow familiar with the process, but we are not even close to truly understanding it! Regardless of what modern science states about what it looks like, it fails to truly explain why and how it's happening, what forces are at play in creating every new generation of cells.

Another huge revelation is that most birth complications are avoidable. Conscious birth assures a healthier child, family and healthier society.

Conscious Procreation, as a general approach, and when it will become a part of mass mentality, is a portal into our species' ability to thrive. It is a big philosophical issue—consider the initial "programming" of humans to experience pain and difficulty as a norm. This programming occurs whether we are aware of it or not, but if we program ourselves to experience nurturing, respect and a sense of safety, we all will benefit from this transformation. We can move beyond the paradigm of continuous conflict and war. There are so many wars going on right now all over the globe. We have also created life-threatening levels of environmental pollution, political systems that don't work, economies that are not capable of sustaining us and social strategies that ignore the needs of the people. We are, clearly, due for change. If we truly understand how we created this mess, we have a good chance to un-create it. One sure way is to change the way we are born.

CONCLUSION

Violence has been a norm among humans for thousands of years. But it is not our true nature. Babies who were protected from the sensory and emotional trauma during their formative period, are free from aggression and are very kind.

It is impossible to have a deep sense of wellbeing if you have never known what it is supposed to feel like. First things first: we need to create that reference point within ourselves. We cannot thrive as a species, unless we create a new generation that was not damaged *in utero* by a high level of stress hormones in the mother's blood stream. The damage persists across generations: if the basic foundation of our emotions is built on our mothers' *anxiety*, *pain*, and *fear*, we must understand that our mothers were once babies, too—they were subjected to *their* mothers' grief. Given the violent history of humankind, probably less than two percent of people who have ever lived have been born peacefully, without high stress.

Do we, the people, want to continue our militaristic behaviours again and again? Can we, instead, establish higher priorities of *love*, *safety*, and *deep connectedness*? Then, as a species, we will truly have a chance for happy life. Aggressive behaviours are rare among healthy, loving people.

Conscious conception and birth are an integral part of conscious living. When parents create a new baby in full awareness of the effect their actions and thoughts have on their unborn child, these non-traumatized children will display an amazing degree of intelligence, kindness, common sense, good health and ingenuity. They will grow to be good communicators, caring, alert, and self-motivated. I truly believe that we can improve the quality of our species in just one generation! Join me in this vision.

[1]This was also the model in the United States in the 1960s when first "hippies," and later feminists, spoke out against this patriarchal model and advocated a return to natural birthing.

[2]Like the proverbial Newtonian apple, imagine how the egg yolk falls into a glass of water and stays round! Now imagine that if it had fallen on the pan, it would have had to obey the law of gravity and go flat.

The logical solution was to have baby's head emerge into water which serves as a buffer zone, giving the brain some time to adjust to the new environment.

[3]This deeper and older level of the brain was named as part of the "triune brain," that represents the oldest part of the brain's evolutionary development. This was named by neuroscientist and medical physician, Paul MacLean, during the 1960s. The reptilian complex, also known as the R-complex or "reptilian brain" was the name MacLean gave to the *basal ganglia*, structures derived from the floor of the forebrain during development (cited in Lewis, Amini and Lannon).

REFERENCES

American Association of Prenatal and Perinatal Psychology and Health (APPPAH). Web.

Buckley, Sarah. *Gentle Birth, Gentle Mothering: A Doctor's Guide to Natural Childbirth and Gentle Early Parenting*. Berkeley, CA: Celestial Arts, 2008. Print.

Chamberlain, David B. *The Mind of Your Newborn Baby*. 3rd ed. Berkeley, CA: North Atlantic Books, 1998. Print.

Chamberlain, David B. "Prenatal Intelligence." *Prenatal Perception, Learning and Bonding*. Ed. Thomas Blum. Berlin: Leonardo Publishers, 1993. 14-21. Print.

Chamberlain, David B. *Windows to the Womb: Revealing the Conscious Baby from Conception to Birth*. Berkeley, CA: North Atlantic Books, 2013. Print.

Emerson, William R. "Birth Trauma: The Psychological Effects of Obstetrical Interventions." *Journal of Prenatal and Perinatal Psychgology and Health* 30.1 (1998): 11-44. Web.

Gaskin, Ina May. *Ina May's Guide to Childbirth*. New York: Bantam, 2003. Print.

Leboyer, Frédérick. *Birth Without Violence*. New York: Knopf, 1975. Print.

Lewis, Thomas, Fari Amini and Richard Lannon. *A General Theory of Love*. New York: Random House, 2000. Print.

Tonetti-Vladimirova, Elena, dir. *Birth As We Know It*. 245 min. DVD. Prod. E. Tonetti. Co-Prod. C. K. Borthwick and George C. Denniston.

Verny, Thomas. *The Secret Life of the Unborn Child: How You Can Prepare Your Baby for a Happy, Healthy Life*. New York: Dell, 1981. Print.

21.
Women Politicians in One
of the World's Most Equal Countries

MAGDALENA ANDERSSON, SWEDEN

ANY DISCUSSION ON WOMEN'S SITUATION and opportunities depends on where in the world it takes place. As expected, it's different being a woman in Sweden as opposed to elsewhere in the world. Sweden is—along with its Nordic neighbours—one of the most equal countries in the world. The World Economic Forum's *Gender Gap Report* often gives Sweden top ranking, and in 2009 Sweden held the number four spot out of 130 countries surveyed (Hausmann, Tyson and Zahidi). Thus, one could argue that it's almost impolite to complain about the situation in Sweden—at least in comparison to other countries that don't have our childcare and professional opportunities for women etc. But let me be clear. There is no "quick fix" in terms of equality. There are no simple solutions and any solution must be adapted to the individual country.

THE SITUATION IN SWEDEN

In spite of Sweden's internationally-recognized equality, there still are great differences between men and women in Sweden. A woman is underpaid compared to a man holding an identical position. Wage drift is almost always advantageous to men regardless of occupation. Women are more often part-time employed than men. Women are also more often over-qualified for the positions they hold. This includes both voluntary as well as involuntary part-time employment.

At the same time, women still assume the main responsibility for unpaid domestic duties such as housekeeping, laundry, cooking, grocery shopping etc. Businesses run by women tend to be smaller, have fewer employees and have lower turnover. Female business owners are outnumbered one to three compared to their male counterparts. Surveys show that women are likely to receive inferior medical care compared to men. Domestic violence is, as elsewhere in the world, a serious problem. Women are left in charge of raising children, and children are more likely to interact with women than with men outside their homes.

Between 90-96 percent of childcare workers, kindergarten teachers and kindergarten supervisors are women. At the other end of life, women represent the overwhelming majority of caregivers for aging parents, both their own and their spouses'. At the same time, girls tend to have better grades than boys in elementary and high school, and are more successful in university.

So, in spite of Sweden's top-ranking equality status, there's still room for improvement. It's therefore of paramount importance that we elect political representatives who see these needs and are willing and eager to change this situation. Women are needed in politics!

Seven parties are represented in our Swedish parliament. We have the Left Party (former communists), the Social Democrats, the Center Party, the Liberals, the Christian Democrats and my own choice—the Moderate Party (considered liberal-conservative or centre-right on the Swedish political spectrum). At present, there is no outright xenophobic or anti-immigrant party represented in Parliament, but there's great concern that this will change in future elections.

THE MODERATE WOMEN—A SHORT INTRODUCTION

The Moderate Women is a network within the Moderate Party. We are a network of women who share a moderate ideology as well as being members of the Moderate Party. We want to form a society for both men and women, where everyone is equally important and equally needed. This train of thought has always been at the core of the Moderate policy platform. We work to encourage women to get involved politically. We believe that our politics will benefit from this development. Founded in 1912, the Moderate Women is independent of the Party in terms of working procedures and organization. Our objective is three-fold: to attract more women into the political process, to increase female representation, and to raise women's issues in public debate. We want men and women to have the same opportunities in life regarding education, professional development and in politics. We feel that it is indisputable that one should be able to combine a professional career with raising a family.

One of the core principles of the Moderate Party is that it shall have competent and diverse representation on all levels. This calls for active participation everywhere—regardless of gender. Many women have knowledge and experiences that are needed in politics. Thus, we'd like the number of women in politics to increase to the point that at least 40 percent of all senior positions are held by women in the coming years.

The Moderate Women is led by a central board of directors. In addition, each county has a regional chairwoman, with her own organization. As well, all local chapters of the Moderate Party have a designated spokesperson on women's issues. On both national and local level, our main tasks consist of political work, e. g., education and training, member recruitment, promotion of female party representatives and raising women's issues in the public debate. Thus, new and better conditions are created that will further extend women's presence within the party in terms of increased female representation.

Together with the party, the local chairwomen design the political activities in accordance with their own preferences, e.g., through local networks or various project teams. The local chairwomen and the board of directors meet at a twice-yearly council, in the spring and fall. Every other year, the spring council is replaced by an assembly of all members. The chairwoman of the Moderate Party is a member of the Party Board of Directors and its executive sub-committee.

THE MISSING WOMEN

No single country in the world—not even Sweden—has a female majority in parliament. There are a number of reasons why female politicians are under-represented in the higher echelons of political power. One is that men prefer to promote other men and women thus become excluded from senior positions. A variety of "master suppression techniques" are used by some men in a systematic fashion to exclude women from the circles of power and influence. [1]

Another reason is the women themselves. A great number of competent and diligent women have been approached and encouraged to run for high political offices, but unfortunately they decline the opportunity. This is often due to lack of self-confidence and the absence of female role-models who can inspire other women.

Some twenty years ago, the Moderate Women realized that further efforts were necessary in order to promote the presence of women in politics more actively. We also wanted more women elected to (high) political offices. Women were under-represented on every level, both locally and nationally. If women weren't represented on the highest levels, women's issues would be lost in the public debate and less likely to get the attention they deserved.

Almost all exit polls from the last elections show that men and women, as demographic groups, have different political preferences when selecting and voting for a political party. Men tend to focus on "hard" issues such as taxes, defense and infrastructure whereas women pay more attention to social issues, environment and equality. Hence, it's not that strange if parties with few women in senior positions also suffer from lack of female support and female voters. Therefore, it should be in all political parties' interest to ensure an even gender distribution in addition to promoting and debating issues that appeal to women.

MANAGEMENT TRAINING

In light of this, the Moderate Women initiated a high-level training program aimed at women in politics. The objective was to provide women with the support, inspiration and encouragement that so many women need in order to develop as politicians. This training program is still ongoing and is one of the most sought-after programs in the Moderate Party.

Every year, some twenty women from all over Sweden are accepted into the program, which lasts for two and a half years and takes place on weekends. It's aimed at women with some political experience, e.g., being a member of a city council, chairing a committee or having gained similar experience elsewhere. The candidate should be inspired by the program goals, have the aspiration to gain additional political knowledge and to grow further politically. These traits are essential if the candidate is to become ready for more challenging political positions.

The program covers a great variety of topics and issues, such as political debating, current affairs, political ideology, influencing the public debate, media relations and leadership skills. Demands are set very high and the program hones the candidates' political skills through idea formulation, shaping the political debate and implementing policy. Attendance is mandatory all through the program and some homework is required.

Other training programs are also offered by the Moderate Women, for example, on how to hold meetings or political rhetoric. We also try hard to assist women who are interested in serving as board members in government-owned companies.

Women holding high political offices often feel isolated. They don't have anyone to talk to. They miss that someone who can provide counsel and support when confronted with hard decisions on both political as well as organizational issues. Therefore, some years ago we launched another program that was solely aimed at women holding high political office at the municipal and county level, i.e. mayors and local governors. We wanted to create a network of women with similar experiences and thus enable them to establish a common platform for future interaction which would, in the long run, aid them mutually. This program became a big success and was greatly appreciated by the participants.

Our program successes are numerous and plentiful. Many of our participants now serve as mayors or local governors. Our present government, which is led by our Moderate Party, includes two female cabinet secretaries, the Minister for International Development Cooperation and the Minister for Social Security. Both have attended our training programs. I myself attended the program in the 1990s. I still think it's one of the best training programs I have ever attended in terms of providing inspiration.

CONCLUSIONS

More women are needed in politics. Not because they are women, but because better decisions are made if the politicians making them represent the *entire* population, instead of just part of the population. It's a huge challenge for all political parties to promote women, to provide opportunities for women and to encourage women to run for high political offices. The utility and value pertaining to our training program efforts cannot be overestimated. Our efforts in this regard were—and still are—invaluable to women and to our party when it comes to supporting and promoting women in politics.

One of my favourite quotations (of many) by Madeleine Albright, the former U.S. Secretary of State and U.S. Ambassador to the United Nations, is this: "There's a place in Hell reserved for women who don't help other women." I myself believe there is a special place *in Heaven* for women who *do* help other women.

[1]Master Suppression Techniques. The following examples include a number of the techniques of domination or negative control observed by Norwegian researcher and former MP Berit Ås. These are (1) Invisibility: those who aren't seen or shown interest feel insignificant

and insecure; (2) Ridicule: made to feel embarrassed, ashamed and uninteresting; (3) Exclusion from information: "being left out of the loop"; (4) Double punishment: "damned if you do, and damned if you don't," e.g., women can be criticized for not prioritizing their children while simultaneously being criticized for neglecting their duties; and, (5) Imposition of guilt and shame: if you feel systematically inferior, it is easy to feel guilt and shame.

REFERENCES

Ås, Berit. *Managing Visions from Invisibility to Visibility.* Amsterdam: Bernardijn ten Zeldam stichting, 1989. Print.

Hausmann, Ricardo. Laura D. Tyson and Saadia Zahidi. *The Global Gender Gap Report 2009.* Geneva: World Economic Forum, 2009. Web.

22.
And God Created Circles

RUFAIDA AL HABASH, SYRIA

The Name of Allah, the Most Compassionate, the Most Merciful

ALLAH'S DESTINY is far beyond any human's ability of understanding and reason. No one knows the hidden secrets of our destiny, or even why it is that sometimes the disasters that fall upon us should be considered a blessing. How is it that one who has lost their home due to misfortune can turn to God and be thankful? We all must struggle to realize that all things have a silver lining, even the worst events in our lives. All of humankind struggle with this at some point in their lives, including myself. In the end, really it is not the disaster that befalls us that should shape us, but how we overcome such a struggle and the path we take to do so. That is what truly makes us who we are. We must always ask ourselves how we can benefit from each situation for the greater good. During my lifetime I have faced many struggles; some I faced alone, and others with my friends, family and neighbours. My story is long and full of both suffering and great joy, but here I will focus on my journey to establish women's freedom in Islam, in the city of Hama, Syria. It was far from an easy journey, but one I look back on with humble pride knowing that I have not only established freedom for women in my generation but hopefully, in many generations to come.

It all began more than 30 years ago when I had to face one of the most difficult decisions in my life, or so I thought. Now looking back, I realize this time in my life was just a stepping stone to many more struggles that I would soon learn to overcome. I was born and raised in Damascus, a fairly large city in a very small country. My city is known as the oldest continuously inhabited city in the world. It is where Jesus once spread his blessings, and where scholars of many great religions once taught. The magic in my city is incomparable to that of any other city. Many people from Damascus have moved on to other parts of the world but the city itself always remains in their hearts. Islam was strong in the hearts of those in Damascus. The muezzin was heard in every part of the city, and to me it was the most beautiful in the whole country. My youth was filled with many happy memories there. My mother and father brought me up in the highest standards of Islam; we were highly educated, and under the constant teaching of God's love and mercy in every aspect of our lives. Family members were well known for their righteousness, wisdom, and high morals. They were well renowned for their ability to deal with people of all levels of faith and backgrounds. My family, friends, teachers, my whole life was in Damascus. I never dreamed I would ever live anywhere else—it was just impossible, and completely unimaginable.

When I had just begun my religious studies at the institute with Sheikh Ahmad Kuftaro, my brothers' friend—also a student of the Sheikh—approached my parents for my hand in marriage. I was very excited for this new stage in my life, but when I learned my husband-to-be was from Hama, a city more than 200 kilometers away, I became confused and reluctant to accept such a proposal. I would have to leave everything behind and begin a new life in a strange city. At that time, travel between the two cities was difficult and much longer than the three hours it is today. And it was certainly far more dangerous. This only increased the difficulty in this decision. I still hadn't finished my college degree at the religious institute and I had no idea what was waiting for me in my new city. To me, Hama seemed a lifetime away, somewhere at the other end of the universe. Yet, it was still my choice to marry this man: how could I resist such a suitable man for me? I decided to embrace this new journey with courage and the strength only God could give me.

When I arrived in Hama in 1976, I found that religious freedom was at its highest point. At each mosque there were *dhikr* circles, classes and gatherings to remember Allah, and even in the homes of the rich and famous people would gather for such events. You couldn't find a nanosecond of time that didn't have some type of religious gathering happening during this time. In some ways it was like a religious paradise. However, even though the people were free to seek Islamic knowledge it was still very biased in regards to women. Women were free to seek knowledge but it was always influenced in some way by Sheikhs and religious men who believed a women's place was in the home. The freedom to learn religion was only surface deep.

Even with all of these religious gatherings, tradition and culture still had their place. Traditionally, women during this time were treated as third class citizens, deprived of their rights and liberties for no reason. The men had all the rights to control everything regarding the women in their families, including preventing them from being educated or leaving the house even to go and see their own mothers. I never had seen such misfortune among women before in my life. These were the minor offences; unfortunately, it would almost always go further and many times women were even denied their rights to their inheritances. Women certainly were not allowed to express opinions; it was the man's opinion at the time that women had no mind of their own, and certainly no comprehension of life. Women were very sad, and hopeless; you could see it in their eyes, feel it in their spirits. The worst of all of this was that it was done in the name of God, under the flag of religion. Men were justifying their decisions and acts as their "religious duty" to keep women in line. It was a man's greatest duty and honour to convince the women that their only purpose and duty on this earth were to serve men and the home, and in so doing, the woman in turn was serving God. Change had no place in this society; things were the way they were and that was that. It was such a contrast to my city which during this same time was religious, even perhaps considered conservative, yet open and much more tolerant of change. In Damascus, women were treated as equals in Islam. We had the right to be educated and to take ownership of our lives, and these rights stemmed directly from Islam.

Fortunately, I was one of the lucky women in Hama during that time, and I thank God everyday that my husband had an open mind, and more importantly that he was well educated in Islam; he knew clearly the proper manner of a man in dealing with his wife and other women in his family according to the and Islamic Law. We both shared the same goal in life, calling people to God's path—the path of peace and love. I felt blessed to have found such a wise man, but still couldn't understand how I would ever spend my life in Hama.

How could I possibly teach women about the love of God, about their rights and freedoms according to Islam in a closed society that has continually been teaching women otherwise? Firstly, how would I even meet the women since they were all locked away in their homes? Secondly, even if I did have the opportunity to meet and gather these women how would I begin teaching them? How was I to ever convince them that what I spoke was the truth? Where to begin when so many of the women were illiterate and merely learned what their husbands and fathers had told them? I soon began to realize that my dilemma in marrying and moving so far away was truly another dilemma in the making, but at the same time I began to understand why I had been sent to Hama. This could only be one thing—God's calling. I had to push forward, and continue the struggle. I could not refuse the path that God had chosen for me. Somehow I had to find a way to free these women from their chains of the traditional culture and customs that had locked them away and kept them from seeing the sun and God's glorious creations in all its beauty. The women of Hama needed to know how important they were in building and developing society, and that this was delegated to them in Islam. These women needed to know that Allah loved them as much as the men, that they too were important and intelligent and capable of learning and having opinions. I had little idea what lay ahead for me, yet I pushed on as that was my duty to God.

CIRCLES OF WOMEN

In the beginning, I held gatherings for women in my mother-in-law's home to teach Qur'an recitation and memorization as well as *Tafsir*, the meaning of the Qur'an. I used the opportunity of women visiting my mother-in-law's home to spread the word that I was available and ready to have such classes. I organized the girls in circles of ten. In contrast to the traditional schools, with young boys sitting in rows learning Qur'anic recitation. I used to sit with them in the circle so that I could see and hear all of them, and so that they could see me. This way of sitting is also useful for the girls as each is also able to see me and notice how I pronounce the letters of the Qur'an—even perhaps without realizing it, they will pay attention to the science of *Tajweed* (proper elocution) indirectly. On the other hand, when the student meets the teacher's eye, she will feel the teacher's closeness and love and be influenced by the teacher's words. This psychological element aids the learning process.

My method of teaching recitation is based on the method of *Talqeen*; that is, I read a short verse loudly, and then the girls repeat it together. Then every girl recites the verse from the Qur'an by herself while everyone listens. Next, the girls close their Qur'ans and we recite together from memory. I then ask "who can recite the verse by heart alone?" I find this method of teaching Qur'an recitation to be very successful, as one after another, all the girls learn to recite the short verse by heart, and my assistants still follow this method of circle recitation.

I had been in Hama for only two weeks before I began my work. This was a very new and exciting experience for me. All my life I had only dreamed of sharing my love of Islam with others; finally I had the chance and the door was wide open. I felt very blessed to be given such an opportunity. It wasn't long before many, many more women joined our gatherings. Yet it sometimes felt overwhelming to have such a responsibility resting on my shoulders. I put all my trust in Allah; I knew firmly that what was meant to be, will be, and continued in my work for the next four years.

In 1980, I left with my husband for a year abroad in France and Belgium. Being away from my work for that year felt like an eternity. When I came back, I immediately returned to my teaching, and the number of students increased rapidly. I saw my classes expand until they were nearly bursting at the seams, and there was just not enough space to hold the amount of people that wanted to attend. Unfortunately, this was all to come to a sudden halt just one year later.

THE TRAGEDIES OF WAR

In 1982, Hama experienced a great tragedy that would change the atmosphere of the city forever. What began as a small gathering of some Muslims grew into a desire to overturn the government of Syria, and the Syrian government quickly swept in to quell this movement. Suddenly everything became forbidden in Hama. We lived under curfews and constant shelling, and it wasn't even safe to venture out of your home. It was truly a living hell. Because the unrest had a religious basis, the government certainly wasn't going to allow any such gatherings, and all religious activities and gatherings came to a stop. People began to question the reality of religious freedom, and wonder if it might be necessary to put some restrictions on religious gatherings and learning. For that matter just gathering for any occasion would be called into suspicion. After sometime, the violence subsided and people began slowly to return to their daily lives. This didn't mean however that the feeling of safety returned with this. People were still wounded and afraid. The scars they bore were deep. Nearly every family lost someone either to death or imprisonment. People began to distance themselves from everyone in fear that they might be somehow linked to matters that were forbidden. Suddenly people were scared to speak about anything, in particular religion.

It was a very scary time for everyone. Somehow they had to return to their normal lives and learn to overcome the fear that had buried itself deep in their hearts. As time passed, ever so slowly people began to return to religious gatherings and classes. It began first as a few, then a trickle, and finally a gush. The Syrian government too felt that it was time to allow religion back into the city of Hama, but with many restrictions and many people watching closely to ensure there would be no repeat of what had happened before. I seized this opportunity and returned to teaching the Qur'an. I soon realized that somehow I needed to obtain a license from the Syrian government to open a small school for the women, as my home could no longer hold the number of women that wanted my teachings. No religious institution had returned to holding classes at this point, and no one dared mention such an idea either. However, I had no other means to continue my work. My goal was to open a similar school to one that my brother had opened in Damascus some time earlier. It should be simple with the goal of sharing God's love and mercy and, I hoped, helping people to restore their lives to the way they were previously.

Unfortunately, applying for and obtaining a license for my institute would prove to be no easy task. No one had the courage to even inquire about such a matter. All religious institutions had been closed after the uprising and, simply put, it was very risky to do such a thing. The uprising had been initiated under the curtain of religion and due to that the government set down tight restrictions on the city's inhabitants and particularly on their religious doings.

This began my three-year long search for a man willing to open an institute with me and bear the risk involved. As a woman, under Syrian law I was not allowed to apply and open an institute in my name. By no means is this an Islamic law, as in Islam women have the full rights as men. I quickly realized no religious man in Hama was willing to muster the courage to join me—I could easily excuse them, as the pain and suffering that the men of Hama endured is unspeakable. There were more than ten thousand men dead, even more imprisoned, and sadly still more unaccounted for. What was left for the men and women of Hama was fear: an unavoidable fear that loomed over the heads of everyone.

THE CHALLENGE OF FINDING SUPPORTIVE MEN

My husband remained a constant supporter of my goal of establishing an institute during this time, but it was beginning to seem an impossible task. I was willing and able to step forward to ask for such a license partly due to the fact that I was not from Hama, but mostly because I believed and trusted in God, and that doing God's work nothing could harm me. I was also a student of Sheikh Ahmad Kuftaro, whose relationship with the government at that time was friendly and cooperative. Sheikh Kuftaro taught us that we must always work together with our government to serve our country for the betterment of all the citizens of our country. We learned that all actions had consequences both good and bad, and every action we take should weigh those consequences and ask ourselves if it bettered the people around us or would cause them undue hardship. He also taught me to avoid conflicts within political arenas, as these were always certain to cause undue hardship.

At this time, the former director of religious affairs in Hama also began helping me in this matter. He saw my sincere desire to help the people of Hama return to normalcy and to religion. So he began introducing my idea to open an institute for women to the many religious men of Hama, but in this time following the uprising, even he couldn't change their minds. The fear the uprising had left behind seemed more powerful than God in their hearts. I knew in the depth of my heart there had to be a way to get past this, and for the sake of the people of Hama I had to find it.

After three years of searching and trying, the ex-director of religious affairs brought a young sheikh, Sheikh Abo Muaaz, from Damascus and introduced him to me; after some time and discussion he agreed to apply for the institute in Hama that I desired so greatly. Finally, I could see through the darkness and begin showing the women of Hama the light and hope that God gives continuously. This young sheikh and I opened the first institute in Hama for men and women after the uprising, the AlAndaluse Institute for Islamic Studies. I thought the difficult part in my journey just might be finally over, and I was bursting with excitement and joy. I had to somehow remind myself that my journey was truly just beginning and that a lot of hard work lay ahead of me. Although I had many followers and supporters in Hama there were still many more who were not so keen on my being a teacher in Hama. Because I was from Damascus, they feared the Islam I taught was "more modern," by which they meant "more freedom for women." Young sheikhs whose faith and education had not even been completed began to work hard to stop my efforts to educate the women of Hama. These sheikhs came from schools that were very conservative and very reliant on old traditions regarding women. They began to realize the power I held in educating women and felt jealousy and fear that perhaps no one would listen to their teachings if I was teaching. They were afraid of losing their status and power, and therefore they exerted every effort to stop me from teaching. Their greatest fear in losing status and power was that they would also lose control over their own women in their families. If the women in their families didn't listen to them then how would anyone else listen? Conservative religious men were (and many still are) used to controlling women and depriving them of their rights under the banner of religion—namely Islam. They began to spread rumors about me of all sorts. They even began to dispute my religion and called me a non-believer. They made every effort to spread the ideas that I was distorting religion and spoiling their women, that I in fact was causing problems and not helping the greater good, that my *fatwa* (religious rulings) were in fact not based in Islam, and that I certainly was not working for the sake of Allah. I was a trouble-maker, and, definitely as a woman, was unable to make any conscious decisions or opinions based on Islam or any other matters in this life.

Many young religious men in Hama still hold views that women should be in the home. I lacked the credibility I so desperately needed to win support from the rest of the city and in particular the local religious men. It didn't help that the fear in people's hearts was still so strong; rumors began to fly that maybe I had been sent as a spy from the government. At the same time, the government too had sent many people to ensure I wasn't encouraging a second uprising. The security agents for the Syrian government had a file that recorded every movement I made. Both sides suspected my motives. I felt trapped between the two sides, but decided to put this matter aside and continue my teachings. All these rumors began simply because I had the courage to do what no one else could do; to open an institute and resume Islamic teachings.

I now had the overwhelming duty to convince each party that my intentions were to improve the lives of the people for the betterment of the country. I had to somehow convince the Syrian government that my intentions were not to destroy them but in fact to support them and bring about a sense of citizenship through my Islamic teachings, like the examples I had learned from Sheikh Kuftaro. I also had to somehow gain trust with the people that I was not there to destroy their lives, but to make them better. This was extremely difficult and it required much patience and endurance. What kept me pursuing my goals was the example that was given by my teacher in his dealings with government authorities all over the world. He was well known for being wise and knowledgeable and peace-bearing. He was never biased and always sought both sides of each story before making any decisions. He was always trying to find excuses for the faults of those around him, reasons why people did the things they did. He always taught us that what makes us better Muslims and better people lies in our behaviour and actions. It was this example that I followed in dealing with the people around me. Sheikh Ahmad Kuftaro also supported me in my actions and behaviours and he was sure of my intentions in Hama. I owe any successes I made during this time to his support; without it I don't know if I could have continued my work.

Women however, continued coming to my classes, and they could see the truth; eventually they were convinced with my ideas and with the proofs that I used from the Qur'an, Sunnah, and the Prophet's biography. They saw and witnessed my struggles with Sheikhs and other religious leaders. They recognized that I faced the same struggles that many of them were facing in their own homes, and that in fact my goals were not status and power but to lovingly serve them, to teach them and in that way to serve God Almighty. The light of God is far brighter than any darkness evil may spread, and this was certainly evident during this time.

This created yet another problem within the conservative families. Many of these families claimed they were protecting religion. In reality they only took what they wanted from the religion and threw out the rest in order to suit their needs, particularly regarding the matter of controlling their women. Women and girls were beginning to see that they had rights and freedoms guaranteed to them in their religion, and one of those rights was to be educated and have the opportunity to express their opinions. Many men in these families were very upset by this, and worse, afraid of losing their power in their homes. These men, who included brothers, fathers, husbands, uncles and even more distant relatives, began to prevent some of the women from attending classes in my institute, fearing that their women would be influenced by my teachings and my way of practicing Islam, and worst of all that their women may also begin implementing these ideas in their own lives. In our society, men (especially religious men) want to force women to accept and to implement their opinions. What the man says goes, and no one should ever contradict what the man says. So you can see the problem I faced. Men wanted control, and women needed their freedom: I was determined to give them that freedom guaranteed to them by Islam no matter what obstacles I faced.

I decided to tackle this head on. I began to think about how I could begin to establish good relations with those Sheikhs and religious leaders who urged men and women in the society to act against me. It was never my path to fight or have confrontations with others. I was always the one that chose the path of least resistance, the middle path—I never sought to make enemies in my life. I knew that truth was on my side and I had the proof in my hands—evidence that no man could argue with. My ideology and my arguments were clearly outlined in the Qur'an and other Islamic texts. I wasn't stating anything new or questionable, in fact, I was merely urging that Islam be reinstated in all matters of life including those matters dealing with women. My thoughts and opinions were based on the scholars' schools of thought; I didn't invent my ideas from my own thinking. These scholars are all well renowned, and they are all men who said that women should have rights as were guaranteed by Islam. Unfortunately, most Sheikhs, preachers, and religious leaders would take from one school of thought and they refused to accept any other thought from any school based on their goals and needs. Most of the time they could form their own opinions to suit their needs, and since the majority of women were illiterate, they had no basis or ability to discuss or hold opinions on any matters.

Sometimes, I wonder if this was the intent: keep the women in the dark in order to keep a hand over them. I decided it was time to request to speak to some of these religious leaders, to discuss with them my ideas and my desires, and to hopefully bring them to accept me. Maybe we could at least come to a better understanding of each other and maybe even benefit from each other.

The reality was this: when I asked for such meetings I was met with hostility and most of them even refused to meet me. Others agreed to meet me only if I agreed to accept their opinions, follow them, and teach them. It was apparent that not only did they have little knowledge of their own religion regarding women, but they also had little knowledge of holding a proper meeting and discussion based on Islamic ideology. It became apparent to me it wasn't just women's opinions that they didn't want to listen to but anyone's opinion that didn't agree with their own. Change was not acceptable then; even today, change can be challenging. Time could only tell what lay ahead of me, and I prayed for God's wisdom continually.

When I finally, after some time, managed to meet with them and open a dialogue to improve the lives of the women of Hama, it seemed of little use. Their goals were still to convince me of their opinions and change my ways. I approached these meetings with an open mind and a willingness to work together. I wanted those sheikhs and myself to be like one hand, agreeing that sometimes we may disagree, but that those disagreements shouldn't stop us in our work for the sake of Allah. Most of the disagreements we had were relatively minor, for example, we disagreed on issues like covering the woman's face, reading the Qur'an, and entering the mosque while menstruating. After many meetings with them, there seemed to be no way to meet in the middle, to set aside our few differences and work together. Every meeting only concluded that they have their way of thinking and I had mine, and we were both free to choose which path or opinion to follow. If they had at least practiced this conclusion then maybe we could have met in the middle. They made these statements with the end mentality of "choose what you like, but our ideas and opinions are still best, and you should discontinue your teachings." They still felt that I had to obey and follow their thinking simply because they were men, and would even quote the verse Surah 4:34 in the Qur'an to substantiate this: "Men are the protectors and maintainers of women."

Having failed in my efforts for open dialogue with these young sheikhs, I had to find another way to establish a good relationship with them. There just had to be some way to restore my reputation that was being so badly distorted. I decided then that I must find the source of these thoughts and teachings. Surely these young sheikhs must have their own teachers, and I set out to find them, to speak with them regarding my ideas and thoughts. I could only hope that if I couldn't influence these young sheikhs then maybe their teachers could help me change their ways.

During my search, I was fortunate enough to find three of the most influential sheikhs in Hama at the time. All three played a great part in shaping society at that time. Not only did they influence sheikhs but also political leaders. One of them specialized in the science of Qur'an. Any young sheikh had to go through him for the Science of reading the Qur'an to be granted a license to teach Qur'an. The second specialized in *Fiqh* (Islamic jurisprudence), and had taught it to most of the scholars in Hama. The third was a scholar of in *Dhikr* and Meditation and was well respected among most young scholars and preachers during this time. I thought for sure that if I could get to these great sheikhs then nothing could stop me. Now if only they would hear me and understand me.

First, I decided to visit the great Sheik who specialized in Qur'an Science. I had three main goals for meeting with him: firstly, to clarify my goals as a teacher of Islam and to allow him to see my sincerity in the work that I did; secondly to clear my name of the falsehoods that had been spread about me; and lastly, to read Qur'an for him to obtain my license for teaching (I was already licensed, but I thought that if I had a license from him, maybe, the young sheikhs of Hama might finally accept me as a partner with them in the service of God). Meeting with this Sheikh wasn't going to be easy, but God gave me answers and directions as God has always done and continues to do. I decided to meet this Sheikh's wife and daughter first and become close friends with them. His wife and daughter were truly great examples of high moral standards and deserved the respect they were given. In the beginning this Sheikh refused to meet with me, but I decided to wait patiently, to persevere for God's sake and for the sake of the women of Hama. When the opportunity finally came, I was able to meet this Sheikh and also managed to get weekly meetings with him. He was a very righteous man, and I grew to respect him dearly. In the end I was also able to get an appointment to meet with him regarding Qur'an reading to begin getting my license from him. I felt comfortable with him and that comfort grew more with the more meetings we had as I slowly began to see that he also saw my sincerity in my work in educating the women of Hama. These meetings increased my faith deeply; we had the meetings in the presence of his wife and daughter, my daughter and sometimes my students.

What I learned from that great man is uncountable, and I will be forever indebted to his time and wisdom. God is truly just, truly All-knowing. Only time would show if the meetings had benefited the women of Hama and my ability to reach them. Did the other young sheikhs believe what this great Sheikh had to say about me? Would the fighting and confrontations lessen? Some scholars respected what the Sheikh said about me, while others' opinions remained unchanged, but I didn't let that bother me, and it definitely didn't stop me in my mission to educate and free the women of Hama.

I approached the second great Sheikh of Hama in the same way. He was the Sheikh and teacher of the Hanafi school of thought in Hama. I requested to be his student, even though I had also finished studying the Shafi school of thought in Damascus. I found his face glowing with light and a smile always on his face. You could feel the happiness and peace within him during our meetings. He welcomed and was generous with me, and I was honoured to learn from him. He even suggested a solution for me to my problems regarding the young sheikhs and religious leaders that had gathered against me. He suggested that I have one more meeting with the Sheikh who had so adamantly stood against me. He suggested that the meeting be in his house and that he would help mediate the discussion. He tried his best to find the common point between me and the Sheikh who was against me. He was very kind and sincere and he wanted us to reach reconciliation and find success in reaching a resolution to our conflict.

However, the Sheikh who was confronting me refused to accept any new ideas or thoughts, and insistently accepted only his way of thinking. He was unconvinced by all the evidence that the scholar of *Fiqh* provided. After leaving, the young Sheikh began to say even worse things about me. He began to tell everyone "She doesn't respect the great Sheikh and she insists on her ideas and opinions even though they are wrong!" I realized there were many more obstacles to overcome. If this sheikh couldn't even listen to his peers, how was I, a woman, going to get any of those sheikhs to approve of me?

The third Sheikh was the remedy for my soul; he supported my efforts and activities and praised me more than I deserved. He said to me once: "You have succeeded in dealing with women, and you have a great influence on them." He defended me against the others. He knew that even he could not educate women as I had done. He did his best to silence the rumours by saying to other sheikhs: "It is more than clear that this woman has been successful in a city in which the men were incapable of educating and empowering women. The great proof for this woman's sincere work is her continuous work and efforts for more than fifteen years although most scholars in the city work against her." The sadness however in this simple statement was clear. The scholars and religious leaders in the city of Hama were capable of serving women, and empowering them just as much as me, but they chose not to empower women due to fear of losing power and status. This third great Sheikh, though, served as my beacon of light in stormy seas. He calmed my heart and gave me great guidance. He was deeply rooted in the spiritual methods of Islam and worshipped God as if he saw Him with his own eyes. It was as if he sat at the feet of God all the time. Whenever I became tired from my work, and the constant spread of rumours about me, I would go to him and just sit. There was no need to speak or complain, just to be near him was sufficient. Finally I had met one man who was a source of peace and not of suffering.

A NEW DOOR UNEXPECTEDLY OPENED

I had now been teaching Qur'an in my institute for twenty years. Although people continued to attack me, this had slowly began to subside. However, many men still couldn't accept a woman of status and knowledge, in particular one who was teaching *their* women. One of these conservative sheikhs sent a bad report against me to the Ministry of Religion, in another attempt to close my institute. This effort again failed for the moment, and with God's good grace my institute continued to grow and empower women of all ages. This opposition had continued for almost thirty years, when finally those conservative sheikhs were successful, and removed my license to teach. The reasons given were unfounded, but I had faith that God's light would shine brightly again soon in Hama as it did before. Thirty years of empowering and teaching women had left a firm mark in all of their hearts, as they were now teaching their children, and their children's children.

It appeared that my teaching in the institute had stopped for the time being, but soon a new door opened. With the help of my students who are proficient in computers and communication, we decided to launch a website to carry our message to all people, and especially women, around the globe. At the beginning, it was not an easy task: I was the first woman in Hama to launch a website and this was in itself a technical challenge. My daughter Sirin, who specializes in communication and design technologies, designed the front page of the website and we began the work of gradually transforming the institute to cyberspace: alandaluse.net. At the beginning it was very difficult, but I was determined to see this endeavour manifest. There were many obstacles socially, financially and technically. AlHamdulillah! Thanks to God and female volunteer students, the Internet expansion of these teachings has begun.

This is a forum intended to attract women from all over the world. If they have any problems or questions, they can contact me directly. It is an honor to offer whatever will be helpful to these women. Also, the forum opens the door for my female students to interact with their sisters and progressive brothers from around the world in order to share experience and knowledge. Although this work began in Arabic, the English version has launched enabling me to interact and benefit my sisters who cannot speak Arabic language.

Through the website, I can upload any article, activity or experience and share it with others. Also, when I attend a conference, I write a report about it with the aim of sharing the experience and learning with my sisters. TV programs can be downloaded from the site. Information on humanitarian activities, for example in Egypt or Tunisia, can be posted—both in the website and in the forum. This enables our circle to grow. Our circles of women joining, praying and sharing our understanding and experience of the Qur'an are expanding. God closed one door for me only to open a much larger door—one using the newest technologies of our age.

THE CIRCLES EXPAND

The warring continues within Syria. It is not safe in Hama and there is no way of knowing how long this will continue. Our Institute was bombed by the military and burned, and it is not safe to gather there. I cannot provide details for obvious reasons, but I can share that the circle work has expanded in yet another manner as we help one another and treat the injured and suffering families in our communities.

But these spiritual lessons, originally practiced in our small circles of women, now have a spirit of their own. They will continue to be passed on from one generation to another. I am continually grateful to God for the honour of carrying messages of love, wisdom and peace. It is an honour to be a woman changing the lives of others. I know my story is one of many stories found throughout this book and also throughout our world.

A women's struggle for liberty is borderless; it knows no difference between religion, wealth, or nationality. I know that with God all things are possible and this is why I keep overcoming difficulties. I look on to my future and the future of all the women, and pray that the lessons of freedom and Islam continue to grow from one heart to the next, one woman to the next one, as we create one large circle of human beings living in freedom and peace.

23.

China

Balancing Gender, Art and the Global Feminism Project

SHARON G. MIJARES, USA/COSTA RICA

THIS CHAPTER INCLUDES a brief historical portrait of influential Chinese women from both ancient and modern times. The stories of three Chinese feminists are portrayed, including, Ge Youli, who has been actively encouraging feminism in urban communities; Zhang Lixi, who has been promoting women's studies in the Chinese Women's University, where she is Vice President; and Gao Xiaoxian, who has been working for the betterment of Chinese women in numerous ways. A multi-dimensional development of feminism is taking place, and its influence on China's economical transformation and its relationship to women's activism is rapidly spreading.

The Western world has little knowledge of the progressive work being done by Chinese feminists nor, for the most part, are Westerners aware of the many women who have stood in powerful leadership positions throughout Chinese history. Although its patriarchal history has certainly influenced the preference of males over females, women have had and do have a lot of power within its social structure. There are also signs of a developing cultural awareness and appreciation of the feminine manifesting in Chinese art forms.

CHINESE ARTS STRENGTHEN OLD PARADIGMS AND REINFORCE NEW ONES

Modern art and film-making reveal cultural concerns and shifts in the portrayal of women. For example, the multi-award winning *King of Masks* depicts an aging street performer respected for his mastery of Sichuan Change[1] who has no male successor to continue his art. As he walks through the market one night, a slave trader, posing as a young child's parent, sells him the longed-for "son." Eventually he discovers that the child is really a girl. How the old man deals with this reflects a shift in cultural perspective as he comes to recognize this young girl as his longed-for heir.

Martial arts films depict an enduring tradition of gender balance—as males and females stand alongside one another portraying the power and beauty of the warrior tradition. In Ang Lee's critically-lauded *Crouching Tiger, Hidden Dragon*,[2] global viewers saw women skillfully fighting alongside men, demonstrating an equality at odds with media coverage of the Far East, which focuses instead, for example, on the vast preference for sons to the point that daughters can be neglected, adopted out, or left to perish. Popular martial arts films throughout the world such as *Hero* (2003), *House of Flying Daggers* (2004), the two versions of *Drunken Master* (1978, 2000),[3] and numerous other recent movies portray a very different image of gender.

The above films led me, an American women's rights advocate and martial artist,[4] to question the impact of these and also other martial arts films on influencing gender balance within Chinese culture. I wondered about the feminist movement in China. This questioning eventually led me to Dr. Wang Zheng, and in our emails I learned about her work with the Global Feminisms project, focused on recording the work of Chinese feminists. In response to my comments on gender balance through the martial arts, Wang explained that women have always participated in Chinese martial arts. In fact, modern national contests in China have included women participants since the early twentieth century. In short, there is a long-standing ancient tradition of warrior women.

Crouching Tiger, Hidden Dragon won over 40 awards and was a very popular film in the United States. In an interview, one of its stars, Zhang Ziyi, reports on a fighting scene in the desert in which she has to not only do a high kick, but also let out a "war-like scream" as she attacks two men:

> That scream was actually one of the harder things to pull off, since that was so against my nature. We did a few takes of that kick, and each time I couldn't get myself to scream like that. I'd jump up, do the kick and open my mouth to scream, but no sound would come out. That happened a couple times, and then I started getting worried about what the director would say if I kept screwing up the scene. Finally, my nerves got the best of me, and on the last shot, I jumped up, threw the kick and this amazing shriek came out.

Zhang had been a dancer and, with a lot of daily training, learned the martial arts movements, but this is an example of a woman finding a voice of command and power from within the dantien.[5] As a young actor, and as a woman, she was awakening to something very deep within her.

Zhang's costar, Michelle Yeoh, has been in many other martial arts films. Her talent and strength are such that she is the only woman that Jackie Chan will allow to perform her own stunts in their films. These actors represent models of powerful women in their art forms, for women of both Western and Eastern cultures. But if as Wang noted, this was nothing new, what does history reveal about Chinese women and their influence on the culture in which they lived?

FEMALE INFLUENCES IN ANCIENT TIMES

There are historical accounts[6] of women credited with great influence over Chinese dynasties, both for their betterment or their downfall. Sadly, many Empresses were primarily concerned with obtaining imperial powers for their sons in order to promote their own goals through maternal influence. This is a weaker use of power. Empress Feng (also known as Empress Wenming) [442-490 CE] of the Xianbei dynasty fostered the position of her stepson. She remained influential in his reign until her death in 490 CE. During the Eastern Han Dynasty [25-220 A.D.], Empress Deng Sui (also known as Empress Hexi) served as regent for both the Emperor's son and his nephew. She is known for her effective rulership, along with her ability to handle the results of natural disasters and also to prevent war. The Empress of Xiaozhuang [1613-1688] Wen's husband died when their son was six-years old. The son died when he was 24, and his male successor was only eight. This Empress was always there, helping both father and son through difficulties. She was also respected for her excellent positions in the political arenas. But these women and other Empresses ruled in the shadows of their husbands' or sons' positions, regardless of their capabilities and related success.

There were Chinese women who stood on their own, such as Fan Ji, the consort of King Zhuang of Chu. She provided wise guidance on his administration, and poetry was written in her honour. Later, the Empress Ziaozhuang, known as the Mother of the Qing Dynasty, took on the role of peace-maker, giving guidance to three separate emperors during her own lifetime. During the Liao, the Empress Dowager Ziao excelled in influencing both politics and military. With an exceptional intelligence she encouraged agricultural development and the cultivation

273

of wastelands. She also commanded armies and personally led soldiers on the battlefield.

. Of specific historical relevance, the Princess Jingheng of the Tang Dynasty [618-907] worked to promote peaceful relationships between the Tibetan regime and the Han people. In an act intended toward peace-building, she married the Zanpu of Tibet, remaining in Tibet for over 30 years. In 773 CE, boundaries were set between the Tang Dynasty and Tibet with agreements not to intrude upon one another, but to, instead, share a collective market. Her influence would certainly be of benefit at this time.

One of China's great cultural achievements, the raising of silk worms and spinning of silk, is attributed to a woman. Although traditional credit for this achievement is given to the emperor Huang Di, it is said that his wife Lei-Tzu not only discovered how to harvest silk, but also developed the way to weave it into a fabric sometime around 2700-2650 BCE. According to legend, she was taking tea in her garden when a cocoon accidently dropped into her tea cup. As she removed it, she discovered it had unraveled into a long thread. Thus, with her ingenuity and that of her husband and their creation of silk fabrics as art, a prosperous and beautiful Chinese tradition was established.

Yet despite this traditional history of women's importance, for the most part women have not experienced genuine equality in Chinese society. Patriarchal influence has reigned in the East, just as it has in the Western world.

GENDER IN THE MAOIST REGIME

On May 4, 1919, Beijing college students gathered to protest a political decision supporting the Japanese occupation of China's Shandong province, which had been previously occupied by Germany. The students' demonstrations were part of a series of events initiating a political and cultural movement throughout the nation.[7] It was a time of great change. Male intellectuals were also reflecting on positions of women in Chinese culture, and considering ideals and practices especially related to gender balance (albeit from a masculine perspective). Women had been the victims of Confucianism and its influence on patriarchal ideology; as in so much of the world, women were deemed second-best. These intellectuals were influenced by their experience with Western or Japanese culture. They were aware of the contrasts between those cultures and China's failures in politics, global and local economics, along with its overwhelming poverty. Thus began a time of reflection on China's standing in the world and the impact of Confucianism's patriarchal ideals on human (including gender) rights, coupled with an appreciation for the ideals of liberty and democracy in the West. Chen Duxiu, who vehemently opposed Confucianism, was one of these radical intellectuals; he eventually became one of the founders of the Chinese Communist Party (Lu).

Historically, the "philosophy of Confucianism emphasized knowing one's place in the hierarchy and assuring that proper decorum was met in order to assure a right harmony between heaven and earth. It contributed to a social moral code for proper behaviours within this hierarchy" (Mijares, Rafea, Falik and Schipper 200). This placed women under the ruler, the male. She was typically relegated to the role of wife or concubine. For almost 10,000 years, women suffered great trauma for the sake of status and marriage, in a culture where tiny feet were considered beautiful (Lim). A woman's future in a patriarchal culture relied on marriage and status—so she had little choice. One could say the cessation of foot-binding in the late 1920s represents a symbolic indication of the changes about to take place as women began the difficult task of regaining their *rightful stance* in the world.

As Dorothy Ko and Xiufen Lu separately suggest, the New Culture movement of May 4th, as a result of the intellectual evaluation of feminism and the Communist revolution, agreed that women had been oppressed. It appeared that positive changes for women were to be the result of the convergence (Xiufen 276). In 1949, Mao Zedong took on the leadership of the People's Republic of China (PRC), holding this position until his death in 1976. Due to the influence of communism, the PRC also became known as the Chinese Communist Party (CCP).

Sadly, Maoist philosophy and its influence upon communistic ideals and practices did not work for the greater benefit of the people. Although feminist revolutionaries had supported more equality, the leveling of the playing field by the CCP led to men and women working alongside each other in common labour as peasants or workers, rather than to a rise in intellectual, economic and social status for women. During the period known as the "Great Leap Forward" women were relegated to agricultural labour, causing many risks to health and well-being.

The All-China Women's Federation (ACWF) was founded on the principle that a quality called *fun'u*—referring to a woman's ability to extend the mothering capacity into society (Koven and Michel)—represented a specific political position in the People's Republic of China. In that this position was considered to be both Marxist and maternalist in origin, it was the basis upon which a number of senior Women's Federation officials understood and advocated for women's liberation in their new organization. If women were to be emancipated, they also had to participate in labour as this represented gender equality. Many believed this push for national production, known as the "Great Leap Forward," would assure a better future for all. In that Mao sought to assure "equality" in family life, the idea that everyone was relegated to similar tasks labour and agricultural work was both established and followed. The ACWF recognized that special allowances needed to be made for menstruating and pregnant women and proposed at least one month's rest from labour following the birth of a child.

By the summer of 1958, women were having to struggle to keep feminists organizations alive as grassroots activities and groups were being disbanded. Senior ACWF leaders, such as Cai Chang and Luo Quong (who had been part of the Long March, but were also recognized for having each chosen their own husbands, contrary to patriarchal tradition), were alarmed and their investigations into this disbanding began. As Wang Zheng discusses, these women recognized the importance of maintaining separate women's organizations in order to assure women's emancipation.

During this era women endured many hardships. There was a lot of controversy regarding whether or not they had benefitted from their efforts, but they were willing to suffer in the conviction that their efforts would eventually bear the fruit of freedom and equality. Even now, in the Post-Maoist era, they are still working toward this ideal. But labour must be balanced by creativity or the soul is out of balance.

Art is the creative expression of both an individual artist and her culture. The Cultural Revolution's driving imperative, to "push forward," meant that artistic expression and art studios were simply shut down, as Xing Lu describes. Everything was intended to serve the purpose of the revolution. Since gender equality was portrayed as the model worker struggling for the cultural ideal, any other emotional or idealistic expressions concerning creativity were suppressed.

THE GLOBAL FEMINISM PROJECT

In early 2002, the Global Feminisms Project (GFP) was founded, with the purpose of recording life stories of activists and scholars from differing cultural and historical settings.[8] One significant goal of the project was to examine "conventional notions of global feminism as the internationalization of the women's movement, which often assumes a transfer eastward of western feminist ideals." Four research teams were created to represent the following nations: China, India, Poland, and the United States. Dr. Wang Zheng became the U.S. based coordinator representing China.

Dr. Zheng was a founding member of the Chinese Society for Women's Studies, established in 1989 to promote women's studies in China and to open channels for dialogue between Chinese women scholars within and outside of China. Her 1995 Ph.D. from UC Davis focused on women and gender in modern China. These and other related endeavours eventually led to the collaborative project of gathering an archive of written transcripts and video-taped interviews from both the women's movement and feminist scholarship.

A spontaneous women's activism began to emerge in the mid-eighties as China moved into the capitalist market economy, and developed more Westernized economic practices. Another primary influence on China's modern feminist movement was the Fourth United Nations Conference on Women, held in Beijing in 1995. These interviews, part of the Global Feminisms Project, were intended as a means of exploring cultural, social and political intentions of Chinese feminism. They provide an illustration of "official, non-official, domestic, and overseas Chinese women activists" (GFP) expressing their diverse visions of gender equality or their process and struggle regarding the very term "gender."[9] The first story to be shared is that of Ge.

GE YOULI

Born in 1962, Ge grew up with an awareness of gender disparities. One of her first lessons in this area occurred on an outing with her brother, who was four years older, and her grandmother. On this outing, the grandmother bought the brother an ice-cream and Ge a Popsicle. Ge questioned why she wasn't given ice cream. It was explained that it cost more and it was natural to give the boy the better of the two choices. This obvious inequity influenced Ge to become a "spontaneous feminist" (Ge *Global Feminisms*).

After graduating in 1988, she obtained a position in the Ford Foundation. The position exposed her to feminism (*nuquan zhuyi*). The associations and emphasis on gender and women's reproductive issues led her to become a "conscious feminist" (Ge *Global Feminisms*) and she began studying the background of feminist theory (*nuquan zhuyi lilun*). Through her associations at the Ford Foundation and contacts with many Western women, she began to recognize that understanding and promoting *nuquan zhuyi lilun* was her ultimate satisfaction. The Ford Foundation was also supporting the upcoming UN Beijing conference. Ge also began to meet with representatives of many NGOs. She continued to research, striving to learn all she could in this area. This growing knowledge had brought her from the depression of her youth, coupled with her realization of gender inequality, to a new cause in life. She began to recognize what she could do to help illuminate, and also liberate other women.

Chinese women needed preparation for the Beijing conference. They needed to learn more about Western ideas, and so an "East Meets West Translation" group was formed to translate concepts of gender and feminist scholarship into a language that could be understood by Chinese women. Concepts such as gender roles, gender orientation, gender relations, gender power relations, etc. became "keys that released us from the things that held us down."[10] These concepts enabled her to look at herself, her identity as a woman, position in society and relationships with men. As time progressed, along with her formal education, she began to focus on issues on gender inequality wherever possible.

At this time she is the China Country Director for the Global Alliance for workers and Communities in Guangzhou. Her work and training through the Ford Foundation, and her position' of Program Officer at the United Nations Development Program in Beijing, prepared her for her numerous feminist endeavours. She has translated feminist texts, facilitates gender awareness training programs and organizes professional women's groups. She illuminates gender imbalance in the workplace, noting where men have the managerial positions and women are predominantly labourers. She points out the wisdom of having women in managerial positions as they understand the needs and working issues related to women—one doorway for men to understand the value in having women in these positions. She defends the rights of migrant workers, and still finds time to contribute to scholarly books and journals.

In a discussion on Chinese feminism, Ge noted,

> I believe that Chinese feminism faces the problem that it must
> consciously unearth its own resources and summarize its own
> thoughts and spiritual value. What I cannot agree with is that
> before we find out what we ourselves have, we blindly reject
> any outside resources ... [yet] it is very important for us to

actively work on our own cultural resources and spiritual resources.... More often people are using their energy to negate other people. I believe that this is useless. When I embrace the west, I am not in any way negating the values in our country.... Currently I have experienced my own country's values as oppressive and exploitative. Do some theorizing, and like the Western feminist theories have done, show me a systematic and rich theoretical resource. Allow me to choose. Of course, I will choose the one that is better for me. The problem is that people have not done any of these things, yet they still negate others. Moreover, other people have spent two hundred years developing such a cultural asset, spiritual asset, and intellectual asset. Why do we want to negate this only because it is Western? ... I have dignity and I am free. This kind of freedom includes being free of anyone restricting my choices. No one should label me. They cannot restrict me with their label of nation, culture or territory. I think I am pursuing or embracing certain kinds of ideas according to my essential needs for life. (GFP, China transcripts)

Ge is a feminist who uses "reasoning" and "rationality" to benefit the good of all.

ZHANG LI XI

Zhang Li Xi is the Vice President of the Chinese Women's College (CWU), affiliated with the All-China Women's Federation, and promotes women's studies in her college. Together the CWU and ACWF train officials on a nation-wide level. In 2001, Zhang Li was responsible for creating China's first Women's Studies Department, and in 2006 she helped create its first Women's Studies major.

Born in 1953, Zhang Li had her own childhood memory foregrounding gender differences. While with Ge it was a Popsicle, with Zhang Li it was a skirt. She wanted to play basketball and knew a skirt would hamper her performance. She was told girls wear skirts as they are "pretty." This incident stopped her from engaging in sports activities, but initiated an awareness that would influence her later work. She had the opportunity to mix with other women scholars in a Canadian program in 1992. She had been limited to sociological courses in China, but was now experiencing training courses such as Women's Studies, Women and Health, and Women and the Environment. One instructor took them out for an experiential study one night. As she looked around she saw many lights on in offices. Upon questioning this she found that women were the labourers cleaning the offices (generally of men). This led to deepened questioning of the factors that led to this inequality that crossed the cultural divide between China and Canada—like the skirt, it had a big impact on the work she would do herself.

China's hosting of the UN conference for women further stimulated her work along with participating in its preparation and membership in the East Meets West group. In her reflections on Chinese culture and patriarchal lineage, she clearly saw how men were honoured, as names, properties, rights, etc., were handed down from father to son and so forth. In particular, she also noticed how even the names given to boys or girls perpetuated this misbegotten belief system. The more she saw of this great gender imbalance, the deeper became her dedication to promoting education in Women's Studies.

As a feminist researcher and scholar (she believes these to be inseparable from activism), Zhang Li gets people to focus on and question marriage and the family, along with marriage and conflict. She also focuses women's health, especially their psychological health. It has not been easy, and there have been obstacles, including from women themselves who argue that a Women's Studies course should not be part of their curriculum. She is also working to convince the Ministry of Education of the importance of Women's Studies being considered an official discipline in its own rights (as it is in many other nations). Her primary goal is to teach what she calls the "Four Selves," which includes the development of self-esteem, self-confidence, self-reliance, and self-improvement (Xi 17). These developments will facilitate gender development.

GAO XIAOXIAN

Yet another exemplar of the feminist movement in China is Gao Xiaoxian, the Secretary General of the Shaanxi Research Association for Women and Family, and also an official in the Shaanxi Provincial Women's Federation. She has created several women's organizations on her own, for the purposes of assuring legal services for women, preventing domestic violence, and encouraging gender awareness and women's development. In particular, she has focused on rural development projects centred on education opportunity for rural girls and political participation for rural women. Her own education has focused on history and sociology. Like Ge and Zhang Li, she was also deeply influenced by a childhood incident awakening her to gender disparity.

Gao is her family's oldest daughter, the child of a father who was an only son. At times she was sent to stay at her paternal grandmother's home in the Guanzhong countryside. Although Gao knew her grandmother loved her, she was aware that the grandmother always told others that her son didn't have any children—disregarding the daughters. Gao would wonder why girls were not considered children as it seemed odd for her grandmother to be making these comments. "I became quite sensitive to gender. But I also grew up with a strong desire to excel. That is to say that I felt that I needed to out-perform boys; I wanted to be stronger than boys. I didn't like it that my grandmother was saying that kind of thing as if girls were not children" (15).

Following the Cultural Revolution, the nation experienced enormous change. The people of the Chinese countryside had many issues to examine. One of these was that women had been bought and sold into marriages. There were women who would rather run away than be forced into some of these marriages. Having experienced the era of the Cultural Revolution, Gao, like many others of her generation, felt a commitment and sense of responsibility to her society. Thus, she began her university studies in the area of social sciences. She had been inspired by democratic ideals and desired political change. She also spent time reading about problems taking place throughout the world. Along with the intention of studying marriage and the family, she also chose to research women's issues. During the 1980s, she learned about the kidnapping and selling of women from the Shaanxi province. She explored the problems and conditions related to women who both worked and cared for a family and examined the effects of the responsibility system on rural women.

As the seventieth anniversary of the May Fourth movement was approaching in 1989, she and others held two gatherings of the "women's salon." A primary theme was "Chinese Women's Liberation and the May Fourth Movement" and the second was "Sex and Commodity Culture." She was branded a "liberal" because of her role in initiating the salon, and in fact, an investigatory team was called in. Many activities were shut down as a result, and her work was quite limited during that time. To place this in historical perspective, 1989 was also the time of the student demonstrations in Tiananmen Square, a time when somewhere between 300 and 10,000 persons (news reports from around the world reported widely varying numbers) were killed and many imprisoned during the regime's response. It was a time of change, challenge and of being challenged.

Gao's employer had recognized her strong administrative abilities, and so she was promoted to research director in 1989. Results included the gathering of "Women's Forty Years in Shaanxi" and "Statistics of Chinese Women" (1949-1989)." Gao was also one of the first women to encourage women's reproductive funds, enabling pregnant women to have prenatal checkups, maternal leave, assistance with delivery and other related needs.

Around this time she met Western educator Susan Greenhalgh, who was conducting a seminar on "Women and Development." Gao began to question many issues regarding the status of women, and formed the intention to work to promote gender equality. Like Ge, she also became involved with social and gender movements initiated by the gatherings at the Ford Foundation, also working to prepare for the 1994 UN conference. She drafted "Legal Principles for Implementing the Women's Law" at the provincial level, but in doing so recognized that principals weren't enough—they also had to be enforced. Far too often ideals and the laws written around them never really create the change they intend. Therefore, Gao dedicated herself to ensuring that disadvantaged groups received the support and services they needed. She recognized the empowering value of recruiting the interest and participation of female intellectuals from within the various institutes. She also believed that a "feminist organization should challenge the hierarchical structure and elitism of masculinist organizational culture" (Xiaoxian 25). She and others created the Chinese Gender And Development (GAD) network and the Shaanxi NGO, a study network. The work required more involvement with and the building of NGOs, which in turn facilitated more networking not only between the various regions and Beijing, but also in the world. The research association now has approximately twenty full-time staff and about one hundred and twenty members, along with university student volunteers.

An important project began around the time of the UN World Conference on Women. Women Presidents from ten regions and cities associated with the Federation had gathered to discuss how to welcome the Conference. They were discouraged that so few Chinese women would participate. They brainstormed ideas for greater participation in the ideal and the promise of this event; Gao knew of the beautiful embroidery that so many rural women practice and envisioned a thousand women working together to co-create a beautiful quilt incorporating traditional designs. She recognized its artistic value, and realized that, if sold, it held the promise of making money for future women's projects: ultimately the quilt held both artistic and financial value. It made a remarkable contribution in many ways, and it also preceded another creative and inspiring endeavour, the "Red Phoenix" project.

Following the UN conference, Gao went on leave and returned to a place of her youth, Linping. She learned of a young woman who, although accepted to a university, could not attend as her family simply didn't have the money. Gao wanted to ensure that the young woman would have what she needed to enter the school. There is a saying in Chinese culture: "hope that a son will grow up to be a dragon and a daughter will grow up to be a phoenix." It was decided that the money from the embroidered quilt would be used to create the "Red Phoenix Project," and the image of the "red phoenix" became a symbol for enabling women to become successful in life.

Next, ways needed to be found to hold gender trainings and to raise more awareness of gender issues into order to recruit the needed funds. Gao reports:

> I hoped that through raising their gender consciousness that these young women would come to realize that being impoverished was not an individual's problem. Instead it is a cultural and a systematic problem. We also hoped that they would return to their hometowns and make contributions there. Moreover I also hoped that the "red phoenix project" could transmit compassion and raise society's sense of responsibility. (34)

Many businesses and groups donated to this fund.

There was a graduation party for the first group in 2000. The students organized everything themselves. They also formed a Modern Dance company and performed a drama—all in that same year. Since then Gao has passed on her position with the Red Phoenix project to Ban Li. It is a transitional time. Her work and her ideals are more focused on international NGO connections and continued research on women's history. She continues to find ever-growing ways to contribute to the development and, now, outreach of the Chinese women's movement.

The combined efforts of these Chinese women and their relationship to women from India, Poland and the U.S., are all part of the Global Feminisms Project so this outreach is an expanding endeavour for all.

At the present time the All China Women's Federation is especially focused the rights and well-being of children—one's own and those of all children. Of course, it also continues to support the equal rights of women.

GENDER AND ART IN POST-MAOIST TIMES

In the abstract to her article, *Gender in Post-Maoist Times,* Jeanne Zhang writes:

> Post-Mao gender discourse readjusts a politicized vision of gender based on Maoist ethics. While rejecting revolutionary concepts of sex equality, contemporary Chinese women embrace a notion of femininity through the revision of a traditional conception of womanhood as well as the construction of new role models. Women poets participate in this construction process with a fresh, powerful voice to express their gender consciousness. In their efforts to (re-)define womanhood, they present radically gendered perspectives via poetic means. (209)

Hung Liu, for example, a woman artist who moved to the United States in the 1980s, honours the worker image and heroic struggles, but also has a feminine touch in that her work emphasizes *relationship*.[11] Another woman, author, Bi Shumin changed career paths from military medical doctor to artistic expression as a writer. At sixteen, she had been stationed in Tibet, and remained there for eleven years. After returning to Beijing, she discovered that writing was the medium she would use to share the caring and zest for life that had awakened within her during her assigned position. She had been profoundly moved by the beauty of the land, and also touched by her experience with people. In her words, "A life of 100 years is insignificant to these mountains. I came away from this with the intense feeling that life is fleeting, and precious—not only my own, but other peoples" (Shumin).

Changes are taking place, and the discipline and creativity inherent within the Chinese spirit are evidenced by all these feminist activists.

CONCLUSIONS: THE ART OF GENDER BALANCE

The *Tao Te Ching,* with all of its wisdom, emerged out of Chinese culture at a significant time in its development. It imparts a wisdom leading to balance and harmony with both heaven and earth. Given its history and the work of all of these dedicated women, China has the potential to demonstrate right balance of male and female—uniting both genders in a state of equality—thereby cultivating a healthy society and creating a peaceful life for all. Like the young actor and martial artist, Zhang Ziyi, Chinese women are awakening to something very deep within them.

[1] *Biàn Liǎn* is translated as "Face-Changing," and is an ancient Chinese dramatic art. It is used in the Sichuan opera where performers "wear brightly coloured costumes and move to quick, dramatic music." They also wear vividly coloured masks, which they change within a fraction of a second. For more information on this art, see <http://en.wikipedia.org/wiki/Bian_lian>.

[2] The martial arts and action scenes were choreographed by Yuen Wo Ping, known for his work with martial art movies. This film grossed more money in the United States than any other foreign film. It has won over 40 awards.

[3] The original, *Drunken Master,* starring Jackie Chan, and directed by Yuen Woo-Ping, appeared in 1978. A later version, *The Legend of Drunken Master,* directed by Chia-Liang Liu, was released in 2000. Although Chan is the dominant artist in these films, the excellent styles of women are also evidenced.

[4] Sharon Mijares has a black belt (Shodan level) in the Japanese martial art and practiced Aikido under a female teacher, Sensei Coryl Crane.

[5] The *dantien* (or *dan tian*) is believed to be a source of energy and power within the lower abdomen. Chinese practices of Chi Gung, Tai Chi and other martial arts draw on their energy for healing, strength and wholeness. In Japanese it is known as the *hara.*

[6] These stories were taken from the historical accounts of ancient Chinese women found on the website "Cultural China," which also provides a useful overview of Chinese history <http://history.cultural-china.com>.

[7] The author is indebted to Xiufen Lu's thorough analysis.

[8] The Global Feminisms Project was funded, beginning in 2002, by a major grant from the Rackham Graduate School, with additional funding provided by the College of Literature, Science and the Arts, the Institute for Research on Women and Gender, the Women's Studies Program, and the Center for South Asian Studies at the University of Michigan. Global Feminisms: Comparative Case Studies of Women's Activism and Scholarship was housed at the Institute for Research on Women and Gender at the University of Michigan (UM) in Ann Arbor,

Michigan. The project was co-directed by Abigail Stewart, Jayati Lal and Kristin McGuire. The China site was housed at the China Women's University in Beijing, China and directed by Wang Jinling and Zhang Jian, in collaboration with UM faculty member Wang Zheng.

[9]Transcripts of interviews can be found at the Global Feminisms Project website.

[10]Quoted from transcripts of interviews to be found at the Global Feminisms Project website.

[11]Examples of her work can be viewed at <www.kelliu.com>.

REFERENCES

Crouching Tiger Hidden Dragon. Dir. Ang Lee. Chor. Yuen Wo-Ping. 2000.

Drunken Master. Dir. Yuen Wo-Ping. Perf. Jackie Chan. 1978.

Gao, Xiaoxian. "Women's Forty Years in Shaanxi." Shaanxi Tourism Press, 1991. Print.

Gao, Xiaoxian. "Statistics of Chinese Women (1949-1989)." China Statistics Press, 1991. Print.

Global Feminist Project (GFP). *Global Feminisms: Comparative Case Studies of Women's Activism and Scholarship*. Site: China. University of Michigan. Web.

Hanna, Judith Lynne. *Dance, Sex and Gender: Signs of Identity, Dominance, Defiance and Desire*. Chicago: University of Chicago Press, 1988. Print.

Hero (Ying ZXiong). Dir. Zhang Yimou. 2003.

House of Flying Daggers. Dir. Zhang Yimou. 2004.

The King of Masks. Dir. Wu Tian-Ming. 1996.

Ko, Dorothy. *Teachers of the Inner Chambers*. Stanford, CA: Stanford University Press, 1994. Print.

Koven, Seth and Sonya Michel. *Mothers of a New World: Maternalist Politics and the Origins of Welfare States*. New York: Routledge, 1993. Print.

The Legend of Drunken Master. Dir. Liu Chia-Liang. Perf. Jackie Chan. 2000.

Lim, Louisa. "Painful Memories for China's Footbinding Survivors." March, 19, 2007. Web.

Lu, Xing. *Rhetoric of the Chinese Cultural Revolution: The Impact on Chinese Thought, Culture, and Communication*. Columbia: University of South Carolina Press, 2004. Print.

Lu, Xiufen. "Chinese Women and Feminist Theory: How Not To Do

Cross-Cultural Studies." *East-West Connections* 5.1 (Jan 2005): 135-151. Print.

Mijares, Sharon, Aliaa Rafea, Rachel Falik and Jenny Eda Schipper. *The Root of All Evil: An Exposition of Prejudice, Fundamentalism and Gender Imbalance.* Exeter, UK: Imprint Academic, 2007. Print.

Sichuan Dance Academy. Taoli Cup performance. YouTube. Web.

Shumin, Bi. "Writer Bi Shumin." china.org.cn. November 16, 2005. Web.

Xi, Zhang Li. Interview. *Global Feminisms: Comparative Case Studies of Women's Activism and Scholarship.* Global Feminist Project (GFP). Web.

Xiaoxian, Gao. Interview. *Global Feminisms: Comparative Case Studies of Women's Activism and Scholarship.* Global Feminist Project (GFP). Web.

Youli, Ge. Interview. *Global Feminisms: Comparative Case Studies of Women's Activism and Scholarship.* Global Feminist Project (GFP). Web.

Youli, Ge. "Violence Against Women: A Global Issue." *Life Monthly* 68 (November1998): 12-22. Print.

Youli, Ge. "When Girls Grow Up, They Have to Get Married?" *Feminist Studies* 22.3 (Fall 1996): 502-505. Print.

Youli, Ge. and Susan Jolly. "East Meets West Feminist Translation Group': A Conversation between Two Participants. *Chinese Women Organizing: Cadres, Feminists, Muslims, Queers.* Eds. Ping-Chun Hsiung, Maria Jaschok, and Cecilia Milwertz. Oxford: Berg Publishers, 2001.

Zhang, Jeanne Hong. "Gender in Post-Maoist China." *European Review* 11.2 (2003): 209-224. Print.

Zheng, Wang. "'State Feminism?' Gender and Socialist State Formation in Maoist China." *Feminist Studies* 31.3 (Fall 2005): 519–51. Print.

Ziyi, Zhang. *Black Belt* interview. September 2001. Web.

24.
Breaking the Power of Patriarchy

Finding a Voice for Ugandan Women

JOY KEMIREMBE, UGANDA

A good Ugandan woman is one who is battered, mutilated and yet remains silent and submissive.

THIS IS THE BURDEN placed on the shoulders of a Ugandan woman. Considering the complexities of Uganda as a country with many ethnic groups, different tribes with each tribe speaking a different language from another, each with deeply rooted culture, a country which has experienced persistent wars for so long, how do we talk of patriarchy in Uganda when there are so many other issues to attend to? How do we transform patriarchy, which is so entrenched in our culture, given the vulnerability of Ugandan women who are often very poor and illiterate? How easy is it to speak of a Ugandan women's unity for global change? In short, it is a big challenge.

Uganda has experienced persistent wars and violent civil conflicts from pre-colonial, colonial, to post-independence periods. These conflicts range from ethno-wars among different ethnic groups and kingdoms, colonial-related conflicts where the British exploited the existing animosity to empower some communities at the expense of others, and religious wars (Christian versus Moslems, Catholics versus Protestants) since Uganda gained independence in 1962. The country has had nine regimes; each has fallen by armed conflict. In all these conflicts both men and women have suffered abduction, loss of lives and property, but it is women who have suffered the most horrific atrocities, such as rape, maiming, and mistreatment of all forms during war and in its aftermath.

At the same time, and not only in times of the scarcity caused by war, they are the ones who are responsible for the care of entire families, for the provision of their basic needs, without any help or support from their husbands.

CULTURE AND PATRIARCHY

Culture is the way of life of people. Its elements constitute the social, economic and political aspects of life. It is the learned part of human behaviour. It is social heredity! Like any other African country, Uganda is a country of culture, and her culture occupies a significant position. Most of the things we do are culturally conditioned, like marriage ceremonies, eating habits, language, the ways we greet, dress, dance, etc. These cultural traditions differ between women and men, from society to society.

Patriarchy is an oppressive system that structures every aspect of our lives by establishing an unquestioned framework within which society views men and women. As women, patriarchy denies us our personhood and is entrenched in our culture, societal norms, division of labour, social roles, and, in fact, every aspect of our lives. For centuries, the patriarchal elements of Ugandan society have kept women subordinate to men, regarded as possessions. The man at best views his wife as one of his objects; she is property, dependent, and he "disciplines" her as he does any of "his" children (a woman had no choice on the number of children to produce andor the type of man she is to marry, for society claims it is a man who should make this choice for her). What women experience now originates from this history. Our tradition dictates that women are the physical property of their husbands, and deprives them of any agency regarding marital sexual relations. Such traditional customs among other things contribute to women's vulnerability to domestic violence.

GENDER-BASED VIOLENCE

Gender-Based Violence (GBV) refers to physical, mental, or sexual violence meted on basis of gender in a domestic relationship. GBV is manifested by forms of defilement, rape, mental torture, sexual harassment, forced sex, physical violence, emotional violence, psychological, social-economical violence. As Ugandan society is largely patriarchal in nature, it is not surprising that, according to the Demographic Health Survey, a higher percentage of GBV is perpetrated by men (UDHS).

"Wife battering tops in Kiboga" (Shaban and Jaramogi). This was *New Vision's* headline for August 6, 2009. The newspaper, one of Uganda's leading national dailies, reported that wife-battering remains the leading form of violence against women in Kiboga (a district in central Uganda, approximately 100 kms north-west of the capital,

Kampala), noting that a survey had shown that approximately 90 percent of the residents in Kiboga were ignorant about their rights in this area. A study carried out by the Foundation for Human Rights Initiative (FHRI) in partnership with Humanist Institute for Development Cooperation revealed that wife-battering remains the leading form of violence against women. Out of every ten women, eight are physically battered by their husbands on a weekly basis, and much of this violence remains unreported to authorities. This reflects a culture that devalues its women.

The 2006 Uganda Demographic Health Survey (UDHS) indicates that 60 percent of women and 53 percent of men aged fifteen to nineteen years experience physical violence, 39 percent of women sexual violence while sixteen percent of women experience violence during pregnancy, 48 percent of married women reported physical violence by their husbands or former husbands. Violence against women has serious consequences for their mental and physical well-being including reducing their productivity.

Gender-based violence also intensifies in situations of armed conflict. It is inflicted on women "because they are women." GBV includes rape, gang rape, forced prostitution, sexual mutilation, and assault, military sexual slavery, as well as forced marriage or forced impregnation or abortion. It should be noted that this type of GBV in armed conflict has been historically overlooked even by the international human rights protective mechanisms. GBV has and continues to be used as a strategy of war and insurgency.

POVERTY AND THE EDUCATION OF WOMEN

Women in Uganda constitute a majority of the rural poor. The Participatory Poverty Assessment in 2002 reveals that women's inadequate control over livelihood assets (such as land, labour, skills and information, networks, technology, and financial capital) remains one of the root causes of poverty. For instance, although 83 percent of women are engaged in agricultural production, only 25.5 percent control the land they cultivate. This creates enormous challenges for the women as they increasingly take on the burden of providing for the family, thus seriously undermining the sustainability of the household livelihoods.

A gender analysis of Uganda National Housing Survey (UNHS) (2002/2003) data indicates that around 20 percent of Ugandan households are chronically poor; more than ten percent of the poorest households moved into poverty between 1992 and 1999. The analysis further shows that a higher proportion of woman-headed households are chronically poor or move into poverty, and fewer have never been in poverty. Selling assets to avoid moving into poverty is more common in female-headed than in male-headed households.

Women additionally continue to suffer very high time burdens in pursuing their livelihoods. The Uganda Strategic Country Gender Assessment (WB) reveals that women work considerably longer hours than men (between twelve and eighteen hours a day, with a mean of fifteen hours) compared with an average male working day of eight to tenhours. They also bear the brunt of domestic tasks, in addition to agricultural and other productive work. The time and effort required for these tasks, in almost total absence of rudimentary domestic technology, is staggering. This has a negative effect on food security, household income, children's schooling, participation in community life, health, and overall productivity.

The high rate of unemployment among women has been blamed on gender imbalances which are limiting economic growth. As reported in the *Daily Monitor,* Microfinance Minister Ruth Nankabirwa, speaking at the Inter-University Female Public Speaking Competition, noted that "women are still discriminated in society which retards the development of the nation" and that "gender inequality persists in access to and control of a range of productive, human and social capital assets." After making this point she added, "But if all people are empowered, levels of corruption will be reduced because men and women will be there to share the different roles hence contributing to national building" ("Job scarcity blamed"). Nankabirwa addressed the problem related to women's land rights and highlighted that this was especially problematic in that "women are the biggest users of land." She explained that women's access to credit is less than men's because financial lenders do not favour agriculture, a sector where most women are employed in rural areas.

Along with the above, according to the 2004 Poverty Eradication Action Plan, there were 1.5 million Internally Displaced Persons (IDP) in Uganda, of whom 80 percent were women and children. The situation they were in and that some are still enduring was and is unspeakable. But, with the relative peace regained in the Northern Uganda sub-region, some people are returning back to their original homes—albeit faced with a lot of challenges.

Because of the patriarchal nature of Uganda society, limited opportunities have been offered to educate women, and as a result many women are still illiterate: fewer than 20 percent of the female population are able to read and write. This limits their capacity to access information and influence national policies and be able to promote favourable laws for women. It also limits a woman's ability to work and earn a living for herself and her family.

The following issues are a small example of gender imbalance. More joy is expressed at the birth of a baby boy than the birth of a baby girl, which continues to be a devaluing message to women. The entirety of domestic work is normally done by women and yet their contributions are rarely appreciated. Women have not been given public or political roles within the community. A man is free to have as many wives as possible, but a woman is allowed only one husband. In case of the death of a husband or father, women and female children inherit nothing. Instead, a widow is inherited by the in-laws. There are also other negative cultural practices and beliefs imposed on women such as female genital mutilation, an act which makes women even more vulnerable than men.

WOMEN, HIV/AIDS AND HEALTH

According to UNAIDS, 51 percent of the people living with HIV/AIDS in Uganda are women, 39 percent are men and ten percent are children under fifteenn years. The overall male to female ratio is approximately 1:1.2. For females in the young age group of 15-19 years it is as high as 1.3. The persistent conflict and post-conflict situations in the country have increased women's susceptibility to HIV/AIDS, hence making women more vulnerable and unable to fight for their rights.

Uganda has a very high maternal mortality rate. Evidence from the Uganda Demographic and Health Survey in 2006 puts maternal mortality ratio at 435 per 100,000 live births. Similarly, the UDHS shows that infant mortality is at 79 deaths per 1,000 births and under five mortality is 137 per 1,000 births. The same day that *New Vision* reported on wife-battering in Kiboga, the same paper published an article headlined "74 percent Lira mothers deliver at home" (Okodia). (Lira is a district in northern Uganda that has suffered heavily from the Lords Resistance Army [LRA] insurgency.)

About 74 percent of mothers in Lira district deliver at home without skilled care. This sometimes results into severe complications or death a survey has revealed. The report on maternal services said the maternal mortality rate in the district was as high as 700 deaths per 100,000 live births. Only 20 percent of Lira women have access to family planning services, leading to a high number of unwanted pregnancies and unsafe abortions the report said. (Okodia)

EFFORTS TO REVERSE THESE TRENDS

Through the efforts of the older generations, many successes have been achieved including the proliferation of professional women, along with an increase in the number of women activists. Women's groups have been established in religious institutions, such as the mothers' unions and other women groups, both at national and grass roots levels. It is important to add that the establishment of alliances with some men partners and also governments promoting women's rights has resulted in some positive changes in both policy and practice.

Over the past decades, Uganda has made significant progress in the advancement of gender equality and empowerment of women in political, economic and social spheres. The Constitution of the Republic of Uganda, adopted in 1995, guarantees equality between women and men before and under the law in the spheres of political, social and cultural life. It prohibits discrimination against women on grounds of sex, laws, cultures, customs or traditions which are against the dignity, welfare or interest of women or which undermines their status. It provides for the reservation of one seat for a woman Member of Parliament for each district, and at least one third of local council seats are reserved for women. This has resulted in increased number of women in leadership and decision-making. The involvement of women in politics has resulted, among other things, in the establishment of a Ministry of Gender, Labour and Social Development, and affirmative action programs in public universities and other institutions of higher learning whereby 1.5 points are automatically given to female students upon enrollment. At the primary school level, the Universal Primary Education (UPE) Program has increased overall enrollment from 2.7 million in 1995 to 5.3 million in 1997 and to 7.3 million in 2002 with girls constituting 49 percent (3.6 million). By 2006, it has risen to 50 percent (3.65 million) (UDHS).

Advancement has been made in other areas as well: women's land rights have been recognized in the *Land Act* and the *Land Acquisition Act*, and spousal consent is a requirement on all matters relating land. The employment status of employed persons aged ten years and above stands at 89.6 percent for the self-employed, with 84.0 percent male and 95.3 percent female in the rural areas 54.3 percent for the male and 68.7 percent female in the urban areas (UDHS).

CREATING CHANGE IN NON-PATRIARCHAL WAYS

The Uganda Media Women's Association, an association of female journalists from government and private media, disseminates information about disadvantaged groups and provides research on issues of concern. It also promotes interactive communication. Another new group is the Uganda Women Writers' Association. They are involved in creating awareness about women rights while promoting reading and writing for women. They also train women writers in order to improve their writing skills and ability to network.

Uganda women have also joined with the intention to provide a safe life for orphans. They empower women groups for foster house holds through training in nutrition, health care and clean drinking water. This provides lifelong skills for orphans and other vulnerable children.

There are also other humanitarian groups such as the Association of Uganda Women Doctors. They improve the health status of women, children and youth. They also conduct career guidance in girls' schools, disseminate of health related information and advocacy for women's health.

Likewise, the Uganda Women's Parliamentary Association provides a forum for women members of parliament to discuss, share experiences and support activities that would enhance women's participation, encourage effective representation and leadership in political, economic and social activities in parliament of Uganda. They carry out sensitization and awareness campaigns, mobilization for political, socio-economic development, advocacy and lobbying.

The Women Initiative for Gender Justice, in collaboration with women victims and survivors of the long-running conflict in Northern Uganda, provides field consultations to inform women about using the International Criminal Court (ICC) to document their experiences. This education assures that women are aware of the Initiative's ideals, priorities and commitment to the pursuit for justice and peace for their communities. They also advocate for gender-based crimes in northern Uganda to be investigated and prosecuted by the ICC. Some other efforts include Uganda Kabong women protesting the rape and detention of women and children in Uganda, and supporting demands against military atrocities. The Uganda Women Entrepreneurs' Association has provided a forum for women to work together as entrepreneurs.

As a result they have facilitated participation of women in international events and trade missions, have provided an effective forum through which government and donor agencies can consult on women in business issues, have established contacts with international women in business organizations, and have focused on training women in modern business and leadership. The promotion of such skills supports the creation of a culture of saving and the development of self reliance with women.

Other organizations are also actively working to empower Ugandan women. The Medical Missionaries of Mary, for example, train women in bee-keeping as an income-generating project. They also make and sell fuel-efficient cooking stoves while offering training in organic farming. Isis WICCE is a global women's organization. In Africa they are committed to fairness, equality and justice in all human relationships. They use strategies like the exchange of skills and experiences information-sharing and networking, and the documentation of women's lives, especially those in conflict zones. Isis WICCE promotes empowerment of women, and the flow of information and ideas, leading to gender sensitivity and equal opportunity at all levels.

The Ministry of Gender, Labour and Social Development has also come up with ways to empower communities, especially marginalized groups who need to realize their potential for sustainable and gender-responsive development. Efforts continue for the formulation of gender-oriented policies, facilitating economic emancipation of women, and the promotion of women's legal and political rights through advocacy, awareness-raising and collaboration with women's organizations.

The faith-based women's groups found in different religious organizations, including the Mothers' Union from the Anglican Church, Uganda Women's Guild from the Catholic Church, Uganda Orthodox Mothers' Union, and the Uganda Muslim's Women Association, promote advocacy, lobbying, production and dissemination of information, including the providing of educational materials for rural women.

A MIX OF SUCCESS AND CONTINUED STRUGGLE

There are many more women's groups, rural and urban, big and small, trying to work together to better themselves but, despite the significant progress highlighted above, challenges to gender equality still persist.

The economic dependence of women on men leaves them vulnerable to abuse and humiliation, particularly on child maintenance issues. Women and girls are amongst the most vulnerable groups in times of conflict. Unfortunately, this abuse is shrouded in silence. The stigma it carries, the powerlessness of the women and the loss of faith in the law, and societies' lack of prioritization of the women's issues accompanied with high levels of illiteracy has made it difficult for such women to come up and speak out.

Even in times of relative peace, women continue to be victims of rape, sexual assault and coercion, as well as harmful traditional practices like Female Genital Mutilation, which is practiced in Eastern Uganda. Trafficking and commercial sexual exploitation, especially of girl children, has been reported. This violence against women resulting from unequal power relations is evident in the home, the community and the nation.

WOMEN'S LEGITIMACY AND CHALLENGES IN PARLIAMENT

When the women's liberation movement was introduced here in Uganda, it was not easy for women to advocate for their rights. This is still the case. Feminists were seen, and continue to be seen, as man-haters, frustrated, unmarried, bitter divorcees, uncompromising, imperialists, lesbians, and so forth. The politics of naming continues to be a hindrance to achieving women's rights. In fact, their human rights are hampered in a variety of ways.

For example, the right to livelihood for young girls has become an issue of concern. Young women and girls' rights are violated through early marriages. According to the Uganda constitution, the age of consent is eighteen, yet sixteen percent of women are married by age fifteen and 53 percent by the age of eighteen. On average, Ugandan girls get married at the age of seventeen years, teenage pregnancy is at the rate of 34 percent, and the average age for women becoming sexually active is 16.7 years compared to men at eighteen years (UDHS). This keeps a woman from knowing her power and also her political influence.

Women in the political arena face numerous constraints preventing them from engaging in the electoral process. Some of these are due to factors such as limited resources for campaigning, spousal control, and the misconception that leadership is a male domain. Low literacy among women, inadequate skills in public speaking, resource mobilization and networking, and limited access to vital information are challenges that undermine their competence. For example, 38 percent of female-headed households own radios compared to 53 percent for male-headed. Cultural factors and poverty constrain the effective participation of women in decision-making.

Legitimacy represents a challenge in advocacy for women's rights. Many coalitions, associations and umbrellas that advocate for the rights of women are often faced with a questioning of their legitimacy. They are often asked "who gives you the mandate to claim that you advocate for women?" This is as a result of poor networking and lack of harmonization between the grass root and the national levels. It is sometimes used to isolate and frustrate the efforts of women's groups, especially when an issue is seen as political.

Most importantly, there is an inadequate institutional framework to ensure the consolidation of gains that women have achieved so far. The steady implementation of affirmative action is needed. For example, the failure of the government of Uganda to establish the Equal Opportunities Commission which would oversee the application of laws ensuring equality for all Ugandans is very telling.

Lack of collaboration and harmony between different "camps" of activists does not contribute to change; those engaged in politics, for example, and those involved in civil society tend to oppose one another. The inadequate support of women parliamentarians on the co-ownership Clause in the Land Bill affected the bargaining power of already small group of women in parliament. At the same time information gaps have also kept women behind. For instance, while a number of Civil Society Organizations are actively involved in research and documentation, there have still been gaps in data collection and dissemination increasing the difficulty of accessing statistics to support advocacy efforts.

A CHECKLIST OF STRATEGIES

There is a need for continuous capacity building for cultural institutions to discourage and condemn, in all forms, harmful cultural practices and prejudices against women. These include: female genital mutilation; denying women healthy foods; and unequal treatment of males and females. These inhumane practices can be changed if women are advised of their rights and men receive more education and sensitization about the well-being and rights of women. Therefore, we also need to assure the following:

- •Women receive equal rights in educational opportunity and that they learn to read and write.
- •Women in rural areas are able to access micro-financial credit.
- •Women are trained to generate income in order to alleviate poverty and economic dependence upon men.

•Legitimacy for women's organizations participating in advocacy at local governmental levels is provided.
•Women receive training in leadership skills in order to obtain equal levels in all of Uganda's decision-making levels.

The above strategies will enable women advocacy groups to have greater opportunities to influence local governments and thereby ensure that policies and activities address gender inequality. As continuous training of women in leadership skills occurs, women will acquire the skills enabling them to compete favourably with men for political positions.

Continuous lobbying of men to support women issues, along with identifying and working with male leaders who are gender-sensitive is needed. When men hear other men defending women rights, they are more apt to listen than when they hear this from women themselves.

Advocacy by both women activists and other civil society is also needed at a national level. It is occurring, but a much greater expansion is needed. We must work to influence the government to protect women from violence in their homes and to prosecute those responsible by instituting relevant laws and regulations from the community to the national level. Our work is to ensure that our government amends or repeals all laws violating women's rights in all aspects of life. We continue to build a constituency of popular grass-roots movements with our advocacy efforts targeted towards law makers, government agencies, and international agencies. In that these groups and institutions respond most to political pressure, the most sustainable advocacy is that one backed at the grass-roots level.

At the time of her death in 2003, the late Satang Jobarteh had risen to become one of the leading women's rights activists in the Gambia. Her deep commitment, courage and vision were focused on ensuring that all women and girls in the Gambia be accorded their rights. This won her the respect of many people, including those who did not share her views. She was a pioneer and a fearless worrier who touched the lives of many young women. She is most remembered for her unwavering passion to end injustices against women. For example, she campaigned to end female genital mutilation in Gambia.

She often came into collision with very powerful figures who opposed her, but she refused to be intimidated on issues she considered to be unjust. She founded an organization called SIMMA Vocational Training Centre to improve economic and social prospects of young women by providing them with information, skills and increased access to information and increased access to resources for self reliance.

Through SIMMA, Satang participated in a number of key international meetings and was also a member of networks such as MAMA CASH, the Women Think Tank and other UN forums. She once said, "The human race is a network in which the single action of one individual has the capacity of affecting all, hence the need for partnership in the human kind for a peaceful coexistence." She reached out to people and put them at their ease. Her ability to make links with others and to work in an empowering way were some of the things remembered most about her.

As women, we must follow her examples and, in turn, prepare ourselves to continue building our own capacity for leadership, and the ability to fully understand the underlying issues of every conflict we face. We must strengthen our skills in negotiation, so that whenever we are lobbying for any space to be heard, we can bear fruits. We should always be prepared and strategically positioned to take up the challenge.

We do not have to do everything at the same time; we also do not have to agree on all the things we are to do. But we need to be strategic, and come together on key issues of importance. We must strengthen the culture of solidarity amongst ourselves as women. Dialogue should be our best tool to use. We need to bring on board the youth, elderly, women with disabilities regardless of our ethnic groups or education levels, religious leaders, as well as men who support us, to map out a clear agenda that we can all subscribe to. Let us understand what we are as women in leadership, whether in parliament, public service, civil society organizations, religious bodies in communities or in families and then together find ways of overcoming these obstacles.

CONCLUSION

Patriarchy is an oppressive system that has structured every aspect of our lives by establishing an unquestioned framework within which society views men and women. Patriarchy denies us our personhood and is entrenched in our culture, societal norms, division of labour, societal roles, and every aspect of our lives. How do we change something so entrenched in every aspect of our lives? By breaking the silence, by campaigning, by writing laws, by changing laws and carrying out transformations. We can do these things and every woman, irrespective of one's nationality, religious affiliation, or education, should participate in this endeavour.

As feminists, we must appreciate the importance of supporting, nurturing and caring for ourselves and each other. Our capacity to create spaces to work, learn, laugh and cry together empowers us all. Let these efforts we have made live forever. Let us acknowledge ourselves that we have made many achievements. Let us try consolidating our gains and making use of the opportunities that exist to reinvent the movement.

REFERENCES

"Feminist Leadership in Eastern Africa: A Report of Eastern Africa Sub-regional African Women's Leadership Institute." Entebbe, Uganda, 22 September-October 3, 2003. Print.

Foundation for Human Rights Initiative (FHRI). "Promoting Sustainable Access to Justice for Vulnerable Women and Children in Uganda: Baseline Survey Report, Kigoba Distric." 19-25 Apirl 2009. Web.

"Job scarcity blamed on gender inequality." *The Daily Monitor* 30 September 2009. Print.

Ministry of Gender, Labour and Social Development. *The Uganda Gender Policy*. Kampala , 2007. Web.

Okodia, Robert. "74% Lira mothers deliver at home." *New Vision* 6 August 2009. Web.

Participatory Poverty Assessment on Safety, Security, and Access to Justice: Voices of the Poor in Uganda. Government of Uganda, 2002. Web.

Shaban, Halima and Patrick Jaramogi. "Wife battering tops in Kiboga." *New Vision* 6 August 2009. Web.

Uganda Demographic and Health Survey 2006. (UDHS). Uganda Bureau of Statistics. Kampala, Uganda, Macro International Inc., Calverton, Maryland, USA, August 2007.

Uganda National Housing Survey (UNHS) (2002/2003). Uganda Bureau of Statistics, 1 November 2006. Web.

Uganda: Poverty Eradication Action Plan (2004/2005-2007/2008). Ministry of Finance, Planning and Economic Planning, Uganda, 2004. Web.

UNAIDS. "Global AIDS Response Progress Report: Country Progress Report Uganda." Kampala: Uganda AIDS Commission, April 2012.

Universal Primary Education Program (UPE), Uganda, February 2006. Web.

World Bank (WB). "Uganda: From Periphery to Center–A Strategic Country Gender Assessment." Report No. 30136-UG, March 2, 2005. Web.

25.
One Woman's Experience in a Changing World

Physical Challenges Do Not Prevent Us from Acting for the Betterment of the World

DIANA RHODES, UNITED KINGDOM

W E EACH SEE THE WORLD through the senses with which we are each blessed. This extends beyond the normal five senses into a sense of compassion, understanding, a sense of community and much more. Disability takes many forms and can be the focus for discrimination, but then, so can being a woman. At this stage of my life I have serious health challenges. I am a full-time wheelchair user due to 27 years of pain and mobility restrictions caused by severe rheumatoid arthritis. I have been unable to eat or drink since the year 2000 and am fed via a pump that supplies liquid nutrition and water directly into the stomach through an external connection point in the stomach wall. I use oxygen 24 hours a day. This sounds rather dramatic when I see it all written down but it's a reminder that who I am is how I act, not how I look or how I maintain a level of function—and how I act is a conscious choice. The ability to affect my experience of life is mine to work with. *I* decide what I can and cannot do despite my limitations and sometimes I achieve things not despite the limitations—but because of them.

Every moment of life is precious; all each of us can work with is the sacrament of each holy moment. This is not a religious connection but rather our connection to a greater awareness of higher good. When one questions self and others it leads to being able to believe in oneself, which is a great skill and a real advantage to achieving the potential of individual, positive participation in life.

None of this is to elicit sympathy but to ask the question: where does the possibility of discrimination begin and where does it end? Being a woman and using a wheelchair brings direct confrontation with attitudes, not just from others but from self, when functioning in a world that is still based largely on patriarchal prerogatives. Even with the *Disability Discrimination Act* in force in the United Kingdom, coping with so-called discrimination, both real and perceived, is a challenge. My view of life is from an all-girl, patriarchal family and attending an all-girl school. I moved on from this limited view to a husband and three sons (who says the Universe does not have a sense of humor?), another male-dominated environment. I kept hens to try to redress the balance! I decided that although being a wife, and particularly a mother is arguably the most important job, it is not the only one.

My personal experience has been one of continual search for higher good. Overcoming discrimination due to disability seems to me to have been greater than overcoming the disability of being a woman. I realized that being a woman was a disadvantage until I accepted who I was. Who I was, was whatever I set my heart on; the lesson was to reach that stage of realization. I live in a culture that does not deny me in any way that, determination, perseverance, hard work and the ability not to take "no" for an answer, cannot overcome.

The restriction is not just being feminine but applies to any discrimination or disability, be it gender, physical, or spiritual/religious differences Is discrimination at least part of the time a perception by the discriminator or discriminatee? I know in my case I needed to learn to grieve for the person I once was and accept, celebrate even, the person I had become or was becoming. I think it may be possible to apply this to anyone in a position of vulnerability for any reason and say "What small steps can I take to becoming who I want to be?"

VULNERABILITY AND DISCRIMINATION

Whilst attending the Millennium World Peace Summit for Religious and Spiritual Leaders in 2000, I sat with a group of followers of "A Course in Miracles." I was in a wheelchair, tube fed—obviously not a perfect specimen of a physical human being. They asked me, "Why would you be invited? You are physically imperfect, maimed, a reflection of the inner spiritual soul." I would not achieve nirvana or whatever names they gave it. I was doomed to oblivion as a warped, unusable specimen. Vulnerability in anyone can be attacked by those living in fear, as a pack of wild animals picks on the weakest or different one in their pack. It needs strength to accept that it is those who attack who are the vulnerable ones, needing forgiveness and understanding as they live their lives in fear.

I do not accept that "I" am disabled, although my body is. My wheelchair means my legs go round instead of up and down, and my feeding machine is my knife and fork. Thus the destructive power of being a victim is removed. When one takes control even in small ways, when one asks, what can *I* do, the answer needs to be *something*, however small. That small movement, like the butterfly's wing, will cause an impact around the world that one may never know about. There is a saying, "One woman can change anything but many women can change everything." Personal experiences such as this have opened my eyes to the real prejudice that less able or less advantaged people have to face.

I believe it is the destiny of women, together with men, to create a balanced, complete whole, and forming ideas of "them and us" may be very dangerous to our advancement. We have been told that men feel threatened by women, emasculated even, and prefer less powerful women. This was a myth presented to women in order for the patriarchal system to maintain its *status quo*. Often women do not think they are good enough and are encouraged, hypnotized by the media, and learn "buying not being" instead of a woman's natural role of "giving and doing." For me, my greatest role has been that of wife and mother, not "instead of" but "as well as." I accept how lucky I am to be able to "fight my corner," to go out and make a mark. The word "fight" is used here in a positive, peaceful, feminine way not in an aggressive, male "hit you first, talk later" way. We women are now our own role models in overcoming preconceived attitudes of inferiority, as more of us take up the challenge and become empowered.

However, I am speaking from a relatively pampered culture and level of society: other levels fare less well. Other countries, through culture, religion, or education, leave women in a position where they cannot rise above the discrimination: they must first realize that there are ways to address the problems that impede them. Some of the ways are very simple, using small steps hour by hour, day by day. This is the method I use in my life.

TRADITIONAL AND MODERN GENDER ROLES

Gender roles are imprinted from the moment a woman knows the sex of her baby. Historical expectations are part of our education as we grow. Traditionally women have gathered, been home builders, worked in the fields in agriculture, gathered fuel and fetched water. Their base and centre is seen as the home, holding that nucleus, nurturing, and maintaining an environment of tolerance and safety. Woman is the anchor of the territory. Historically men are the hunters, confronting danger, standing alone, gathering and generally working from a perspective outside the home. This has been necessary and in some instances still is. The women needed to multi-task, to remember which water hole was safe, where the best berries were to be found and were the children safe, and the men needed to be single-minded, to forget the fear and danger when hunting, to focus on one task and to perform "the kill." Modern civilization has moved on and recognition of the need to expand these traditional roles to fit the pressures of community living is now an accepted fact.

Women are still perceived as gathering together to work for better life conditions, in such endeavours as parent/teachers associations, children's playgroups, self help groups, charitable and caring groups, and working at the grass-roots level—often unpaid. These skills of cooperation and "getting things done" are greatly needed in decision-making positions such as large corporations, governments, and financial institutions. Freedom and democracy cannot exclude the female role if it is to be truly free and democratic. The world is populated by men and women and our means of running the world needs to reflect that and be people-centred, not merely male centred.

As in the past, "looking right" and "acting right" to please men is too often the goal; one result of this is a tendency for many young women to experiment with binge drinking and "lad" culture as an attempt to fit in with patriarchal dominance. That minority forgets to honour the women who have worked so hard, from suffragettes to women's liberation to get to today with votes for all and human rights.

Why do we say, as my Grandmother used to, "Necessity is the Mother of Invention?" Because traditionally women have had to refuse to see a problem and only see a solution, or the family and thus the community would break down. Women and this approach are the core to overcoming and resolving the needs of our families, our communities. A "good" wife happily and willingly devotes her time and energy to her husband and subsequently their children as her part in the survival of the species. The United States and the United Kingdom are wealthy countries and yet poverty, homelessness and starvation are not uncommon in certain areas and sections of society, exacerbated by poor wages for women compared to men.

Education is our first line of progress: it starts in the womb. Mothers, and I was one of them, perpetuate the role of male "superiority" through the cultural tendency to encourage male prowess. A male child is treated differently from a female child. Girls are given doll babies and boys are given guns, and boys are forgiven aggression far more easily than girls because we are taught it is innate in their makeup. I know these are generalizations (and I do not like generalizations) but everyone will have experience of these attitudes. Education is probably the most influential societal force shaping young people. This is why we need to look closer to home than legislation and look to the education of a spiritual, mental revolution to see through the experiences of cultural, personal, religious and spiritual eyes and our emotional and intellectual response to what we find. This I felt was where I could begin to play a part in the process.

MY INTRODUCTION TO EDUCATION: WHO TEACHES WHOM?

In the early 1970s, I worked in the first multi-racial playgroup in the United Kingdom. Women were the highest contributors to change in the community as increasing multi-culturalism required a new approach to facilitate integration. The influx of Pakistani and Indian immigrants chose Bradford, my hometown, as one of their first places to settle. This created a situation that needed help to integrate the different communities. I loved the work and the children, especially their honest communication. Nothing was held back. The children com-municated through facial expression, body language, and even what seemed sometimes like telepathy. Language and words were actually a barrier, not just to the foreign children, but to the English ones as well, and this word-free communication created an atmosphere of tolerance and acceptance for whom each of us were. This playgroup played a huge role in not only integrating the children but allowing the mothers in particular to learn the language through their children and incorporate new customs into their new life. The men were out working and becoming integrated through their work, and those families were then able to live more comfortably and feel more at ease in their new home.

When I feel comfortable with who I am, then I can begin to feel comfortable with who you are. When I feel comfortable with who you are, I remove the basis of conflict. When conflict is removed then the need for aggression is removed. When the need for aggression is removed, then the need for violence is removed. When the need for violence is removed then the need for war is removed. War is not just absent but obsolete. From this foundation we are able to build tolerance and understanding, feeling comfortable with our differences. When this level of comfort is reached we can allow our differences, then we will achieve lasting and sustainable peace. The diversity of all humanity can express itself in all its beauty. This is my mantra.

The success of this playgroup gave me the confidence to move on and, with a colleague, set up another playgroup for local children near our homes. There was nearby a closed-down infant school, and we approached the local council who agreed to let us use the facility for our project. When we left four years later we legally handed the playgroup over to the local community. Some 30 years later it is still running with the addition of several other community-based projects, such as mother and baby classes, health support groups and more. It is very fulfilling to realize that we had planted the seed, and a great learning situation that small beginnings can grow into something so worthwhile.

Following on from this project I trained for and achieved my Teaching Certificate. I was a mature student earning the qualification to teach Infant/Junior children. In order to do this I had to give up the short-term fostering of vulnerable children I had been engaged in. Even this small job, working at home and caring for these individual children alongside our own, had the potential to change these children's lives and thereby the lives of those with whom they came into contact. At this time I did not have the health challenges I subsequently acquired and was a very active and physically involved person in many fields, including the study of spiritual matters. I have always wanted to know about other people's beliefs and relationships and would absorb everything and anything in order to find what it was that I did or did not wish to incorporate into my philosophy.

In 1978, I moved to Wales with my family, and was unable to teach Infant/Junior as I was not fluent in Welsh. My secretarial qualifications, however, came into their own and I taught typing and Business Studies at the local Secondary School and the College of Further Education, happily involving the boys as well as the girls. In the age of computers, keyboard skills have proved to be essential, removing the traditional role of women as "office worker." During my teaching, I had discovered that members of my family, although highly intelligent, were struggling with dyslexia, at that time a newly-recognized phenomenon. I researched and trained in this new subject and eventually worked with the Headmaster of a large local secondary school in a University town. The Headmaster and I—he with his contacts and me with my knowledge and experience of the subject—put pressure on the Welsh Joint Education Committee who then allowed those students, formally diagnosed with dyslexia, to have extra time to check their spelling when sitting their GCSE/O Level exams. The gateway to their life. Another small step that positively affected the three million population of Wales.

The inability to read and write costs us dearly. The frustration and pent-up abilities in young people are not always recognized by our education system, and United Kingdom prisons are populated by non-readers (75 percent of the inmates are illiterate). At the age of seven, my youngest son told me, "I don't want to frighten you Mummy but I can't read as well as other children in my class and I think that something is pressing on my brain so that I am not able to learn as easily." At seven this child thought he had a brain tumor! He did however pass the MENSA test at the age of twelve, putting him in the top two percent of the population. Whilst I was training I asked the tutor when would we be taught how to teach reading? The reply: children are not taught to read, they catch it like measles! Yet again my small efforts have tried to rectify this for at least some children.

IQ VERSUS DIVERGENT THINKING

I have taught individual children with different abilities, from dyslexia to mild brain damage, and had results that prove beyond doubt that these children have the potential to be our geniuses, despite the fact that they tend to score low on conventional IQ tests. Their brain software is different—we need to appreciate this and allow room for it to blend with the academic emphasis in our world. Highly academic people are not always practical and are not better than people with different learning processes, they are just different. I have taught children labeled by the system as non-examination material, a potential death sentence as far as education and job prospects are concerned. These children, with the right educational approach, have gone on to achieve MAs, work in the field of advanced medical research, university, and/or maybe a happier more confident path in life. We are missing that potential if we do not work with the creative, divergent thinkers of our world who may have the answers to many of the world's ills.

During the 1990s-2000s, I produced a newsletter (titled "The Newsletter") reporting on alternative views on many issues including health, the effect of depleted uranium weapons in use in Iraq and Afghanistan, and other issues of concern, together with stories of the good things happening in the world. There were 100 subscribers to this newsletter. I received a phone call from an older lady who had read a copy whilst she was in a waiting room in a small village in India and had responded to the information presented about aspartame and as a result "cured" a life-inhibiting illness. I have no idea how this newsletter found its way to such a distant place, but this emphasizes how we can never know the results of our actions. Small is beautiful. It may not produce financial riches but it does produce coherence and compassion in our communities however far-flung.

As I railed internally against the negative situations I saw around me, I began consciously to try to affect my environment. I became involved with working with the Elders of the Native American traditions to bring the Sundance Ceremony to Wales to link with Celtic Spiritual traditions. My role was that of the "office:" advertising, organizing, responding to, booking and keeping records of those attending, including the sixty Native American dancers, participants and cooks needed to carry out the Ceremony. Six weeks before the planned date the Native Americans withdrew from the project due to financial difficulties. I was in a state of shock with 100 people from around the world booked and expecting to attend. I felt my only option was to still hold an Event but to change its focus and concentrate on peace, healing and understanding for humanity. I contacted everyone and explained the situation and was thrilled that all 100 people who had booked for the Sundance still attended what became known as "The Gathering," under the banner of The Seed of Life Peace Foundation, the name I had given to the work and venture I had decided to undertake. The remit of the Foundation was and is to cross all cultures, all creeds and all barriers. The abandonment of the Sundance was my first real experience of something planned not happening, and my first enlightenment that so many beautiful and inspirational things could be spun from the planning and organization even as it took a different route.

It was a most profound and inspirational time. In an attempt to link more people, I wrote, emailed, or spoke to many—World Leaders, organizations, groups, schools, individuals—asking them to send words of encouragement to be turned into a Scroll which would be unfurled and read in the World Linking sessions held on the twelve days of the Gathering. These physical written links were then passed around for people to read or use during this Gathering time. Many countries were involved: Australia; Barbados; Belgium; Canada; Czechoslovakia; China; Cyprus; Denmark; England; Egypt; France; Granada; India; Ireland; Japan; Lithuania; Mexico; Netherlands; New Zealand; Nigeria; Oman; Russia; Scotland; South Africa; Spain; United States; Wales. Each contributor was asked to approximate how many people their contribution represented; astoundingly the final total was five million.

This was why the Peace Scroll became a book: in order to incorporate the response and the numbers represented, including Nelson Mandela, His Holiness The Dalai Lama, His Royal Highness Prince Charles, prisoners in State Penitentiaries, individuals and children. The subsequent Peace Scroll books continued with that World Linking for the following four years. The third and final Peace Scroll was dedicated to the Millennium World Peace Summit of Religious and Spiritual Leaders and was blessed by and the Foreword written by His Holiness the Dalai Lama. This Gathering Event continued to be held for four years, in accordance with the original commitment that would have been four years for the Sundance. It was held in the Native American tradition of a circle, without hierarchy and each person present being honored for their presence. We also incorporated the World Peace Prayer Society's Peace and Flag Ceremony with representatives from the European Division, currently directed by Caroline Uchima, present at the Gathering to conduct this Ceremony. The World Peace Prayer Society[1] also presented a Peace Pole to the Seed of Life Peace Foundation, which was placed in the centre of the Seed of Life symbol in the garden and spreads the prayer *May Peace Prevail on Earth*. The Ceremony invites people from every race, religion and culture to join in one voice and spirit to pray for peace in every country of the world. The repercussions of linking and hope and tolerance that spread around the world were incalculable, small beginnings with profound implications.

We asked ourselves as the Gatherings came to an end, were they a success? How do you define success? People came carrying fear, anger, rejection, many emotions. At the Gathering they found a safe haven in which to confront and release these limitations. People came and found knowledge, information, sharing. They came lonely—perhaps a little lost—they found new family and friendship, caring and love. They came seeking and found hidden depths to their being, strengths that they didn't know they had, adding meaning to their lives. People came and linked to millions round the world. They returned home with potential and ambition to be more understanding, more compassionate, more aware of the impact of our thoughts, words and deeds on the whole of humanity. They left determined to foster the self-discipline to be aware of every thought, word and deed, not to be depressed if it doesn't always work but to try to cultivate this way of living until it becomes second nature. Success is different in different situations but to my way of thinking, this was success on a grand scale.

Small steps, gaining confidence, perseverance and dedication to a project brings results. We decided to print fifty copies of the first Peace Scroll books—as we were making that decision, I received a telephone call from Elinore Detiger—she had heard my talk about the forthcoming event and what I hoped it would achieve at a Wise Women's Association meeting in London (which I had attended through a tireless worker furthering connectedness, Shauna Crockat Burrows of Positive News), and wanted to know how the Peace Scroll was progressing. With Elinore's support and encouragement we had 700 books printed, and she herself took three boxes of these to deliver around the world. Elinore is a "behind the scenes" woman, the epitome of humility, and I think her role in the world is to be a typical Mother—Divine Mother—a role of linking, connecting, encouraging and supporting any women with whom she comes into contact. It was she who asked me to dedicate the second Peace Scroll to the United Nation's University for Peace and from that developed a relationship with that prestigious establishment and with the Earth Charter Secretariat and the exceptional women working there. This led to another invitation to attend the launch of this Earth Charter and ultimately to an invitation to the Millennium World Peace Summit of Religious and Spiritual Leaders. These religious positions of power are unfortunately dominated by men, with so few of the world's religions headed by women.

Some years later I received a phone call from a lady in Cornwall, who had attended one of the talks I had given regarding the Gatherings. At the time she was not a spiritual person and had merely accompanied a friend. At the talk I spoke about how we cut a thirty-foot Seed of Life symbol into the turf of the land and everyone present took part in the placing of pure white stones around the outlines of the interlocking circles. This created a permanent energy centre that continues to be maintained. Many of the Starseed spin-off groups around the world chose to set up and organize events to run in conjunction with the main Gathering. In Cornwall there was the synchronicity of an identically-sized Seed of Life symbol, on similar sloping land, cut in the turf. In Ipswich a full camp experience was organized on very similar lines to the Gathering in Wales. A Peace Festival was held in Hawaii under the banner of the Seed of Life during the twelve day period. In Spain, a special acoustically-designed Dome in Alcalali was open for a week of intoning, song, prayer and meditation. At the Findhorn Community in Scotland a symbol was created in flower petals and in Western Australia, in drought conditions, 40 people round a gum tree managed rain! Native American tradition says if it rains on your prayers the gods have heard. These were just a few of the wonderful ways in which the Event was celebrated throughout the world.

The lady of my phone call became more and more involved with the work. She now helps organize four ceremonies a year around the symbol in the spirit of the original Seed of Life teachings. As the group has grown they have extended their venues and in 2010 were going to Glastonbury to hold a ceremony. She wanted me to send her information regarding the start up of the Seed of Life Peace Foundation and all it stood for. The talk she had attended had been the means for her to understand that what she had thought was a spiritual quest was in fact the means to a practical commitment to higher good in the world. She said, "I've visited Australia, Germany and America where Seed of Life symbols have been created along with active groups in those countries and I know for a fact they are all over the world. I want to remind everyone how it was started and the legacy you have left behind, Diana."

I sat still when I came off the phone and contemplated that conversation. What I had started, when the Sundance did not manifest with the Gatherings taking over, had transpired into what I had originally set out to do. Each group had gone away and adapted it to their own situation and beliefs, no dogmas, no creeds or beliefs set in stone. It was a great enlightenment to realize that I had achieved what I had hoped and wanted to: diversity, tolerance and the ability for that to be sustainable and the ability to adapt to different cultures and spiritual beliefs, like a fledgling able to leave the nest and create its life apart from its original nest. It never even entered my thought process that each day's work would eventually encompass and encircle the world when I started the project. Small steps following small steps.

IF A MIDDLE AGED, SEVERELY DISABLED WOMAN
CAN ACHIEVE SUCH A LINKAGE THEN THERE IS HOPE

All women taking small steps can and will turn around the world as they affect the entrenched patriarchal ways of working that are failing to alleviate the inequality, the disparity through greed and experimentation, not least of which with the manipulation of our food and health.

It is time for religions to look at their organizations in a new light and include the integration of women who can stand up and declare "God has no Religion." Religion is the interpretation of God's words through many prophets and holy people and holy texts. When we can celebrate these holy people and yet allow God to stand above them all, we will see a release of fanatical tension. Our lives must be led by a living God, a God who is still present, a continuous Creator. Creation did not cease when these holy texts were written. These words are sacred but not to the exclusion of new words that fit the times in which we live. This does not detract from the holiness of our heritage but celebrates God's continuous creation as we use our free will and choice to extend the spiritual awareness of higher good. Women have the power to intuit the way forward and I see this happening in ways that are blossoming in the UK in religious and spiritual fields.

Through my small efforts at trying to make a difference I was invited to join with Professor T. Daffern at the International Institute of Peace Studies and Global Philosophies in organising a Peace Conference – Peace and Justice, War and Terrorism? The Implications of September 11th to Faith and Education Communities. The group of people involved, together with the MP Lembit Opek held the first meeting in the Houses of Parliament where an All Party Parliamentary Group was formed to study Peace and Conflict Resolution/Transformation. The UK has for many years had a Department for War; a counter-balance was needed and thus from these initial meetings the Ministry for Peace was formed and continues its important work. I was not the only woman involved in this process and was listened to with respect, the discrimination I encountered was not due to my gender. Whilst attending this meeting in Westminster Houses of Parliament I required a visit to "the Ladies" facility. I had to be escorted by a security guard down corridors and up and down lifts, and this process took 25 minutes. As I returned to the meeting the Chairman apologized on my behalf for my delay. He was rather abashed as he remarked,

"This is the twenty-first century in a Parliamentary Government building and we have in force a *Disability Discrimination Act*. How can we expect it to work elsewhere when Government is so negligent in its duty?" The next project I became involved in was to move on from the decade of Conference and Summits with a new innovative approach. With the help of an American colleague we brought together a forum, "The Creative Forum for Conscious Action" to be held in Costa Rica. Its aim was to be to bring together people working at the grass-roots level within communities, from many different countries. Its remit was to spread viable, proven, working models—not workshops but working models—that would introduce these excellent role models to the world, allowing us to influence or even bypass the conventional decision makers of the world, giving direct access to working in a way that fostered peace, tolerance, understanding and vitally, self-empowerment.

The Forum was planned with immediate support from Miriam Vilela, the Earth Charter Secretariat and the United Nations University for Peace, and also support from Costa Rica's former President and Nobel Peace Laureate Oscar Arias, and then Presidential-candidate Oton Solis. Support from many others quickly followed. We had meetings with Ambassadors, Government Ministers, Organizations, and Heads of Political Parties who all offered support. Even a prestigious Hotel and the National Theatre had penciled in the forthcoming dates. Costa Rica was a country where I met and worked with more highly motivated and influential women than I have come across anywhere else. Dame Dr. Jane Goodall had been the main speaker at the Peace and Conflict Resolution meeting in St Deiniols, Wales, and she was fully supportive. She is a wonderful female role model of what can be achieved from small beginnings. Her worldwide Roots and Shoots program was to be one of the main working models alongside many others.

Unfortunately the American colleague withdrew her partnership and support. I could not organize this alone, which meant the Forum could not take place. I tell this story of failure to show that something not happening, as with the Sundance, that could be thought of as a failure was not. The contacts made during this period had a huge impact, even without the Forum, as people listened, took notice and in many cases took action. I am told that the idea behind this Forum is being considered again by another group of people. The work, the ideas, the contacts are never wasted they are the catalyst for future events and ideas to manifest.

When working alone one does not necessarily see the fruits of one's labour, but the work does go on, many times manifesting above and beyond the original idea. The wheels that are set in motion go on spinning their own web of development and perpetual, advancing progress.

PATRIARCHY AND MATRIARCHY RESOLVED

Leadership in the patriarchal sense is no longer sustainable. The twenty-first century needs even more of a feminine, intuitive, nurturing, compassionate, commonsense approach. This is not confined to women but is far different than patriarchy. We do not need the academic, Newtonian, male, mechanical view—but notice I do not advocate a matriarchy. It is time to forego both matriarchy and patriarchy in our leadership at whatever level that may be. The yin and yang symbol is the symbol of balance and harmony. The male/female principle and combination of both these strengths will be the ultimate answer to equality. I know men who do not know about patriarchal ways, who exhibit compassion and nurturing qualities. I also know women who wallow in the patriarchal world and use their sexuality to get what they want and then as an excuse when they do not achieve their aim. It can then become the glass ceiling, the burden of child rearing, or the "casting couch" to use a film cliché. Women cannot challenge men on the same ground; they need to find a neutral area and like any negatively viewed condition, have to work harder to prove their worth. It was not accepted that the gender difference might offer the greatest benefits, it was that the benefits had to be proven as beneficial before being accepted. This is slowly changing as women take on more powerful, effective roles.

THE DESTINY OF WOMEN IS THE DESTINY OF THE WORLD

My journey has not been confined to working with a particular woman's group. I have at all times been involved with both men and women. Women I find, as I examine my life, have played a greater part in offering me the opportunities to move further and faster with my ideas and projects. It has been said that "the destiny of women is the destiny of the world." I would like to expand on that to say that the destiny of the world is the destiny of the mothering instincts, of care, compassion, understanding, tolerance and the connection to the spiritual, intuitive energy that all human beings, not just women, are capable of accessing. Our destiny awaits us as we join hands and move toward it.

My great joy at the moment is *Grandma's Garden*. During the Gathering Events, people found it hard to leave the atmosphere that had been created. They brought favourite plants from their own garden to plant in the garden so that they felt they had a physical link with the energies, memories and changes that had taken place for those that had participated. We called this our little Peace Garden. As it grew, I added sculptures and areas of interest with the idea of linking cultural and spiritual beliefs from around the world. The rest of the Garden, which belonged to our business, incorporated a small Country House Hotel and Chalet Park and was a natural arboretum with over 50 species of tree and shrub. The Garden grew as we rediscovered forgotten areas and naturally it evolved into its name—Peace Garden, Arboretum and Sculpture Park . I applied to the Community Capital Grant Scheme and received a grant of £10,000 which gave the whole project a tremendous boost and allowed me to add and create seven small sensory gardens, "Gardens for the Human Condition," through which the seven conditions of being human are expressed. As I became more limited in my abilities, this project allowed me to sit still. Day and night I spent planning, thinking, analysing my motive and philosophy.

Garden one: focuses on the senses of sight, scent and touch. A "sight and light" garden particularly relevant to those with a hearing impairment. *Garden two*: a garden of sound, scent and touch, of particular appeal to those with a sight impairment. *Garden three*: Mother Nature's Magic Garden focuses on edible plants such as herbs, fruit bushes, nettles and seeds that succour and heal humanity, with symbols of sun, moon, water and wind to emphasise their necessity to support life. *Garden four*: a Garden of Other Dimensions, offers an insight and encouragement to explore fairies, angels, Celtic history and Mabinogion mythology. *Garden five*: a Children's Enchanted Garden that leads the child along a yellow-brick road to discover characters from classic stories and nursery rhymes. The garden has a multi sensory approach using all the senses to stimulate imagination. *Garden six*: a Garden of Infinity. A small brick-paved figure eight, the sign of infinity, just large enough to allow the walker to concentrate on the simple but complex task of experiencing limits within life's path and to accept those that are necessary. And last but not least, *Garden seven*: Humanity's Destiny. Humanity is asked to "Dream the Vision of Man Uniting," with a small circle of "friends" linking arms atop a north, south, east, west circle, representing all the corners of the world.

It was my small grand-daughter who insisted that it was Grandma's Garden, not Peace Garden, no more no less, and indeed it has proved to be a good name as visitors realize it is accessible to all, young and old. Grandparents have grandchildren after all.

The physical dimension of the garden had to be tackled by those who had the physical ability and I became the "Sitting Foreman." As the garden progressed my husband and I built a "retirement" bungalow (specifically adapted for my needs) in the Garden. This home allowed us to "walk our talk" as we incorporated geothermal energy for heating and photovoltaic cells to produce electricity that minimized our carbon footprint. Whatever view we hold regarding global warming and climate change we cannot deny the need to clean up our environment when one in ten children in the United Kingdom suffer from asthma. In this new home I was able to oversee and enjoy even more the progress of the Garden as my ideas flowed freely. Poems I have written over the years are placed in the seven sensory gardens in order to encourage people to stand and stare, and in fact they have deep spiritual effects on the readers.

HUMAN BEINGS NOT HUMAN DOINGS—THE EFFECT OF LANGUAGE

I try to embody a fusion of all and every spiritual and religious belief that I know works for me. I like to think of the garden as just *Being*. As with the playgroup children, language can be a stumbling block to understanding. When we ask "Are you happy?" we have to think about it and the connection with the experience of being happy is lost in the search for the word that we use to convey that state of being. We have suddenly lost the experience of being happy. Although science has proven differently, our vocabulary, our concepts of sunrise and sunset leaves us with the misconception that we, the earth, are the centre of the Universe. The sun appears to be moving around us, as if we are rising and setting. If we stop for a minute, we remember that we move around the sun. We are a speck of dust that in spinning towards and away creates what we name as sunrise and sunset. Because we cannot see or feel it we revert to its name and then find ourselves confronted with the idea and conception and not the truth. Our ideas only become reality when they reflect reality. This is a classic example of when we name something we do not experience it. Language in our relationships is often what makes or breaks that relationship.

As visitors walk and experience the gardens the potential exists to take that experience back into their every day world and into the society that they inhabit. There is a stone circle surrounding water forming a wildlife pond, with a central island reflecting the stones, the sky, the clouds; a bog garden illustrates the need to conserve the peat as a carbon reserve; sculptures of the Stag as the representation of the Christ consciousness; Buddha symbolizing compassion; a pair of cranes, the Japanese symbol of peace and longevity; Dolphins and their demise through low frequency sonar waves used by the world's navies; Aquarius, the age through which we are at present passing; and most recently a beautiful 36-foot diameter labyrinth as in the design of Chartres Cathedral. All offer information to further the visitors' understanding of the world.

The money raised by the garden visitors is donated each year to local and national charities and worthy projects. The Garden is fully accessible to wheelchairs and is visited by groups of blind and visually impaired people and hearing impaired people who all gain great comfort and solace from the atmosphere and peace that is inherent in the garden. In fact it is the effect on people of all ages who visit that is its major contribution—the financial donations are just a bonus, the icing on the cake.

Each year for the last ten years the business and Garden at Dolguog have received the Gold Award for Conservation from Professor David Bellamy's Conservation Scheme and in 2004 David himself came to open and dedicate Grandma's Garden. We felt blessed and honoured by his support. In 2009, a new award was set up. Instead of adding another hierarchical award to the Gold, Silver and Bronze, it was decided to give a Special Award of Distinction. The new award is designed to highlight special efforts to protect and enhance the natural world, with responsibility for careful management, good neighbourliness, community involvement, and the Garden's place as a centre of education for conservation are all taken into account by the independent Assessors. Our Assessor came from the Wildlife Trust, looking for the highest standards of conservation practice and awareness. In the first year of the new Award, only fourteen Special Awards of Distinction were given in the United Kingdom, with these participants having been deemed to have gone considerably beyond the standards of environmental care expected of winners and having made exceptional achievement in areas judged for the competition. Grandma's Garden was honoured to receive one of these special awards. The garden has been and will continue to be the catalyst for others around the world to create Peace Gardens, be they window boxes or large estates.

SACRED LIFE

This whole philosophy of the garden and way of living addresses the spiritual needs of humanity and teaches us that social action, life and death decisions by those in power, those in a position to understand the consequences of those acts and those decisions are paramount. Government above all needs discipline, as we all do. Not authoritarian discipline but self-discipline, old-fashioned willpower, to have the discipline to employ integrity, to take decisions to look beyond the immediate, to understand the outcomes and consequences. Governing, positions of power, cannot be separate from spiritual/humanistic ideals. Spiritual evolution is always for the higher good. We need the ability to retreat for seconds or minutes to consider that moral, caring individuals are not just consumers, perpetuating the myth of economic growth at the expense of a more tolerant, contented community.

Schools are introducing meditation periods for even very young children. We now have the proof that prayer and meditation in the community alters the crime rate dramatically. The Garden supports clubs and organizations and schools in integrating woodland skills, gardening and food-growing, and helping and caring for others. Our local Secondary school has just involved all children in running a mile for Sport Aid and thereby acknowledging and realizing the disparity and the horrendous conditions that some children have to endure in other countries. How more graphically can this be learnt than through direct involvement? This takes us back to "small steps," one step leading to another step, on to another. We are achieving so much through this approach where children are exposed to the reality of "what can I do?" and in the acceptance of this question can then act and become empowered. Their visits to Grandma's Garden opens up the school curriculum to include practical, educational, fun visits to see the benefits of caring.

I know these approaches work. I spent seven years, twice a year, attending a School of Ancient Wisdom where I confirmed the sacredness of life and that personal transformation allows progress toward the betterment of the world, and I try to utilize this knowledge in the projects and ventures with which I become involved. The task of the individual is to live a life so that it fulfills its own highest meaning and touches on every other life throughout the allotted time span.

DREAMING THE VISION

I would like to think that this chapter is not about preaching to the converted but that it might spark a note reminding the reader of how each individual can make a difference by taking such small steps. Each person, each small thing, builds the momentum to transform our global outlook toward the earth and each other. I believe this book is about what is happening now around the world. It is about women and their gifts of multi-tasking, compassion and spiritual links to the rhythms of life, and their ability to apply these skills at a practical level, affecting the advancement, the evolution, of the human race.

The 2012 Mayan prophecy of the end of the world is a metaphor for the end of the world as we know it, as women take their rightful and much needed role alongside the men, both of whom realize the absolute necessity of this equal partnership for the survival of a sustainable, tolerant, sharing world, where greed and selfish motives are abandoned.

The following story encapsulates and brings home the need for recognizing the impact of each person's actions hour-to-hour, day-to-day throughout each of our lives as we ask, "What can I do?"

An old man walking the beach at dawn noticed a young man ahead of him picking up starfish and flinging them into the sea. Catching up with the youth he asked what he was doing.

"The starfish will die if they are still on the beach when the sun roasts them with its mid-morning heat" came the answer.

"But the beach goes on for miles, and there are millions of

starfish," countered the old man. "How can your effort make
any difference?"

    The young man looked at the starfish in his hand then threw
it to safety in the waves. "It makes a difference to this one,"
he said.

I do not intend this chapter to sound as though I think my achievements
are any greater than others. It is an account of a very personal experience
of responding to a world that begs us to care. I tell it in the hope that
others will look at what they themselves have done and realize what a
great contribution everyone has already made. With encouragement and
dedication we can keep taking those small steps to fulfillment. Perhaps
this would be a good place to include my poem of destiny.

"Dreaming the Vision"

Dream the dream of man^2 uniting.
Dream the dream of man held dear.
Dream the dream of life unfolding.
Dream the dream and hold it clear.

Bring your soul and give it freedom.
Bring your love and let it share.
Make your choice and let it blossom.
Spreading joy from here to there.

Bring your thoughts and give them power.
Plant the seed and let it grow.
Bring the grace of choice and prayer.
Helping nurture what you know.

Dream the dream and take its knowledge.
Watch your thoughts and keep them true.
Step inside with faith and courage.
Live your life in every hue.

Take the dream into experience.
Make it yours to live and own.
God is joyous, full of beauty.
Create your path as he has shown.
Spin the dream upon earth's axis.

Watch it form as it revolves.
Yours is choice and yours is freedom.
Take that choice as it evolves.

Dream the dream as love intends it.
Dream the dream of man's release.
Here's the chance to own your beauty.
Live in love and light and peace.

Dream the dream as you create it.
Dream the dream that is foretold.
Own the fact that you are holy.
Dream the dream you now can hold.

[1]"The European Division of the World Peace Prayer Society is headed by Caroline Uchima and the many woman working with her in their profound role of expanding conscious involvement through prayer and action.
[2]The term "man" is used here as a generic term for all humankind, to fit the rhythm and metre of the poem.

26.

Voices from Venezuela

Women's Paths to Recovering Power

AURA SOFIA DIAZ AND CECILIA VICENTINI, VENEZUELA

MERGING OUR STORIES

There came a silence after one woman spoke about her fears. All of a sudden another woman burst into tears and started sobbing and the other, next to her, touched her shoulder and then tears came down in some of us. There was respect, solidarity in the air and little by little a murmur grew out of their mouths. First it was like a plaint, then little by little, it grew into a rhythm and women started a rocking movement, and finished singing in a very soft voice, a lullaby.... Afterwards, a feeling of being at ease filled the air and they stood up and left the room.

This encounter took place in a house along the road to a very small town in the eastern part of Venezuela, where we were giving a workshop dealing with empowering strategies, and the ambiance was filled with feelings wanting to come out. We became conscious of the value of women coming together, and the strength that emerges when they share their stories. Sharing became an opportunity to let go all of the repressed tenderness, the unexpressed love, the hidden warmth that women carry within themselves. In many life situations women are unable to show feelings let alone share them because of lack of protected spaces to do it.

Aura and I (Cecilia) first met at a meeting held at a family therapy association in Caracas in 1990, where she was a member of the board of directors and I had recently arrived from working at a University in the Venezuelan Guyana. Her directedness, her capacity to focus and her fluent and straight manner of speaking drew my attention. In my up-bringing, I was taught to behave in a more subtle manner, not to be outspoken, and not show self-pride. Today, I believe Aura's characters and skills are valuable for both, women and men because they allow the expression of our wanting and desires, and encourage us to act towards achieving them. After working together for several months, Aura presented to me a multidimensional model of human beings that is crucially important in my life. She then showed me three beautiful flags coloured blue, red and yellow, each one representing a part of the brain system, the neocortex, the limbic or emotional system and the basic or R-system brain. And our journey then began.

We have been working in Venezuela promoting human development with women and men for over 21 years. During these years we have come to realize that Western civilization, as we know and experience it, fails in providing explanations and answers to the multiple crises humanity has been experiencing. The current paradigms used for processing our realities as human beings, have remained the same in spite of recent scientific and humanistic discoveries. Rational approaches to life have been predominant, ignoring other forms of knowing, such as making free associations, spatial knowledge and the power of imagining and visualizations, experiencing through our senses and using intuitive ways of accessing inner realities. We are taught to believe that we must accept old parameters, in order to adjust to a male-designed world and be able to conquer spaces in it.

The main purpose in our work is to increase awareness of the power that emerges when women come together. This power creates a path that enables us to see and value other perspectives of accessing knowledge and of gaining a better understanding of the world and the web of relationships in which we are immersed, because old ways of thinking, based on patriarchal paradigms, are unable to offer answers to the complex situations men and women are facing today.

There are many ways to introduce human life experiences and find meaning in them. In the following pages, we integrate the narratives of Venezuelan women with our own stories, outlining the patterns we adopt to handle the emotions elicited by frustrations and sadness, as well as fear, guilt, and worries.

The portraits contained in the stories represent images, patches of our lives, and have helped to clarify and realize what we want, as we defend our wanting and desires thereby expanding our ability for love. Our life experiences are embedded in our bodies, sometimes as non-expressed feelings, sometimes as memories which also carry feelings within. Some are happy ones; some are hurtful. What is evident is that when women get together, their "narratives are woven into the fabric of their bodies" (Mijares). These testimonies are tainted with our own vision and perspectives, since, as we researchers and social activists believe that when observing human realities we become part of the observed. We also believe that the act of observing and asking questions also modifies our observations. Questions like, how to deal with our actions as women? How to handle unsafe environments? How to handle feelings of anger, sadness, worry, fear and guilt that rob our energy? How to heal those feelings? Those were questions that were always in the air, explicitly or implicitly.

We have placed ourselves, together with the woman we have been involved with, at the center of these narratives, knitting a tapestry of experiences. We approach the narratives from a perspective that establishes deep connections between ourselves and the women we are interacting with. We want to maintain an awareness of how we are affected by the stories we are hearing along with the environments the stories come from, the culture and common behavioural patterns and the shared values. It has become an enriching dance of perspectives, our own experiences are dancing with theirs.

OUR LIVING CONTEXT

These women's stories come from different parts of Venezuela, a Latin American country facing the Caribbean, well known because its main economic activity is centered in the exploitation of oil reserves. We are immersed in the paradox of being a rich country with a significant percentage of the population still living in poverty, lacking basic services and living in violent environments. Although recent studies reveal that the ratio of poverty has decreased, the number of people that have come out of it is rather small if we compare it with the high amounts of money spent by the government on social programs. During the last ten years, extreme poverty decreased only by three percent and non-extreme poverty by five percent, according to a study performed by Luis Pedro España.

Venezuela lives in a political turmoil, with confrontations common between those who support the government and those who oppose it. We are witnessing how social, political, financial, and environmental crises steal personal and collective power from people, both women and men. We have come to the conclusion that nowadays our main problem, added to poverty, is the lack of safe environments for citizens, causing an abandoning of public spaces and retirement to private spaces of living.

When exploring cultural factors, it is noticeable that patriarchal structures still perpetuate, and dominate the relationships among men and women. There are many ways to silence women's voices, sometimes to the point of making them invisible, in family life and work as well.

From a legal standpoint and from a perspective of human rights, Venezuelan women enjoy equal status with men, but reality tells us otherwise because social mores and costumes still demand more of women to change. The implicit contract is that if women want and/or need to work outside their homes, it is expected that they keep caring for their children and living spaces. Even though changes in habits have started to occur and there is an increase of situations where both men and woman share all chores and tasks, inequalities prevail.

Census data reveal that one-third of Venezuelan families have a single parent structure, mainly headed by women. Generally the single mother either lives alone with her children or (most often) the grandmother moves in to help with the children. Whether she lives alone or with a partner, it is the woman who is expected to take care of the household, even if she has a full work schedule. Women have a heavy work load, a fact that is ignored or taken as natural by our patriarchally-oriented society, and this trait seems to cross social strata. A portrait of an urban, working-class Venezuelan woman depicts a person who works eight hours a day, leaves her children at school or other child-care arrangements, picks them up at the end of the day and arrives home to go on working. She gets few hours of rest and sometimes the feeling of tiredness fills most of her days. If you add up poverty and deficient means of public transportation, plus living far away from working places, then you have a serious threat to women's health.

PREPARING FOR CHANGE

Being aware of these problems, we started providing workshops for both, men and women, so they could become more conscious of the lives they were living and their potential for self-empowerment and change. This was facilitated through experiential learning exercises and the practice of strategies that allowed them to make changes and to become more conscious, based on Elaine de Beauport's ten paths of intelligences.[1]

Sharing spaces has made us become progressively aware of our multi-dimensionality. With this approach, our goal is to expand our minds, to better handle our feelings, and to become more conscious of our actions. We value our rational competencies as well as our capacities to associate ourselves with people, music, art works, nature; we are becoming more aware that we are capable of creating internal as well as external images and, at the same time, we are learning to be confident of our intuition. We acknowledge our emotional capabilities and are developing the ability to let ourselves be affected by nature, a song, a poem. We feel our unity with one another, become more aware of the emotions that steal the peace from our hearts. And, finally, this experience enables us to identify the importance of each behaviour, recognizing basic behaviours that favour or impinge on our lives, behaviours we approach easily or we attempt to move away from. Most importantly, we recognize our power to make changes, to transform our own lives. We also acknowledge that we need to know what we want from life and design parameters that protect these intentions and desires, and that we can change behaviours on behalf of our lives.

EMOTIONS, BEHAVIOURS, FAMILY PATTERNS AND SELF-DEVELOPMENT

The findings of prior research concerning the importance of emotions conducted by the co-author, Aura Sofia Díaz, includes relevant testimonies of how Venezuelan women of differing backgrounds became aware of the ways emotions affected their individual self development. Díaz concluded that recognition of emotional states increases women's awareness of themselves and their abilities to heal and learn from emotions, such as sadness and anger, as well as hurtful memories. Understanding our feelings also has an impact on health, spirituality, inner peace, regaining personal power, inner motivations and improving relationships. Diaz reflects on perspectives on women emotions:

> To be emotionally conscious means being able to feel feelings in order to access their information; be appreciative of the emotional dimensions of others, sense basic needs and signals related to health; heal past emotional hurts; feel the power of my life; motivate myself; feel my internal states of consciousness; feel the spiritual connection and relevance of my actions, and be able to guide my internal system to live the highs and lows of daily energy. (i)

325

Getting together, bonding, participating in workshops to train others, as well as ourselves, has been an enriching experience. Exploring our beliefs, our thoughts, building images, encouraging ourselves to be confident of our intuitions, learning how to be affected by finding out what moves us in life and most of all, learning how to handle the ups and emotional downs of our lives has played a significant part in bringing back our hidden power, but more importantly, in learning learn how to love, its nuances and obstacles. We could not have accomplished this without entering the shadows: those patterns rooted beyond consciousness, beyond light, that formed way back in our childhood. Therefore it was also crucial to learn to identify and recognize our patterns and build parameters to protect our actions, feelings and thoughts.

BECOMING AWARE OF LOVE AND TRUST

We have learned that if we are to trust one another we have to know each other first, if not, when we get together it takes time to open up and it is difficult to go beyond of what others would think and say. Moreover, the process of trust is slow if women have focused more on developing the neocortex (the "thinking" brain). When women live near nature, and become conscious of their bodies and the context they live in, when they need others to survive, then critical thinking does not prevail and it becomes easier to open up when they are together. Diaz believes that the more complex our thoughts become, the more difficult it is to access feelings. When love is felt, then trust flourishes and reveals itself. Trust emerges from love.

Love is the feeling that keeps us alive. It is a key emotion that motivates and makes us go on with our lives. Love for the bus that gets me where I want to go and brings me back home, love for my sunsets, for the pond where I can swim, love for my mother that takes care of me and cooks good and tasty meals, for the music my neighbour plays every afternoon when I arrive from work. To fall in love with another human being is no nonsense. And remember, love has three faces, to appreciate one another, to be a companion to our beloved, and to feel the love. All other feelings are not as important as love. Trust is important and gives us security, love comes from our heart.

The following stories come from Cecilia's experiences when developing a program for women in different regions of Venezuela, as well as Aura Sofia's research, and provicde evidence of how women are working through these issues and related developments.

BECOMING AWARE OF OUR HEALTH PATTERNS

Sometimes health becomes a cumbersome issue in our lives, due to experiences from the past. Margarita, a higher education professor, is very much appreciated by her students. From her early years she saw many illnesses at home; she told me about seeing her mother suffering serious asthma attacks and her father dying of cancer. Later as an adult, whenever she had an issue with one of her family members, she would stay hooked into fear, afraid of speaking out her emotions, getting sadder and sadder and isolating herself until she became short of breath and physically ill with high blood pressure. She describes herself as a "hypochondriac" and reports that her family was neither healthy nor knowledgeable of how to deal with illnesses. After consciously sharing and learning about emotions she says she feels freer and healthy. To have gone into the experience of feeling her feelings, being able to get in and out of them, gave her great freedom, and she is not afraid anymore of having to deal with them. Feelings of wellbeing, expansion and pleasure have brought her health under control. She is on a journey exploring her family patterns of dealing with illness and now recognizes that when she feels stressed, and feels her blood pressure going up, she has many choices. She relaxes by putting on some music, letting herself be affected by it and by the beauty of the flowers she is now used to having on her desk. She says she feels expanded.

FEAR OF LONELINESS

Rosa, a 60-year-old woman living near Río Caribe, a small town facing the sea in the north eastern part of Venezuela, is an important and appreciated figure in her community. One afternoon at one of our meetings we could sense a feeling of expectation among the women because some men were coming to see what we were doing. The women asked, "What should we do?" I proceeded to invite the men to join us, but they refused and stood outside leaning to the fences. It was early afternoon and the sun was burning hot outside, but it was fresh inside. There were sixteen women, ages 16 to 60, who had agreed to get together to speak about their lives, to share experiences and see if we could find some answers. When we asked them what did they want to talk about, all the women turned their faces to Rosa, the eldest.

Part of our work that sunny afternoon involved finding out and defining who we felt we were; we asked Rosa if she wanted to be the first to speak, and she agreed. When confronted with the question

"Who am I?" tears came to her eyes, she raised her hand and said "I am a wife, a mother, a sister, a friend...." and she wanted to go on mentioning the roles she played, but then we gently asked, what she did for herself, she answered "I cannot see Rosa, because she went down a big black hole a long time ago." A mixture of feelings erupted, sadness and anger came out. When asked what she had lost, she said: "*myself*." When we explored ways to heal sadness and anger seeking to find out if she wanted to regain the self she had lost, she said "yes." She wanted time and space, and she craved solitude. What she didn't realize was that while loving and protecting her loved ones, making a very comfortable and stable home for them, she had forgotten her own needs. She didn't think of herself as a woman, or even as a human being, and she had repressed her own wishes and dreams. She was upset because her husband used to play music at a very high pitch on weekends, when she wanted, and also needed, to rest. That music was so loud that she got sick to her stomach. She wanted to build a small house on top of the hill so she could get away when he was drinking and making noise; she wanted moments alone. The other women told her that they doubted she could have the courage to do it, because he could get angry at her, leave, and she would then be alone. I asked her if she really wanted that and she nodded affirmatively. Rosa did it and, surprisingly, the husband didn't leave her, her family respected her space.

NEW WAYS OF BEING WITH OTHERS:
A CULTURE OF COMPLEMENTARY LIVING

We strongly believe that we need to work towards the construction of a new civilization as Edgar Morin suggests to collectively become involved in the design of a new blueprint for living together and being with others, at a planetary level like the late Thomas Berry has so beautifully proposed. That is a *great task*, which we have to undertake if we really want to live in peace. Instead of accepting views that separate us, that lead us to see ourselves as being opposed and thereby responding in confrontation, we can strive to build common grounds, as Elaine de Beauport and Aura Sofia Díaz propose, integrating our visions, looking for complementary views. The story we just told about Rosa (which can be found in my report to the National Council of Women) (Vicentini *Report of Project of Self-Development*) presents a beautiful narrative of a woman who integrated her dream of solitude with family and couple life—seeing both as complementary rather than oppositional.

We, as women, need to become aware that we are experiencing the emergence of a new culture where we are taking the first steps in the practice of gender complementarities, instead of competing and fighting with each other, thereby amplifying suffering. We are walking new paths to explore the depth of our differences, approaching togetherness in what we are alike and appreciating our differences.

Getting together has become an invitation to get involved in a culture that, in Jurgen Habermas's phrase, "includes the other," and we believe that this is crucial if we want to become planetary citizens. Latin American culture sometimes makes it difficult for women to participate and include themselves in building new ways of being together, in making creative changes that can make a difference in the lives we are all living. Because of lack of opportunities and because we live within a social structure still only oriented by patriarchal patterns, instead of practicing complementary thinking and acting, we are in need of finding our own ways to make our lives more meaningful.

The sociopolitical and cultural pattern makes it difficult for women to reclaim their power. They are frequently lost in an emotional battle between what they want from their lives, their dreams and what their life partners, families, and society in general, expects from them. We firmly believe that getting together to share our stories was and is a powerful tool for empowerment and can lead us to contribute to *a life worthy of living*. For this to happen, women must come together in a journey of transformation, not substituting one behaviour for another, but conceiving it as a change process, one that has to start by accepting what we are in present time, being aware of our situation, thinking and imagining new ways of being and living together, of constructing new and open realities for women and men. With this purpose in our minds and letting ourselves be affected by it, we can take actions to continue changing, to promote change by adding to our lives instead of being centered in our losses, a change that brings satisfaction and pleasure, so that new behaviour patterns become rooted in our souls. Emphasizing and practicing new behaviours will allow a movement that spreads, transforming the old ones, and, finally, establishing new ones. Our emotional caring enables this change.

BECOMING AWARE OF THE POWER OF EMOTIONS

There is new and increasing research and information, as Bruce Lipton discusses, coming out about the meanings of emotions in our lives, and how it relates to our biology, to our health. At different occasions and through our sessions we have had the opportunity to go back to our early years and revisit painful experiences, like this one related by Cecilia, who shared an experience with her father:

> If I go back to my childhood years I have a feeling of uneasiness, of fear, of sadness rooted in my mind and heart, a lack of understanding of the things that happened around me...
> I remember laying down in the grass and falling asleep feeling that I was going to die and waiting to die while asleep, waking up one or two hours after, in an open field while waiting for my father who was hunting birds which he used to collect and then place in a huge cage. I hated seeing them deprived of their freedom. I usually went with him to get away from home, and at that time I didn't know why and when I became conscious of why I was able to better understand all the lack of information that plagued my early life.

This is the voice of a woman who is a social worker, helping people who live in poverty, in Venezuelan communities. Using a hermeneutic approach[2] to interpret her story we can identify family patterns of helping people, especially the poor, but beyond interpretation, what we would like to stress is the images these words evoke and the process of understanding and identification that took place between the women that were listening when she told this story, the connections they made, the feelings elicited and all that was shared about what Cecilia could do from that moment on.

HEALING SADNESS AND ANGER

The narrative of Beatriz, a 27-year-old woman living in the rural town Tacarigua of the Lagoon, on the Caribbean coastline, where we were working with female elementary school teachers (Vicentini *Building Bridges*) tells us about women's suffering. We were at a meeting with the purpose of planning activities for the children, when she suddenly stood up and said she had something to tell. Tears came to her eyes as she spoke:

> I cannot work today and make plans for the children, I am very sad and also very angry, what is in my mind and heart at this moment is how to deal with my husband. You all know he is a fisherman, and has trouble fishing because of the dry season,

and therefore is selling less and less. Because I am earning more than him and our societal patterns dictate that he is expected to provide more than me, he feels ashamed and has gone away. He told me that he will be back when he finds the way to support his family. Please, tell me what to do with the pain I am feeling here [touching her chest] and what can I say to convince him to come back!"

She then insisted that she was angry because of the community's expectations towards men, which she afterwards was able to identify as the patriarchal structure of society causing him to leave her. She was sad because she missed him.

The situation gave us the opportunity to experience first-hand the teachings of de Beauport and Diaz. They teach that anger and sadness are twin emotions, that is an internal movement where we are constantly switching from *I can* to *I can't,* from *I could* to *I won't.* This emotional conflict causes us to be separate from our inner power, and also separates us from an authentic path of love. We have learned that being in the path of love starts by becoming conscious and identifying our wanting, our feelings, our desire and capacity to feel warmth, to practice the expansion of the self and attain the desired. This leads to a greater sense of power as we merge with feelings of joy, content, happiness, and satisfaction. This can also lead us to love and to the belief that we can all be successful in life.

Unfortunately we do not always remain in this route of love and there are frustrations that take us off the road that leads to centeredness and resulting peace within ourselves. In those cases de Beauport and Diaz tell us that we can expand when we feel contractions, and contract when expanded, in a movement that portrays the ways our heart, lungs and stomach function, following nature's paths. Sometimes we fight, and others we contract. The expansion to fight can be healthy, but we have to figure out how to return to the highway of love, otherwise we are bound to fall into anger, to make it a habitual response. If we do not heal our anger, then the road to hate and violence is easy to follow. If we have a pattern of contraction, like many women do, we could fall into sadness and if not dealt with we end up in depression because of a lack of power and agency on our own lives. This can produce illness, making it difficult to identify where we lost our power, where we lost the ability to love ourselves. Sometimes, the symptoms of illness can mask the real need, which is how to recover our power.

We explored with Beatriz what she could do to heal sadness and to enable her to face her "I can't." She found that she could talk to other women about what she was experiencing. At that moment, some women stood up telling her that they understood what she was going through because they were feeling the same emotions. They invited her to get together and figure out what they could do to cope with the situation. The feeling that she was no longer alone yielded to a feeling of hope that something could be done. Their solution was to work together to facilitate the needed changes. Therefore, everyone benefitted.

Emotions are a means of relating. We all know the importance of tears, the relief that they can offer to the body. As Elaine de Beauport so expressively said, tears are "a language of the Limbic Brain" ("Self Care") and they show how profoundly moved women and men can be.

EMOTIONS IN THE WORKPLACE

We are aware that we need to act in order to build a more humane and complementary platform from which to start a transformation. Although a significant number of women have access to education, there still are women suffering from discrimination in workplaces. For instance, when two people apply for a job, generally if women are offered the job, they are paid less than men doing the same task. There are places where they ask you, in a very informal way, if you are married or have children, because facing the decision to hire a highly competent woman and a not-so-highly qualified man, they choose the man or the woman that is not married.

Violeta, a highly successful businesswoman related her manner of handling emotions at her office, following one of our workshops. She expressed that the knowledge of emotions clarified certain aspects of her relationship at work. It was a two-way emotional movement, sometimes bringing her closer to some of her working mates, and creating a distance from others. She is firm and clear about what she wants in her working relationships, and accepts that some of her companions may not like this new person that is emerging since her experience in the workshop on Emotional Intelligences.

She also recognized that without proper information understanding emotions can be very confusing. She expressed that when she is worried about something at work or in her family, she goes within herself to provide a focus for inner guidance. She became aware that some people misinterpreted this, thinking she was upset or worrying. So now she explains her emotional process, and manner of expressing emotions. Before the workshop she hadn't felt a need to provide explanations to others. Now she recognizes that clarifying emotional processes can be very helpful for the people she works with and express concern. She is now able to both recognize and make judgments about issues with her working relationships. She found that after the training in "dealing with emotions" she has been able to respond more effectively to both men and women at her job. She has more "mind flexibility," being able to go deep inside and explore what her feelings are and reaching out to others when she or they need it. She is also able to share her knowledge and offer help as needed.

Aura Sofia Diaz found it rewarding, as a facilitator of the course on emotions, to hear Violeta say that now she has the freedom to get upset at work, the freedom to lock her office door and cry for ten minutes if necessary, to relieve the stress.

As previously noted, de Beauport's theory states that *wanting and desires* are the avenues to the connection within our own selves and also with the other. If we know *what we want*, she says, we can go for it, and we can learn, move and stay moving until we reach our goals. The women we worked with were surprised when they heard the new meanings of emotions. Tears came to their eyes when they learned that sadness meant that they have loved and cherished deeply, that there was a loss of an opportunity, of a loved one, of an experience, and that acknowledging this is the first step to healing. We also learned to explore and re-experience our fears and we became conscious that they are signs to stop and direct our steps to safer grounds. All these feelings and emotions can be dealt with when we, as a whole living community of women, decide to engage ourselves in creating and building "peace in our minds." In order to truly create a "gender-balanced" world, we need to become more truly human, as Virginia Satir used to say.

KNITTING OUR MURMURS

Women are indeed opening channels for global transformations. Social, political, work, and family contexts are important environments from which women's stories can continue to be told, and we need to assure spaces in which to share them. In our work we are getting together in different ways, through the use of conversational strategies, carrying out workshops, doing qualitative research, and through innovative ways as meditation groups, movement and dance groups that integrate body, mind and heart. In a collective way, new forms of awareness are emerging. Through different paths we are learning that, even coming from different environments, perspectives, economical and educational backgrounds, when we put those differences aside for moments, we have similar joys and grievances, worries and motivations concerning our own lives and the lives of our loved ones.

Venezuelan women share the same sociopolitical climate, independent of our political preferences. We are all sharing the certainty of uncertainty and the security of insecurity. Being always alert for physical survival is a subject we are all immersed in. There is an increase of aggressive and violent behaviour, in public spaces and also in private realms. The causes are multiple, but what is evident is a growing feeling of frustration and loss of personal power that a significant percentage of the Venezuelan citizens are experiencing. Life itself seems to be losing meaning, living is a daily threat because of violence, and there is evident restriction of freedoms and basic liberties. In this milieu women continue to love, raise children, work and fight for moments of leisure according to their possibilities.

We firmly believe that peace in our country is seriously threatened, even though we continue to promote peace in our minds, hearts and bodies through the path of amplifying our intelligences and capabilities as de Beauport and Diaz state. It is from this perspective that we have told the stories of some of the women we have worked with.

Venezuela is undergoing a very critical situation, where life often seems to have lost its value, as can be seen in the weekly balance of deaths produced by confrontations within community realms where those who are killed are mostly men 20 to 50 years old. We are witnessing these situations through the media, and we see mothers, sisters and daughters crying for their lost loved ones. We are a society in need of new ways to manage our thoughts, our emotions and our actions. We believe that Venezuelans as a whole need to re-think, re-feel in order to re-build our lives and women can play an important role in this task.

We firmly believe that we can no longer afford to ignore the power of emotions and that the door to our emotional world is often closed due to painful experiences. We need to learn how to feel, to let ourselves be affected by our life experiences. It is through this lens that we explored the life experiences of Venezuelan women. There were moments you could feel the intensity of the emotions, where deep and intuitive inner knowledge became evident through words and body expressions. There is no doubt that we were creating a net for enhancing human understanding, recognizing the web of inter-subjectivities involved, and some of the women have started new journeys that have given all of us strength to manage our emotional environments.

Seeing Venezuelan's life through the eyes of women and hearing their voices, sharing moments and spaces where we talked about the lives we are living, certainly made a difference in our lives. We strongly believe that providing spaces where women can come together has a tremendous impact on living together in peace in the global community.

[1]The ten paths of intelligence of de Beauport are represented by ten intelligences that she offers in her program as a way to a more conscious life. Those paths-intelligences are ways to deal with the world though thinking, feeling and acting. The thinking paths are rational, associative, spatial (visual and auditive), and intuitive. The feeling paths are: letting ourselves to be affected by, dealings with our emotional scale, where there are five emotions that steal our energy: anger, sadness, fear, worries and guilt. Finally paths related to action and behaviour such as: basic behaviours that humans exhibit as the capacity to approach or get away from people and situations in an appropriate manner; identifying our behavioural patterns and being able to change them in favour of our lives and the lives of others; and the paths of identifying rhythms, routines, and parameters that sustain and protect our thoughts, feelings, and actions.

[2]The term *hermeneutics* covers both the first order art and the second order theory of understanding and interpretation of linguistic and non-linguistic expressions. As a theory of interpretation, the hermeneutic tradition stretches all the way back to ancient Greek philosophy (*Stanford Encyclopedia of Philosophy*).

REFERENCES

Berry, Thomas. *The Great Work. Our Way Into the Future*. New York: Bell Tower. 1998.
de Beauport, Elaine. "Self Care." Caracas. 1997. Workshop.
de Beauport, Elaine. *The Three Faces of Mind*. With Aura Sofia Diaz. Wheaton, IL: Quest Books. 2008. Print.
Díaz, Aura Sofía. *In What Ways Are Emotions Important to Self-Development?* Diss. The Fielding Institute, 2000. Print.
España, Luis Pedro. *Detrás de la pobreza. Diez años después*. Caracas, Venezuela: Publicaciones UCAB, Asociación Civil para la promoción de estudios sociales, 2009. Print.
Habermas, Jurgen. *The Inclusion of the Other: Studies on Political Theory*. Cambridge, MA: The MIT Press, 1998. Print.

Lipton, Bruce. *The Biology of Belief*. Santa Rosa, CA: Mountain of Love/Elite Books, 2005. Print.

Mijares, Sharon. "Narratives and Neural Winds." Seishindo.org. 1996. Web. 10 Jan. 2010.

Morin, Edgar. *Pour une politique de civilization.* Paris: Arléa, 2008. Print.

Satir, Virginia. *The New Peoplemaking*. Mountain View, CA: Science and Behaviour Books, 1988. Print.

Stanford Encyclopedia of Philosophy. Web.

Vicentini, Cecilia. *Executive Report on Building Bridges Program*. Caracas: Universidad Metropolitana de Venezuela, 2006. Print.

Vicentini, Cecilia. *Report of Project of Self-Development with Venezuelan Women*. Caracas: National Council of Women, 1994. Print.

27.
From Devotion to Action

The Sufi Women's Organization

NAHID ANGHA, USA

LIFE IS A JOURNEY that begins from a station towards a destination. Every moment is the beginning of a new chapter that leads us closer to our goal; hands of destiny embrace our being, gently and smoothly shaping every second of our space and time. We play our part on this magnificent stage of life, we mark our way into cultures and civilizations, and we participate and become an essential part of this harmonious journey. Our paths cross, we meet a while, we exchange greetings, some will take our imaginations to distant times and place, some have within themselves the potentiality to lead us to a greater world of human heart, some open the door of possibilities by creating goals and promoting progress, some build obstacles preventing us from going forward, some influence and infuse our life with richness, and others become distant memories as soon as they are out of our view. I have been fortunate! I have met and come across many honourable fellow travelers, trustworthy friends, sisters and brothers in the truest meaning, and worthy acquaintances on my path of life and in this journey of becoming. What a humbling experience!

As individuals, we continue our direction towards our own destination. Time-era, culture, gender, geographical environment, social status, religion, and otherwise become secondary to the heart of this journey. "We are an embarking entity" before we "fall under categories and are labeled as one."

Perhaps the most valuable of our fellow travelers and companions are those who "stand for what is right" for humanity and oppose "what is not." This is the very core of human heart, these are the ones who lead civilizations to a favourable destinations, whose conviction to the well-being of humanity is strong, who honour every human's rights to a peaceful life, life that is given to all equally by this magnificent universe.

I am not sure if we choose our convictions or the convictions choose us; I am not sure if the stories we tell transform communities or communities plant the seeds of transformation that grow into lasting stories; I am not sure if every step we take is predestined or we freely create our own choosing. It does not matter—what matters is that I am born into this journey, into this "space in time" that I can claim as my own. It is with this realization and acknowledgement that I cultivate a longing to serve humanity, as an offering, an appreciation to this magnificent Being that has given me this "space in time," an irreplaceable chance of life. How can I remain indifferent to it?

It is from this view that I would like to tell the story of the International Association of Sufism, a gender balanced organization, and, its Sufi Women's Organization.

For a long time, during the late seventies and early eighties, Dr. Ali Kianfar, my life's partner, and I had been cultivating the idea of inviting Sufis from around the world to a forum, to open a line of communication and dialogue amongst Sufi Schools, to provide educational programs for the public to become more acquainted with the treasure of Sufism, and to publish a journal devoted to Sufi practices and schools. Sufis have made great contributions to human rights, education, art, freedom, literature and equality throughout history, and it was time to create a forum so that we could all come together as an international and global spiritual family, exchange information, and gather together and stand for humanity. We thought it was unfair if Sufi communities remained outsiders to each other's teachings and spiritual pursuit, and if the interested members of societies remained unaware of the treasure of Sufism, in its totality, diversities and colours and forms. So we embarked on a new journey: establishing an international organization inclusive of all Sufi schools and teachers, Sufi writers and artists, scholars and those interested in the discipline of Sufism. To my knowledge this was the first time in the history of Sufism that an organization was established for this goal: bringing Sufis from around the world to a forum.

Sufism, a mystical school born from the heart of Islam in the seventh century, has been one of the most influential spiritual paths that has contributed to the advancement of civilizations, from science to literature, art to architect, poetic conversation to political stand, medicine to mathematics, astronomy to the most fascinating story-telling and poetic pursuit, with a universal language that talks to the human heart. Perhaps it is because of its heart-felt language and universality that Sufism has been welcomed by many cultures and become an essential part of the fabric of traditions.

To take a journey of such magnitude seemed like an impossible dream. It required extensive research to identify, locate, contact, communicate, invite, to understand all diversities, personalities, politics, while ultimately remaining truthful to the goal of coming together in the spirit of harmony and friendship for the sake of education, human rights and equality. It has been one of the most valuable journeys of my life. The idea was welcomed by many Sufi masters and Schools, and proved to become a gathering of harmonious spiritual families connected in this world that is so consumed by materialist ideology.

Being reminded by my maternal grandmother's advice: "the world is an open forum, to stand for what you think is a worthy pursuit, you must first qualify yourself for the endeavour; otherwise you would be pushed aside." So I began my journey with extensive research and learning; with each step, my personal world expanded into a universe of deeply valued devotion manifested in many colours and forms. What a magnificent treasure unlocked by the hand of my destiny! Yet this journey was not without its limitations. Sufism, that has welcomed women's leadership from its very beginning of its history, sometimes had to face the dictates of cultural traditions and political practices. So this was an obstacle that I had to face. Being a woman, taking on such an endeavour was not always appreciated or tolerated, so I faced some small pebbles on the road.

For the last decade we have seen in the international as well as nation-wide context, developments and progress that have addressed women's rights, equality, and improvement in the life of female generations through equal opportunity in education, positions and professions. In male-dominated patriarchal societies, women themselves have been a great asset in such progress. They continue to strive to create a forum of equality for all to benefit. Yet nothing is accomplished without its challenges and women themselves have taken great responsibility to lead the road towards equality and improvement in the lives of women.

FORMATION OF THE INTERNATIONAL ASSOCIATION OF SUFISM

Challenges and limitations are reminders that help us to remain strong on our journey. Women, who have made great advancements in the fields of education, literature, sports, music, entertainment and politics, have yet to overcome the traditional institution of religion or cultural traditions. These fields have remained the most difficult domains to enter, and whether or not these domains will truly welcome women with open arms remains to be seen. Perhaps the great resistance lies in the stories told in religious traditions where Eve, the mother of all living, has been portrayed as "an addition" rather than an independent entity, whose cunning causes disobedience. It does not matter, we do not have to dwell in the old stories; we do not have to live them but let them remain as old stories, nothing more. What matters is that we have seen progress in different sections of our society, even though the institution of religion has remained a challenge to overcome in order to create an equal opportunity for leadership amongst its members, male and female.

Fortunately, progress in technology and formation of global interaction, on a very human level, has opened the door towards the greater understanding of human self, human potentiality, and human values. The old stories are gradually losing their influence, a new understanding is being embarked, and women have developed interests and see possibilities of their own spiritual leadership, and have found a mutual respectful ground for interaction with their male counterparts.

One such example is the formation of the International Association of Sufism (IAS), a non-profit, was founded in October 1983 in California. IAS is also a United Nations' Non-Governmental Organization with the Department of Public Information (UN NGO/DPI). IAS is a gender-balanced international organization with membership, representations, and chapters around the world, many years of service, hosting an annual Sufism Symposium since 1994. It has developed eleven departments, including the Sufi Women Organization (SWO), many programs and projects, closely worked with global interfaith and interreligious organizations, and remained truthful to its gender-balanced mission to the present time. The coming together of Sufi masters and scholars, men and women, in a mutually respectful ground, within the Annual Sufism Symposia events, have formed an acceptable place for honoring Sufi women's leadership, re-examining their historical movements in the creation of cultures, their cultural identity, history, politics, and women who have established leadership in patriarchal societies. Their narratives have become the focus of books and studies, and their contributions to the development of civilizations are being recognized and acknowledged. With every progress and acknowledgment we came closer to the formation of the Sufi Women's Organization.

SUFI WOMEN'S ORGANIZATION

The Sufi Women's Organization was not born overnight; it took me many steps, a great deal of thoughtful cultivation, facing challenges and sometimes intolerance. To make our point, to walk towards our goal, to make sure equality is preserved, sometimes we have to be bold, to take action, to remain respectful and require respect. Hesitation is not always our friend, and doubtfulness may not work to our benefit. We have to stand for what is right, stand strong, and stand for all humanity. Following my own advice, in the global forum of that first annual Sufism Symposium in 1994, I made my point for Sufi women's leadership, wherever they are.

Bringing together Sufis, Sufi Schools and prominent leaders into the first Sufism Symposium (1994) required over ten years continuous work. Finally, Sufi masters and practitioners, Sufi scholars and artists, many Sufi schools and traditions, from the coasts of Indonesia to the boarders of West Africa, gathered for a weekend of conversation, presentation, communication, meditation, prayers, and *Zikr* (Sufi chanting). The seed was planted, communication began to flourish, and the impossible dream was made possible. I have made sure that Sufi women present their views side by side with their male counterparts from the very beginning of these Symposia.

Throughout its history, Sufi women have made great contributions to the teachings of Sufism and spiritual pursuit; traditionally, however, the center circle of Sufi chanting has been reserved for Sufi male masters and leaders. It was in that first international Symposium that I took a memorable step, a bold endeavour, and sat in that center circle leading meditation, with my Sufi brothers and leaders. This was a devotional act, Sufi women leadership was emerging once again, and equal rights of leadership was acknowledged one more time. My fellow travelers and brothers in that Symposium remained respectful and welcoming of this endeavour. A new historical and global chapter began to emerge, women were welcomed (back) as Masters and renowned teachers, they claimed their rightful seat at the center, and the story travelled to far away cultures through my Sufi family, brothers, and sisters. That act opened a door of equality within schools that were not traditionally accommodating. My brothers, those Sufi masters who recognized and approved the need to welcome women's leadership to their own spiritual family, opened the door. This was an unprecedented achievement. The International Association of Sufism began and remained a gender balanced international organization and its departments and programs continued to honour such pursuit.

One of the most significant objectives was the creation of the International Sufi Women's Organization. I worked towards the formation of the Sufi Women's Organization for many years and in

1993 I proposed the idea and began a campaign to officially establish such organization. The idea was welcomed and became a global pursuit through the efforts of many women from diverse backgrounds, nationalities, traditions, education, Sufi schools, age groups, and so forth. The Sufi Women's Organization (SWO), a humanitarian, non-political, non-sectarian organization, was officially established in 1994, the Sufi Women Dialogue became an on-line conversation in 1996, and the SWO Luncheon program began the same year and continues to the present time. In that year, many of us decided to gather to develop programs during a weekend retreat, held in the beautiful scenery of Marin County, California. Our early morning walks, fresh air, sunshine, silent meditation, evening talks, midnight star watching, and roundtable discussions gave us more determination to develop focused and global programs for such a devotional organization. So we decided and finalized that Sufi Women was founded in order to introduce, disseminate, honour and acknowledge the contribution and service of Sufi women to the world civilization. The mission was and is to come together free from human prejudice to share the knowledge, wisdom, experience, and concerns of Sufi women of the past and present with our societies and time, remembering that the essence of the human being, regardless of gender or colour, time or place, has been regarded as reverent, dignified, and respectful by teachers of humanity. Such magnificence, we determined, was and is the gift of Being: recognizing such magnificence is learned. The Sufi Women's Organization has come together as a group of honourable and responsible women in order to serve as educators, guides, advisors and friends to support, protect, and educate for such learning. Sufism requires great vigilance and sustained continuous self-improvement efforts.

We began by opening a global dialogue amongst Sufi women whose mission was/is to take peaceful actions towards common causes with focus on women and children's rights. Ever since that remarkable weekend retreat we have made great contributions towards world peace, education, health, human rights and policy-making.

The accomplishments and achievements of any group that makes a difference in communities and leads towards advancement, are the result of the efforts of many, and SWO is no exception. The list of what SWO has achieved through the efforts of those who have volunteered their devotion, time, energy, and expertise is long that I can mention only a few.

The Sufi Women's Organization began its membership draw, and, before long its presence was extended internationally, with enthusiasm and a spirit of global friendship and sisterhood. We started our mission in 1997 by drafting a "Code of Ethics" for members to honour, in the spirit of offering guidance rather than mandating or regulating conduct. After eight months work of over one hundred women from around the globe, we finalized the Code. Our primary humanitarian goals included women's rights, education, and social awareness. We extended these endeavours into a second list of "what to support" and "what to refuse" which included a list of products and companies that generate earth-friendly goods, and a list of products manufactured by war-associated organizations, business with unfair practices, etc.

We have made a significant positive change for women's leadership, from leading Islamic prayers to opening the door for equality, conversation and education, and tirelessly created a peaceful space for Sufi women to come together with other Sufi Masters, Interfaith leaders and spiritual scholars in the spirit of harmony and understanding, making positive change in recognizing the leadership role of women in communities.

We were able to take active leadership roles within the global community through interfaith organizations, Amnesty International, Habitats for Humanity, UNICEF, UNESCO, and the United Nations, and have worked with diverse community services programs. We have been able to provide classes and lecture series for Sufi women introducing Sufi women's accomplishments in art, literature, poetry, teachings, and practices in publications distributed internationally and through the SWO Quarterly Newsletter, Luncheon Programs, and annual Sufism Symposium meeting.

Sufi Women Dialogue, our online listserve, opened unprecedented possibilities with a global family beyond our imaginations. We began to converse, discuss, seek ideas, request support, and open the door of friendship, creating a forum for exchanging ideas, traditions and teachings among Sufi women from different schools and cultures. These endeavours resulted in a two-day conference "Women's Wisdom: Women in Action" where over 200 women spiritual leaders from across the United States as well as SWO Chapters participated and addressed an audience numbering several hundred. Among the projects developed at that conference was a youth project entitled "Community Service with Interfaith Reflection," where youth and young adults joined in regular community service projects such as work with homeless, environment, Habitat for Humanity, etc. We promoted and assisted to establish Voices for Justice, a youth organization to stand for and work towards justice and the rights of young adults.

Over the years we have been able to create and continue programs such as the Prison Project, where our therapists volunteer their time, assist the under-served female population incarcerated in jails and prisons, conduct workshops, provide therapy, and donate books for the women, their children and family member visitors.

We became the 151st organization to sign in support of the Global Women's Peace Petition; participated in action with Amnesty International and in The High Commission for Human Rights.

We have contributed to different organizations to help women and children in need around the world, including Project Amigo, Mexico, providing school supplies and assisting after-school programs

We helped to build and repair an orphanage for girls in Jakarta, Indonesia, through SWO Indonesian Chapter and the contributions of SWO members. We provided assistance and financial support to a project that provides free medical attention, clean water to refugees in Ethiopia.

We worked with humanitarian and educational international organizations such as UNICEF to provide immunization to children in sub-Saharan Africa, and to provide school supplies to children in war zones.

With the help and leadership of our Egyptian Chapter, SWO was also able to provide education for young women in need.

SWO compiled and published the first volume of the biography of the Sufi women masters of the present time, a scholarly book on the story of *hijab*, and created classes and lecture series to educate for the prevention of domestic violence.

We campaign tirelessly and write letters to advocate for women whose rights have been violated.

Our members were able to establish a vocational school for low-income young women as well as literacy projects including tutoring services for low-income families.

We have sponsored a homeless program: "Friday coffee" that provides one year of hot beverages and food for the homeless population in northern California (homelessness is global).

We have provided abuse-prevention services for transitional housing residents and created lecture series and workshop programs for domestic violence awareness and prevention specifically for women within the Islamic community.

And our work continues....

Life is a journey that begins from a station and proceeds towards a destination. Every moment is the beginning of a new chapter leading us closer to our goal; hands of destiny embrace our being, and gently and smoothly shape every second of our space and time. We play our part on this magnificent stage of life, we mark our way into cultures and civilizations, and we participate and become an essential part of this harmonious journey.

Yet, true equality becomes a characteristic of an ideal universe, spiritual or not, where we hide behind or are haunted by the old stories told in traditions, whether we are dominated by many kinds of battles and refuse to find solutions in peace, we are on the crossroad of decision making and we are responsible for the outcome. Do we have the capacity to honour all humanity and protect every individual's rights to a peaceful life and equality? The decision is based on our personal morals, and the answer remains to be seen. Whether we are visionaries, humanitarians, advocates, even inspirations to a few and leaders to others, it takes more than just a few to fulfill a centuries old dream, and to understand the morality and necessity to promote equal rights in order to recover from our own failings, which are the failings of most of humankind.

28.
A Dawn of a New Era[1]

ALIAA RAFEA, EGYPT

E GYPT IS KNOWN and respected for its ancient civilization. It holds a distinguished cultural place in the Middle East given its contributions to both ancient and modern history. Women have always contributed to Egyptian culture, from its powerful mythological feminine deities to the ancient female Pharaohs, Hatshepsut to Cleopatra, and into recent years. Moreover, Egypt had women-liberating movements early in the twentieth century when Egyptian women, supported by courageous men, went out of their way to bring the society from the dark ages to enlightenment.[2] The 1952 Revolution opened numerous avenues for women. They were encouraged to get into a variety of professions that had previously not been allowed, and for the first time they were given the right to vote and to get elected in the Parliament. As a result, women now occupy a variety of leading positions, and have equal opportunities in many social areas. But alas, Egyptian society is witnessing a backlash; women are practicing self-oppression, and retreating from the public to the private sphere, imprisoning themselves once more in limited gender roles. To counter this withdrawal, women's organizations have begun to deal with the modern women's situations from different angles. The Egyptian revolution brought women to the middle of that event. I believe that the impact of the revolution will have lasting impacts on the Egyptian women's self image. One of the women is quoted as saying: "The Revolution has changed us. No one sees you as a woman here; no one sees you as a man. We are all united in our desire for democracy and freedom." Where in previous protests women had accounted for, at most, ten percent, in Tahrir Square that number stood at about 40 percent to 50 percent in the eighteen days leading up to Mr. Mubarak's resignation (January 25-February 11) (Biggs).

As a co-founder of a women's group within the Egyptian Society for Spiritual and Cultural Research (ESSCR), I would like to demonstrate how spiritual guidance has been empowering women to find and cultivate their skills and talents and use them to serve and help other people and other women. This chapter also sheds lights on how cultural dogma prevents women from expressing their aspirations and limits their participation in society. I conclude that, without awakening the spiritual root of the human soul, humans are likely to be deceived by pseudo-religious rhetoric, and worn-out traditional values. The Egyptian Revolution shucked stagnant ideologies and rejuvenated the deep spiritual power within the Egyptian heart. Thus women, many of whom had never before shared in protests and demonstrations, came forth to share in this historical moment. Will this spirit continue or will be defeated? This question cannot be easily answered as Egypt is passing through a transitional phase which may take some years to mature.

UNIVERSALITY VERSUS PARTICULARITY

I would like to discuss women's issues in Egypt from a human rights perspective that cannot be separated from a spiritual dimension. Men and women share this experience of being human and deserve to enjoy equal rights. Regardless of their biological differences, the world needs their contributions in order to bring peace and prosperity to the whole of humankind. However women have been for the most part deprived from participating effectively in social, political, or intellectual change. If that is true for the world at large, it is also true for Egyptians.

As a woman who has watched human rights violations perpetrated under the claim of the necessity to respect cultural particularity,[3] I would like to deal with gender issues in a manner that goes beyond any specific cultural definitions, and sets both women and men free to be who they really are, rather than conform to norms that society and culture dictate. This approach does not deny cultural differences, but considers that cultural values that block individual human potentials need to be reconsidered and criticized from within that particular culture.

However, as an Egyptian Muslim, I clearly see where universal human rights are violated and where specific cultural values are respected. That is to say, to acknowledge cultural variations does not necessarily contradict with universal principles of human rights. For example, when women in Egypt are denied the right to be employed as judges, under the spurious claim that our culture protects women from harsh situations and great stress so therefore they should not enter such professions. I consider this to be a denial of their human rights, and a loss for the whole society. Other women in other areas in this world have proven that women are capable of dealing with complicated cases, and to be successful as judges.

On the other hand, I do not agree that gender freedom equates to sexual freedom, a practice seen in some other cultures. Young people in Muslim countries are taught that sex is a sacred relationship between a man and a woman, and thus should only be practiced within marriage: I honour this view. I may have my own reservations on different perspectives and practices in other cultures, but I understand that they have their own moral justifications that should be revered as long as it does not abuse human dignity and self pride.

There has been much discourse regarding "Islamic dress" or "veiling," the act of covering one's hair. Most Egyptian women today wear head scarves, believing that they follow Islamic teachings. For some outsiders, this style of dressing may be seen as a sign of oppression. Though I do not wear a headscarf, I honour women's freedom to choose their dress styles. I do not and cannot see any contradictions between this act as a sign of modesty, and women's freedom to be active in various social roles. Actually I become critical when women reduce themselves to being sexual objects, revealing their charm and beauty with the intention of seduction. On the other side of the coin, I do not feel comfortable when women are ashamed of their bodies, feeling guilty, just because they are women. Accordingly, they try to hide under veils. Both cases reflect a negative self-image that contradicts human dignity and integrity.

In Egypt, we have these two extreme cases. In the middle, there are women who adhere to modest clothing, but are not committed to traditionally-defined Islamic dress (wearing scarves and loose garments). There are also women who consider the scarf to be a sign of religiosity but do not give up their social roles and prestigious positions. However, there is a stereotype about hair-covering among westerners, that all women who wear scarves are not free to choose. British Muslim singer Sami Yusuf illustrates this stereotype as a dialogue between a Muslim woman and a westerner in the lyrics to his 2005 song "Free":

So don't you see? I am truly free. This piece of scarf on me, I wear so proudly, to preserve my dignity, my modesty, my integrity. So don't judge me. Open your eyes and see. Why cannot you just accept me?

This ethnocentric perspective ignores the variety of meanings given to cultural symbols. Actually veiling was part of a social movement in the seventies and eighties (Rafea 1983, 2001). As I have reported in my other work, against outsiders' expectations, veiling empowered young women by giving them a sense of cultural identity backed by ideological perspectives of a wider social reform (I may disagree with these women, yet I respect their will to actively share in the process of changing society). Veiling is also seen within the context of creating a safe private space in work environments. Symbolically, as Fadwa El-Guindi points out, the veil defines the boundaries between women and the external world and gives them a sense of protection that increases their self-confidence. Attention should be given not to what women wear, but rather to how they think and act. It is because of this that I am concerned about the increasing number of women who stress their religiosity by covering their whole body from head to toes, including their faces; they are called *mutanaquibat*. They choose dark plain colours for this dress style, and wear gloves, so nothing is seen from them except their eyes. I believe that there must be an underlying ideology supporting this new phenomenon that requires deep investigation. Covering women's faces is a continuation of the same ideas that demean women's bodies. Because these ideas are framed in religious rhetoric, defining women's bodies as *awra* (shame) has power over women, compelling them to lean on religious instructions that advocate for the *necessity* of wearing *niqab*. *Niquab* is different symbolically from hair-covering. It completely veils the identity, and certainly will hinder face-to-face interaction. I consider this practice similar to burying baby girls alive, a practice that had been common before Islam. Veiling the face denies the uniqueness of each women and her right to communicate with the outer world.

The educator Ken Robinson places great emphasis on individual uniqueness and the importance of self-discovery, or finding what he calls the *Element*. He believes that each individual should be given the chance to develop his or her potential differently. The element is the point at which natural talent meets personal passion: "When People arrive at the Element, they feel most themselves, most inspired, and achieve at their highest levels" (15). How could a woman who hides under a wide, dark garment, covering her face completely, who walks in the streets anonymously like a ghost, be able to discover and unfold her potential? This tendency to be isolated and withdrawn goes against not only the right of being oneself, but also against the Egyptian cultural roots represented in Egypt's Ancient Civilization, and against all revelations' basic spiritual messages, including that of Islam.

Fortunately, Egypt's Element was revealed collectively by the revolution, when Egyptians came to a moment of self-discovery. At that fateful event, the authentic Egyptian soul, which was buried for several decades, witnessed resurgence. This was revealed in the revolutionary behaviour in Tahrir Square, which served as a model that was repeated everywhere in Egypt.

It was worth watching a Christian woman helping a bearded religiously-committed man in ablution before prayers. In holy places, as they did in Tahrir Square, women and men stood beside each other in prayers. All barriers disappeared: sheikhs from Al-Azhar with their traditional garment walked hand in hand with priests in their formal dress. Christians guarded Muslims during their prayers, and Muslims chanted while guarding Christians during their prayers. Young couples celebrated their weddings amongst the protesters, considering all the attendants in the square as family. Some mothers of martyrs came to hug and encourage young people, calling them their sons and daughters. Stories of the revolution are endless, but with a singular theme: coming together as one family. This is the spirit of the ancient Egyptian civilization.

Unfortunately, the wonderful utopian society of Tahrir Square and its counterparts all over Egypt was gradually vanishing as a result of continuous attempts to diminish young people's enthusiasm, and gradually inhabit the Egyptian People's aspirations. It started by diverting people's attention from a focus on the realization of the Revolution's goals to a debate over accepting or rejecting constitutional amendments. Meanwhile the Supreme Council of Armed Forces (SCAF) took every possible opportunity to detain activists. Women were especially targeted. As early as March 9, 2011, after army officers violently cleared the square of protesters, at least eighteen women were held in military detention. They were beaten, given electric shocks, subjected to strip searches while being photographed by male soldiers, forced to submit to "virginity checks" and threatened with prostitution charges ("Egypt bans"). Women continued to be targeted in many other incidents. In December 2011, in a powerful and graphic video watched around the world, soldiers are visible beating and dragging a woman along the street during a protest. Her clothing is ripped by helmeted soldiers, her midriff exposed and her blue bra is clearly on show as a soldier stomps on her. This woman was one among many who were detained and humiliated in a nearby building of the People's assembly. As reported in Canada's *National Post,* more than ten thousand women marched Cairo streets, chanting against the military and raising their voices in protest: "the Women in Egypt are a red line." (Higgins). It is not easy to put any expectation at the time being on how the situation is going to be like. On one hand, the Egyptians' dream of a free society with justice and equality faces great challenges. On the other hand, the Egyptians have broken the fear barrier, and will continue their struggles. As their ancestors could cultivate the land around the River Nile, and survived to create a great civilization, they seem to be going through jumping over obstacles with determination. At least I carry this spirit, and would not let it go.

THE BALANCE BETWEEN MALE AND FEMALE ASPECTS
IN ANCIENT EGYPT

Ancient Egyptians perceived male and female aspects of the universe united in one whole. The Sky (*Nut)* and the earth (*Geb*) met at the edges of the universe to complement one another. Together they embrace human and natural worlds. This harmony continues on different levels: *Ma'at* represents the truth, and is symbolized as a feminine body with an ostrich head. She stands in the underworld with *Osiris* (a male figure) on the Day of Judgment to reward or punish the deceased. For Ancient Egyptians, feminine aspects mixed gentleness and power. Storms were personified by *Sakhmet* and *Tefnut. Hathor*, another ancient deity, was associated with pleasure, but also had the power of destruction. It seems that the Ancient Egyptian were aware consciously and unconsciously of the integrations between male and female aspects on a cosmic as well as individual level. That awareness was likewise reflected in their lives. In social and political arenas, Egyptian women such as Queen Hatshepsut were accepted as rulers. Her reign lasted twenty-two years (1479-1457 BCE) and witnessed major accomplishments. She established trade networks with neighbour countries, and most Egyptologists agree that her expeditions were for trade not war, and that she kept peaceful relations with other countries. Nefertiti (ca. 1370-1330 BCE), who was well known for her beauty, reigned for approximately twelve years with her husband Ikhnaton (or Akhenaten) , but she was, perhaps, one of the most powerful queens to ever rule. During her reign, Egypt underwent many radical religious changes. She promoted Ikhnaton's call for Monotheism courageously but smoothly, and helped avoid seemingly inevitable religious civic confrontations. As mothers, wives, or sisters, women also shared with Pharaohs' decision-making (although that is not to say that all Pharaohs had women as a power behind the throne). That Ancient Egyptian world view was in accord with the analytical psychology of Carl Gustav Jung, who explained how every male and female have an opposite-gendered inner aspect on the unconscious level. A balanced human being is one who is in harmony with this opposite aspect. That is to say, a man should seek harmony with his *anima* (the female aspect of self), and a woman should find that harmony with her *animus* (the male aspect of self). This harmony is part of a process that Jung called individuation.[4] Within Jungian psychology, feminine and masculine aspects of the psyche are not rigidly defined, and do not point to mentally and socially constructed attributes, but are metaphorically used to denote two separate but integrative opposite collectivities of the unconscious. In Taoism these two aspects are called Yin and Yang. I consider the process toward individuation as a way of spiritual fulfillment. I use the term "spiritual fulfillment" rather than "religion" or "faith" because those terms have become contaminated with dogmatic ways of thinking. This will lead us to differentiate between religiosity as socio-cultural phenomenon, and religiosity as a spiritual process. This clarification is essential in relation to explain how oppressive, worn-out traditions in Egypt and elsewhere are legitimized under the disguise of religiosity, and to show on the other hand how religiosity when inspired by one's inner voice can be a liberating force.[5]

THE PARADOX BETWEEN NATURE AND CULTURE

Women have suffered from the belittling of their abilities and weakening of the self-esteem that is necessary for them to unleash their potential and contribute in public sphere. Likewise, men have been denied their right to express emotions, to admit to vulnerability and therefore to seek help when needed. In social psychology, our ideas about ourselves are formed through the process of social interaction. A child may think s/he is stupid, ugly, or otherwise because his/her parents treat him/her as such. Self-image is the idiom that is used to denote to those ideas of who we think we are. The image and self-image of who we are, and what we are capable of doing is based on cultural assumptions defining masculinity and femininity according to what is considered "natural."

In 1972, Ann Oakley introduced the term "gender roles" to discuss the socio-cultural impact in defining male/female roles. When the term "gender" was introduced to social sciences in relation to social roles, it challenged the myth of "natural" roles. Women proved to be capable of taking the lead in many scientific, political, and social spheres. Although the roles of women have been slowly changing in various parts of the world, this continuing dogma about fixed natural roles of women threatens the women of Egypt. As a result, the achievements of the Egyptian women's movements, which took over a century to accomplish, are facing great peril.

In her research, Hind Khattab has shown that a great many Egyptian women in rural areas, as well as others in urban areas, believe that they were created "weak," "incompatible with men," and "having limited intellectual and physical abilities." Some of these women believe that their biological ability to bear children determines their main role in life. They literally say "that is how we are created." Many women of the younger generations are convinced that they received education simply for the purpose of helping their children to study their lessons, and to support their husbands. They believe that they should surrender to these roles because that is what God/nature wanted them to do. As a professor who teaches about the Egyptian Women's Movement, I have asked my own students what they want to do with their lives after graduation; many reply that they preferred to get married and settle at homes with their families.

Of course motherhood is exclusively nature's gift to women, and therefore should be revered, but this reverence should not lead to the conclusion that women are created merely to care for their families. Both men and women should care for each other, and for children within the family. Many people around the world have been realizing this reality, but the tendency amongst younger Egyptians is to support earlier cultural tendencies, in the mistaken belief that it is a religious duty.

Thanks to research in the social sciences, it has become obvious that what is considered "natural" is often socially and culturally constructed (see Oakley). In sociology as well as in psychology, "collective consciousness" is an outcome of shared cultural values. The worldview of what is "natural" is the outcome of historical accumulations that shape the collective consciousness. That is partly a result of acknowledging biological differences between men and women, and defining their roles accordingly; the emphasis on specific roles is transmitted from generation to generation, and became part of collective consciousnesses.

This hypothesis regarding natural roles of men and women had restricted Egyptian women from participation in the public sphere in the nineteenth and early twentieth centuries. Women conformed to harem culture, where women had their own space in the household, with no access to the outer world: it used to be said that a woman went outdoors twice: once for her marriage, and once for her funeral. The change came slowly, started by the then-revolutionary call of Refe'a Al Tahtawy (1805-73) for women's education in his book *Al Murshid al-Amin Lilbanat wa Albanin* ("Honest Guidance for Girls and Boys"). Special schools were opened to teach women what was believed to be helpful to their community, such as a school for midwives. Gradually, women enrolled in the normal educational system but were not allowed to attend universities. In 1929, the first woman was admitted to schools of higher education, opening the doors to the many women who would follow.

In the wake of the 1919 Revolution, women's consciousness underwent a noticeable shift. As participants during the Revolution, women started to be aware of their civic rights and duties. The well-known activist Huda Sha'arwy and her colleagues established the Egyptian Feminist Union (EFU) in 1923. The Union called for political rights for women, major reforms in family law, equal education, and expanded professional opportunities (see Badran), but the new constitution fell far short of Union's expectations, with none of these changes incorporated.

More than nine decades later, this mentality is still at work. In February 2010, with a majority of votes, the State Council refused to employ new female graduates under the claim that women's so-called "natural traits" make them vulnerable to political pressures. The premise is that women are emotional and biased by nature; therefore their ability for rationality is limited. The international rights organization Human Rights Watch condemned this decision, describing it as an extension of discrimination against women. Their report states: "women are still barred from serving as judges in other state bodies, including criminal courts.... The continuing discrimination insults the many Egyptian women who are fully qualified to serve as judges." Sometimes the proponents of this theory use verses from the Qur'an to support with their views. It must be clear that those claims are specific interpretations that do not necessarily represent the guidance of the Islamic teachings. The rise of President Morsi and the Muslim Brotherhood to power in the wake of the January 25 Revolution has worsened the situation. They have their own way of interpreting and using the Qur'an and Sunna to manipulate public opinion. Since Morsi was inaugurated as a president and till June 30, 2013, he has been continuously violating the terms of his election. In November 2012, he gave himself the illegal right to issue a constitutional declaration, appointed a prosecutor general through unconstitutional procedures, immunized the Shura Council and the Constitutional Assembly, and challenged court verdicts. The promise made by Morsi, that all factions of the society will be represented in the constitutional assembly, was ignored, leaving women, Christians and minorities at large, unprotected. Egyptians felt that there was a plan to steal their country, and if they didn't remove MB from power, they would be humiliated, marginalized, and overruled forever by this fascist regime. A group of young people established a campaign under the name *Tamorrod* (the word means rebel). By collecting 22 million signatures to call for early presidential elections and bring an end to the fascist MB rule, and giving enough time to mobilize the masses, they created the ground for unprecedented massive demonstrations with estimates ranging from 17 to 33 million protestors in the streets The army was duty bound to respond to the demands of the people of Egypt and to maintain stability. Otherwise, a civil war could have erupted. This event was a continuation of the January 25 Revolution. It is obvious now for any one who would come to power, that Egyptians are determined to reach their goals "freedom, dignity, and social justice." For the majority of Egyptians, religion (Islam) should not be mixed with politics. If the Muslim Brotherhood continued to be in power, women's rights would have deteriorated enormously.

The way that Prophet Muhammad (Peace be upon him) treated women is at odds with the interpretations of fundamentalists and Islamists, and renders them illogical within the context of the Islamic guidance. For example, the Prophet trusted his wife Khadija's wisdom, and she was the first to know about the Revelation. Moreover, history tells us about women warriors who fought hand-in-hand with men. One of those warriors sacrificed her life to save the Prophet's life in Uhud. Considering Egypt's cultural roots, whether in Ancient Egypt or within Islam, it is surprising to observe this tendency to defend what are claimed to be "natural roles" of women and men.

It is not easy to explain the Egyptian mix between traditions, as religiosity, liberalism, and the influence of westernization are very complex. Defining the "natural" role of women has become a common denominator between rich and poor, rural and urban, religious and liberal. The decline in women's participation in politics has been phenomenal. In order to face this noticeable withdrawal, the government passed a law to reserve at least 64 seats for women out of more than five hundred in Parliament for the 2010 election. This law is not the first of its kind; in 1979 election 30 seats were allocated to women.[6] Although this appears to be a minimal number of seats for females, it still carries significance. The revolution has changed the situation, and the temporary constitutional declaration left the quota of the women in the Parliament open. That is to say, the declaration does not mention certain number of seats that should be allocated to women, instead it says "allocation of a certain parentage of women in the parliament is negotiable."

The legal system in Egypt encourages women to get involved in the labour force, and to be employed according to their educational qualifications. Women have the right to maternal leave for two years, which can be renewed further if needed. Women can go back to their work positions and promotions are granted. For the sake of family solidarity, women as well as men can take leave from their work if one spouse is appointed to a position outside Egypt without the other losing his or her job. It is worth noting that this legal arrangement, which includes working women, provides a positive addition to the cultural premise that women are mothers and care-givers. Parenting is seen as women's main responsibility, but professional positions are still respected. Men are completely excluded from parental leave.

Despite these benefits, there is a tendency for women to use self-defeating mechanisms. Unless this idea of "natural roles" and religious dogma change, women will remain excluded from sensitive and important positions and places where gender balance is needed. Educating women to learn how to be free is a necessity. This is the core message of all spiritual revelations, including Islam—simply because humans cannot be true believers of spiritual guidance through indoctrination or oppression.

FACING THE CHALLENGES

Religiosity—as practiced today—has political, economic, cultural, and social aspects. Historians and political analysts agree that what was called a religious revival in the seventies emerged as a response to the ideological void following Egypt's defeat in 1967's Six-Day War, where religion replaced nationalism for Muslims and Coptic Christians alike.[7] There were other factors that contributed to strengthen the Islamic groups and formalize and crystallize their ideologies. As President Anwar Sadat started to encourage the brand of political Islam represented by the Muslim Brotherhood to counter the popularity of Gamal Abdel Nasr and to build his own popularity, many young people joined this trend. On the other hand, the open-door policy encouraged migration to Saudi Arabia and other Gulf states. Migrants were exposed to other types of religiosity in these countries, and they returned to Egypt with differing values and attitudes. Added to this, the turmoil of events in Iran and the establishment of Iran's Islamic Republic encouraged differing Islamic groups to build foundations for their political ambitions.[8] Within these contexts, women's roles, as understood by interpretations of Islam, became a major issue of discussion. There was no consensus on defining these roles, so the trend of encouraging women to take limited social roles was confusing to many women.

Recent history reveals the complexity and difficulty of these changes. Civic and governmental efforts have been taking place in an attempt to transform the crippling situation. In 2000, the National Council for Women was established by a decree from former President Hosni Mubarak. This Council was linked directly to his office, and headed by the former First Lady, Suzanne Mubarak. The Council still functions and serves more or less the same goals. One of the many objectives of this Council is to propose public policy matters for society and its constitutional institutions. This includes the development and empowerment of women enabling them to contribute to economic improvements, while integrating their efforts in comprehensive development programs.[9] One of the council's most noticeable achievements is the institution of a law enabling women to initiate divorce proceedings, a step that frees women from their husbands' domination. Unfortunately, and against all expectations, after the January 25 Revolution Islamists started to launch campaigns against that law, and other hard-earned advances for women.

At the grass-roots level, there are many women's organizations working in Egyptian society, advocating for women's issues. These organizations focus on a variety of remarkable endeavours. Arab Women's Solidarity was established in 1982 with the aim of gathering women around common goals, rooting the movement within Islamic contexts in an attempt to build a new religious discourse that empowers women. The Society of Earth's Daughters, also founded in 1982, draws attention to rural women and their status. The Center of New Woman Studies, now The Foundation of New Women (FNW), began is activities in 1984 as informal study group, initially formed by a number of women who were activities on issue of democracy and social Justice. The organization has since evolved to embrace numerous activities as well as different generations. It has also taken on different legal forms and was recently registered with the ministry of social affairs in 2004, and the Egyptian Center for Women's Rights (1996) encourages women to participate in politics. Mohamed Abdel Fatah Mohamed gives a comprehensive breakdown (in Arabic) in his 2008 book *Al-Jami'iyat Al-Ahliyya Al-Nisa'iyya*.

These are but some examples, demonstrating the turmoil of ideological conflict and attempted resolutions in Egyptian society currently taking place.

ALIAA RAFEA

THE BIRTH OF A SPIRITUAL MOVEMENT

With great respect to the efforts that have taken place to support women on their way to liberation legally, economically, socially, and ideologically, spiritual education also needs attention. It is through changing the outlook of who we are as male and female that both women and men will find their way to freely decide what they want to do in their lives.

As long as religion is used to indoctrinate, to paralyze people's ability of making their own decisions, women and men lose the ability to see clearly what they want in life. Instead, they respond to what other people tell them what God wants them to be, and thereby lose their connection with their inner voice—a God-given gift. Unlike these extremist religious teachings, spiritual training and education respects the uniqueness of each person. By rejecting absolutism, and encouraging free dialogue, a person finds a way to listen to the inner voice, and to discover what s/he really wants.

As a co-founder of the women's group within the Egyptian Society of Spiritual and Cultural Research (ESSCR), I have found interaction among women to be very meaningful. Participants in this society act as one family. As a family they care and support one another. Although women in this group are of different ages, occupations, cultural and social backgrounds, they are able to communicate and feel close to one another. Our attendees wear different dress styles; some cover their hair, others do not; some wear traditional dresses, other wear fashionable dress styles. Differences are not barriers: on the contrary, they enrich our experiences. Some men have started to attend our meetings, and they are increasing in number. We welcome them and feel enriched by their presence. Men and women share in the ESSCR cultural forums, and work together as one team.

Within the ESSCR environment and through meetings and discussions—inspired by the spiritual teaching of Islam—*fixed roles* of men and women are diminishing. Mercy and love within the family are emphasized. This clarity of vision among women challenges a rigid way of thinking. Therefore, women are advised to gradually change their setting by being patient, not weak; loving, but not subordinate; able to voice their position, but not to fight. Young couples are facing many difficulties in their day-to-day lives, but their way of dealing with these struggles is based on comforting one another, rather than competing with each other. Even those young women who choose to leave their jobs in order to take care of their youngsters do so out of love, rather

358

than because it is a woman's expected duty. Instead, it is with the consciousness that their social participation can take many forms and make many contributions. They are more concerned about their skills and talents and how to develop them, than acting according to society's expectations.

Women are also inspired to find varieties of ways to fulfill their innate spiritual urge towards fuller spiritual awakening.[10] With loving spirit, they stretch their hands to each other on different levels. Experts in different fields train other members voluntarily. For example, lessons in the English language, Arabic grammar, and computer skills were all voluntarily offered as part of the society's activities. Informally, we financially support each other, not with charitable intent, but with the idea of keeping the spirit of oneness flowing by paying forward, not paying back. Well-off people on certain occasions accept gifts from others, who may have less fortune, with gratitude. Those who receive express their thanks and gratitude through seizing opportunities to offer services or money whenever needed within or outside the group. This flow of support is rooted in the flow of love and oneness where class classifications diminish.

As a group who cultivates their talents and skills, women within our spiritual circle are inspired differently to interact with the greater society. Women artists hold exhibitions; each one has her own spiritual experiences that manifest through her work. For example Maha Gohar was inspired by the ninety-nine names of God to make beautiful jewelry, using principles of bio-geometry. Ines Amer's experience with nature, peoples, and symbols has enabled her to hold successful exhibitions. Amany el Mofti is a professional artist who holds her degree from France; her spiritual experience has an impact on her drawings. She also teaches art privately in her studio, and uses her teachings as a way to spread spiritual culture. Other women use literature as a vehicle for spiritual expression. to disseminate the spiritual culture. Nevine Sidki wrote two novels, one of them was turned to a theatrical drama, and played in different theatres. Dr. Magda El-Mofty wrote a book called *Al-Kinz* ("The Treasure") that focuses on how one can cultivate positive energy.

Alternative medicine attracts many members in the society who seek to combine spiritual knowledge and scientific findings. Magda Serry is an optician, for example, but she is involved in many fields of alternative medicines, such as homeopathy, reiki, and body mirrors. She is helping so many people. Amani El-Mofty explores the possibilities of verses of the Qur'an and the process of healing through meditation.

Some women initiated non-governmental organizations to help marginal segments of society. Azza El-Sharnobi and Basma Nour established an organization to support disadvantaged and spiritually-poor students in governmental schools. Afkar Mohammed established another organization to support poverty-stricken single women by teaching crafts. Ola Nour helps her in marketing the products.

A group of young women who were interested in education initiated the idea of a project for the teaching of ethics. In response to their enthusiasm, Sayeda Aisha Rafea developed a program, titled "Be Yourself ... Be Happy" based on our spiritual teachings. The program can adjust to different cultural differences. Many people in our group have been trained to teach this program, and many have started to practice it in orphanages and various schools in Egypt. Also, Sayeda Aisaha was invited to train teachers to implement this program in Saudi Arabia early in 2010. Another female member, Sayeda Ma'aman Rafea, developed a course in art for children. She considers art to be an essential activity for the psychological and spiritual well being of the soul.

In 2011, I founded another NGO, the Human Foundation (www. hfegypt.org), to incorporate these programs and others and move them to wider scale. I consider this foundation an extension of my work at the ESSCR, transforming our spiritual path into service. The idea of turning spirituality to action has motivated me through my life. I found my chance to widen my activities through a foundation that mediates between human growth, sustainable development, and education. It is a seed that I hope will grow to be strong enough to challenge religious dogmas, and enlighten people's lives. Our spiritual group, gathered through the ESSCR, continues to work for this foundation and it has become a channel to attract more friends who have similar endeavours. We have now, in addition, two other projects. The Asl Wa Wasl Project, based on the vision of the Egyptian artist Hamed Said, is meant to connect people to their spiritual past through organized trips to Egyptian sites, explaining the continuation of the spiritual path that has flowed through history. Said reads the underlying message of Egyptian heritage as materialized in arts and architect. The Asl Wa Wasl project is conducted by a group of young people who have different professions; two are artists and had direct contact with Hamed Said, one is a tourist guide, and a young woman who is an architect. The other project is called *NABD*, which, in Arabic, means "palpitation of the heart." The young people who started this project have designed a program of educating people about the relationship between science, ethics and development.

Our spiritual gathering has been empowering each and every one of us using this energy, individuals move in a variety of different directions. The impact of these organizations are not measured by the number of people who share in their activities, but rather by the amount of effort they put in their field of expertise to spread the spiritual awareness and work. Teachers, medical doctors, engineers, civic servant employees, housewives, and students, are using this manner of spiritual perspective to guide their steps in diverse activities.

On the personal level, I have greatly benefitted from the positive energy and the exchange of knowledge that we share. I am indebted to Master Ali Rafea, our Guide within ESSCR, not only for the knowledge he provides, but also for his style of leadership. His modesty is remarkable, and his openness to consider other points of view is so inspiring. Through the courses I teach, I indirectly train my students to see beyond the academic objectives of the course, and to make connections between the subjects of study and their lives. The Egyptian Women's Movements course opens the door wide to navigate in different areas of women's history in Egypt and elsewhere, and to search for ways to get out of the box and dream freely, and plan to achieve goals.

Cognitive anthropology is one of my favourite courses because it focuses primarily on how culture structures our ways of thinking. I consider the ability to look at one's own culture from a distance to be a spiritual training in itself. Actually, if the process is successful, a person is going to be freed from pre-conceived assumptions, and able to see different ones. This training activates the critical mind that is linked also to our primordial core of existence: a core that is veiled through socialization; an enculturation based on indoctrination. By removing layers and layers of veiling and encouraging the freshness of our inquisitive mind, the innate spirit guides us in directions that express our inner personalities, helping us to accept differences, while at the same time being able to see and share links between other cultures, civilizations, and religions.

I was surprised to find out that the model of interaction that was cultivated in our spiritual circle manifested in Tahrir Square during the Revolution. It was a classless structure–a free and non-ideological gathering, yet highly organized, greatly motivated, and spiritually inspired. It was so impressive to see how people from all walks of lives became One, supporting one another, helping each other, creating a station for tending the wounded, and even preparing a surgical station. Food was distributed; blankets and tents were brought to those who resided in the open air. It was amazing that every person shared creatively to ensure the project continued. I, our group members, and members of our families were there. My son Mohammed and more than ten people from my family and friends were eye-witnesses and participants in the battle that took place on February 2. On that day, paid thugs with their camels and horses, armed with Molotov cocktails, attacked the unarmed peaceful protestors. Snipers on nearby roofs were shooting people. Young women from my family were involved; they insisted to remain despite the dangerous environment. They could have been died on that day among others. Those peaceful protestors courageously fought, and miraculously won, and kept their place in Tahrir Square.

The Egyptians' realization that they can achieve their goals without using violence will be present in their spirit for years to come. They cherished freedom over living, and sacrificed their lives to provide a better place for the whole of Egypt. This spirit will free men and women from dogma, and bring them together to build a new era. Even though we are passing through a difficult time, this spirit has been at our backs. It manifested on a large scale in the Egyptian Revolution and it will survive with our hard work.

CONCLUSION

The culturally-conceived "natural role" of women is an elusive idea that has influenced numerous generations and framed perceptions. Men and women are deprived of inner freedom as a result of being imprisoned in cultural frames. Their consciousness must be shaken and awakened.

As much as religion can be an awakening force, it also can be used as a suppressive one. New terms are needed to convey the same core message of authentic revelations that came to awaken humans' consciousness to who they are as human beings and to make them feel their connections to one another and to the whole.

From a spiritual perspective, human's rights' realization is accomplished and grounded in practice when both men and women are given the chance to self-realization through Carl Jung's process of individuation. Neither culturally nor socially driven, individuation is intuitively and inwardly developed. The more that the individual is liberated from cultural constraints and, instead, searches for one's core personality, the more she is able to understand her direction in life. In Egyptian society, Islam should be re-introduced with its spiritual dimension.[11]As we suggest in *Islam from Adam to Muhammad and*

Beyond (Ali and Rafea), Islam can and should be a liberating force. In the realm of spirit, there are no men or women, no colours, no names of religions: there are only human beings who would reap according to their deeds. Islam should be introduced as a path, not a name of a creed. This is the point of departure which should direct attempts to change the dogmatic way of thinking that has been standing in the way of liberating the Egyptian Soul.

In a society that is based on this spiritual culture, I envisage men and women supporting one another on all levels of activities—family as well as societal—paving the way for the feminine spirit to rise, embracing the whole world with love, and directing the coming change. Women are not the only carriers of the feminine spirit, but unless women are given the chance to be treated on an equal basis with men, mercy, compassion and all known feminine qualities will remain dormant and the world will be deprived from this power. Women need to appreciate who they are, and to find their unique way of acting within the world. Spirituality rather than religiosity is our hope for a new era in our human history.

I am so grateful that a new era has started in my country, where barriers were removed as love and peace were cultivated among the millions who stood firm—facing tyranny with non-violent resistance. Our slogan was "*selmiyya,*" meaning "*we are peaceful.*" I hope that this start continues despite the set-backs that we have experienced by the coming of Islamists into power. Whenever I see young people who conquer fear through this revolution, my hope grows stronger. I pray that peace overwhelms my country and the whole world.

[1]When I chose the title of this chapter, I was not aware that my individual unconscious was picking up from the collective unconscious the idea that Egypt would witness a radical change, and a beginning of a new era. The Egyptian Revolution that started on January 25 surprised the Egyptians as it surprised the world by its high morals and nobility. Egyptians were so peaceful, yet very determined to reach their goals. Egypt for us is identified as our mother, or the young beautiful woman that never gets old. The motherhood archetype overwhelmed the sphere of the revolution. Everyone was protective, caring, and selfless. I am sure this will not vanish.

[2]The feminist movement in Egypt started in the early twentieth century and had a great impact on the Arab World. It awakened women's consciousness of their civic rights, For example, The Arab Women

Union was founded as a second step after the establishment of the Egyptian Women Union, and was led by the Egyptian feminist Houda Sha'arawy in 1935.

[3]Each culture has its particular value system and norms that may violate certain items in Human Rights' Declaration. For example, the cast system in India is obviously against the first item in the Universal Declaration of Human Right "every human being is born free."

[4]For a concise and useful summary of Jung's contribution to analytical psychology, see Anthony Stevens' *Jung: A Very Short Introduction.*

[5]As a matter of fact, the founders of social sciences paid great attention to religion as a social phenomena throughout history, and demonstrated how religions impact the lives and world-views of people. Although they had different theories, they agreed that religions have their way of shaping the perception of "reality" and direct people's behaviour accordingly. See, for example, Emile Durkheim *The Elementary Forms of Religious Life,* Karl Marx and Friedrich Engels' *The German Ideology,* or Max Weber's *The Protestant Ethics and the Spirit of Capitalism.*

[6]In 1976-79, six women held parliamentary seats. In 1984-87, 30 seats were reserved for women, six women won their seats. In 1987, eighteen women held seats in parliament ("Bringing Gender Justice...").

[7]Egyptians of all faiths shared the idea that because they did not seek God's support, depending instead mainly on their military strength, they were defeated. In 1968, the reported appearance of Virgin Mary on a church situated in one of Cairo's suburbs was very significant for Muslims and Christian alike. The faithful spent days and nights near the church in the hopes of receiving her blessings. The Qur'an narrates stories of women who made an impact on the people, such as the Queen of Saba, who is praised for her rationality, wisdom, and courage. The Virgin Mary is mentioned side by side with other Prophets in a Sura (chapter) that carries her name.

[8]During the 1970s, two military coups were attempted. In 1981, Sadat was assassinated.

[9]The Council's objectives are available on the NCW website: http://www.ncwegypt.com/index.php/en/about-ncw/presidential-decree.

[10]Out of our experience as a group of people who gather together, making our lives meaningful by filling our heart with love, each one of us is inspired to act in certain directions, responding to his or her inner voice. We call this a "spiritual urge."

[11]In another co-authored work, the authors dealt with Islam, demonstrating its liberating force. The book presented an approach that

emphasized the commonality between revelations from within Islamic perspective (Ali and Rafea).

REFERENCES

Ali, Aliaa and Aisha Rafea *Islam from Adam to Muhammad and Beyond*. Book Foundation, 2004. Print.

Badran, Margot. *Feminism, Islam, and Nation: Gender and the Making of Modern Egypt*. Cairo: The American University in Cairo Press, 1996. Print.

Biggs, Cassie. "Women make their power felt in Egypt's revolution." *The National* 14 Feb 2011. Web. 7 Jul. 2012.

"Bringing Gender Justice to the Egyptian Parliament." *IDS in Focus Policy Briefing* 30 (December 2012). Web. 5 Sept. 2013.

Durkheim, Emile. *The Elementary Forms of Religious Life*. Trans. Karen E. Fields. New York : Free Press, 1995. Print.

"Egypt bans forced virginity tests by military." *Aljazeera* 27 Dec. 2011. Web. 13 Jul. 2012

"Egypt: Open All Judicial Positions to Women." Human Rights Watch. Web. 20 Aug 2010.

El-Guindi, Fadwa. "Veiling Infitah with Muslim Ethics: Egypt's Contemporary Islamic Movement." *Social Problems* 28.4 (1981): 465-85. Print.

Higgins, Michael. "Police beating of 'girl in the blue bra' becomes new rallying call for Egyptians." *National Post* 20 Dec. 2011. Web. 7 Jul. 2012.

Khattab, Hind. *The Silent Endurance: Social Conditions of Women's Reproductive Health in Rural Egypt*. Amman, Jordan: UNICEF, 1992. Print.

Khattab, Hind. *Women's Perceptions of Sexuality in Rural Giza*. Cairo: Reproductive Health Working Group, 1996. Print.

Marx, Karl and Friedrich Engels. *The German Ideology*. Moscow: Progress Publishers, 197. Print.

Mohamed, Mohamed Abdel Fatah. *Al-Jami'iyat Al-Ahliyya Al-Nisa'iyya: Qhadhaya wa Mushkilat*. Alexandria, Egypt: Al-Maktab Al-Jami'i Al- Hadith (Modern University Office), 2008. Print.

Oakley, Ann. *Sex, Gender and Society*. 1972. London: Gower, 1985. Print.

Rafea, Aliaa R. "The Students Islamic Movement: A Study of the Veil (Hijab)." Master DegreeMaster's Thesis, the American University in Cairo, 1983.

Rafea, Aliaa R. "Unraveling Different Meanings of the Veil." *Feminist Movements: Origins and Orientations*. Ed. Fatima Sadiqi. Publication of the Faculty of Art and Humanities, Dhar El Meharaz, Fès, Morocco, 2001, pp. 25-52. Print.

Rafea, Ali, Aliaa Rafea and Aisha Rafea. *Islam from Adam to Muhammad and Beyond*. London, UK: Book Foundation, 2004. Print.

Robinson, Ken. *The Element: How Finding Your Passion Changes Everything*. New York: Viking Penguin, 2009. Print.

Stevens, Anthony. *Jung: A Very Short Introduction*. New York: Oxford University Press, 1994. Print.

Weber, Max. *The Protestant Ethics and the Spirit of Capitalism*. New York: Charles Scribner's Sons, 1950. Print.

Yusuf, Sami. "Free." *My Ummah*. Awakening Records, 2005. CD.

29.

We Honour Her Beauty, Now It's Time to Embody Her Power

SHARON G. MIJARES, USA/COSTA RICA

THE UNITED STATES HAS BEEN a forerunner of change for the last three-hundred years. Although some of this change has been for the good, at the same time, due to its ethnocentricity and goal of global superiority, it has also created numerous problems around the world. On the positive side, the United States has been a leader in times of environmental disasters; for example, it contributed more aid to restore Haiti following the devastating earthquake in 2010 and likewise to Indonesia and nearby nations following the 2005 Tsunami than any other nation in the world. Yet at the same time, the U.S. has perpetuated a paradigm of political and economic supremacy ignoring, and/or often stifling, the unique qualities of cultures different than our own. Through the spread of global trade, travel, the Internet, media, and, in particular, Hollywood and MTV-style videos, the United States has impacted the world more than any other nation. But there is also a big loss in this paradigm, as the uniqueness of each culture—its specific ways of praying, eating, dressing, expression of dance and music, along with its philosophical understanding and ways of communicating—may soon be nothing more than a historical memory. Despite the history of U.S. *exceptionalism*, an increasing number of its women are reaching out in new ways, creating friendships rather than enemies—joining with other women around the globe, via the Internet and conferences, with the shared intention of healing our human family. This chapter will discuss some of the ways that American women are connecting with women from both within the U.S. and also with other nations by honoring diversity rather than repeating the ethnocentric behaviours of the U.S. past. We want to honor and to learn from the unique understanding and experience of women from around the world. We also want to give respect to multi-cultural ideas of feminism as opposed to following old theories developed from studies of white, educated, middle-class women and what may represent limited cultural perspectives (Weedon). The ongoing challenge will be that of relinquishing any introjected patterns and attitudes of superiority initiated by this tendency of viewing ourselves as models for others. One great example of this is the fact that the U.S. was not always the first nation to create positive changes for women. For this reason, we, the editors of this book, have gathered women from various cultures to share their stories. The goal of progressive women's movements should not be hierarchical—nor should it be built upon corporate structures bringing women together primarily for the purpose of commercial gain.

Other authors in this book have noted the numerous obstacles they face in their unique contributions in the effort of gender equality. In particular, this author believes that the biggest obstacle in U.S. women's endeavors is the danger of creating structures built upon a *for-profit* model—as this is the paradigm of our patriarchal past. Instead, we need to gather others in the name of shared, feminine power. Our work is that of balancing feminine power and beauty—for the benefit of all. It is an egalitarian model open to new ways of living and being, because the current models—based on consumerism and hierarchical power--are failing. It is so easy for groups to fall into this pattern, as it has been the model we have followed for several thousand years. True feminism emanates the beauty of caring and the power to create change.

UN RESOLUTION 1325

This resolution was adopted on October 31, 2000. It marked another step in the progress of gender equality as the resolution affirms the importance of women in the prevention and resolution of conflicts, peace negotiations, peace-building, peacekeeping, humanitarian response and in post-conflict reconstruction and stresses the importance of their equal participation and full involvement in all efforts for the maintenance and promotion of peace and security (Office of the Special Advisor).

Given the long-time history of global patriarchal (namely *male*) dominance, it remains a slow, ongoing and arduous task to actualize this intention. But, as the authors in this volume demonstrate, it is up to women to join in the effort of creating a more positive world for future generations.

My own contributions have primarily come through writing and workshops. In 2003, I invited Dr. Aliaa Rafea, an Egyptian Muslim; Rachel Falik, an Israeli Jew; and, later in 2006, Jenny Eda Schipper, a new age yoga teacher, massage therapist and poet, to join with me in pointing out the evils of a patriarchal social structure along with the importance of women's role in global transformation through co-authoring a book, *The Root of All Evil: An Exposition of Prejudice, Fundamentalism and Gender Imbalance*. We began this not long after the events of 9/11 and the attacks on Afghanistan and Iraq. The idea of Christian, Jewish, Islamic and New Age co-authors was an effort of unifying women of diverse backgrounds in the shared goal of peace. Our research affirmed the balance and healing that women's presence can bring in political, economic, religious and other social arenas in life—along with the need for gender balance. We also demonstrated a method for working together, despite differing backgrounds and beliefs.

A few years later, when doing some research for an article I was writing for the journal *Adaptive Options*, I learned that Eleanor Roosevelt had noted the importance of gender balance as a way of resolving many of the world's problems in her own book, *This Troubled World*.[1] She emphasized the role of a love that extended beyond one's personal relationships to include the entirety of the human family. She noted that this would be our saving grace and that women were capable of this because of their inherent *maternal* qualities.

Nurturing qualities do not have to be limited to the birthing and caretaking of one's own children—but rather the caring for the entire human family. But women have to "wake up" and recognize the potential depth within this inherent relational quality. Far too many young women are content to play the role of sexual objects (as evidenced through various media). The U.S. media and its wide viewership tends to give more attention to the behaviours of a young movie star than to educate about the atrocities happening to women and children around the world.

Many women prefer to remain in oblivion, and they do this through a variety of means. Example include women hiding behind their husbands (how many of us have heard others say that a leader's wife is running things behind the scenes) and/or blindly accepting religious, economic and social limitations. Thus, women's overall presence and participation is limited and gender balance denied. Many women are still content to be "second-best"—abdicating their capacity for research, thought and action, and therefore the power for decision-making to men. If we look at the current state of the world, where power for its own sake and financial interests rule, it becomes obvious that something more is needed.

In a patriarchal culture someone always has to be superior to another. If the woman is on the bottom rung, due to the modeling of those above her, she is more apt to belittle and demean others in an attempt to rise higher on the ladder (however misguided this may be). But if her heart is open to a deeper level of caring, she has much to offer as long as she resists the temptation to take power for its own sake, for example, making the women's movement one of corporate intent as opposed to creating *sustainable* relationships and ways of living.

THE FIRST WAVE OF FEMINISM AND WORK FOR GENDER BALANCE

On August 26, 1920, the 19th Amendment to the U.S. Constitution was ratified and women were given the right to vote. This amendment is also known as the *Susan B. Anthony amendment* due to her amazing courage, willingness and work to assure that women would have this right. But she was but one woman, among many, as this victory was the result of almost a century of work by its numerous advocates. The women's suffrage movement was influenced in its beginnings by Francis Wright (1795-1852) and Ernestine Rose (1810-1892). Wright had emigrated from Scotland in 1818, bringing her beliefs in the value of universal equality and feminism to the U.S., whereas Rose had emigrated from Poland in 1836. Both worked diligently for women's suffrage. Later, women such as Lucretia Mott, Margaret Fuller, the ex-slave Sojourner Truth, Elizabeth Cady Stanton, Lucy Stone, Susan B. Anthony and numerous other women were willing to be jailed, beaten, and/or to suffer public humiliation for the cause of gender equality, and, in particular, the right for women to make decisions in governance of this country—to vote. Not all women supported equal rights. Many believed this arena to be the realm of men, and men alone, adhering to patriarchal ideology. This same struggle, the women's suffrage (civil right to vote) was not just taking place in the U.S., nor was the United States the first to obtain it for in 1893 New Zealand became the first country in the world to grant women the equal right to vote.

Women of the United States have not been the first to obtain equal rights in a variety of areas. Although U.S. women are quick to either criticize and/or to genuinely feel sympathy for women's suppression in other countries, they often fail to realize that it has been a relatively short time in American history that women have had the right to own property or to divorce. Many women are unaware that until the mid-1800s U.S. women did not have the right to own property separate from their husbands. In *The Root of All Evil*, we noted that,

During the early history of the United States, a man virtually owned his wife and children as he did his material possessions. If a poor man chose to send his children to the poorhouse, the mother was legally defenseless to object. Some communities, however, modified the common law to allow women to act as lawyers in the courts, to sue for property, and to own property in their own names if their husbands agreed. Gradually, the states granted women limited property rights. By 1900 every state had granted married women considerable control over their property.[2] (158)

In our research, we also learned that women had not been allowed the right to execute a will until 1809. Then, in 1839, "Mississippi passed a law granting women limited property rights, the beginning of a serious of successes—part of a long arduous struggle" (Mijares, Rafea, Falik and Schipper 158).

The feminist movement revived itself in the 1960s. Women began to speak out against sexual hypocrisy, such as the "double standard" for males and females when it came to sexual permissiveness or the like. Many symbolically burned their bras in university campus demonstrations. (During this era, gender rights issues were also present in China, France, Germany and other countries as well.) The rise in U.S. feminism was also in alignment with the Civil Rights movement—as both African Americans and women demanded equality. Many women and men spoke out against the Vietnam War—and the act of warring itself. Women began to expand professional opportunities, beyond that of caretaking professions. This included managerial positions. Yet, despite decades of awareness and united effort, males are still at the pinnacle of administrative positions—often earning higher wages for the same work as women.

There have been many stigmas propagated in response to feminism. Many people feared the relationship between feminists' ideals of equality and socialism.[3] The term "feminist" also became associated with "angry" and "aggressive" women. *Such rumors suggested a negative association and were spread as a way of demeaning a feminist.* These insinuations still have a certain amount of influence by disregarding a women's right to have a voice, to speak out against injustice or to simply expect equality. If she is associated with the image of an "angry feminist" than her words (their intention and meaning) are negative. If these feminists had not spoken out and taken positions against patriarchal power, positive changes for women would not have occurred.

THE SECOND WAVE OF FEMINISM:
THE AWAKENING OF THE FEMININE

In 1984, I was introduced to a new book, *Goddesses in Everywoman*, by Jungian psychiatrist Jean Shinoda Bolen. Other friends were reading this book and we often had discussions as to which of these archetypal Grecian Goddesses might have the largest impact in our own lives. Were we led by *Hera*, the devoted wife archetype or *Demeter*, the mother with her associated maternal instincts? Or were we impelled by the archetypal influences of *Artemis* or *Athena*—virgin Goddesses representing wholeness in oneself? Prior to this time there was little, if any, discussion of *Goddesses*—let alone thoughts about their actual influences in our lives.

Women began reading books, such as the earlier 1976 edition of Merlin Stone's book, *When God Was a Woman*. This book documented stories of Goddesses from numerous ancient cultures—stories very different than the Biblical rendition of Eve, destined to be the Judeo-Christian scapegoat for all sin, born from Adam's rib and then causing all woe to befall humankind. No one had ever told us that there were other versions of this tale such as the one of *Lilith*, Adam's first wife. We did not know of *Sophia*, the Greek name for the ancient Hebrew Goddess of holy wisdom, *Hokhmah*.[4] Women were waking up to previously unknown revelations.

Patriarchal religions had denounced Goddess-worshipping cultures, or ignored them completely because they were *paganistic* (honoring a variety of deities instead of an ultimate source of creation—proclaimed to be male). Many women learned that in earlier times the divine was believed to be feminine, because of the fact that women birthed life. In many earlier cultures, for instance, Roman and Greek, Goddesses were equal to Gods. Goddesses reigned in Celtic and ancient European eras. In Shamanic cultures, the Shaman (Medicine person, healer) can be either male or female—but generally this person has gone through an inner process that initiates gender balance as part of awakening to the Shamanic gifts. Ideas of gender were changing. Women were re-discovering themselves and a very different identity was being revealed.

Marija Gimbutas, an archeologist revealing ancient findings from the Neolithic era showing the existence of women-centered (matristic) civilizations built around a feminine deity (or deities) also had a big influence on this awakening. Archeologists were finding sacred replicas (statues and so forth) representing the feminine as divine. These stories had simply not been told, yet we would soon learn they were abundant in every culture—negated by patriarchal religions, being damned as part of our pagan past. Women were beginning to have a very different image of what it meant to be a woman. The images of powerful birthing Goddesses acknowledging the feminine who brought life into the world—propelled a new strength into feminism and feminist action. Added to the concerns for equality and human rights—feminism began to recognize it was holy. She was also *sacred!* The emphasis was on the beauty of women, the earth and the capacity for birthing new life.

Women's groups formed, simply to share and discuss our feminine identity, and to acknowledge our feelings as women and as mothers. They also affirmed our sexuality. These stories about Goddess cultures were shared (Mijares "Tales of the Goddess"), and women began to have a stronger sense of a healthy feminine identity—a new sense of beauty.

In my own groups, I often focused on women learning to trust and to share their vulnerability with one another. This was a major issue for many women had internalized much of the long-held influences from biased religious teachings. We were psychically controlled by patriarchal images and teachings instilling mistrust in one's feminine self while creating barriers between ourselves and other women. Also, as noted in the Introduction to this book, if women were placed "below" the male, one way of feeling superior would be to demean another woman. Women's gatherings sought to change this irrational behaviour and create an environment of trust and support.

The United States has always had its share of women's groups associated with religious communities and/or political parties. There are certainly numerous women's associations focused on helping the poor, or deprived children and many other very important causes. But these groups have not deliberately focused on awakening the feminine within and empowering women to connect with one another. This second wave of feminism differed because of this shift, but the next wave of feminism would bring connectedness to a whole new level.

THE THIRD WAVE OF FEMINISM:
PROMOTING UNITY FOR GLOBAL CHANGE

In 1993, the group *Women of Vision and Action* (WOVA) formed in response to a Middle Eastern woman sharing her story of the death of family members during a civil war. Her tearful request was to "call the women together" and begin a much-needed change (WOVA). Rana Vernon listened and within two years a conference, *Women of Vision:*

Leadership for a New World was held in Washington, DC. I remember attending WOVA groups in San Diego in those early years. In fact, I presented a talk on women and healing at one of their conferences as did another author in this volume, Dr. Deva Beck.

Eventually, WOVA transformed itself into the *Gather the Women* (GTW) movement in 2001. Since then it has continued to grow—with the intention of gathering women from around the planet although the primary membership is U.S. women. GTW sees and uses the Internet as a means of connecting and global outreach. The primary focus is on feminine connectedness—building relationship. GTW differs from women's NGO groups that focus on a specific cause, such as preventing violence against women, empowering women in war-stricken areas, environmental concerns, trafficking, or other significant needs, as GTW primarily desires to build on the strength of the many. The intention is one of promoting connectedness and support for its growing membership.

Likewise, another group, Jean Shinoda Bolen's *Millionth Circle*[5] movement, based upon her book with the same title, emphasizes "the power of the many" to create change and social connectedness. Bolen has continued to have a large influence on women since her book, *Goddesses in Everywoman*, was released in 1984. As a psychiatrist, author and leader, she has been one of the larger influences in this female-affirming movement.

These social connections, along with the Internet, represent a powerful tool for both informing and connecting. The third wave of feminism has utilized this power to spread its message. Many women are providing various means to empower the movement. Another example is *World Pulse*, located in Portland, Oregon. It provides a *free* on-line magazine that introduces its reader to various women throughout the world who are making a difference in their communities. The magazine's intention is to "broadcast and unite women's voices from around the world into a powerful force for change."

More recently, the Internet has been used to promote a wider movement in this area. It began with a large e-mail campaign noting an opportunity to gather with well-known new age authors and leaders via a "live" call-in web-cast. These speakers discussed the vision of women, men and children joining to create much-needed change. The discussions were recorded so that the archives were available to all and that could be accessed at any time. Notices of each live call-in were sent out in vast emails and social networks were encouraged to pass them on. The primary draw (besides an opportunity to be on the phone line with popular teachers) was engaging in a large movement to empower women motivated to create change.

Social connectedness via the Internet appeared to be activating women's capacity to help transform the numerous global problems facing this humanity—but with one little glitch. The emailed notices began to include the announcement of ongoing, in fact, several weeks of training in the area of feminine empowerment—for a fee.

A pattern had emerged. First, thousands of emails were sent out to announce the opportunity—that of electronic networks providing a means of connectedness with other women. Popular leaders and/or influential women's groups were used to draw in likely participants. The initial connection, typically a free one to two hour call-in each week or so develops a good data base as word of these tele-courses spread. This list was then used for commercial reasons as "for-profit" workshops were offered in the guise of spirituality and transformation, leadership and self-empowerment.

The marketing appears to have been a success, but does our nation, and our world, need more of the same thing—*wherein the bottom line is the dollar*? It appears as though U.S. women might simply be following the capitalist ideal—the model propagated by the male majority.

This is a capitalist society—often referred to as *corporate America*. But this ideology comes at a cost considering that our humanity and environment are seriously threatened and we can no longer afford the continued patterns of our patriarchal past. This structure does not represent *feminine power*. Our efforts need to arise from a deeper feminine caring, something deep within each woman. We need to create new ways, especially in these times of economic unrest.

Change-bringers *need to first* free themselves from the corporate influence that makes everything—including this precious endeavor of gender balance for the good of humanity—yet another commodity or another hierarchical power structure. I have seen far too many women endeavoring to both initiate and lead large global gatherings to unite women while following masculine models with strong leadership "at the top."

Matthew Arnold's belief that "*If ever women gathered together simply and purely for the benefit of [hu]mankind that it would be a force such as the world had never known*" goes far beyond the "profit" motive. In fact, my concerns about these issues initiated the idea for this book. I awakened one morning with the idea to bring numerous women together to share their stories and experience—contributing to an egalitarian dialogue—without a bunch of *hoopla*.[6] The goal was to simply provide examples of what women around the world were doing—each in her own way, and according to the needs to their culture. No corporate structure, funding or the like would be necessary—simply the reaching out to invite women in various nations around the world to share their stories, their obstacles and their successes.[7] In fact, this feminist model of "power with" influenced all of my prior books. I knew I could do the research and write the chapters, but I would rather those with expertise in specific areas share their stories. This is especially powerful when bringing people together from differing cultural, racial and religious backgrounds. It represents yet another egalitarian model, which has been the goal of every wave of feminism.

AN EMPHASIS ON POWER AND BEAUTY

As discussed, the feminists of the '70s were portrayed as a group of "angry women," but there were good reasons to be angry. Their important efforts often went unseen as the "angry feminist" rumor gained more power than what the women were attempting to point out and change.

Far too many people fall for the projected images put out by those who would maintain the status quo (to keep things as they are). And, far too many women want to be *nice* to assure approval, rather than to express—or even be conscious of—what they really believe. This is not an authentic representation of feminine beauty nor does it indicate the presence of feminine power.

The great ethnologist, Konrad Lorenz, noted that aggression was an innate expression meant to protect and preserve life. It is found in some form or another in all species. It is generally acceptable as a male trait. The mother instinct alone should make women angry enough to join in the cause to preserve future generations. We don't have to rant, rave, growl or swear—or go to war against another nation—but this "caring" energy can be harnessed to speak for *truth*, and to gather for the sake of all life in order to create change. In this way, the anger and motivating aggression transforms and becomes a great *force*—one that is motivated by love and wisdom. This earth-moving fire within us will be ignited as all nature moves toward right balance. Remember Mother Earth has fire at the center of her core. Nature demonstrates a variety of forces—and this model is available to empower us as we are her offspring—the children of heaven and earth (spirit and form).

Yes, the women of the United States need to free themselves from the corporate influence that makes everything a commodity. And, we also need to discard the illusion that the United States is superior and that it is *the* example for all to follow. Every culture, with its unique environment, heritage, religion and so forth has something to contribute to this human family. We must each free ourselves inwardly and outwardly from the shackles of patriarchy and its bedfellow, corporate power, wherein something or someone always has to be better than another.

Women must also individually and collectively heal our relationships with one another. Mothers, daughters and sisters must unite. Early and latter developments in feminism need to learn from one another. If each generation disregards the efforts and personhood of others, we have a disconnect—a split that weakens our efforts to improve conditions wherein equality and goodness will be available to all human beings and all life. When we individually take responsibility for our motivations and behaviours, both with ourselves and with others, discernment and self-knowledge result. Authentic self-knowledge is an empowering influence that spreads—initiating healing and impacting upon relationships in positive ways.

In the Introduction I shared an experience that had occurred in response to an assignment in a Creative Writing course. I chose to allow the words of the Earth Mother to flow through me—spontaneously—without thought or reflection. I will end this chapter by repeating the message that preceded the synchronistic earthquake.

> *You walk upon my paths, and acknowledge my beauty.*
> *But you do not know my power—*
> *the power to push forth mountain peaks and open valleys for oceans to fill.*

We need to find this right balance of power and beauty and let it be what leads us, creating a new paradigm for the good of all. Nature will guide us.

---

[1] In my article "Adapting to Change is a Gender Issue," I referenced Eleanor Roosevelt's book *This Troubled World* (New York: H.S. Kinsey & Company, 1938). Her insights were profound.

[2] Excerpted from *Compton's Interactive Encyclopedia*, *"Women's History in America,"* Compton's NewMedia, Inc. and posted on http://www.wic.org/misc/history.htm.

[3] They still do! Thus, a strongly conservative political party with a

fundamentalist religious leaning could take the U.S. into a similar state as some of the Islamic nations this same group.

[4]*Hokhmah* is the focus of Proverbs 8 where wisdom is clearly described as a feminine deity calling to and guiding the people. Professor Dvora Weisberg describes *her* influence for Jewish women at a 2004 conference (see http://www.eewc.com/Conferences/2004Panel.htm). *Sophia* has also become a significant influence for many Christian women as discussed in Wikipedia page on Christian feminism noting their belief that "She" is the Holy Spirit in the Christian Trinity.

[5]This book is based upon the idea of the 100th monkey and its influential power to evoke change.

[6]According to an on-line free dictionary this term as the following meanings. The first relates to being boisterous, having jovial commotion or excitement and extravagant publicity. The second meaning regards a talk intended to mislead or confuse. See http://www.thefreedictionary.com/hoopla.

[7]Actually I have used this model with other books, even though it is far more work than to simply write a book on my own. For example, I have to be at the mercy of everyone else's timing and so forth so it takes a lot of patience and communication. My first (edited) book was a response to the immense influence of pharmaceutical companies on mental health care. The idea was to show different meanings and healing influences from the world's religious traditions. As I contemplated the book I decided that even though I could do the research and writing of each chapter, the book would have far more validity if the persons who represented these traditions wrote the chapters. Each one had something special to bring to the book. Thus began a pattern of bringing other voices to share in the message given in each of my first four books. Also, I learned right away that there would be minimal money earned, especially in comparison to the time and efforts given to each project—so the goal was clearly to fill the need for the book's message.

REFERENCES

Bolen, Jean Shinoda. *Goddesses in Everywoman: A New Psychology of Women.* Rev. ten-year anniversary ed. New York: HarperCollins, 2004. Print.

Bolen, Jean Shinoda. *The Millionth Circle: How to Change Ourselves and the World. The Essential Guide to Women's Circles.* Berkeley, CA: Conair Press, 1999. Print.

Lorenz, Konrad. *On Aggression*. New York: Bantam Books, 1967. Print.

Gimbutas, Marija. *The Language of the Goddess*. San Francisco, CA: HarperSanFrancisco, 1991. Print.

Mijares, Sharon. "Adapting to Change is a Gender Issue." *Adaptive Options* 5.1 (Spring 2010): 13-18. Print.

Mijares, Sharon. "Tales of the Goddess: Healing Metaphors for Women." *Modern Psychology and Ancient Wisdom: Psychological Healing Practices from the Worlds Religious Traditions*. Ed. Sharon Mijares. New York: Routledge, 2002. 71-96. Print.

Mijares, Sharon, Aliaa Rafea, Rachel Falik and Jenny Eda Schipper. *The Root of All Evil: An Exposition of Prejudice, Fundamentalism and Gender Imbalance*. Exeter, UK: Imprint Academic, 2007. Print.

Office of the Special Advisor on Gender Issues and Advancement of Women. "Landmark Resolution on Women, Peace and Security." New York: United Nations, October 31, 2000. Web.

Stone, Merlin. *When God Was a Woman*. New York: Harcourt, Brace and Company, 1976. Print.

Weedon, Chris. "Key Issues in Postcolonial Feminism: A Western Perspective." Presentation at Gender Forum: Gender Realizations, 2002. Web.

Women of Action and Wisdom (WOVA). Web.

World Pulse. Web.

30.
Conclusions

Envisioning a Balanced World

ALIAA RAFEA, EGYPT AND NAHID ANGHA, USA

WOMEN HAVE BEEN AN ESSENTIAL PART of the mosaic of life; they are the major contributors to the development and rise of nations, cultures, and establishments from the very beginning. We want to acknowledge their work and contributions towards the world's civilizations. In this book we have read the stories of many women from many cultures. We became acquainted with their works, endeavours, visions, leadership, and contributions in honouring humanity, in all its divisions and colours, for the sake and hope of an honourable and better world for generations to come. This has been a great journey!

This book is about a promising future. In reading their stories, we became familiar with women who have been working to create a balanced world—one that honours all of its members, and thereby offers an environment for all to live in harmony and peace. These women have endeavoured and overcome many obstacles; they live lives of aspiration and are achieving their goals. It is valuable to recognize that each woman began with an idea and has devoted her life to seeing it flourish. They have shared their stories with us, cultivating seeds of hope and confidence within our hearts through their endeavours to create a better future.

The inherently inclusive nature of the feminine spirit cultivates endurance, understanding, and peace rather than prejudice and conflict. It is the design of nature in giving women (and feminine nature) the responsibility and the ability to carry life, to hold and care for its vitality and existence. Nature has bestowed not only a great strength on this sex, but also an undeniable trust ... so just imagine if ever the women of the world can come together to cultivate the seeds of hope and peace and lead humanity to a favourable station ... *it will be a force such as the world has never known*!

It must be clear that we are not taking a reductionist approach that envisions women's leadership as a solution for the world's misery and conflicts. Rather, the solution is that of equal partnership, of equal opportunity. The world cannot remain indifferent to this great strength and power. When women are given an equal opportunity to share in world leadership, changes, directions and possibilities, there will be greater harmony. We need to balance masculine and feminine aspects on both unconscious and conscious levels. By excluding women for approximately 4,000 years,[1] the masculine model of leadership has created an overwhelming imbalance, blocking the powers and strength of compassion, care for life, kindness and understanding in human destiny.

Our hope is to transcend gender differences and inequality, thereby opening new opportunities that allow each human being to choose a way of inner and outer peace. In her introduction, Sharon Mijares wrote about the need for men and women to work side-by-side to create a better world. In this conclusion we will have an opportunity to recap the authors' core experience told in their stories. Each chapter of this book illustrates a different way of contributing to change within our world. This chapter is not a summary but rather an overview of the contributions of these women.

GLIMPSES OF THE FEMININE SPIRIT

In our recent history, the world has witnessed glimpses of the feminine spirit in political movements; for example, Mahatma Gandhi and Martin Luther King Jr. are examples of men whose work was for the benefit of all beings. Just a few decades later, we see an acceleration of this innate feminine spirit inspiring other peaceful movements. For example, in the latter twenty years of the twentieth century, peaceful resistance in the Philippines, beginning in 1986, resulted in the overthrow of the dictatorial regime of Marcos. It was called the *People Power Revolution* because of its massive scale of participation. In East Germany, peaceful political protests led to the fall of the Berlin Wall in 1989, a prelude to the German reunification a year later. Even though China's Tiananmen Square Protests were crushed in 1989, the peaceful nature and courageous spirit of the Protests are still remembered in annual gatherings. After the demise of the Soviet Union, starting in 1991, non-violent civil movements were initiated in Poland, Hungry, Bulgaria, Uzbekistan and other Warsaw Pact nations and former Soviet republics. The Arab Spring Revolutions are a continuation of this spirit. Although this was not the case in Libya, in other nations such as Tunisia, Egypt, Yemen, and Bahrain, non-violence was the norm for the people who initiated these movements. There was a sense of equality supporting both men and women demonstrators. Tragically, the successes of these revolutions vary from one country to another, and seem to change by the day, but their peaceful features remain, indicating a paradigm shift in our human consciousness.

The power of the feminine is expressed in many different ways in this book. The story Leymah Gbowee relates is remarkable as she plays a major role in turning Liberia from a dictatorship to a democratic country. She led women to defy a feared warlord, Charles Taylor, and pushed for peace during one of Africa's bloodiest wars. She helped bring a woman, Ellen Johnson Sirleaf, into the presidency of her country. In 2011, both Leymah Gwobee and Ellen Johnson Sirleaf were awarded the Nobel Peace Prize. Tenzin Dhardon Sharling's chapter describes Tibetan women's peaceful struggle for justice for the Tibetan people. As she writes in Chapter Ten, "Tibetan women, who have lost everything, survived decades in prison, and braved a perilous escape across the Himalayas have managed to transform the brutality of invasion into a community of compassion and courage, of devotion and defiance." Parvin Ardalan, a courageous woman from Iran, has been closely involved in resistance movements and taken into custody several times. Regardless of the circumstances and in the face of great danger, these women have continued their efforts to better their nations.

A LONG WAY TO GO

Women around the world are taking steps to transform our world and to make a difference both locally and globally. Their experiences, as narrated in this book, are powerful and inspiring, to the extent that we (the editors) envision that their stories will be widely accessible to all. Each one brings hope and vision to readers. As stories from differing traditions are told, they create bonds, motivating us all—the citizens of this globe—to join hand in hand and make a difference. Small steps here and there may grow to form greater alliances, changing current policies of domination and control as the spirit of superiority and hegemony transforms into ways of equality and peace.

It requires hard work to truly create a world of equal opportunities for all. However, history teaches us that great changes and transformation start with a dream, a vision and the perseverance to actualize the inspiration. It was Rosa Parks who initiated the Civil Rights movement in the United States in 1955 by refusing to move to the back of the bus because of her race. Although she was arrested for civil disobedience, she was later called "the mother of the modern Civil Rights Movement." She stood against racial discrimination and her perseverance motivated African American leaders to gather, and to take a stand for equality in what is known as the "Montgomery Bus Boycott." During that time, a young Baptist minister, Dr. Martin Luther King Jr., stepped forward. The rest is well known history.

Rosa Parks and other women have shared such dreams, resisting discrimination and opposition, and paving the way to greater changes. In Egypt, Nabaweyya Musa challenged her family traditions of not educating girls by choosing to go to school. Her challenges continued and she initiated the education of girls from the status of dreams to realities. She established schools for girls' education in many provinces around Egypt (Badran 38–45). Changing regimes in different countries begins as dreams. We—the people of this century—would have never reached the technological development we now experience without the dreams and imagination of such innovative people.

Therefore we envision a world void of discrimination against gender, colours, nationality, religion, or race. This opens the door for creativity and innovation from all human beings. It is an old dream, yet many of the stories shared by authors, points to the fact that there is still a long way before reaching such goals. While it is well known that dictatorships in many parts of the world coincide with discrimination against women, it is surprising that some *democratic* countries still have problems with creating an egalitarian society. Authors from Sweden, Italy, Mexico and many other nations illuminate the struggle that women are still taking in order to be treated equal to men.

Compared to the reset of the world, both Sweden and Norway have achieved one goal toward gender equality by promoting women to higher status. For example, Sweden was one of the first nations to sponsor a movement towards equality of women in parliament. Yet, at the same time, Magdalena Andersson explains in Chapter Twenty-One that "Women are left in charge of raising children, and children are more likely to interact with women than with men outside their homes"; moreover, women face great challenges to reach high political positions. Andersson explains that although "female politicians are under-represented in the higher echelons of political power" noting the problem of males preferring to promote other males and thus excluding women from opportunities for more political influence.

Along similar lines, author Rosane M. Reis Lavigne describes the pressures and successes of women working in the Brazilian judicial system to promote democracy. We continue to see how women are struggling against powerful oppositional forces that are determined to maintain the power structure as it has been. In examining this problem, Italian contributor Paola Conti uses official documents to demonstrate how women are paid less for the same work task, and showing how few women have leadership positions. Annie Imbens-Fransen reports that according to the World Health Organization, fifteen percent of Japanese women in urban area experience physical or sexual violence in their lifetime.

In Russia, women are still struggling to have control over birthing processes to assure healthy peaceful births for their children. Elena Tonetti-Vladimirova narrates in detail the story of the Russian doctors' uncaring attitudes and medical practices when dealing with women during delivery or abortion, not only abusing women's bodies, but also their dignity as equal human beings. They were exposed to medical complications as a result of negligence and bad treatment. In another manner but in the same vein, Maria Luisa Sánchez-Fuentes discusses her work with women in Mexico struggling for control of their bodies and decisions about birth control.

Although we did not include stories about female genital mutilation in our book, this remains a practice of violence against women in many countries around the world, such as Uganda, Egypt, Sudan and others. In general violence, against women world-wide remains a major cause of death and disability. Women are facing serious challenges in order to have control their bodies, minds and souls.

Hana Kirreh describes how Palestinian women are faced with two parallel movements; the first is related to establishing their own national state and the second is to be liberated from male dominance, enabling them to realize equal rights. In Israel, women also suffer, first as a result of fear of their Palestinian neighbours; and secondly because their role as *producers* of soldiers and fighters is considered top priority, both politically and culturally. Gal Harmat explains how this use of a women's inherent ability to birth life dehumanizes them as they are treated as mechanical agents for human production.

In Venezuela, Costa Rica, and definitely in other countries, women are burdened with the complete responsibility for domestic work, thereby depleting their energy or crippling their contributions to the wider society. Ana Marcela Garcia Chaves of Costa Rica notes how inequality of income puts many women in jail. Joy Kemirembe clearly demonstrates the ways that women struggle in the midst of religious and political differences in Uganda, and yet still find ways to achieve their goals—step by step.

In Iran, Syria and other parts of various Muslim countries, Islam is misinterpreted and used by many men to dominate and bring women to a lower status in a variety of ways. Syrian religious scholar Rufaida al Habash has been involved in an on-going courageous battle to defend her rights to teach jurisprudence and other religious subjects to women. In Iran, Islam (or rather the misinterpretation of the religion) has been used as a political tool against women. Women are denied Islamic jurisprudence and religious leadership. Parvin Ardalan has been closely involved in resistance movements in Iran. Parvin narrates her story with what is known as the movement of the "One Million Signatures Campaign to Change Discriminating Laws." She discusses the impact of this movement on the everyday culture of the society, as well as on the inter-relations among activists.

TRANSNATIONALISM VERSUS COMMON GOALS

This book is not about cross-cultural comparison between women's status in different parts of the world, but to emphasize the importance of women's struggles around the world as a way of creating global balance by countering gender imbalance. At the same time, and from a scholarly point of view, as we live in a post-modern era, we understand that there is no one solution that fits all, nor one theory that can explain everything. Therefore, when we acknowledge the common struggle and suffrage of women, we are also aware that the key to overcoming and eliminating suffering and to reaching a satisfying and safe destination may be in the hands of those who suffer. Each nation has its own unique experience, and it is not acceptable to judge other nations according to one's own value system. Mijares grapples with this issue in her chapter when she criticizes the assumption that the U.S. value system should be a reference for the whole world. We stress that there is no single national value system considered as a universal reference.

Diversities in cultures began to be welcomed by twentieth century anthropologists, who came to realize that each cultural particularity should be honoured. Peoples' values systems are intrinsically woven in their choices of how to solve social, political or economic problems. It was due to the American school of anthropology and its famous pioneer Franz Boas (1858-1942) that the racist approach within social sciences came to an end. Boas introduced the concept of cultural relativism, bringing to the discipline a new theoretical framework in the study of peoples and their cultures. He opened the way to other social scientists, such as W.E.B Du Bois (1868-1963), Margaret Mead (1901-1978), Allison Davis (1902-1983), and others to study the construction to racist ideologies, and consider the dynamics of hierarchy. In the late twentieth and now in the twenty-first centuries, cultural variations are considered assets to the enrichment to humankind heritage. UNESCO places "culture" at the heart of any development. Despite appreciation of cultural variations, equality, justice, human rights are honoured beyond particularities of cultures, yet each culture has its own way to express its values.

Within this context, women's movements around the world have recently been studied with emphasis on "transnational perspective," acknowledging the different experiences and at the same time breaking the cultural, ideological, political or religious barriers, to form decentralized global movement(s).

This perspective is crystallized in what is called "transnational feminism." This term was coined in the mid-1980s and early 1990s. Transnational feminism is an academic term that describes the global unidentified, non-structured, ideologically free women's movement(s) (see, for example, Moghadam). This book is transnational in the sense that it gathered stories from around the world, transcending nationalities, ideologies, classes, and religions. Each contributing author has provided a unique perspective from her part of the world. These women have already begun the work of changing their social/ human/ecological environments. They are contributing toward creating a peaceful, egalitarian, harmonious, and prosperous world—in both small and larger contexts.

Breaking barriers will allow us to work as one human family, respecting our diversity and enriching our experiences. From this perspective, as we emphasize common problems, we also acknowledge creative and unusual experiences, such as the work of Japanese author Yumiko Otani who has devoted her life to promoting healthy nutrition in ways that both benefit human beings and also our Mother Earth. Sustainable living is necessary in order for continuance of life, therefore, promoting environmental care as described by Despina Namwembe of Uganda represents a growing endeavour manifesting in many parts of the globe. Modern eco-feminists clearly note the disparaging of the feminine equates to the horrible care we have given our Mother Earth.

As a matter of fact, readers of this book may be amazed by the different ways that women contributors merge their specific stories with global issues, while providing a holistic view to human conditions. The urge to transcend geographical as well as ideological limitations is very impressive in many of the stories. For example, at the very beginning of her chapter, Deva-Marie Beck shared her hope of creating a world well-being network of like-minded friends for the sake of strengthening our collective ability to transform dreams into realities. As an outcome of this ideal, Deva became a leader promoting Florence Nightingale's Initiative Global Health movement that includes more than twenty-three thousand nurses and other people from 110 nations. This group cares about global health needs and promotes them in a holistic way, including other social variables, such as education, economic status, environment, and so on.

Anahata Iradah from Brazil shares a story conveying a message of love and compassion that she believes to be one way of changing the world, and affirms that we are able to radiate our loving compassion into the world for the benefit of all beings everywhere, without exception. It is evidenced in her attitude and in her promoting of the Dances of Universal Peace. A similar, yet differing vision is seen when reading Elly Pradervand's vision of human history as a march toward unity and the consciousness of the oneness of all forms of life. She believes this march towards unity is possible if the spirit of service manifests worldwide.

Renuka Singh addresses rural women, noting their struggles, endeavours and available wisdom. Aura Sofia Diaz and Cecilia Vicentini from Venezuela, working with local women, express a similar meaning. They share the importance of working towards a new civilization and collectively becoming involved in the design of this new blueprint for living together and being with others at a planetary level. Their chapter specifically focuses on emotional healing by providing a forum for women to tell their stories as a step to realizing this goal. As women build inner peace and become whole, they can lead the way in creating a world as one community.

SPIRITUALITY IN ACTION

This book also contains the thoughts, stories and experiences of women whose stories primarily focus on "spirituality" as the core of their experience. For example, Elena Tonetti-Vladimirova from Russia considers giving birth as a major spiritual experience, a miraculous event, rather than as a mere biological or mechanical one. Susan Masten, an aboriginal American from Yurok Tribe, highlights the tribal White Deer Skin Ceremony and the *jump dance*— prayers to the Creator to keep balance in the tribe. Native traditions recognize that balance is important for the well-being of the tribe as well as for the well-being of the world. Rufaida al Habash considers freeing Syrian women from the chains of the traditional culture and custom to be a way to enable them to experience *divine* beauty. Whereas young males traditionally sit in lines learning Quranic recitation, al Habash had girls sitting in circles learning this process of spiritual recitation. Annie Imbens-Fransen from the Netherlands emphasizes the role of spirituality to be a stimulating and empowering source of strength, enabling individuals to become aware of mechanisms supporting unjust practices as well as seeing the suffering these social and political mechanisms cause. Her chapter and life work demonstrate processes for increasing appreciation of diversity.

Although there are many other examples of spirituality, a strong example is given by Diana Rhodes' story of establishing *The Seed of Life Peace Foundation*. The remit of the Foundation has been one of crossing all cultures, all creeds and all barriers, but her spirituality is most evidenced in *how she has lived her life*. Despite ongoing physical challenges, Diana has continued to contribute to the good of humanity.

Spirituality is illustrated throughout this book through its examples of working for humanity, rather than isolating oneself in a monastery. For example, Renuka Singh from India demonstrates how women have been attempting to remove the divide between secularity and spirituality, and to synthesize the sacred and the mundane through the principle of non-violence. This resolution is an extension of the work that Gandhi started in his resistance movement. Sharmin Ahmad from Bangladesh is able to draw a hard line between how religion (in her case, Islam) has been politicized as a way of domination and control, and how religion can, instead, be a liberating force and a source of divine love. This compassionate and inclusive love is the human way to sustainable peace, prosperity and development.

The editors of this book share the vision that spirituality is intrinsically related to creating better living conditions for human beings. That is, it influences changes in every dimension of society. Nahid Angha brings "conviction to the well being of humanity" as the core of Sufism (or the core of human heart, according to her own expression). In her chapter she describes those who work for humanity as those persons who lead civilizations to better ways of living and being. Against the stereotype of spiritual devotees known as Sufis as often being those who abandon the *mundane life* for the sake of life in the hereafter, Angha affirms that Sufis have made great contributions to human rights, education, art, freedom, literature, architect, medicine, mathematics, astronomy. Sufis also have had their political stand in revolting against tyranny along our human history.

Mijares synthesizes between politics, feminism and spirituality. She widens the scope in examining political, cultural and economic aspects. For example, promoting the feminist movement as a means of influential power and financial gain simply replicates the consumer and corporate model. If Sharmin Ahmad explains how Islam has been misused to suppress women's voices, Mijares points the danger of feminists using their ideology in a commercial manner, for example *selling* specific workshops as a means for empowering women. She defines the way to bring the feminist movement to its authenticity, in describing how change-bringers need to first free themselves from the corporate influence that makes everything—including calling for gender balance—yet another commodity. Sincerity, honesty, and clarity are needed for the noble goal of resolving gender imbalance.

I (Aliaa) believe that the feminine spirit is an active energy manifested in tangible events. In my own chapter describing what is occurring in Egypt, I emphasize the importance of spirituality in activating the feminine archetype on the collective unconsciousness, along with the importance of integrating the masculine archetype. From my point of view, that is the force that leads us to a new era.

By thinking positively, and working enthusiastically, we influence the collective consciousness. The style of the anticipated leadership will gradually emerge, to fulfill the description of what Jean Lipman-Blumen defines as "connective leadership." This sort of leadership

> ...derives its label from its character of connecting individuals not only to their own tasks and ego drives, but also to those of the group and community that depend upon the accomplishment of mutual goals. It is a leadership that connects individuals to others and others' goals. (183)

In this conclusion, we have tried to compare and identify similarities and differences in the stories, and pursued the underlying messages and wisdom. We are sure that more messages and wisdom can be found. We salute each and every one of the contributors for their role in the process of giving birth to a new era.

So, here we are. We have read the stories of endeavours, obstacles, and triumph; we have learned about visions, journeys, and hopes. We walked with women step by step; we salute their perseverance and we acknowledge their strength. Their goals and missions have opened the door of hope, planting the seed of encouragement that we, too, may stand strong for what is right so all humanity may benefit from the bounty and richness of this world and have an opportunity to contribute to the development of civilization.

We are members of families, cultures, traditions, and histories. We cannot underestimate the strength and perseverance of our mothers and grandmothers who long ago began the journey toward women's equality and rights. It is their ambition, their vision, and their strength that has been overcoming inequality, preparing the way for the next wave of women to bring in life-supporting feminine consciousness across the earth. We have seen Iranian women walking for women's rights to vote, black women standing against racial oppression, Egyptian women working for the right to an education, and Liberian women transforming a nation from one at war into one at peace. We also see the political role of women in India, Africa, and Scandinavian nations as well as women of the United States challenging the traditional idea of women as homemakers as women emerge in various forms of leadership, including political. Our deepest homage is to the women of our past history, of our cultures, of our religions, of our family: they are the personification of leadership in its truest form, a global vision for all humanity.

No individual stands alone, and we are honoured, grateful and fortunate to journey on this road towards equality accompanied by the women of our past generations. We bring forth these stories of women as inspiration for all in creating a meaningful and healthy transformation throughout the world to benefit all life.

[1]According to scholar Riane Eisler, anthropological explorations of Paleolithic (around 20,000+ to 8000 BCE) and Neolithic (approximately 8000 to 4000 BCE) gravesites suggest egalitarian cultural values whereas excavations of post-Neolithic gravesites reveal that the practice of burying wives, children, animals, etc., along with the deceased male indicate a shift accompanying the rise of patriarchal ideologies. Historian Gerda Lerner argues in her 1987 book, *The Creation of Patriarchy*, that "male dominance over women is not 'natural' or biological, but the product of an historical development begun in the second millennium B.C. in the Ancient Near East." She adds: "The period of the establishment of patriarchy was not one 'event', but a process developing over a period of nearly 2500 years, from approximately 3100 to 600 B.C. It occurred even within the Ancient Near East, at a different pace and at different

times" (8). The patriarchal system of organizing society began over time and therefore can be ended as a historical process. In *The Root of All Evil*, Sharon Mijares, Aliaa Rafea, Rachel Falik and Jenny Eda Schipper note numerous quotations from religious scriptures of the changing era elevating the positions of the male gender, while demeaning the status and intelligence of women. For example, the *Hebrew Bible* and Vedic scriptures known as the *Rig Veda* have numerous passages exemplifying these changes.

REFERENCES

Badran, Margot. *Feminists, Islam, and Nation: Gender and the Making of Modern Egypt*. Princeton, NJ: Princeton University Press, 1995. Print.

Eisler, Riane. *The Chalice and the Blade: Our History, Our Future*. 1987. New York: HarperCollins, 1995. Print.

Lerner, Gerda. *The Creation of Patriarchy*. Oxford: Oxford University Press, 1987. Print.

Lipman-Blumen, Jean "Connective Leadership: Female Leadership Styles in the 21st-Century Workplace." *Sociological Perspective 35* (Spring 1992): 183-203. Print.

Mijares, Sharon G., Aliaa Rafea, Rachel Falik and Jenny Eda Schipper. *The Root of All Evil: An Exposition of Prejudice, Fundamentalism and Gender Imbalance*. Exeter, UK: Imprint Academic, 2007. Print.

Moghadam, Valentine. *Globalizing Women: Transnational Feminist Networks*. Baltimore, MD: Johns Hopkins University Press, 2005. Print.

Contributor Notes

EDITORS

Sharon G. Mijares is a licensed psychologist and a graduate of the Union Institute and University. Her education, psychotherapy practice and life have all centered on gender balance, and she has led groups and workshops on women's development for decades. Sharon is a member of the Sufi Ruhaniat International, the International Association of Sufism's Sufi Women's Organization, Gather the Women, the American Association of Anthropology's Anthropology of Consciousness and the Global Peace Initiative of Women. She is a visiting professor with the United Nations University for Peace, teaching in the Sustainable Peace through Sports and Sustainable Peace in the Contemporary World Master's Programs. She is also a core adjunct faculty member of National University's leadership and psychology departments and Brandman University's Psychology program. She teaches Eco-Psychology and other courses for the California Institute for Human Science. Publications include, *The Root of All Evil: An Exposition of Prejudice, Fundamentalism and Gender Imbalance* (2007); *Modern Psychology and Ancient Wisdom: Psychological Healing Practices from the World's Religious Traditions* (2003); *The Psychospiritual Clinician's Handbook: Alternative Methods for Understanding and Treating Mental Disorders* (edited with Gurucharan Singh Khalsa, 2005); *The Revelation of the Breath* (2009); and *Fragmented Self, Archetypal Forces and the Embodied Mind* (2012). She lives in both California and Costa Rica. She has two children, four grandchildren and four great-grandchildren. Email: <sharon.mijares12@gmail.com>.

Aliaa Rafea is a full Professor at Ain Shams University, Women's College, a writer and spiritual activist. She authored and co-authored many books, among them: *Egyptian Identity: An Anthropological Study of The School of Art and Life*; *Islam from Adam to Muhammad and Beyond* with Ali Rafea and Aisha Rafea; *The Root of All Evil: An Exposition to Prejudice, Fundamentalism and Gender Imbalance* with Sharon Mijares et al. As a visiting professor, she taught at Randolph-Macon Women's College on Islam and the World, and on the universal message of the Egyptian civilization. She also worked as a consultant for the Arab League in the Project of Youth empowerment. She wrote a weekly article for *Nahdt Misr Newspaper*, and is a member of the Egyptian Women Writers Society, the American Anthropological and Sociological Societies, and a fellow at the Society for Applied Anthropology. She is a co-founder of women's activities within the Egyptian Society for Spiritual and Cultural Research (ESSCR), and a founder and Chair of The Human Foundation.

Nahid Angha is co-director of the International Association of Sufism (IAS), the Executive Editor of the quarterly journal, *Sufism: An Inquiry*, and founder of the International Sufi Women Organization. She is the main representative of the IAS to the United Nations (NGO/DPI), a Marin Women's Hall of Fame Inductee, and the recipient of Visionary Marin 2012. She is an internationally published author, featured in a variety of media and publications, including *White Fire: A Portrait of Women Spiritual Leaders in America* and *Women in Sufism: A Hidden Treasure*. She is one of the major Muslim scholars of the present time with over fourteen published works. Her dedication to peace has led her to serve as in various leadership roles in large-scale international interfaith organizations. Angha, a professor of Middle Eastern and Islamic Studies, has given lectures and taught classes nationally as well as internationally, and created a cooperative educational partnership with the Dominican University of California, where she also teaches, through Building Bridges of Understanding Conference and Lecture Series that has featured prominent leaders.

CONTRIBUTING AUTHORS

Sharmin Ahmad immigrated from Bangladesh to the United States in 1984. She has a MA in Women's Studies, was awarded fellowship, and was the first recipient of Women's Studies Scholar award at George Washington University. She also completed graduate studies in Early Childhood Education at GWU. The Soroptimist International of the Americas club, Washington, DC, presented her with a "Woman of

Distinction" award for her "outstanding contributions in the field of international goodwill and understanding." She has been involved with children's education for nearly two decades. *The Rainbow in a Heart* is her first published bilingual book (Bangla-English), which is aimed at promoting female empowerment, universal motherhood and peace-building among children, parents, educators and those who strive for peace at home and around the world. Sharmin co-produced a children's peace dance drama, *The Rainbow in a Heart*, based on her book, which has been performed on stage internationally. She is a co-founder and former director of Minaret of Freedom Institute, a progressive Islamic policy research think tank that promotes human rights. She has also served on the steering committee of Women in Development and Samhati, two organizations providing help to destitute women. Sharmin's recently published book, *Daughter of Bangladesh Liberation Witnesses Tahrir Emancipation,* is a first-hand account of the mass revolution in Egypt. Her next book, a historic memoir, *Tajuddin Ahmad a Leader and Father,* is forthcoming in 2014. Currently, Sharmin travels to many countries promoting peace education, human rights, goodwill and understanding among various faiths and cultures. Email: <reepia@ hotmail.com>.

Magdalena Andersson was a member of the Committee of the female wing of the Moderate Party in Sweden from 2003-2005, and was its chair from 2005-2009. Since 2003, she has held the following positions: Member of Parliament, representing the Moderate Party; member of the Standing Committee of Health and Care, and Deputy of the Standing Committee of Labour, 2003-2010. In 2006, she joined the Standing Committee of War, and was also Vice Chairman of the party group in the Parliament, member of the Parliament executive board and of the Board of the Moderate Party in the county of Jönköping. From 2010 she was Member and the Moderate Party's spokesperson in the Standing Committee of Civil Affairs and Housing. In November 2012, she became Governor of the Västerbotten region. She is married and has a daughter. Email: <magdalena.andersson@lansstyrelsen.se>.

Parvin Ardalan received her BA in Communications and MA in Women's Studies from the University of Allameh Tabatabai in Tehran. She is a journalist, blogger, researcher, a women's rights activist, and one of the founders of "One Million Signatures Campaign to Change Discriminating Laws" for changing discriminatory laws in Iran. She was recognized for her activism in 2007 and was the recipient of the

Olaf Palme Prize and Ramon Rubial Award in 2007. She is the co-author of *The Senator* (2003), a biography of the Iranian Women's struggle during the past 100 years by focusing on the life of one of its distinguished personalities. She is on the editorial staff of *Women Magazine* in Iran, in addition to writing for feminists journals such as *The Second Sex* and *The Women's Journal*. She and some of her colleagues established the "Women's Cultural Center," an NGO that educates women about their rights. Ardalan was editor-in-chief of the Women's Cultural Center's website newsletter, the *Feminist Tribune*, for two years. Later she became a staff writer for the Center's Internet magazine, *Zanestan (Womenville)*. Both these online journals were shut down by the government. Currently, she is editor-in-chief of the online journal, *Change for Equality*, which is part of the One Million Signatures Campaign website. Ardalan was one of the organizers of the women's public gathering (demanding women's rights) in May 2005 and 2006, which landed her in prison for activism against the regime. She and four others were sentenced to three years in prison. The case is still in the courts. She was sentenced to six-month suspended prison term for being active on the aforementioned websites. Parvin is currently at Lund University, Middle Eastern Studies, working with the Iran Working Group on a monograph about women's movements in post-revolutionary Iran, with emphasis on the years followed the Iran-Iraq War (1989-2009).

Deva-Marie Beck, Ph.D., RN, is a Nightingale scholar, nurse, author, multi-media developer and global ambassador for the worldwide nursing community. She is International Co-Director of the Nightingale Initiative for Global Health (NIGH), which was created—in Florence Nightingale's name—as a grassroots-to-global movement to increase public concern and commitment by engaging and empowering nurses and concerned citizens to advocate for the pressing global health issues of our time. Her recent focus is encompassed in NIGH's global awareness campaign: "Daring, Caring & Sharing to Save Mothers' Lives" at <www.NIGHtingaleDeclaration.net>. Having resided in several places in North America, Beck currently lives and works in Neepawa, Manitoba, Canada. She has officially represented NIGH at two NGO Civil Society Development Forums convened parallel to United Nations Economic and Social Councils (ECOSCO), in 2009 for *Global Health* in Geneva, and in 2010 for *Women's Issues* in New York. She currently oversees a team of New York city-based NGO DPI Youth Representatives at the United Nations. She has keynoted at major nursing and health conferences around the world and has represented NIGH at regular WHO global nursing leadership meetings in India, Zambia and Switzerland. Her work has been featured in numerous articles and websites, as well as in *China Peoples Daily* in Beijing and *Times of India* in Mumbai. During 27 years of clinical nursing experience, she practiced in a wide variety critical-care and home-care settings. She is an award-winning co-author of *Florence Nightingale Today: Healing, Leadership, Global Action* (2005) and has written numerous related articles and textbook chapters that have contributed new scholarship on Nightingale's extensive community and global work for health, recommending how Nightingale's legacy can inform and empower twenty-first century nursing practice, women's empowerment worldwide and global citizenship efforts toward achieving a healthy world.

Ana Marcela Garcia Chaves was born in San Jose, Costa Rica where she completed undergraduate and graduate programs majoring in criminal law at the University of Costa Rica. An attorney at law for the past five years, she has litigated in family law and penal law, experiences which have given her a broad vision and understanding of her native land and society. Her graduate studies and work experience have allowed her to work closely with women secluded in penal institutions. It is particularly because of these experiences that she has developed a deep sense for human dignity: that is, women's dignity and pride, for who women are, for what they do, and wherever they may be.

Paola Conti, sociologist, has a Master's degree in integrative medicine and long experience of projects aimed at developing individual and organizational well-being, alongside organizational innovation and skill development. Currently, she directs a research program for the development of appropriateness in interventions based on gender in occupational health for the National Institute for Work Insurance. She conducts adult training workshops on skill development in health and stress management, and self-empowerment through mindfulness, integrating autobiographical and reflexive methodology. For the past 30 years, she has been involved in human rights protection and development particularly for women, both nationally and internationally, working in Europe, Central America, the Middle East and Africa. She is a member of the Italian Society of Psychoneuroendocrinoimmunology and Vice President of the Center for International Studies on Health *Hu YaoZhen*. She practices as researcher, consultant, trainer and counselor, focusing in traditional and integrative medicine with a particular interest in traditional Chinese medicine and Taoist, Buddhist and Sufi spirituality. She is author of several books, including *Gender and Work-Related Stress: Two Opportunities* (2009), and co-editor with Antonella Ninci of *Health and Safety at Work: A Matter of Gender* (two volumes, 2011). Since 2006, she has been the Managing Director of Sintagmi srl. She lives in Rome, Italy. Email: <paolaconti09@gmail.com>.

Aura Sofia Diaz is a specialist on the teachings of emotions, and energy as well as the brain applied to daily life, to human development and also to family therapy. After training with Virginia Satir, family therapist, and then with Dr. Elaine de Beauport on the 500 hours of the Self Care and Multiple Intelligence Programs, she organizes conferences and facilitates workshops for teachers, parents, and for industries. She is a facilitator of the DNA of Peace (Dialogue, Negotiation and Agreements) at the Central University of Venezuela under the auspices of the Elaine de Beauport Chair "Coexistence, Cognition and Consciousness." She has co-authored the book *The Three Faces of Mind* and is a co-founder and Vice-President of the Instituto MEAD de Venezuela, as well as a member of AVANTA, the Virginia Satir Global Network. She is also a member of the Council of Advisors of the Eugenio Mendoza Foundation, an NGO in Caracas, and Honourary Member of the SVPNI Venezuelan Society of Psiconeuroimmunology.

Leymah Gwobee, 2011 Nobel Peace Laureate, is a Liberian peace activist, social worker and women's rights advocate. She is the founder and President of the Gbowee Peace Foundation Africa, the Liberia Reconciliation Initiative, and co-founder and former Executive Director of Women Peace and Security Network Africa (WIPSEN-A). She is also a founding member and former Liberia Coordinator of Women in Peacebuilding Network/West Africa Network for Peacebuilding (WIPNET/WANEP). In addition, Gbowee serves on the Board of Directors of the Nobel Women's Initiative, Gbowee Peace Foundation and the PeaceJam Foundation, and is a member of the African Women Leaders Network for Reproductive Health and Family Planning. She holds a MA in Conflict Transformation from Eastern Mennonite University (Harrisonburg, VA), and a Doctor of Laws (LLD) *honoris causa* from Rhodes University in South Africa and University of Alberta in Canada. Currentoy, she is a Distinguished Fellow in Social Justice, a Visiting Transnational Fellow at the Center for Research on Women and Fellow in Residence at the Athena Center for Leadership Studies at Barnard College. She is also the *Newsweek Daily Beast's* Africa columnist.

Further, she serves as a member of the High-Level Task Force for the International Conference on Population and Development. She is also a board member of the Federation of Liberian Youth. Gbowee's leadership of the Women of Liberia Mass Action for Peace—which brought together Christian and Muslim women in a nonviolent movement that played a pivotal role in ending Liberia's civil war in 2003—is chronicled in her memoir, *Mighty Be Our Powers,* and in the documentary, *Pray the Devil Back to Hell.* Gbowee was honoured as a flag-bearer for the opening ceremony of the 2012 Olympic Games in London. She is based in Monrovia, Liberia, and is the proud mother of six children. <https://www.facebook.com/leymahgbowee>.

Rufaida al Habash is the President of Al Andaluse Institute for Islamic Studies in Hama, Syria. She has a BA in Islamic Legislation from Damascus University, a BA in Da'wa Studies from Abo Alnoor College, an MA in Islamic Studies from Pakistan University, and a Ph.D. in Islamic Studies from Alquraan Alkarim University, Om Darman, Sudan. The author of *The Prophet's Wife: Aisha, Asma' Bent Omais; The History of Eve; Adabany Raby; Hamasat Asheka*; and *A Comparative Study: Women's Work and Status in Islam and Other Religions.* She is a spiritual leader, a humanitarian activist, a member of the Sufi Women Dialogue Group, the International Muslim Scholars Union, the International Muslim Women's Union, and the Global Medium Forum. She has spoken nationally and internationally on Islamic topics and women's issues, and has been awarded the title of Ideal Mother in Hama. She resides in Hama with her husband and three children: Ghaith, Bara' and Sereen.

Gal Harmat is a gender and peace-building specialist. She has extensive experience in training, conflict analysis, dialogue facilitation and gender empowerment and gender mainstreaming research. As a group facilitator she has conducted a large number of trainings on Reconciliation, Dialogue and Gender. She has also facilitated many Jewish/Palestinian encounter groups for teachers and students, and has worked as a group facilitator for the Seeds of Peace International Co-Existence training in Maine, USA and for Jewish/Palestinian, India/Pakistan and Balkan multicultural groups. Since 2004, Harmat has been teaching conflict transformation and gender and is Co-Director of the Social Justice and Peace Education Teachers Training Program of the Kibbutzim Teachers College in Tel Aviv. Today she also continues facilitate Peace Dialogue between Jews and Arabs in the Middle East. In the past twelve years, she has given hundreds of Peacebuilding and Gender equality and empowerment trainings in conflict zones around the world. She is a lecturer at the UN-mandated University for Peace in Costa Rica and the UN-awarded European Peace University in Austria. She is also a regular consultant for intergovernmental organizations such as the Organization for Security and Cooperation in Europe (OSCE) and peace organizations such as the Peres Centre for Peace (founded by President of Israel and Nobel Peace Prize Laureate, Shimon Peres). Harmat holds an MA in Gender and Peacebuilding from the University for Peace in Costa Rica and is currently a Ph.D. candidate in Gender Analysis of Peace Education Dialogue encounters at Nitra University (Slovakia). Email: <Gal.harmat@gmail.com>.

Annie Imbens-Fransen lives in the Netherlands. From 1979-1983, she studied at the Theologisch Catechetisch Instituut, Tilburg (connected to Tilburg University) and the Universities of Utrecht and Nijmegen. In 1986, she founded the Dutch Foundation for Pastoral Care for Women to provide pastoral care and counseling to sexually abused women with religious trauma. She has served as a member of the board of the Dutch organization Interuniversitaire Werkgroep Feminisme en Theologie and of the European Society of Women in Theological Research. As well, from 1979-1996 she has given numerous lectures and taught courses on women, religion and society. In 1996, she became Coolidge Fellow of the Association for Religion and Intellectual Life. Since 1997, she has been involved in the inter-religious organization United Religions Initiative (URI), organizing conferences all over Europe. She has published extensively on the impact of a religious education on the lives of women, among them *Godsdienst en Incest* (Christianity and Incest), *God in de beleving van vrouwen* (God in Women's Lives). She has three children and seven grandchildren.

Anahata Iradah is a senior teacher in the Mentor Teacher's Guild of the International Network for the Dances of Universal Peace. She is a versatile and gifted musician, teacher, composer, songwriter, meditator and documentary film producer. The revered Buddhist teacher Shinzen Young has been her personal guide in the path of Vipassana meditation. With his encouragement, she has combined the Dances of Universal Peace and Buddhist meditation techniques and teachings. Iradah was the former Artistic Director of Tara Dhatu. She directs humanitarian outreach programs in India, Nepal and Brasi and travels the world teaching sacred dance and meditation. She currently resides in Georgia. Email <anahatara@mac.com>.

Joy Kemirembe was born in Kyenjojo district, Mwenge County, Nyantungo sub-county in Uganda. She lost her mother at the age of four during the fall of one of the regimes. Her father also passed away when she was eleven. Under the care of several cousins, she was able to complete her schooling and received a diploma from the Secondary Education of the Institute of Teacher Education Kyambogo (ITEK) 1999. In 2000, the Uganda Orthodox Church employed her as their National Education Secretary, where she became independent, and in 2001, she enrolled at Makerere University and subsequently graduated in Educational Administration and Evaluation in 2004. In 2006, she became the national coordinator of the Peace and Good Governance Department where she worked with the member organizations such as the Inter-religious Council of Uganda and the Uganda Joint Christian Council. Currently, Kemirembe is working with Inter-Religious Council of Uganda as a program officer for peace justice and governance.

Hana Kirreh is a Palestinian woman living in East Jerusalem with her husband and two sons. She was born and educated in Bethlehem, graduated from the Bethlehem University, with a degree in English Language and Literature. She is an English teacher, working in several schools in East Jerusalem. Through Wi'am center, a Palestinian program devoted to conflict she has learned much and worked for women rights and the challenges facing women in Palestine. This has led to participation in numerous conferences, seminars and consultations associated with women's empowerment. As a woman activist, she was the Middle East representative of the Women Peace Program Working Group (WPPWG) in Holland. Kirreh conducts workshops and training on leadership and communication, gender, conflict resolution and non-violence. Email: <samkirreh@yahoo.com>.

Rosane Maria Reis Lavigne has an MA and an MBA from the Judicial Branch of the FGV Direito Rio. A Public Defender, she is in charge of the second Public Defender's Office of the 6th Criminal Chamber of the Court of Appeals of the State of Rio de Janeiro. She is a member of the research group Judicial Branch, Human Rights and Society (DHPJS), which is linked to the School of Law at the State University of Rio de Janeiro (UERJ). She is a feminist and member of several organizations including Articulação de Mulheres Brasileiras, Comissão Mulher Advogad, Brazilian Bar Association/RJ and other governmental and NGOs working on gender issues and women's rights. She was a member of the consortium of NGOs and experts that drafted Law 11340, enacted on August 6, 2006, the *Maria da Penha Act*, which provides mechanisms to prevent domestic and family violence against women. She is a founding member of the discussion group Fórum Justiça.

Susan Masten, past Yurok Tribal Chairperson, resides in Northern California. She currently serves as Vice Chair of the Yurok Tribe, Vice Chair, National Center for American Indian Enterprise Development and Chair, Indian Law Resource Center. For 32 years, Susan Masten has advocated for the rights of Native peoples in her community and across the nation. After graduation from Oregon State University, she returned home to the Reservation and found herself on the front lines of the salmon wars, a battle to protect her people's natural resources, cultural identity, tradition and fishing rights. Susan Masten was instrumental in securing the Yurok's fishing allocation rights to the Klamath River Basin, which were reaffirmed in her uncle's U.S. Supreme Court case *Mattz v. Arnett*. She has been selected "Outstanding Young Woman of American," Humboldt County's "Outstanding Citizen," Del Norte County's "Young Woman of the Year" and is the Founder/Co-President of Women Empowering Women for Indian Nations (WEWIN) a national Native women's organization. At home, Susan Masten is active in traditional Yurok practices including fishing on the Klamath River and caring for her family's basket collection and dance regalia. She lives with her husband, Leonard, and has a son, a daughter and is the proud grandmother of eight. Email <susanmasten04@gmail.com>.

Despina Namwembe was born and raised in Eastern Uganda. She has a Bachelors degree in Social Sciences and is currently working on a Master's degree in Peace and Conflict Studies. She has a diploma in public administration, certificates in Women's Involvement in Peace-Building, Gender and Development Economics, HIV and Counseling Skills among others. She also has memberships with African Women of Faith Network–Uganda Chapter, the Circle of Concerned African Women Theologians, the Women's Interfaith Network of the United Religions Initiative, Think Peace Organization, the Uganda Joint Christian Council, and the Uganda Orthodox Mother Union. She has managed projects sponsored by the National Environmental Authority (NEMA) in Uganda. Nanwembe is currently working as the Sub-Regional Coordinator for the United Religions Initiative in the Great Lakes Sub-region in Africa, coordinating the work of over nineteen self-organized interfaith organizations in the sub-region, emphasizing interfaith dialogue, human rights and environmental protection.

Yumiko Otani, "Tubu-Tubu Grandma Yumiko," is the creator of "Tubu-Tubu Peace Food." She graduated from the Industrial Design Department of National Chiba University's Faculty of Engineering. In 1982, she began studying traditional Japanese foods, and has since been a vegetarian, establishing an NGO, "Tubu-Tubu" (formerly ILFA). In 1996, she published *Mirai-shoku (Future Food): Surviving the Age of Environmental Pollution,* and started the "Life Seed Campaign" under the concept of "changing kitchens and farmland to enrich the Japanese diet with native grains." She began organizing "Tubu-Tubu Peace Food Seminars" to teach her theories and skills with regard to foods that can revitalize the body. In 2000, she began introducing her concepts to international audiences, and by 2004 Tubu-Tubu Peace Food was introduced at "Terra Madre," a slow-food conference of 5,000 producers. More recently, Yumiko has found that Tubu-Tubu Peace Food has a significant meaning, allowing women to undergo a spiritual awakening, and this prompted her to start holding "Tubu-Tubu Tennyo Seminars" on female empowerment. She has written over 30 books on native grains and recipes using them. Her most recent books are *Simple Tubu-Tubu Gohan for Babies and Moms, Tubu-Tubu Cooking Start Book* (Gakuyo-shobo) and *Gohan no Chikara* (KK Longsellers). Yumiko is now a member of the Millet Society of Japan. She currently manages the Fu Future Living Labo Inc., which organizes seminars, and Team E, which manages restaurants and cafes, as part of her efforts to understand the relationship between the universe and humanity. She can be reached via <http://tsubutsubu.jp/global/index.html>.

Elly Pradervand is a Swiss citizen of German origin, mother of two married children and grandmother of four. She has been active for the past 30 years in the field of public education for development and advocacy for women and children's rights. In 1991, she founded the Women's World Summit Foundation (a humanitarian, not-for-profit, lay organization with United Nations consultative status) serving as an international NGO network for the implementation of women and children's rights. Pradervand created and directs the annual WWSF Prize for women's creativity in rural life (385 Laureates awarded since 1994); the World Day of Rural Women (15 October), an annual awareness-raising campaign to increase knowledge and empowerment, declared a United Nations Resolution Day in 2007; and the White Ribbon Campaign Switzerland, to mobilize men and women to pledge not to commit, condone or remain silent about violence against women. In 2000, she also launched the World Day for Prevention of Child Abuse

(19 November), a Prize for innovative prevention activities, and in 2011 the annual campaign "19 Days of Activism for Prevention" (1-19 November).

Diana Rhodes is a devoted wife, mother and grandmother. She is a teacher and educator, and a tireless worker for the peace process. Despite, or perhaps even because of, serious ongoing health challenges she has a passion for her work. Her work has involved the education of less able children and those in need of specific educational understanding. Her total commitment to linking millions of people around the world to work for peace and understanding has included an annual gathering and world prayer for peace and healing. She has compiled and edited three books of words of peace and encouragement from around the world, the last book, *The Peace Scroll,* being blessed by His Holiness the Dalai Lama writing the Foreword. She, with her loyal and supportive husband, has created an award-winning Peace garden and sculpture park, Grandma's Garden, in the grounds of their natural arboretum. Despite her severe physical difficulties she has helped organize and attended peace initiatives around the world and continues to work with her garden raising money for local and national charity and worthy causes. She has written her autobiography, *No Ordinary Life*, which is found in teaching libraries and university libraries, and provides inspirational insight into disability and health challenges for those in the medical professions and for those training in these fields.

Maria Luisa Sánchez Fuentes is an economist by training with an MA in Public Administration, specializing in population, reproductive health and management both from the University of Washington. She was the Executive Director of the Grupo de Información en Reproducción Elegida (GIRE) (Information Group on Reproductive Choice), founded in 1992 to promote and defend reproductive and sexual health and rights, particularly abortion rights, from a human rights perspective, through the promotion of a legal and policy framework that guarantees women's freedom of choice. Sánchez Fuentes has specialized in strategic planning, political advocacy, negotiation, conflict resolution, message development, and strategic public interest litigation. She participated in the preparation of the Technical Guidelines for Health Systems (World Health Organization) and in a comparative analysis to improve health regulations for the legal termination of pregnancy in Latin America coordinated by International Planned Parenthood Federation. In addition, she acted as an External Reviewer for the International

Development Research Centre project "The Politics of Abortion in Latin America." She has received the following awards: Eleanor Roosevelt, from the Feminist Majority Foundation; 21 Leaders for the 21st Century 2009, from Women eNews; and, Salud, Dignidad, Justicia, from the National Latina Institute for Reproductive Health.

Tenzin Dhardon Sharling is a second-generation Tibetan born in exile after her grandparents were forced to escape to India in the aftermath of the brutal and illegal occupation of Tibet by the Chinese Communist regime in 1959. Dhardon is today the youngest elected member of the Tibetan Parliament based in exile India. She has served as an executive board member of Tibetan Women's Association, the most powerful women's organization in Tibetan history that advocates human rights for Tibetan women in Tibet and also works to empower Tibetan women in exile. At TWA, Dhardon published many research books on the situation of Tibetan women including *Tears of Silence,* a report on China's family planning policy and its impact on Tibetan women, and *Light in the Abyss,* the story of the fourteen nuns who served as political prisoners in the notorious Drapchi prison in Tibet. In 2012, she was elected as the co-chair of the steering committee of International Tibet Network. Dhardon has an MA in Communication studies from an Indian University and an MA in Counseling studies from the University of Edinburgh, Scotland. She travels around the world for speaking engagements and is today an avid spokesperson for the Tibet movement. Email <dhardonsharling@gmail.com>.

Renuka Singh has a doctorate in Sociology from Jawaharlal Nehru University, New Delhi. For the last 30 years, she has been working in the field of Gender Studies. She has been a fellow at Oxford University and UGC Research Scientist at JNU. Currently, she is an Associate Professor at the Centre for the Study of Social Systems, Jawaharlal Nehru University, and also the Director of Tushita Mahayana Meditation Centre, New Delhi. Renuka Singh is the author of *The Womb of Mind* and *Women Reborn* and has co-authored *Growing Up in Rural India.* She has compiled and edited *The Path to Tranquillity; The Transformed Mind; The Little Book of Buddhism; The Path of the Buddha; Many Ways to Nirvana; Becoming Buddha*; and *Buddhism: The Message of Peace.* These books have been published in several languages.

Cecilia Vicentini is a sociologist, professor of social and community psychology, and civic commitment, author of a chapter on a book that addresses inequity in Venezuelan higher education, co-author of a book on an educational agenda for equity in education. She is a member of the Chair "Coexistence, Cognition and Consciousness," at Universidad Central de Venezuela, and of the Board of Directors of Instituto Mead de Venezuela, and coach of a training program called "Mind and Peace." She recently developed a training program called "Free Movement and Dance," centered on becoming conscious of our bodies, acknowledging that all our parts are connected and that moving as an integral human being, allows us to become more conscious of our outer and inner spaces.

Elena Tonetti-Vladimirova has been working in the Birthing Field of Conscious Procreation since 1982 and was one of the pioneers organizing birth camps at the Black Sea in Russia, where women gave birth in shallow lagoons, in the presence of wild dolphins. In 2006, she directed a revolutionary documentary, *Birth As We Know It,* about the correlation between birth trauma and the quality of life, and about what it really takes to prepare for conscious birth and to deliver a baby gracefully, minimizing trauma for all involved. The film, already in 57 countries, without any marketing or advertising, has been translated into twelve languages by local volunteers, making a huge difference for hundreds of thousands people, who are self-organizing into grassroots movements for empowered approaches to childbirth. In 1986, she was a facilitator in business seminars called "Games," extremely effective brainstorming for economic changes to the USSR. At the same time, she was one of the key players in "Citizen Diplomacy," an underground political organization aimed at putting an end to the Cold War. Since 2003, she has been facilitating Birth Into Being workshops in ten countries per year on average. She has over 200 apprentices in 22 countries and maintains her leadership of the constantly expanding international organization, The Sentient Circle, dedicated to conscious evolution. Elena offers a very effective healing modality called Limbic Imprint Re-Coding (LIR), which helps adults heal their emotional trauma received during pre-cognitive formative period, from the earliest developmental stages and through their entire childhood. For more on Elena's work visit <www.birthintobeing.com>.

purely and simply for the benefit of all life...